KNOWLEDGE INTO ACTION

KNOWLEDGE INTO ACTION

Research and Evaluation in Library and Information Science

DANNY P. WALLACE AND
CONNIE VAN FLEET

 LIBRARIES UNLIMITED

AN IMPRINT OF ABC-CLIO, LLC
Santa Barbara, California • Denver, Colorado • Oxford, England

Library of Congress Cataloging-in-Publication Data

Wallace, Danny P.
    Knowledge into action : research and evaluation in library and information science /
Danny P. Wallace and Connie Van Fleet.
        pages cm
    Includes bibliographical references and index.
    ISBN 978-1-59884-975-2 (pbk.) — ISBN 978-1-61069-266-3 (ebook)
1. Library science—Research—Methodology.   2. Information science—Research—
Methodology.   3. Libraries—Evaluation.   4. Information services—
Evaluation.   I. Van Fleet, Connie Jean, 1950–   II. Title.
    Z669.7.W35   2012
    025.0072—dc23   2012010396

ISBN: 978-1-59884-975-2
EISBN: 978-1-61069-266-3

16   15   14   13   12   1   2   3   4   5

This book is also available on the World Wide Web as an eBook.
Visit www.abc-clio.com for details.

Libraries Unlimited
An Imprint of ABC-CLIO, LLC

ABC-CLIO, LLC
130 Cremona Drive, P.O. Box 1911
Santa Barbara, California 93116-1911

This book is printed on acid-free paper ∞

Manufactured in the United States of America

CONTENTS

List of Figures   vii

Introduction   1

1   **Knowing, Research, and Evaluation**   5

2   **Research and Evaluation Processes**   39

3   **Ethics and Politics in Library and Information
       Science Research and Evaluation**   67

4   **Published Reports and the Professional as Consumer**   97

5   **The Project Plan or Proposal**   113

6   **Measurement, Populations, Samples, and Sampling**   135

7   **Historical Methods**   159

8   **Descriptive Methods—Questionnaires and Interviews**   179

9   **Descriptive Methods—Observation**   211

10 **Experimental Methods**   227

11 **Bibliometrics and Citation Analysis**   241

12 **Data Analysis and Presentation**   265

13 **Descriptive and Inferential Statistics**   291

14 Funding for Research and Evaluation 331

15 Research, Evaluation, and Change 343

Glossary 353

Bibliography 365

Index 377

LIST OF FIGURES

Figure 1.1	Major approaches to learning	9
Figure 1.2	Induction and deduction	13
Figure 1.3	Essential characteristics of research and evaluation	19
Figure 1.4	Desirable characteristics of research and evaluation	21
Figure 1.5	Manifestations of the characteristics of research and evaluation	22
Figure 1.6	Levels of research and evaluation	23
Figure 1.7	Families of research and evaluation methods	31
Figure 1.8	Benefits of research	32
Figure 2.1	The research and evaluation process	40
Figure 2.2	Origin and preplanning	42
Figure 2.3	Origins of research and evaluation ideas	43
Figure 2.4	Purposes of the literature review	45
Figure 2.5	Planning	47
Figure 2.6	Methodology definition	49
Figure 2.7	Data gathering	52
Figure 2.8	Data analysis	54
Figure 2.9	Processing results	55
Figure 2.10	Reporting	57
Figure 2.11	From the professional literature—components of a research report	58
Figure 2.12	Decision making	59
Figure 2.13	Action	62
Figure 3.1	Beneficiaries of ethical practices in research and evaluation	70
Figure 3.2	The Nuremberg Code	71
Figure 3.3	Fundamental principles of the Belmont Report	75
Figure 3.4	Criteria for IRB approval of research	79
Figure 3.5	Grounds for exemption from IRB review	81
Figure 4.1	Criteria for evaluating published reports	101

Figure 5.1	Purposes of plans and proposals	114
Figure 5.2	Typical proposal elements	117
Figure 5.3	Project Gantt chart	122
Figure 5.4	Research and evaluation checknote: Bibliographic style	127
Figure 5.5	Research and evaluation checknote: Citing sources 1—style manual variations	129
Figure 5.6	Research and evaluation checknote: Citing sources 2—the dangers of copy and paste	131
Figure 6.1	Measurement scales	138
Figure 6.2	Nominal measurement scale	139
Figure 6.3	Ordinal measurement scale	140
Figure 6.4	Interval measurement scale	141
Figure 6.5	Ratio measurement scale	142
Figure 6.6	The NOIR mnemonic	142
Figure 6.7	How to lie with measurement scales	144
Figure 6.8	Sample size table	150
Figure 6.9	Contingency table model	151
Figure 6.10	Table of random digits	153
Figure 6.11	Stratified random sample	155
Figure 6.12	Proportional random sample	155
Figure 6.13	How to lie with populations and samples	155
Figure 7.1	From the professional literature—historical method 1	169
Figure 7.2	From the professional literature—historical method 2	170
Figure 7.3	Time series table from *ARL Statistics 2007–2008*	174
Figure 7.4	Time series graph of selected academic library indicators, 1992–2008	174
Figure 8.1	From the professional literature—combined survey and interview method	185
Figure 8.2	From the professional literature—survey method	196
Figure 8.3	From the professional literature—secondary analysis	204
Figure 9.1	Research and evaluation checknote: Using professional standards and guidelines	213
Figure 9.2	From the professional literature—direct observation	216
Figure 9.3	From the professional literature—qualitative method	217
Figure 9.4	From the professional literature—ethnographic method	220
Figure 9.5	From the professional literature—transaction log analysis and observational interviews	222
Figure 10.1	From the professional literature—experimental method 1	229
Figure 10.2	From the professional literature—experimental method 2	234
Figure 11.1	Lotka's Law example	244
Figure 11.2	Lotka's Law graph	244
Figure 11.3	Zipf distribution graph	245
Figure 11.4	Bradford distribution table: Applied geophysics	246
Figure 11.5	Idealized Bradford distribution table	246
Figure 11.6	Bradford distribution graph	247
Figure 11.7	Bradford distribution semilog plot	248

Figure 11.8	Bradford distribution semilog plot for knowledge management journals	248
Figure 11.9	Typical obsolescence graph	250
Figure 11.10	Obsolescence graph with immediacy effect	251
Figure 11.11	Reference versus citation	252
Figure 11.12	From the professional literature—bibliometric analysis	258
Figure 12.1	The data matrix model	269
Figure 12.2	Data matrix example: Time to answer each of three reference questions	269
Figure 12.3	The data matrix model implemented in a spreadsheet	271
Figure 12.4	Using a spreadsheet to calculate a mean—the average function	271
Figure 12.5	Using a spreadsheet to calculate a mean—calculated mean	272
Figure 12.6	The data matrix model implemented in a statistical analysis package	272
Figure 12.7	SPSS variable view	273
Figure 12.8	Using a statistical analysis package to calculate a mean—selecting variables	273
Figure 12.9	Using a statistical analysis package to calculate a mean—results	274
Figure 12.10	Table layout basics	275
Figure 12.11	Table layout example	275
Figure 12.12	Improved table example	275
Figure 12.13	How to lie with tables	276
Figure 12.14	Column graph	277
Figure 12.15	Multiple column graph	278
Figure 12.16	Stacked column graph	278
Figure 12.17	100 percent column graph	279
Figure 12.18	Bar graph	280
Figure 12.19	Pie chart	281
Figure 12.20	Scatter plot	282
Figure 12.21	Scatter plot with trend line	282
Figure 12.22	Line graph	283
Figure 12.23	Multiple line graph	284
Figure 12.24	Impact of scale on a line graph	284
Figure 12.25	Impact of perspective on a line graph	285
Figure 12.26	How to lie with graphs	285
Figure 12.27	Thematic map	287
Figure 13.1	Centrality and dispersion	295
Figure 13.2	Data matrix example: Time to answer each of three reference questions	296
Figure 13.3	Frequency distribution table: Time to answer each of three reference questions	297
Figure 13.4	Calculating the median: Time to answer reference Question 1	298
Figure 13.5	Calculating the mean 1: Time to answer reference Question 1	298
Figure 13.6	Calculating the mean 2: Time to answer reference Question x	299
Figure 13.7	How to lie with measures of centrality	300
Figure 13.8	Calculating the standard deviation: Time to answer reference Question 1	301

Figure 13.9	How to lie with measures of dispersion	302
Figure 13.10	The normal curve	302
Figure 13.11	Normal curves	303
Figure 13.12	Areas under the normal curve	304
Figure 13.13	Negatively skewed curve	305
Figure 13.14	Positively skewed curve	305
Figure 13.15	Logarithmic (J-shaped) curve	306
Figure 13.16	Traffic fatalities, 2009	307
Figure 13.17	Traffic fatalities and blood alcohol concentration, 2009	307
Figure 13.18	Null hypothesis truth table	308
Figure 13.19	Degrees of freedom: One cell	310
Figure 13.20	Degrees of freedom: One-cell solution	310
Figure 13.21	Degrees of freedom: Two cells	311
Figure 13.22	Degrees of freedom: Two cells, known row totals	311
Figure 13.23	Degrees of freedom: Two-cell solution	311
Figure 13.24	Degrees of freedom: Four cells	312
Figure 13.25	Degrees of freedom: Four cells, known row totals	312
Figure 13.26	Degrees of freedom: Four-cell solution	312
Figure 13.27	Success in answering reference questions, 50 librarians	314
Figure 13.28	Data needed for chi-square analysis, success in answering reference questions, 50 librarians	314
Figure 13.29	Critical values of chi-square	315
Figure 13.30	Success in answering two related reference questions, 100 librarians	316
Figure 13.31	Expected values, success in answering two related reference questions, 100 librarians	316
Figure 13.32	Positive correlation	317
Figure 13.33	Negative correlation	317
Figure 13.34	No correlation	318
Figure 13.35	Nonlinear relationship	318
Figure 13.36	Results of success in answering paired factual/interpretive question, 10 librarians	319
Figure 13.37	Tables of values for calculating Pearson correlation	320
Figure 13.38	Is bread causing global warming?	322
Figure 13.39	Results of success in answering pretest/posttest questions, 10 librarians	324
Figure 13.40	Regression line	326
Figure 13.41	Regression line calculation	326
Figure 13.42	Outlier example	327
Figure 13.43	Box plot	327
Figure 14.1	IMLS schedule of completion	334
Figure 14.2	Library funding programs of the Institute of Museum and Library Services	337
Figure 15.1	Factors in putting results to work	344
Figure 15.2	The evaluation action plan	350

INTRODUCTION

The unexamined life is not worth living.

—*Socrates, Apology 36a*

WHY THIS BOOK?

The focus of *Knowledge Into Action: Research and Evaluation in Library and Information Science* is the application of research principles and methods to the understanding of library and information science processes and the solution of problems related to library and information science. Although the book is designed for use in graduate programs in schools of library and information science, any student of the profession, whether enrolled in a formal course of study or learning independently, can benefit from learning about research and evaluation.

Knowledge Into Action is an introduction to library and information science research and evaluation, not a research manual or statistics textbook. It is a practical guide for practitioners in library and information science who have specific research interests or institutional evaluation needs. Research and evaluation are the foundation of evidence-based practice. Every library and information professional will at some time in his or her career be called upon or will elect to engage in evaluation activities. Understanding the nature and methods of evaluation and the close linkage between research and evaluation will inevitably strengthen the evaluation of library services and processes and thereby strengthen the good that libraries provide to the publics they serve. It is the authors' hope and expectation that this book will also inspire professionals who might otherwise not have attempted broad-based research to take a step beyond the solution of local problems and venture into the arena of benefiting the profession as a whole.

Recognition that research and evaluation are closely related is the guiding principle for this book. Research and evaluation are interwoven throughout the text. Although the distinctions between research and evaluation are addressed and explained, the premise of this book is that research and evaluation are two sides of a single coin. Although a coin with only one side may be of value to a collector, only the coin with both sides is valid as currency. Research and evaluation are at their best when they constitute a cyclical process. The relationship between research and evaluation is itself cyclical. Research informs the selection of methods and tools for evaluation, while effective evaluation serves as an inspiration for research.

Even library and information science practitioners who have no responsibility for evaluation and are not actively involved in research have a need to understand the nature and benefits of research and evaluation. A goal of this book is to educate practitioners in the basics of being effective consumers of the research and evaluation literature. A critical consumer is better positioned than a casual or uninformed consumer to make use of the published literature and to benefit from conference experiences.

This is not a book about research for purely academic purposes, although it has value for students working on thesis, dissertation, or other individualized research projects. For such students, this book will not serve as a substitute for the requirements and guidelines of individual universities.

ASSUMPTIONS OF THE BOOK

Knowledge Into Action is built on a number of core assumptions. For most readers, this is a first book in the systematic application of research and evaluation as an approach to problem solving. Students who have completed an introductory research course as part of a program of study at the bachelor's or graduate level in a different discipline may need a complete refresher experience and may additionally need an opportunity to overcome and even unlearn content that is more applicable to that other program than to library and information science.

Most students enrolled in professional programs in library and information studies will pursue careers primarily or exclusively as practitioners rather than as researchers; students who enter careers that explicitly include a research role will fulfill that role as part of a broader range of responsibilities that are mostly non-research-related. All library and information professionals are at some time in their careers involved in evaluation activities and decisions that will be strengthened by an understanding of research methods and systematic approaches to evaluation. An ability to understand and apply research results in an evaluation context is useful for all library and information professionals and essential for most.

ORGANIZATION OF THE BOOK

Knowledge Into Action is designed to be a textbook and a guide for independent learning. Examples drawn from the literature are used liberally, both in the narrative and as From the Professional Literature boxes that summarize specific research or evaluation publications. Research and Evaluation Checknotes call attention to areas of concern or interest for further exploration. Each chapter concludes with a Think About It! section that raises questions for reflection and a Do It! section that presents targets for independent investigation. The Think About It! and Do It! features are not intended as study guides for quizzes or exams. Their purpose is to encourage individual thought and action. How to Lie features expose the potential dark side of research and evaluation and serve as guidelines for how to avoid unintentional dishonesty or misconduct. The book includes a Glossary and a Bibliography.

Knowledge Into Action comprises 15 chapters. Chapter 1 explores the nature of knowing, research, and evaluation, grounding research and evaluation in approaches to learning and knowing, and introduces key research and evaluation concepts, including the quantitative and qualitative paradigms for research and evaluation, the nature of validity and reliability, and the major families of research and evaluation methods.

Chapter 2 is built around nine flowcharts that encapsulate the essential steps of the research and evaluation process, including the origin of a project, preplanning, planning, methodology definition, data gathering, data analysis, processing results, reporting, decision making, and action.

Chapter 3 examines ethics and politics in library and information science research and evaluation. Ethics and practical ethics are defined, major ethical dilemmas are explored, policy and legal documents are summarized, and tools for addressing ethical threats are presented. The chapter concludes with a discussion of the roles and challenges of politics in research and evaluation in library and information science.

Chapter 4 is a practical guide to published reports and the professional as consumer. The nature of publication in library and information science and the roles of differing kinds of publications are discussed, the essential elements of published reports are outlined, and a set of pragmatic criteria for evaluation of published reports are presented.

The project plan or proposal is the focus of Chapter 5. Project planning is presented as a requisite for project success. The purposes of research and evaluation project plans and proposals are discussed and the elements of project plans and proposals are detailed. The chapter concludes with guidance on writing plans and proposals.

Chapter 6 defines and explains measurement, explores the nature of measurement, and explores populations, samples, and sampling. Population definition, the role of samples in research and evaluation, selection of an appropriate sample size, and approaches to selecting a sample are explored in detail.

Chapters 7 through 11 explore specific families of research methods. Quantitative and qualitative methods are integrated to emphasize the interlocking roles of the two investigative paradigms. Historical methods are the focus of Chapter 7. Chapters 8 and 9 address descriptive methods, with Chapter 8 concentrating on interviews and questionnaires and Chapter 9 addressing observation. Chapter 10 presents the nature of experimental methods and models for experimental design. Chapter 11 covers the nature and applications of bibliometrics and citation analysis, two areas of particular interest in library and information science research and evaluation.

Data analysis is the focus of Chapter 12, which explores the purposes of data analysis and data analysis concerns. The data matrix model is presented as a tool for visualizing relationships among quantitatively measured phenomena. Quantitative and qualitative tools for analysis are presented, along with basic guidance and rules for presenting data visually in tables, graphs, and charts.

Chapter 13 is a gentle guide to the nature and functions of descriptive and inferential statistics. The distinction between descriptive and inferential statistics is explored. The chapter concludes with hypothesis testing and examples of inferential statistics procedures.

Funding for research and evaluation is the topic of Chapter 14. Internal and external sources of funding are explained. The chapter focuses on targets for external funding, including governmental and quasi-governmental agencies, foundations, professional associations, and corporate sources.

Knowledge Into Action concludes with a chapter on research, evaluation, and change, which returns to the purpose of research and evaluation explored in Chapter 1 and provides a different take on research, evaluation, and the informed consumer. The characteristics that make research and evaluation useful are explored. The core value of creating a personal or institutional culture of research and evaluation is presented in the context of research, evaluation, and managing change. The book concludes with the relationships among research, evaluation, and the reflective practitioner.

CAVEATS

A single book can provide a useful introduction to research and evaluation but cannot be comprehensive. The emphasis of this book is on gaining familiarity with a broad range of research concepts and methods and their application to evaluation activities and decisions, not on building skill in specific research methods or research tools. Although quantitative methods and statistics are introduced, *Knowledge Into Action* is not designed as a quantitative methods book and is not intended to build expertise in statistical methods. Some readers may feel intimidated by this book, particularly by the discussion of the research and evaluation processes in Chapter 2. Readers should remember that it isn't necessary to know and understand everything from the beginning: the purpose of the book is to build understanding.

1

KNOWING, RESEARCH, AND EVALUATION

The outcome of any serious research can only be to make two questions grow where only one question grew before.

—*Thorstein Veblen, "Evolution of the Scientific Point of View,"*
University of California Chronicle, *1908*

Evaluation is creation. . . . Valuating is itself the value and jewel of all valued things. Only through evaluation is there value: and without evaluation the nut of existence would be hollow.

—*Friedrich Nietzsche,* Thus Spake Zarathustra, *1883*

In This Chapter

The nature of research and evaluation

Facts and proof

Approaches to learning

Validity and reliability

Definitions of research and evaluation

Characteristics of research and evaluation

Levels of research and evaluation

The traditional research dichotomy

Major research and evaluation paradigms

Families of research and evaluation methods

Benefits of research and evaluation

Divergence and convergence in research and evaluation

THE NATURE OF RESEARCH AND EVALUATION

The Problem of Truth

Research and evaluation are methods for asking questions in a systematic way and developing an analytical approach to deriving and assessing answers. It is very tempting to equate this with a search for *truth*. Unfortunately, *truth* is a very ambiguous and situational concept. The very long history of the study of epistemology—the study of knowledge—and ontology—the study of the nature of being—as subdisciplines within philosophy indicates that the notion that truth can be observed, captured, and verified cannot itself be ascertained to be a genuine representation of the nature of truth. Truth can vary in a variety of ways including the following examples.

Chronological Influences

Truth changes over time. Most learned Europeans in the early 16th century accepted as fundamental truth the principle that the Universe revolved around the Earth. Nicolaus Copernicus's theory of a heliocentric Universe with the Sun at the center, first formulated in 1513, was a direct challenge to prevailing assumptions of truth. Scholars and scientists did not begin to give general acceptance to the truth of the Copernican theory until the middle of the 17th century. The theoretical base necessary for widespread acceptance of the Copernican theory wasn't in place until Newton formulated the theory of universal gravity in 1687. Even though most educated people at the beginning of the 21st century probably reject the notion that the Earth is the center of the Universe, however, few would actually accept Copernicus's notion that the Sun is the center of the Universe. In the initial era of public libraries in the United States, there was a shared understanding among library professionals that the purpose of a public library was to support education for adults. Children were not viewed as being a legitimate component in the clientele of a public library. In the late 19th century, public libraries began to accept children as being a part of their clienteles. By the mid-20th century, children and young adults were a primary focus of public libraries.

It is tempting to assign values of right and wrong to changes in truth over time: the old way of thinking is quaint, misguided, and *wrong* while the new way is accurate, informed, and *right*. To do so is to fall into the trap of *historicism:* interpreting and judging the past using the assumptions and values of the present.

Societal Influences

Truth is in large part a social, human phenomenon rather than a physical or biological phenomenon. What is true for one culture or societal niche is not necessarily true for another. An obvious example of social variation in ascribing truth is that of religion. Religions are complex social systems that to a considerable extent revolve around structures for determining truth. Governments also establish systems, both formal and accidental, for determining and establishing official truth. Aesthetics is another area in which there are significant societal differences. Keats' *Ode on a Grecian Urn* contends that beauty is truth, but beauty is defined in a vast number of ways by various societal groups. Berger and Luckmann's *The Social Construction of Reality* was a pioneering work in the field of the sociology of knowledge that attempted to differentiate between the objective and subjective aspects of knowledge, broadly defined, and worked to establish a model of societal structure that embraced both objective and subjective viewpoints while making it clear that reality is largely a societal rather than a physical phenomenon.[1]

Library and information professionals share a conviction that libraries of all types are a fundamental public good. That belief is not immune to challenge as communities and institutions today have many sources of information readily available to them, competition for resources is fierce, and administrations are demanding evidence of the value and contribution of library services.

Personal Influences

Truth can be a very personal matter, especially when human emotions are attached to understanding what is or is not true. Every individual ascribes validity to truths that cannot be verified through external examination and may defy explanation to others. The acceptability of given assertions as true varies not only among individuals but may vary within a given individual over time. It is, for instance, not unusual for a child to view the role of Santa Claus in delivering holiday gifts as undeniable truth, but it is normally expected that the child's view of this particular truth will be altered with maturity.

Library and information professionals typically subscribe to the tenet that more information is better than less information and that all views should be available to all members of the library's public. That tenet is not necessarily shared by members of the public, members of the staff, or government officials. Differing personal views of access to information frequently lead to disagreement and conflict. As a profession, library and information science has at least a loosely defined worldview and mental models that shape the profession's collective outlook and differentiate the profession from other professions and from the general public.

While some personal truths cannot be externally verified, some individual perceptions of truth may be so internally convincing that they defy overwhelming external verification. Phobias are sometimes so deeply ingrained that they constitute absolute truth even though the individual affected by the phobia knows it to be unreasonable.

"We Hold These Truths to Be Self-Evident . . ."

Ultimately, what is true or not true can be adequately perceived and understood only within the context of one or more value systems. Truth is not an absolute and is never truly self-evident. The evidence for truth lies in some combination of the value systems at work and the tools for understanding truth that pertain to those value systems. Truth, then, can only be understood in context. To the extent that research is a search for truth, the success of the search can be assessed only within the constraints of the context within which the search is conducted.

IS THAT A FACT?

The concept of truth is frequently conflated with the concept of a *fact*. The *Oxford English Dictionary* provides several definitions of *fact*, the most pertinent of which is

> Something that has really occurred or is actually the case . . . as opposed to what is merely inferred, or to a conjecture or fiction; a datum of experience, as distinguished from the conclusions that may be based upon it.

In the research and evaluation contexts, a fact is an item of evidence that has been verified and replicated, and that can therefore be generalized. There is an element of objectivity inherent in the concept of a fact—it implies alignment with the physical reality of the universe rather than with a subjective value system. An important element of the *Oxford English Dictionary* definition is the distinction between the objective fact and the conclusions that may be associated with that fact. A fact is generally considered to be a matter of observation and confirmation rather than interpretation, but a conclusion is fundamentally an interpretation of one or more facts. Many investigators consciously avoid the use of the word fact because it tends to imply a definitive and immutable interpretation of truth.

PROVE IT!

Many people who are new to research and evaluation associate the search for meaning or the identification of facts as being a matter of *proof*. Proof as a concept is closely associated with *truth*. If something has in some sense been proven, it takes on the status of being definitively, immutably, and irrefutably true. Proof as a concept and process is essential in mathematics and in civil or criminal law. The notion of proof has very limited applicability in research and evaluation. The problem with proof in the research and evaluation context is that a search for proof, unlike a search for facts or meanings, implies that the investigator knows the answer from the outset. A research or evaluation project that has as its mission an attempt to prove something to be true is extremely susceptible to bias, deceit, and dishonesty, whether intentional or unconscious. Most professionals experienced in research and evaluation very consciously and rigorously avoid the use of the term proof, preferring to speak in terms of evidence.

APPROACHES TO LEARNING

Research and evaluation are about learning. The motive for conducting a research project or implementing an evaluation program is a desire to *know*. That desire for new knowledge may be a matter of curiosity, may be a response to an imposed need such as the requirement to complete a thesis for a master's degree, or may be driven by an immediate, pragmatic problem in need of a solution. The processes of research and evaluation are essentially the same regardless of the specific motivation.

The search for knowledge—the process of *learning*—can take many forms. Some of the most prominent are experience, belief, deduction, and induction. In many cases, the perception of knowledge is derived not from one of these approaches to learning but from some combination of approaches. Such combinations may be formally designed and implemented or may be essentially accidental and mostly unconscious. The major approaches to learning are summarized in Figure 1.1.

Experience

Personal Experience

Experience is a very important avenue for pursuing and assessing new knowledge. Every individual relies on personal experience as an approach to learning. The actual number of experiences necessary to acquire and integrate knowledge is variable. An extremely pleasant or intensely unpleasant experience may result in a very quick and perhaps unreliable

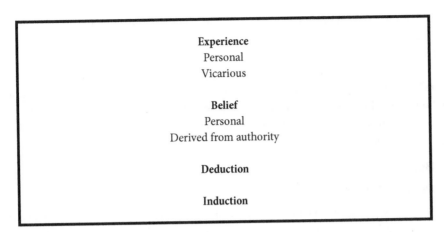

Figure 1.1 Major approaches to learning.

assignment of personal understanding. A child whose experimental curiosity leads him or her to extend a finger into a flame may immediately conclude that the tendency of fire to burn and cause pain is essential knowledge. Less dramatic, less traumatic experiences may involve a longer transformation from experience into knowledge. A child who does not learn from experimental curiosity may lead a very traumatic life and require protections from parental guidance or societal interventions that are unnecessary for most children. Lifelong patterns of failure to learn from personal experience are associated with psychopathic or sociopathic personalities.

A librarian may find that his or her behavior during an interaction with patrons—smiling, asking welcoming questions, engaging in active listening—results in positive and productive experiences. That librarian may find that not only are the reactions of patrons more positive in response to such behavior, but that his or her professional experiences are enhanced. A librarian who does not learn from such experiences may develop a pattern of behavior that is counter to both successful interaction with patrons and to norms of professional behavior.

Vicarious Experience

A second form of experience is vicarious experience—knowledge derived from the experiences of others. No individual can experience everything, nor is it desirable for everyone to experience everything. Every society throughout history has generated and perpetuated some means of imparting knowledge through vicarious experience. Even those societies that emphasize a potentially traumatic rite of passage build readiness through sharing collective experiences with those individuals who must undergo the rite. Both the news media and the entertainment media play significant roles in building knowledge through vicarious experience. The professional library and information science literature provides vicarious experience by providing access to the programs, philosophies, and activities of parallel institutions. Orientation and training for new professionals is another prominent source of vicarious experience, as are professional conferences and meetings, continuing education activities, and the formal education provided by schools of library and information science.

One of the potential negative outcomes of vicarious experience as an approach to acquiring knowledge is that the division between reality and fiction is not always adequately clear. On October 30, 1938, thousands of listeners panicked in response to a radio broadcast describing an invasion of New Jersey by Martians. Many people did not realize until much later that they had been listening to a very convincing radio play of H. G. Wells's *War of the Worlds.*

The "we have always done it this way" syndrome and the "we tried that and it didn't work" argument in professional service are also negative outcomes of vicarious experience. In both cases, the listener is being invited to accept the message without question or argument. Methodical exploration and critical analysis, however, frequently reveal that neither message is accurate.

Belief

Personal Belief

Belief is experience augmented by additional contextual information. Belief is frequently very closely related to experience—the dividing line between knowledge derived from experience and knowledge derived from belief is not always readily apparent.

Belief can be directly derived from personal experience. The child who has burned a finger by touching a flame will very probably conclude that other parts of his or her body are also susceptible to pain from the same source; only a very unusual child would repeat the same experiment with another finger to determine whether the principle of pain associated with heat is a general one, although such an experiment would facilitate the transition from belief based on limited experience to empirical knowledge based on a systematic series of experiences. Furthermore, the burnt child may reasonably conclude that all human beings are subject to pain, even though he or she cannot directly experience the pain felt by others.

Belief derived from experience may extend further as well—the child who has been burned may conclude that pain will also be felt when inanimate objects such as toys or stuffed animals come in contact with fire. At a greater extreme, the child may conclude that fire is inherently and without exception a *bad* thing that should be eradicated. This could turn into a lasting phobic fear of fire or a pathological belief that could shape the child's approach to adult life.

A professional who finds that welcoming behaviors are productive and rewarding in interactions with patrons may develop the positive belief that such behaviors are similarly productive when interacting with colleagues, administrators, and the public in general. These behaviors may not only be effective in professional life, but may extend to situations outside the workplace. A professional whose experience leads to a belief that the best solution to every encounter is to engage in behaviors that please others may develop patterns of behavior that are counterproductive to the professional endeavor. A librarian who responds to all challenges to library materials by acquiescing, for instance, may be acting on a belief that avoiding any semblance of conflict is always desirable.

Belief Derived from Authority

In addition to belief derived from personal experience, belief derived from authority plays an important role in assessing knowledge. A responsible parent may engage in appropriate efforts to limit a child's direct personal experiences by introducing beliefs that are backed by parental authority. Although some experience of pain is perhaps an essential learning experience, teaching a child to avoid some painful experiences is critical. Belief derived from authority also pervades systems of religion, education, government, and professions. The imprimatur of the Library of Congress, the American Library Association, or another institution to which professional status has been conferred may cause professionals to believe—in some cases unquestioningly—that the practices and views of that institution are necessarily representative of truth.

Professional standards and guidelines are encapsulations of belief derived from a combination of experience, authority, and sometimes research and evaluation. The American Library Association's *Code of Ethics* represents a set of beliefs derived from the collective experiences of library and information professionals issue under the authority of the Association.[2] The Reference & User Service Association's *Guidelines for Behavioral Performance of Reference and Information Service Providers* explicitly identify the importance of approachability, interest, and listening/inquiring in conducting a reference interview.[3]

Formal Logic

Experience and belief are natural, primarily informal processes that are a deeply ingrained part of human life. Two additional major approaches to determining knowledge are more formal and systematic. Although they cannot be entirely separated from experience and belief, they provide structured frameworks within which experience and belief can be positioned and examined.

Deduction

Deduction is the systematic application of general principles to specific cases. If it is true that fire burns human beings, then it can be assumed that fire will burn any individual human being. If welcoming behaviors work effectively for most library and information professionals, they can be assumed to work for all such professionals. The traditional logical structure of deduction is the syllogism, an argument with two premises and a conclusion:

Premise:	All human beings are mortal.
Premise:	Melvil Dewey was a human being.
Conclusion:	Melvil Dewey was mortal.

In any syllogism the truth of the conclusion is a dependent function of the truth of the premises and of the logic of the syllogistic structure. The premises of the preceding example are both true, therefore the conclusion is reasonable and acceptable.

If one or more of the premises is false, the conclusion is necessarily false as well. In the following example, the second premise is false; as a result the conclusion, although it is an appropriate logical extension of the premises, is false as well.

Premise:	All gods are immortal.
Premise:	Melvil Dewey was a god.
Conclusion:	Melvil Dewey is immortal.

Although Melvil Dewey may to many people in the library world be a figurative god, and his works may indeed possess a substantial element of immortality, this syllogism cannot be taken as literally true because the second premise is not literally true.

Truth in the premises is not a guarantee of truth in the conclusion. The following syllogism contains true premises. The conclusion is true as well, but fails to follow logically from the premises.

Premise:	All human beings are mortal.
Premise:	Melvil Dewey is dead.
Conclusion:	Melvil Dewey was a human being.

Deductive logic is an important formal structure that has played a long history in the development of scientific and scholarly thought. Deduction is the basis for most of Aristotelian logic, which was the fundamental principle of scholarly reasoning up until the Scientific Revolution. In the deductive reasoning process, general principles or theories are applied to specific situations. The literature review and analysis that is an appropriate first action for both research and evaluation plays a deductive role by identifying relevant general principles and theories that may apply to a specific situation. Deduction in modern research and evaluation is used primarily for generating questions and hypotheses and for testing established theories or principles. It is generally not used in research as an approach to gathering or analyzing data.

Many approaches to evaluation are fundamentally deductive in nature. Comparing local library performance to standards published by professional associations or governmental agencies is a deductive process in which a general principle—a *standard*—is used to draw conclusions about a specific case—a particular library. List checking to assess the quality or comprehensiveness of a collection is also a deductive process. A library may routinely compare its collection to sources such as the *Fiction Catalog* or *Reference Sources for Small and Medium-Sized Libraries*. List checking of this sort relies largely on acceptance of the authority and competence of the publisher, editors, and contributors who prepared the list.

Induction

Induction is the formulation of general principles based on information about specific cases. In the inductive reasoning process, evidence from specific situations is used to generate a general principle or build a body of theory. Induction is closely associated with the Scientific Revolution in general and with English mathematician and scientist Roger Bacon in particular. Where deduction is primarily logical and qualitative, induction is very closely associated with quantitative methods.

The basic principle of induction is that observation of a suitable subset of some phenomenon of interest—a *sample*—may substitute for observation of the phenomenon in its entirety. Some level of induction occurs naturally and automatically as part of the human experience; individuals categorize and summarize their personal experiences, vicarious experiences, and beliefs, and formulate general principles based on that analysis. The distinctive factor in systematic induction is an attempt to divorce the observational process from personal values and beliefs and to create a dispassionate body of knowledge.

Induction is very closely linked to both experimental and survey research. Effective inductive analysis requires identification of an appropriate and manageable approach to observing the phenomenon of interest, selection of those characteristics of the phenomenon that will be observed, determination of a minimum or optimal number of observations, gathering data related to the selected characteristics for the target number of observations, summarization of the gathered data, and formulation of conclusions that may serve as general principles for understanding the phenomenon. Researching and writing a typical term paper is an inductive process in which a student identifies and gathers pertinent sources, synthesizes the content of the sources, and draws a conclusion or formulates an argument based on that synthesis. The annual Association of Research Libraries' *ARL Statistics* is a survey that gathers numeric data on the collections, resources, and staffs of all 123 ARL member libraries. In addition to making available data for individual member libraries, the *ARL Statistics* includes calculated statistics such as the mean and mode. The mean number of volumes held by ARL libraries in 2008–2009, for instance, was 4,528,262.[4]

The Induction–Deduction Cycle

Deduction and induction are used together in the research and evaluation process in a cyclical manner. The cyclical nature of the relationship between induction and deduction draws upon the strengths of each logical model and uses the strengths of each to balance the weaknesses of the other. Figure 1.2 provides a graphic representation of the induction–deduction cycle.

The induction–deduction cycle applies both to evaluation and to research, but works a bit differently for evaluation programs and research projects. The induction–deduction cycle is a model, not a rule, and applies in a variable manner depending on the nature of the specific problem or question to be addressed.

The Induction–Deduction Cycle and Evaluation

A fundamental characteristic of evaluation as it is applied in this text is that it focuses on a local environment and is intended to solve a specific problem and add understanding for purposes primarily internal to a single institution. The following is an example of the induction–deduction cycle applied to an evaluation process.

1. The cycle usually begins when a general interest in some phenomenon is derived from informal inductive observation of the phenomenon, frequently through direct contact between a professional and a process or product for which that professional has some

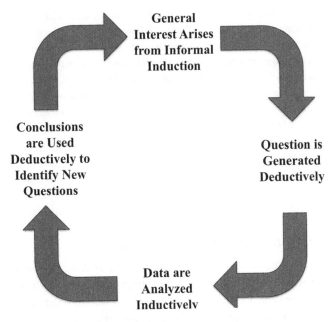

Figure 1.2   Induction and deduction.

assigned or natural sense of responsibility. The motivation for evaluation is frequently an observation of a real-life phenomenon that reveals the existence of a definite or potential problem. A university librarian, for instance, might observe that both the number of questions asked at the reference desk and the number of books circulated in that specific library have been declining in recent years. This informal observation, based on data that may be incomplete, leads to speculation as to the nature of the decline.

2. Working from the inductive, informal observation, and using that observation as a tentative general principle for initial understanding of the phenomenon of interest, a research question or hypothesis (or more than one of either or both) is generated deductively. The research question or hypothesis serves as a general principle for understanding the phenomenon that plays a temporary role pending systematic gathering of data for use in an inductive examination of the nature of the phenomenon. For the example presented in step 1, the informal, inductive observation of data related to declining reference and circulation activity leads to the formulation of a question: are these declines indicators of an overall decline in the use of the library? The broad question serves as a tentative conclusion that may lead directly to deductive speculation regarding subquestions, examples of which might include:

   • Is use of the library's digital resources also declining?

   • Are the library's patrons interacting with reference staff in modes other than face-to-face?

   • Are the indicators in use by the library the most appropriate for effective management and decision making?

   • Are there differences in use among faculty, graduate students, and undergraduate students?

   • Are there differences among users from different colleges in the university?

   • Are there differences between full-time and part-time student use?

   • Are there differences between residential and commuter student use?

3. Using the formulated question as a guide, observational data related to the phenomenon are systematically, formally gathered and then analyzed inductively to formulate conclusions. The question "are these declines indicators of an overall decline in the use of the library?" suggests a need to examine additional sources of data, some of which may be readily available as preexisting routinely gathered figures. It may additionally be necessary to gather new data about use of the library to supplement data already available. The introduction of subquestions in addition to the major question frequently leads to the need to gather additional data.

4. The conclusions are used deductively to assess the performance of the library, to make decisions regarding library policy and practice, and to identify further targets for evaluation. The evaluation process may, for instance, reveal that overall use of the library has not declined, but that numbers of reference transactions and circulation counts are of declining importance and need to be routinely accompanied by other measures.

The Induction–Deduction Cycle and Research

A directly parallel process is typical of research. A primary difference between evaluation and research is that a single library, which is the legitimate and primary focus of evaluation, is at best a limited convenience sample for purposes of research, which is focused on more universal concerns. The cycle, however, is fundamentally the same.

1. Again, the cycle begins with a general interest in some phenomenon derived from informal inductive observation of the phenomenon. To parallel the example used in discussing the induction–deduction cycle and evaluation in the context of research, a university librarian observes that both the number of questions asked at the reference desk and the number of books circulated has been declining in recent years. This informal observation, based on data that may be incomplete, leads to speculation as to the nature of the decline. Unlike the evaluation example, however, in this case the speculation focuses on the possibility of a general decline in the use of academic libraries.

2. A research question or hypothesis is generated deductively from prior understanding of the phenomenon. The observation regarding declines in reference transactions and circulation in the local library leads to the question: Is use of university libraries declining? The act of formulating the question implies the possibility of a general conclusion that use is in decline. This question can easily lead to the same subquestions identified in the evaluation examples, but can also lead to additional subquestions such as

   - Are there differences between Association of Research Libraries members and non-member libraries?

   - Are there differences between comprehensive universities and liberal arts colleges?

   - Are there differences between state-supported institutions and private institutions?

   Ultimately, addressing these and other questions may lead to the need to address more fundamental questions that have meaningful implications for both research and evaluation, such as

   - Does circulation of print materials accurately reflect use of library resources?

   - Do guidelines and practices designed for face-to-face transactions effectively translate to a digital environment?

3. Observational data related to the phenomenon are gathered and analyzed inductively to formulate conclusions. Some data may be readily available from published sources such as the *ARL Statistics* and the annual surveys conducted by the National Center for Educational Statistics. It may also be necessary to gather additional data to support all aspects of the question and its subquestions; these data will need to be gathered from some appropriately selected sample drawn from the universe of university libraries.

4. The conclusions are used deductively to inform the field and perhaps the broader public and to identify new targets for research. Research results generally do not directly guide local policy, practice, or decision making, but may serve as motivators for specific evaluation programs.

VALIDITY AND RELIABILITY

Validity and reliability are concepts that apply to all kinds of research and evaluation (historical, descriptive, experimental). The terms are most frequently associated with quantitative approaches to research and evaluation, primarily because explicit tools and techniques for assessing validity and reliability in quantitative research and evaluation have been developed and tested. Validity and reliability are frequently discussed in relationship to approaches to measurement or tools used in measurement, although the meaning of the terms is actually broader than that.

Validity

Validity refers to the extent to which conclusions accurately reflect reality. Another way of interpreting this is that validity has to do with the extent to which conclusions are true or accurate.

1. Internal validity has to do with the extent to which relationships among variables are accurately described. A variable is an observable entity of interest to the investigator, the value or nature of which is not known at the outset of the research project. The essential nature of a variable is that its value or nature can vary. Imagine that the hypothesis of a study is "there will be a positive correlation between scores for the analytical portion of the Graduate Record Examination and the number of correct answers to a selected list of known-answer factual reference questions." The implication of this hypothesis is that there is a systematic, predictable relationship between the abilities measured by the analytical GRE score and the ability to answer factual questions. The results of whatever approach is taken to testing the hypothesis are very dependent on the extent to which the two variables (GRE scores and correct answer scores) are truly related and the extent to which the true relationship is revealed by the research and evaluation process. Ensuring internal validity for this hypothesis requires appropriate and careful data gathering, appropriate and accurate measurement, and appropriate analysis. It is very easy to deliberately undermine internal validity. It would be possible, for instance, to manipulate the relationship between GRE scores and question-answering ability by selecting only participants with high analytical GRE scores or by framing the questions such that they deliberately match the abilities assessed by the GRE analytical test.

2. Construct validity refers to the extent to which variables are accurately identified and described. The GRE analytical test certainly measures *something* and has been linked to success in a variety of academic disciplines. It was not, however, designed as a test of reference ability and may be a poor indicator of reference ability even if the hypothesized relationship is supported by the research and evaluation project. The ability to answer factual question is one important component in reference ability but cannot be considered a comprehensive indicator of reference performance. Construct validity is largely a function of the extent to which the investigator is cognizant of and honest about the limitations of operational definitions of variables. A failure to ensure construct validity is always a direct threat to internal validity.

3. External validity is the extent to which conclusions can be generalized and applied to other environments. There are three common approaches to ensuring external validity: (1) carrying out the research and evaluation project in a real-life or realistic setting, (2) gathering data in a manner that constitutes a representative sample, and (3) replication of the research and evaluation project in a different environment.

Reliability

Reliability refers to the extent to which conclusions are repeatable or replicable. A basic principle of reliability is that if the same approach to gathering and analyzing data is repeated with an acceptable level of precision in a directly comparable environment the results will be the same. The definitive test of reliability is direct replication. Although that test is rarely actually applied, the charge to the investigator is to present the results of research and evaluation in a manner that would make it possible for a reader of the research and evaluation report to replicate the study.

Reliability is closely related to measurement, which is addressed in Chapter 6, "Measurement, Populations, Samples, and Sampling." The ability to measure phenomena accurately and consistently is essential to ensuring reliability in research and evaluation. Intercoder reliability, also known as interrater, interobserver, or interjudge reliability, is a concern in any research or evaluation project in which more than one individual is responsible for observing, recording, or describing data. Intercoder reliability is a measure of the extent to which two or more observers agree on what has been observed and how to describe what has been observed. Imagine an evaluation study in which library patrons are asked to provide open-ended answers to the question "Are the library's operating hours adequate?" The most obvious answers are "yes" and "no," but the open-ended nature of the question allows for a wide range of answers, including "most of the time," "I guess so," "I don't know," and others. If multiple research team members are responsible for coding and consolidating those answers, there must be some set of rules for ensuring that they agree in their interpretations of answers. Where one coder may automatically interpret "they're just fine" as being a wholly positive response, another coder may interpret the same expression as meaning barely adequate.

The Relationship between Validity and Reliability

Validity and reliability are very closely related; both are important aspects of quality research and evaluation. There are three possible relationships between validity and reliability:

1. Conclusions are valid and reliable. This is the desired outcome of all research and evaluation. If either the validity or the reliability of the conclusions drawn from a research and evaluation endeavor is in question, then the conclusions themselves are in question and the research and evaluation as a whole cannot be accepted as a useful basis for either understanding or action.

2. Conclusions are reliable but not valid. If an instrument used in measurement is inherently but consistently flawed, it will yield the same results whenever it is applied but those results will always be incorrect. A ruler that is an eighth of an inch short will consistently produce measurements that are incorrect by an eighth of an inch. A question that can be misinterpreted may be consistently misinterpreted. If an operational definition fails to accurately represent the concept being defined, results based on that operational definition will be consistently wrong. Replication of a study that yields invalid conclusions may lead to extensive reproduction of the same invalid conclusions. The situation in which conclusions drawn from research and evaluation are reliable but not valid is one of the most difficult to detect and correct and is one reason that research and evaluation designs tend to focus more on validity than on reliability.

3. Conclusions are neither valid nor reliable. If an instrument is flawed in a manner that produces inconsistent or random results, the conclusions drawn from the use of that instrument will be neither valid nor reliable. Similarly, if an operational definition results in a representation of reality that is overly flexible, results based on that definition will have an unacceptable level of variability. When conclusions cannot be established as being either valid or reliable, they must be rejected and the research and evaluation project as a whole must be rejected as well.

Note that there is a fourth relationship that is not listed (conclusions are valid but not reliable). All valid conclusions are to some extent reliable; if conclusions are not reliable, however, validity may be difficult to ascertain. Again, the investigator has an obligation to present in the research and evaluation report those details that make it possible for the reader to ascertain validity.

DEFINITIONS OF RESEARCH AND EVALUATION

Research

The *Oxford English Dictionary* provides the following definitions for research:

1. The act of searching carefully for or pursuing a specified thing or person; an instance of this.

2. Systematic investigation or inquiry aimed at contributing to knowledge of a theory, topic, and so on, by careful consideration, observation, or study of a subject. In later use also: original critical or scientific investigation carried out under the auspices of an academic or other institution.

3. Investigation undertaken in order to obtain material for a book, article, thesis, and so on; an instance of this.

4. The product of systematic investigation, presented in written (esp. published) form.

The second definition is most directly related to the focus of this book, but the other three are pertinent as well. Research is properly both a process and a product.

Herbert Goldhor, in *An Introduction to Scientific Research in Librarianship,* which was among the earliest comprehensive attempts to describe the real and potential roles of research in the study of library practice, defined research as "any conscious premeditated inquiry."[5] The fundamental point of Goldhor's definition is in the elements of consciousness and premeditation. Goldhor, who was for many years director of the Library Research Center at the University of Illinois, frequently lamented that librarians are constantly engaged in activities that are almost research—gathering data, compiling statistical reports, searching for new ways to do things more effectively—without adding the elements of "conscious premeditated inquiry" that would turn those activities into research.

Evaluation

The *Oxford English Dictionary* definitions of evaluation are:

1. The action of appraising or valuing (goods, etc.); a calculation or statement of value.

2. The action of evaluating or determining the value of (a mathematical expression, a physical quantity, etc.), or of estimating the force of (probabilities, evidence, etc.).

Evaluation in the context of this book spans both of these definitions. Evaluation has to do with assigning value to things, institutions, processes, or individuals. The central purpose of evaluation is improvement of service in a specific environment or institution, although evaluation may address more than one environment in a comparative manner and may produce results that are of interest beyond the specific institution. Nietzsche's depiction of evaluation as creation in the quote at the beginning of this chapter is appropriate and illustrative: evaluation is a creative activity intended to bring about improvement.

The process of assigning value is perhaps the essential difference between research and evaluation. Research primarily describes what *is* and provides evidence to support general conclusions and to guide understanding and theory development. Evaluation balances factors in a given situation to determine best use of results to achieve desired outcomes.

THE CHARACTERISTICS OF RESEARCH AND EVALUATION

Research and evaluation are characterized by a number of essential factors. The explicit and conspicuous presence of these factors is an indicator of quality and attention to detail in a research project or evaluation program. Their absence signals the potential for flawed research or evaluation and is suggestive of limitations in the extent to which results can be trusted and to which decisions can be made or actions undertaken. The essential characteristics of research and evaluation are summarized in Figure 1.3. These shared characteristics of research and evaluation may assume very different manifestations; the differences in manifestation are summarized further on in Figure 1.5.

1. Research and evaluation are *planned* activities. Research and evaluation are not natural or organic phenomena and do not just occur. The ultimate success and value of any research or evaluation activity are embedded in the planning process. Sloppy planning almost always results in sloppy implementation, sloppy conclusions, and sloppy decisions. Planning for research is generally focused on achieving overall research integrity and ensuring validity, which is a measure of the extent to which conclusions accurately reflect reality, and reliability, which measures the extent to which conclusions are repeatable or replicable. Planning for evaluation, although it should also take into account validity and reliability, is primarily carried out in the interest of ensuring that data are sufficiently accurate to provide a sound basis for decision making and that measures have a pragmatic value.

2. Research and evaluation are *systematic*. There are two meanings of the word *systematic* that apply to research and evaluation. The first has to do with carrying out work in an orderly and methodical manner, which is an essential component in reliable evaluation and research. The second has to do with systems thinking. A fundamental

---

Research and evaluation are

Planned
Systematic
Controlled
Objective
Goal oriented
Aimed at increasing understanding

Figure 1.3   Essential characteristics of research and evaluation.

aspect of planning for research and evaluation is identification of the systems and structures within which the research or evaluation effort will take place. Understanding the systematic context of the phenomenon to be examined is essential to research and evaluation processes. Research generally explores the relationship between the phenomenon of interest and universal or general systems; in this context, the systematic nature of research is a direct tie to building or expanding an appropriate theoretical base. Evaluation is much more focused on establishing, assessing, and improving local systems.

3. Research and evaluation are *controlled*. The extent to which the process is controlled and the ways in which it is controlled vary according to the general and specific methodologies used to carry out research or evaluation. Some forms of research and evaluation, such as those characterized by ethnographic methods, may appear to be less controlled than others, such as those reliant on experimentation. Regardless of the methodological base or the specific purpose of the project, some aspect of control must be exerted for the results of the project to be both valid and reliable. The role of control in research has primarily to do with assuring validity and reliability. The most obvious aspect of control in research is the use of control groups in experimental research as a check on the validity of an experimental treatment. Control in evaluation usually focuses more on assuring that the evaluation effort itself is appropriately cost-effective and that human factors in the institutional environment are appropriately respected and supported.

4. Research and evaluation are *objective*. In traditional thinking, scientific research can basically be reduced to an assessment of physical reality—of what *is*; that which can be observed. The principle of objectivity does not violate the basic principle that truth and values cannot be completely separated. Objectivity in practice has to do with matching the research or evaluation process to the context of the phenomenon being examined. Objectivity in research is primarily a function of minimizing intentional or accidental bias in the research process; random sampling is a prime tool of objectivity in research. Avoidance of bias is also essential in evaluation, but objectivity in local evaluation may also have to do with ensuring that project design, analysis, decision making, and reporting support fairness and equitable treatment for all constituents. Evaluation tends to be more political and value-laden than research, which may make objectivity more difficult to ensure.

5. Research and evaluation are *goal oriented*. As attractive and amusing as the image of the investigator bumbling around until he or she produces some unexpected beneficial result may be, it is not an accurate portrayal of the way in which research and evaluation really happen. Research and evaluation tend to be very highly focused toward the attainment of very explicitly stated, verifiable goals and objectives. This is especially true of evaluation, which is undertaken to solve specific problems or facilitate explicit decision making, but it is also true when the motivation is simply curiosity about some unexplained phenomenon. The central goal of any research project is ensuring that a carefully defined and precisely stated research question and/or hypothesis is explored in a manner that yields valid and reliable results. The fundamental goals of evaluation are ensuring and improving organizational effectiveness.

6. Research and evaluation are aimed at *increasing understanding*. The role of research and evaluation as approaches to learning is essential. Research and evaluation are not idle or casual endeavors. Even if the goal is very specific and local or even essentially personal in nature, the factor of gaining a better understanding of the phenomenon

under consideration is fundamental. Increasing understanding for purposes of evaluation may be intensely immediate and even transitory, but value cannot be assigned without understanding. Activities that do not lead to increased understanding cannot truly be considered to be research at all. Research and evaluation are somewhat different in that universal or general understanding with a pure goal of increasing knowledge is a legitimate and desirable goal of research, where the increased understanding that characterizes evaluation takes the form of concrete knowledge that can be used for purposes of effective decision making.

In addition to the six essential characteristics of research and evaluation, there are four characteristics that are highly desirable. These characteristics can be thought of as factors that add value to research and evaluation. The four value-added research and evaluation characteristics are summarized in Figure 1.4.

1. Research and evaluation may be *predictive*. There is a special appeal to research and evaluation projects that produce results of a predictive nature. There is an obvious added value when the results of a research initiative or evaluation program can be used to predict future outcomes or influence future decisions. This is true even if the predictive nature of the results is limited or incomplete. The predictive role of research leads to identification of future trends and their implications for the profession and/or society. The predictive role of evaluation identifies targets for future decisions and actions and targets future evaluation needs.

2. The results of research and evaluation may be *cumulative*. As results of similar research efforts or repeated evaluations are assembled and summarized, there is the potential for a cumulative synergetic impact that greatly exceeds the benefits of any of the individual projects. Cumulation of results is especially important in building and testing bodies of theory and in evaluating progress over time. Time series are an especially important component in evaluation. Cumulation in research can lead to expanded understanding of the field and the field's role in society. Cumulation in research builds effectiveness and robustness in the institution's decision-making toolkit and helps make future evaluation more efficient and more effective.

3. Research and evaluation processes and results may be *transferable*. Transferability is closely related to the factor of prediction. Transferability and cumulation in research and evaluation are very closely related and mutually supportive. The outcomes of evaluation are transferable when a process used in one environment can be effectively and usefully replicated in another environment or when the results of a project conducted in one environment have direct implications for decision making or action in a different environment. Transferability in evaluation is most effectively manifested when

---

Predictive
Cumulative
Transferable
Used as a basis for action

Figure 1.4   Desirable characteristics of research and evaluation.

results produced in one institutional environment can be applied in a parallel institutional environment. Transferability in evaluation means that an evaluation process may not have to be carried out across the entire institutional base; instead, a particular department, division, or branch can serve as a test-bed for evaluation with a reasonable expectation that what is learned in the test-bed setting can be directly applied across the institution. Transferability in evaluation may lend support to the development of best practices—accepted approaches to action that are based on the shared understanding and collective evaluation outcomes of a professional body. Transferability in research is heightened when the results of a research endeavor suggest enhancements to understanding closely related phenomena and particularly when the results of research suggest targets for future research.

4. Research and evaluation results may be *used as a basis for action*. Action and decision making are especially important roles for research and evaluation in library and information science. An obvious focus of research and evaluation in any professional field is the generation of approaches and methods for improving professional practice. Results may also have meaningful policy implications. A series of studies carried out by Lance and others documents a positive correlation between school library media center resources and student reading scores, a finding that has substantial implications for school administrators and community leaders.[6] Research results are sometimes a direct basis for action, but are more frequently a guide to targets for and approaches to local evaluation. The outcomes of research are transformed into action when new questions are generated, targets for theory development and testing are identified, or new methods of exploration are generated. Action based on effective decision making is a fundamental goal of evaluation. Although some concrete change or improvement is frequently an anticipated outcome of evaluation, a positive decision to preserve the status quo is also a form of action.

Characteristic	Manifestation	
	Research	**Evaluation**
Planned	Assurance of integrity, validity, and reliability	Assurance of accuracy and pragmatic benefit
Systematic	Grounded in universal systems	Grounded in local systems
Controlled	Assurance of validity and reliability	Assurance of economy and human factors
Objective	Avoidance of bias	Assurance of organizational integrity
Goal-oriented	Grounded in research questions and hypotheses	Grounded in improvement of organizational effectiveness
Aimed at increasing understanding	Universal understanding	Knowledge for decision making
Predictive	Focused on future trends and expansion of knowledge	Focused on future decision making and future evaluation needs
Cumulative	Expansion of the field	Expansion of bases for decision making
Transferable	Applicable across institutions and environments	Applicable across a single institution
Used as a basis for action	Indirect, as a guide to local evaluation	Direct, as a basis for local decision making

Figure 1.5 Manifestations of the characteristics of research and evaluation

LEVELS OF RESEARCH AND EVALUATION

Research and evaluation occur at varying levels of complexity, from extremely simple to intimidatingly complex. The typology presented here and summarized in Figure 1.6 is adapted from Simon and Burstein's general categorization of research goals and methodologies.[7] Each category adds to the previous one to yield an order of increasing complexity.

1. Description is a basic process that is essential for all research and evaluation. A phenomenon that cannot be described at least provisionally cannot be understood even provisionally. The goal of description in research and evaluation is to generate a general understanding of a phenomenon of interest by encapsulating the fundamental characteristics of the phenomenon, usually in the form of a narrative. That narrative may be as brief as a single word or short phrase or as long as a complete and detailed case study. In some research and evaluation projects, description is a preliminary step prior to other activities. For other projects, description may be employed as the sole and fundamental activity. Some disciplines, such as anthropology and ethnography, rely very heavily on description as a core research process.

2. Classification is the process of assigning different manifestations of a phenomenon to discrete categories as a means of understanding fundamental differences or variations within that phenomenon. Classification is most frequently undertaken as part of a larger process, but may be a legitimate activity in and of itself. The development of specific, detailed taxonomies is a classification activity that is especially important in the biological and biomedical sciences. Classification plays a special role in library and information science that is most commonly associated with collocation and retrieval of information but can also play a research and evaluation role.

3. Measurement and estimation are used to establish the size or extent of a phenomenon. Effective measurement requires reduction of the phenomenon of interest to some set of summary characteristics. That reduction process inevitably results in the loss of the richness that is an advantage of narrative description. The most difficult aspects of measurement are determining which characteristics to measure and developing the tools and metrics for measurement. Some phenomena are more amenable to measurement than others; those that are most easily measurable are frequently those of least interest. Use of library materials can to some extent be measured in terms of circulation, counts of items left on tables, interlibrary loan requests, and similar counts. Usefulness of library services is a much more elusive concept that mostly defies direct or accurate measurement. It is convenient to distinguish between substantive phenomena that can

Description
Classification
Measurement and estimation
Comparison
Relationship
Cause and effect

Figure 1.6   Levels of research and evaluation.

be directly measured and insubstantive phenomena that can be measured only through indirect means that yield estimates rather than precise measurements. Measurement is addressed in greater detail in Chapter 6.

4. Comparison is the extension of measurement to multiple manifestations of the phenomenon of interest. Comparison combines the elements of classification and measurement. This may involve time series, in which some phenomenon is measured on a recurring basis over time to assess chronological trends. Libraries frequently use time series as a fundamental component in evaluation. Alternatively, the comparison may involve multiple similar cases. Comparing use measures for libraries of a similar size and type, for instance, may yield interesting results about patterns and variations in use.

5. Relationship research focuses on the ways in which different characteristics or manifestations of a phenomenon are related to each other. The search for relationships is a step toward understanding not only the nature of the phenomenon but also exploring the root causes of the nature of the phenomenon. A relationship study of use of library materials might explore whether circulation varies in public libraries of similar sizes as a function of whether they are located in urban, suburban, or rural areas.

6. Cause and effect is a special kind of relationship in which the search is not only for the existence of a relationship but for evidence that one characteristic or factor systematically and consistently influences another. Causation is in practice very difficult to determine except in experimental research. Even if there is a consistent, predictable relationship between the setting (urban, suburban, rural) of a public library of a specific size and the volume of library materials circulated, it is a long step from that observation to a conclusive demonstration that that setting in and of itself causes a particular pattern of circulation.

THE TRADITIONAL RESEARCH DICHOTOMY

Research is often categorized into a dichotomy that distinguishes between basic research and applied research. In this scheme, basic (pure, theoretical) research is aimed at increasing knowledge, with no specific practical application in mind while applied (action oriented, decision making) research is aimed at improving some body of practice. Evaluation is most commonly associated with applied research and applied methods, while research is frequently associated with more academic or theoretical motives.

In reality, the distinction is not that clear-cut. In Pasteur's words, "There are no such things as applied sciences, only applications of science."[8] Although pure research is unquestionably a very real phenomenon and many investigators are employed in the pursuit of increased learning for its own sake, research ideas do not arise in a vacuum but in the tangible environment of the real world. It is difficult to envision an investigator engaged in a project for which there is truly no specific desired outcome that can be applied, especially in professional disciplines such as medicine, law, engineering, and library and information science.

At the same time, effective evaluation that is directly oriented toward decision making, even in the confines of a very specific local environment, must have the outcome of yielding new understanding of some phenomenon that has the potential for being added to the cumulative knowledge base related to that phenomenon. At the very least, good evaluation draws on relevant research. This is the juncture that ties research to evaluation.

Ultimately, the distinction between pure and applied research is not so much in what is done but in the motivation for doing it, and even then the distinction is frequently excessively subtle.

MAJOR RESEARCH AND EVALUATION PARADIGMS

A *paradigm* is a model or pattern used in understanding a particular domain of interest. Thomas Kuhn, in his book *The Structure of Scientific Revolutions,* used the term paradigm to describe the mental image or model scientists employ to understand a body of knowledge.[9] Two major research and evaluation paradigms that are sometimes viewed as competing for dominance are the quantitative model and the qualitative model.

Quantitative Methods

Quantitative (scientific) methods focus on measuring and summarizing the characteristics of the entities being studied. Observations tend to fall into predetermined, precise categories. Quantitative methods are very closely related to the use of statistical methods as analytical tools. Quantification is essential to exploring relationships and especially to exploring cause and effect relationships. The quantitative model is characteristic of most research in the physical, biological, and behavioral sciences. Quantification is also characteristic of most approaches to evaluation.

The quantitative model is sometimes linked to *logical positivism,* a school of philosophical thought that arose in the 1920s. A basic tenet of logical positivism is that knowledge (or truth) can be derived only from a combination of formal logic and empirical experience. By extension, logical positivism is frequently taken to imply that there is an objective, verifiable universe and that the essential purpose of research is description of that universe. Taken to an extreme, logical positivism assumes that the investigator is a completely objective, neutral observer of natural phenomenon and plays no role whatsoever in influencing those phenomena. The neutral role of the investigator is such that any other investigator can be expected to view the phenomenon in exactly the same way.

Quantitative Methods and Data Reduction

Data reduction is a term used in quantitative research to describe "any technique used to transform data from raw data into a more useful form of data."[10] Data reduction—the process of reducing a complex concept to a simpler, more manageable representation—is essential to quantitative research. A frequently employed quantitative approach to patron satisfaction with library services involves distribution of a questionnaire followed by a tally of responses in predefined categories. Such a survey frequently uses some form of scale to allow respondents to assess levels of satisfaction with various services. Satisfaction with services is inherently a complex personal judgment. Many patrons may be unaware of any level of satisfaction with library services prior to being asked to provide an assessment. When a decision is made to implement a quantitative representation of satisfaction in the form of a rating scale, the investigator has accepted, at least tacitly, the necessity of reducing the complexity of the concept in the interest of obtaining numeric assessments that can be readily tabulated for comparison across patrons. Data reduction is revisited in Chapter 6, "Measurement, Populations, Samples, and Sampling," Chapter 8, "Descriptive Methods—Questionnaires and Interviews," and Chapter 13, "Descriptive and Inferential Statistics."

Qualitative Methods

Qualitative (naturalistic) methods focus on in-depth examination of the nature of the entities being studied. Qualitative methods tend to emphasize depth and complexity rather than quantity. Observations are unpredictable and open-ended. The qualitative model is characteristic of much research in the social sciences, particularly in disciplines such as anthropology and ethnography and has in recent years played an increasing role throughout the social sciences. Given has provided a comprehensive, in-depth overview of qualitative research methods.[11]

A qualitative approach to assessing patron satisfaction with library services may take the form of a focus group experience. A focus group brings together representative constituents in a free form, open discussion that centers around a specified service, function, or concern. Very general questions are asked to stimulate discussion, but there are no predefined answer categories. Results are not summarized or tallied, but are presented verbatim.

A substantial emphasis of the literature on qualitative research, particularly in those fields where the quantitative model has historically been dominant, has focused on explicit rejection of quantification. The backlash from the quantitative school has frequently denigrated qualitative methods. This has resulted in a state of tension and conflict that has tended to have a largely negative impact. As approaches to qualitative research have matured and become more widely applied, an increasing number of investigators have begun to combine quantitative and qualitative methods to more fully understand phenomena of interest.

The Qualitative Paradigm

The nature of the quantitative paradigm is relatively easy to understand in that applying numeric values to phenomena is a familiar process that is deeply embedded in education from early childhood through postgraduate experiences. The qualitative paradigm is somewhat more difficult for the uninitiated to understand, in part because it is an emergent way of approaching research and evaluation.

Synonyms and Near Synonyms

The research tradition has its deepest roots in scientific models and modes of inquiry. The emphasis is on objectivity and exploration of the physical environment. Quantitative analysis and statistical tools are applied as means of ensuring objectivity and to provide consistency and comparability in describing what is observed. The emphasis of most reports of quantitative research studies is on summarization of the ways in which manifestations of the phenomenon being studied are alike or different.

Qualitative research comprises a family of methods that deemphasize quantification in favor of studying the fundamental qualities of phenomena. The emphasis of most reports of qualitative research is on explication of specific manifestations of the phenomenon being studied.

Quantitative research and qualitative research are sometimes viewed and treated as being opposites or even as being opposing armed camps. Another point of view is that there is a continuum that extends from entirely qualitative studies through various mixtures of qualitative and quantitative methods to purely quantitative studies. It may be more accurate, however, to view quantitative and qualitative research as being differing perspectives. Just as historical research focuses on the past and descriptive research focuses on the present, quantitative research focuses on examination of the quantifiable aspects of a phenomenon of interest and qualitative research focuses on the nonnumeric qualities of a phenomenon. It is quite reasonable to expect that any given phenomenon can be examined from either a quantitative or a qualitative perspective or from both perspectives simultaneously.

One of the characteristics frequently ascribed to qualitative research is the principle that the research need defines and shapes the nature of the research. Qualitative research tends to be more exploratory than conclusive in nature. The focus is on the particular rather than the generalizable. There are many closely related terms in the general domain of qualitative research. The definitions given below overlap and are not necessarily subject to universal agreement.

1. Qualitative research is a broad term that serves as a summarizing and unifying name for a very broad range of methods and tools. Just as there is no one historical research method, there is no unitary qualitative research method.

2. Naturalistic research, also known as naturalistic inquiry, is frequently used as a general synonym for qualitative research but can also have a more specific meaning related to the naturalistic paradigm. One of the earliest proponents of naturalistic inquiry, Herbert Blumer, described naturalistic research as research built "on patient, careful and imaginative life study, not quick shortcuts or technical instruments. While its progress remains slow and tedious, it has the virtue of remaining in close and continuing relations with the natural social world."[12] The basic notion of the naturalistic paradigm is that there is no one objective reality but instead are as many realities as there are interpretations of reality. The goal of naturalistic research in this narrower definition is exploration of the ways in which reality is understood and in which interpretations of reality are derived and articulated.

3. Feminist research "shares many of the tasks of traditional research but approaches those tasks from a radically different perspective, one that explicitly identifies the investigator's emotional involvement with the subject; sees investigators as participants who are often not neutral; gains ethos not from objectivity but from community; and embraces pluralistic, rather than definitive, theories and conclusions."[13] Feminist research challenges the Aristotelian concept of logic and the Baconian model of scientific research as being essentially masculine concepts that may be of limited value in studies of a gender-specific nature.

4. Artistic research is a term that has multiple meanings. One prominent use of the term is to describe the contributions artistic or other creative activities make to the advancement of knowledge. Design research is a specific case of this definition of artistic research and refers to the application of systematic principles to the processes of designing, developing, and refining products. Design research has been explored in such diverse arenas as architecture and information systems ergonomics. A second use has to do with the application of principles adopted from the arts and humanities to the kinds of questions more usually explored through quantitative research. Humanistic research is a specific case of this definition in which the emphasis is on examination of cultural systems and artifacts to address questions that fall into the domain of historical or descriptive research. Humanistic research raises "questions about the meanings of consciousness, conduct, and culture in a context of diversity and change."[14] A third definition focuses on "research into artistic practices and materials."[15]

5. Impressionistic research is research conducted to produce an overview or general sense of the phenomenon of interest. No attempt is made to assess the extent to which manifestations of the phenomenon are alike or different nor is there any effort to explore or describe the phenomenon in depth. Impressionistic research tends to be used in an essentially definitional manner and is frequently a precursor to some more detail-oriented qualitative study.

6. Nonnumeric research and nonquantitative research are terms that are used to describe qualitative research without explicitly naming it. This appeals to some investigators who feel that applying a name constricts and confines research.

Foundations of Qualitative Research

1. Reality. If there is an opposite to qualitative research, it is experimental research. A fundamental principle of all approaches to qualitative research is the exploration of phenomena in naturally occurring environments, rejecting the artificial and controlled settings critical to experimentation. Nearly all qualitative research, then, is aligned with the purposes of descriptive research and the goal of describing current reality.

2. Complexity. While data reduction is a fundamental component in quantitative research, a basic principle of qualitative research is the value of understanding the raw data in all their dimensions. Qualitative research tends to emphasize data expansion and the derivation of meaning from complex sources of data.

Purposes of Qualitative Research

Peshkin described four basic purposes or functions of qualitative research: description, interpretation, verification, and evaluation.[16] Validation is a fifth purpose slightly different from any of the four described by Peshkin.

1. Description is the core purpose of qualitative research. Description in qualitative research is typically detailed and expressive and emphasizes systematic exploration of the complexities of the phenomenon of interest.

2. Interpretation is the process of applying meaning to the phenomenon being described. Qualitative research tends to emphasize interpretation as a dialectic process in which the investigator asks questions about the phenomenon, derives answers, and uses the answers to build further questions for which answers are also sought.

3. Verification involves testing beliefs, assumptions, theories, or previous interpretations.

4. Evaluation is frequently associated with qualitative research, especially in the context of a strict interpretation of evaluation as the process of assigning value. Qualitative evaluation tends to emphasize personal, social, or societal value rather than matters of productivity, effectiveness, or efficiency.

5. Validation combines elements of interpretation, verification, and evaluation to lend support to conclusions or generalizations. Where verification focuses on confirming the accuracy of preexisting conclusions or interpretations, validation has more to do with placing conclusions or interpretations in a larger system of understanding.

Focuses of Qualitative Research

There are a number of focuses that are frequently described as being characteristic of qualitative research. Hard-core qualitative investigators tend to think in terms of these factors of characteristics that distinguish qualitative research from quantitative research. An alternative view is that these are aspects of research that are reflected in different ways in different research modalities.

1. Rejection of logical positivism. Logical positivism was an early 20th-century movement to apply the precision and predictability of mathematics to all areas of understanding and particularly to philosophy. An essential element of logical positivism is

that a statement about any phenomenon is meaningful only if it can be verified. This combined with the emergence of large-scale scientific research to produce a substantial emphasis on quantification as an essential approach to verification. Qualitative research places greater emphasis on small-scale research and speculative rather than positivist approaches to understanding.

2. Emphasis on description. As mentioned earlier, qualitative research is very oriented toward description of phenomena, often to the extent that a report of a qualitative study tends to be primarily a descriptive narrative with a much lesser emphasis on analysis and interpretation. Qualitative investigators frequently avoid drawing conclusions, preferring to let the reader draw his or her own conclusions.

3. Context. Although understanding the context in which a phenomenon exists is important to all research, qualitative research tends to place greater emphasis on the intimacy of the relationships among the context, the phenomenon, and the investigator. The context, the phenomenon, and the investigator are a triad in which each informs and influences the others. The context is therefore fluid rather than fixed and must be observed and understood in a dynamic manner. The challenge to the investigator is to develop an approach to continuously updating understanding of this three-way relationship.

4. Symbolic interactionism. Symbolic interactionism has to do with the role of symbols in social interaction. Symbolic interactionism is a school of thought based on the propositions that (a) symbols are the primary basis for society and societies are basically symbolic in nature, (b) individual self-perception is closely tied to maturity in the use of symbols, and (c) individual self-perception is largely a matter of learning to see oneself as one is seen by others. The central theme of symbolic interactionism is that the universe as it is known to any individual, rather than being defined primarily by physics, is defined primarily by society.

5. Perceived reality. Logical positivism is closely tied to the assumption of an objective reality that is subject to examination and verification. Qualitative research tends to accept the notion of a more intense relationship between reality and perception and allows for the notion that there may be many realities, each a function of the interaction between an individual or group and the physical and social environments within which the individual or group exists. Symbolic interactionism and perceived reality are closely tied to phenomenological studies.

6. Research as a cycle. The notion that research is a cyclical, progressive process is fundamental to most research paradigms. What makes qualitative research different is a more intense perception that the cycle *is* the research and that no project is ever truly completed since each project is only part of the larger cycle. Each project is essentially like a snapshot of an evolving reality or an isolated frame from a motion picture, with no intrinsic value outside the totality of the cycle, which can never be perceived as a whole.

These different views of reality lead to the potential for a revised relationship between induction and deduction. Quantitative research tends to view the process as beginning with inductive analysis of a substantial body of data, from which general conclusions or assertions are produced. Those general conclusions then become the basis for deductive formation of conclusions about similar phenomena. Qualitative research works much the same way, except that induction is based on smaller bodies of data that are understood in much greater detail. The general conclusions induced from the data are therefore more tenuous and the role of those conclusions in forming conclusions about similar phenomenon is not assumed to be precise or permanent.

Theory building is a role frequently ascribed to qualitative research in a manner very different from theory building in the quantitative domain. A theory is a body of interrelated assumptions, facts, laws, and hypotheses that can, as a whole, be interpreted as a summary of a particular area of interest. Theory building in quantitative research is usually closely related to hypothesis testing. As a hypothesis is tested and retested, conclusions are drawn that can, over time, be synthesized into a general theory that can be verified and validated by further hypothesis testing. Theory building in qualitative research frequently begins with an open question rather than a hypothesis and seeks to identify the theoretical base that explains the data gathered in the process of seeking an answer to the question. Qualitative investigators sometimes refer to the role of *emergent* theory that arises from understanding the phenomenon of interest and *forced* theory that is derived from acceptance of a preformulated hypothesis. Emergent theory is best represented in the very structured context of grounded theory. Grounded theory is a social sciences process, first explored by Glaser and Strauss, in which theory is derived from data.[17]

Research and Evaluation Paradigms in Library and Information Science

The history of research in library and information science is typical of professional areas grounded in the social sciences and is closely parallel to the history of research in education, psychology, and the behavioral sciences. True research in library and information science was practically unknown prior to the 1930s. The establishment of the Graduate Library School at the University of Chicago in 1926 was triggered in large part by the perceived need to establish a research paradigm for librarianship. The faculty of the Graduate Library School were drawn primarily from other social sciences disciplines and brought with them the paradigms of their own disciplines, which were largely quantitative in nature.

The emphasis on quantitative research, which was viewed as essential to validating the research base, completely dominated research in library and information science until the emergence of interest in qualitative methods in the 1980s and to a significant extent is still dominant. The growth of interest in qualitative research in library and information science has been slow and cautious but meaningful, and a small number of investigators in library and information science have made very good use of qualitative methods.

FAMILIES OF RESEARCH AND EVALUATION METHODOLOGIES

A research or evaluation methodology is a specific plan for conducting a project. In a very real and meaningful sense, each project has its own methodology. Although investigators and scholars frequently refer to the experimental method or the historical method, there is no unitary definition that dictates how research or evaluation in any methodological area must be conducted. A method, then, can be understood to be a general approach to research while a methodology is a specific plan for an individual project. It is useful, however, to establish a set of basic focuses of research and evaluation methodologies. Research and evaluation methods can readily be divided into three fundamental categories or families based on the focus of the research. These research and evaluation methods families, which are summarized in Figure 1.7 are (1) historical, (2) descriptive, and (3) experimental.

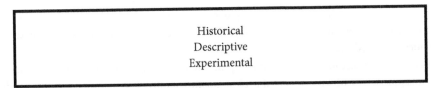

Historical
Descriptive
Experimental

Figure 1.7   Families of research and evaluation methods.

Historical Methods

Historical methods are based on observation of the past. The basic question of any historical exploration is "what happened?" Although there is a strong emphasis in historical research on examination of primary source documents or gathering information from direct witnesses, any research or evaluation project that consciously focuses on the past is fundamentally historical. Historical studies are a critical part of the research base of library and information science but constitute a fairly small portion of the research literature. Time series are an important historical component in many evaluation programs. Historical methods are addressed in depth in Chapter 9.

A historical study of the arrangement of materials in public libraries would naturally look at the transition from closed to open stacks, the move from subject departments in major public libraries to integrated nonfiction collections, and the rise of fiction collections as a major focus of public library services.

Descriptive Methods

Descriptive methods are based on observation of the present. The basic question is "what is happening?" Some people equate descriptive methods with the use of surveys and particularly of questionnaires, but there are actually a wide variety of methodological tools that can be used in a descriptive mode. Note that descriptive research is not bound by Simon and Burstein's definition of description as a level of research. Descriptive projects frequently involve measurement, comparison, and the search for relationships. Most of the research literature of library and information science reports the results of descriptive studies. Most library and information science evaluation makes use of methods and techniques from the descriptive family. Descriptive methods are the focus of Chapter 10.

A descriptive study of the arrangement of materials in public libraries can logically focus on patron preferences, asking questions designed to determine whether patrons prefer a single alphabetical arrangement for fiction as opposed to genre subcollections, the extent to which patrons understand the distinctions among general fiction and genre fiction, patron use of multiple genres, and related matters of perception and preference.

Experimental Methods

Experimentation is based on manipulation of the present. The basic question is "what might happen?" Experimentation is the only family of research methods that has real potential for exploration of cause and effect relationships. Experimental methods have long dominated the physical and biological sciences. Experimentation has been an important but frequently elusive target for the behavioral sciences and education. Experimental research constitutes a very small portion of the research literature of library and information science.

Experimental methods are sometimes employed as evaluative tools in library and information science and have the potential for playing a much larger role in evaluation. Chapter 11 provides a detailed overview of experimentation.

Baker studied methods of displaying popular fiction in public libraries, using an experimental approach in which a standard pretest–posttest control group design was used to determine the relationship between placement and display and circulation of genre fiction. Her experiment found that the impact of placement and display was at least in part a function of collection size.[18]

BENEFITS OF RESEARCH AND EVALUATION

Why do people undertake research and evaluation activities? Engaging in a research project or designing and implementing an evaluation program is time consuming and mind stretching. Many library and information professionals derive no direct, tangible reward from their research or evaluation activities, but nonetheless are involved in research and evaluation on an ongoing basis. There must be some set of benefits associated with research and evaluation. The following categorization of benefits, summarized in Figure 1.8, is adapted from Simon and Burstein.[19]

To Society
Improvement of quality of life
Reduction of expense
Removal of danger

To the Profession
Theory testing
Surprisal
Action
Universality and generality
Cumulation
Linkage
Human factors

To the Institution
Increased efficiency
Reduction of expense
Managerial effectiveness
Achievement of goals
Public relations

To the Researcher
Personal
Professional

Figure 1.8   Benefits of research.

Benefits to Society

1. Improvement of the quality of life. Improving the quality of life of consumers of library and information services and of the population in general is a major focus of research and evaluation in library and information science. The role of libraries and information systems is primarily that of a public service or even a public good. A library or information system that functions at an enhanced level of quality or produces an increased volume of output is an obvious and desirable outcome of research.

2. Reduction of expense. Reducing the cost of providing library and information services is a second desirable benefit to society, especially if it can be coupled with a demonstrable improvement in those services. Cost-effectiveness and cost-benefit studies focus on the relationship between quality of service and cost of service.

3. Removal of danger. Although the role of libraries and information systems in reducing danger may not be prominent in the minds of either practitioners or the clienteles they serve, removal of danger is in fact a significant benefit of quality library and information services at both the micro- and macro-levels. At a very specific level, access to appropriate and useful information at the time it is needed and in the form in which it can be best employed provides clients with the tools for avoiding errors in personal or professional life. An obvious example of the role of library and information services in removing danger is the inclusion of biomedical librarians in clinical treatment teams. At a broader, more conceptual level libraries and information systems play a critical role in reducing ignorance and increasing citizen access to government and society. Research and evaluation activities that improve the timely delivery of accurate information or improve public access to information play a very direct and meaningful role in ensuring public safety. The removal of danger benefit can also apply to the library as an entity; policies are designed to protect the institution from harm on a number of levels.

Benefits to the Profession

1. Theory testing. The search for an explanatory, general theory base to explain a discipline or professional field requires that theories be not only formulated but also tested to determine the extent to which they are accurate and universal. Although theory testing doesn't generally play a very significant role in library and information science it does retain some importance as a benefit to the field. Some theories pertinent to library and information science, such as Chatman's Small World Theory, Kuhlthau's Information Seeking Behavior Model, and Price's Cumulative Advantage Theory, have been extensively tested to the benefit of both research and practice.[20]

2. Surprisal. Surprisal is the process of producing unexpected results. These may be results that lie outside the boundaries of established theory or that appear to be in conflict with shared experience. The potential for learning something new and surprising is one of the greatest attractions of research and evaluation to an individual with a curious mind. The formulation of the "55 Percent Rule" constituted a major surprise for many professionals by suggesting that only slightly more than half of factual reference questions are answered correctly.[21]

3. Action. Translating research and evaluation results into action is especially important in an area of professional practice such as library and information science. Finding better ways to do things or justifying elimination of unnecessary activities is an obvious and essential benefit of research and evaluation. Unobtrusive assessment of reference service similar to that used in formulating the 55 Percent Rule has also been used very successfully in improving reference services in specific library environments.

4. Universality and generality. Demonstrating that an approach to understanding some phenomenon has universal application and can be treated as a general rule adds both to the theory base for the field and to the potential for improving professional practice. Library and information professionals frequently feel that they are working in isolation from their peers and have poor access to information related to whether the problems they face and the solutions they employ have general applicability. Research and evaluation activities that confirm that phenomena apply across environments and experiences have substantial potential for alleviating that sense of isolation. The development of broadly applicable standards and guidelines for professional practice both builds on and contributes to the development of universal and general principles.

5. Cumulation. The cumulative impact of research and evaluation is closely related to universality and generality but also has to do with simply building confidence in results. As results are accumulated and synthesized it becomes possible to identify definitive patterns and variations that add to the depth and breadth with which the phenomenon can be understood.

6. Linkage. Linkage is the process of making associations and identifying relationships. If, for instance, it can be demonstrated that a baseline measure such as circulation-per-capita is more closely associated with size of library rather than type of library, there is the potential for forging links that cut across library types and lead to shared solutions to common problems.

7. Human factors. Improving the quality of life for practitioners in the field is a frequent byproduct of research and evaluation. Projects that explore ways and means of improving library and information services to the public can be expected to additionally result in benefits to practitioners. A further example of human factors benefits is the commonly noted phenomenon that workers simply feel better about their jobs if they know someone is making an effort to effect improvements.

Benefits to the Institution

1. Optimized effectiveness. Effectiveness has to do with achievement of goals and objectives. Evaluation is primarily a matter of ensuring achievement of goals and objectives. Every institution has a major investment in serving the needs and desires of its clientele. Establishment of appropriate goals and objectives is an essential component in meeting those needs. Local evaluation of the extent to which goals and objectives are met and broader research into the ways in which goals and objectives are set and the extents to which they are met are fundamentally beneficial to individual institutions.

2. Increased efficiency. Efficiency is a goal of all institutions. Efficiency is an indictor of the appropriateness of resource allocation. Analysis of efficiency looks at the ways in which resources are used to address needs and provide services to determine whether resources are being used in the best possible way. Within any institution there are many ways in which goals and objectives can be met. Efficiency analysis tends to assume that goals and objectives are fixed and are therefore not a part of the efficiency equation. The basic issue in efficiency is thrift: questions that address whether a particular task can be accomplished less expensive, more quickly, or with fewer employees all address efficiency. The assumption is that valuation of competing approaches to meeting goals and objectives leads to the selection of the most efficient modes of operation.

3. Cost-effectiveness. Cost-effectiveness balances achievement of objectives against expense. Cost-effectiveness and efficiency are sometimes treated as synonymous, but they actually are not. Where efficiency addresses thrift, cost-effectiveness addresses

optimization. The fundamental question is "are objectives being achieved in the context of an optimum level of expenditure?" A cheaper, faster, less labor-intensive approach to solving a problem may be fundamentally efficient, but may fail to meet goals in an optimal manner. A service model for a university library reference desk that relies entirely on graduate students to answer all questions may be admirably efficient, but may compromise the achievement of goals and objectives related to support of faculty and student research.

a. Managerial effectiveness. Just as there are multiple ways of assessing the achievement of goals and objectives, there are many ways in which management and administration of an institution can be implemented. Evaluation of local administration and management and comparative assessment across institutions are important ways in which evaluation and research can benefit the institution.

b. Public relations. Research and evaluation activities are meaningful ways by which institutions can demonstrate accountability to the publics they serve. Although public relations is sometimes assigned a rather cynical role, there is a meaningful benefit in demonstrating that the institution is engaging in activities that assess and document its benefit to its clientele. Outcomes of research and evaluation processes can be particularly compelling as arguments in favor of the benefit of the institution to its public and can be instrumental in ensuring organizational survival.

Benefits to the Investigator

1. Personal satisfaction. Knowing that one has done something good, improved practice, or solved a meaningful problem can constitute an appreciable personal benefit. Some people are just driven to know, explore, or find out. For those individuals in particular, carrying out research and evaluation activities can take on the role of adding to the basic quality of life. Although the era of the individual investigator operating on his or her funds or with the support of a wealthy sponsor is probably long past, there are still people who invest in their own research or evaluation activities simply because doing so carries a direct sense of reward. Evaluation of library services and processes helps build personal confidence and can be a source of energy for the professional.

2. Professional achievement. Research and evaluation in many cases constitute the most appropriate approach to solving professional problems. Although some problems are so small, obvious, or immediate that addressing them via a true research project is inappropriate or unfeasible; most large or long-term problems are very amenable to solution via research methods. Systematic evaluation is always more meaningful than ad hoc or casual evaluation. Knowing when and how to employ systematic techniques can add greatly to an individual's value as a library and information science professional. Some professionals, including many university librarians holding faculty status, have no choice—engaging in research activities is a defined part of the processes leading to promotion and tenure. Most professionals in library and information science have responsibility for evaluation activities.

RESEARCH AND EVALUATION: DIVERGENCE AND CONVERGENCE

Research and evaluation have typically been treated separately in the library and information science literature, particularly in books, and in the focuses of professional activities such as conferences, meetings, and workshops. Not all research is conducted in the interest of evaluation, although it is clear that in a service-oriented professional area such as library and information science there is a substantial need for research that contributes to evaluation. There are many bibliometric and social informatics research techniques that are aimed more at understanding the role of information in society than at evaluating information products, processes, or services.

Similarly, not all evaluation activities are grounded in research. For instance, although it is to be hoped that formal standards for performance such as those formulated by government agencies and professional associations have a basis in research, benchmarking local performance against published standards, while a legitimate and sometimes essential approach to evaluation, is not research. Many management techniques and tools, such as Six Sigma and Total Quality Management, have no more than a quasi-research origin, but they have proven to be useful in an evaluation context.

The founding premise of this book is that research and evaluation are more similar than dissimilar and that the most well-founded approaches to evaluation have an origin in, a link to, or at least recognition of the nature and value of research. The remainder of this book explores research and evaluation as an integrated set of processes with a common, although not always identical purpose, many shared questions, and closely aligned approaches to seeking answers.

 THINK ABOUT IT!

1. Provide examples of ways in which the major ways of knowing discussed in the chapter influenced your decision to pursue a career in library and information science.
2. How does the old saying "seeing is believing" relate to belief and formal logic as ways of knowing?
3. Describe how the essential characteristics of research and evaluation can guide your experience as a student of library and information science.

 DO IT!

1. Identify a personal information seeking problem or gap you have recently experienced; how does the choice of either a quantitative or qualitative approach influence the ways in which the problem can be understood and a solution identified?

2. Several researchers have identified a gender gap in the use of libraries by teens; how can this problem potentially be explored using (a) historical, (b) descriptive, and (c) experimental methods.
3. Lance and others have described the positive impact of school library media centers on academic performance; how can studying this relationship benefit (a) society, (b) the library and information profession, (c) an institution in which you work or would like to work, and (b) yourself personally and professionally.

NOTES

1. Peter L. Berger and Thomas Luckmann, *The Social Construction of Reality: A Treatise in the Sociology of Knowledge* (New York: Doubleday, 1967).

2. American Library Association, *Code of Ethics of the American Library Association,* http://www.ala.org/ala/issuesadvocacy/proethics/codeofethics/codeethics.cfm (accessed May 30, 2011).

3. Reference and User Services Association, *Guidelines for Behavioral Performance of Reference and Information Service Providers,* http://www.ala.org/ala/mgrps/divs/rusa/resources/guidelines/guidelinesbehavioral.cfm (accessed June 20, 2010).

4. *ARL Statistics Tables 2008–09,* http://www.arl.org/bm~doc/09tables.xls.

5. Herbert Goldhor, *An Introduction to Scientific Research in Librarianship* (Washington, DC: U.S. Department of Education Bureau of Research, 1969), 8.

6. Keith Curry Lance, "The Impact of School Library Media Centers on Academic Achievement," *School Library Media Quarterly* 22 (Spring 1994): 167–70; Keith Curry Lance, "Still Making an Impact: School Library Staffing and Student Performance," *Colorado Libraries* 25, no. 3 (Fall 1999): 6–9; Keith Curry Lance, "Impact of School Library Media Programs on Academic Achievement," *Teacher Librarian* 29, no. 3 (February 2002): 29–34; Keith Curry Lance and Becky Russell, "Scientifically Based Research on School Libraries and Academic Achievement: What is It? How Much of It Do We Have? How Can We Do It Better?" *Knowledge Quest* 32, no. 5 (May/June 3004): 13–17; Keith Curry Lance, Marcia J. Rodney, and Bill Schwarz, "The Impact of School Libraries on Academic Achievement: A Research Study Based on Responses from Administrators in Idaho," *School Library Monthly* 36, no. 9 (May 2010): 14–17.

7. Julian L. Simon and Paul Burstein, *Basic Research Methods in Social Science: The Art of Empirical Investigation,* 3rd ed. (New York: McGraw-Hill, 1985), 36–57.

8. Louis Pasteur, Address to the Congrès Viticole et Séricole, *Compte Rendus des Travaux du Congrès Viticole et Séricole de Lyon* (Lyon, 1872).

9. Thomas Kuhn, *The Structure of Scientific Revolutions* (Chicago: University of Chicago Press, 1962).

10. *IEEE Standard Computer Dictionary: A Compilation of IEEE Standard Computer Glossaries* (New York: Institute of Electrical and Electronics Engineers, 1990).

11. Lisa Given, ed., *The Sage Encyclopedia of Qualitative Research Methods* (Thousand Oaks, CA: Sage, 2008).

12. Herbert Blumer, "What Is Wrong with Social Theory?" in *Symbolic Interactionism: Perspective and Method,* ed. Herbert Blumer, 140–52 (Englewood Cliffs, NJ: Prentice Hall, 1954).

13. Elizabeth Tasker and Frances B. Holt-Underwood, "Feminist Research Methodologies in Historic Rhetoric and Composition: An Overview of Scholarship from the 1970s to the Present," *Rhetoric Review* 27, no. 1 (2009): 54–71.

14. Scott D. Churchill, "Humanistic Research in the Wake of Postmodernism," *The Humanistic Psychologist* 33, no. 4 (2005): 331.

15. Simon Sheikh, Simon. "Objects of Study or Commodification of Knowledge? Remarks on Artistic Research," *Art and Research* 2, no. 2 (2009). http://www.artandresearch.org.uk/v2n2/sheikh.html (accessed February, 2011).

16. Alan Peshkin, "The Goodness of Qualitative Research," *Educational Investigator* 22, no. 2 (March 1993): 23–29.

17. Barney G. Glaser and Anselm L. Strauss, *The Discovery of Grounded Theory: Strategies for Qualitative Research* (Chicago: Aldine, 1967).

18. Sharon L. Baker, "The Display Phenomenon: An Exploration into Factors Causing the Increased Circulation of Displayed Books," *Library Quarterly* 56 (July 1986): 237–57.

19. Simon and Burstein, *Basic Research Methods in Social Science.*

20. Elfreda A. Chatman, "Life in a Small World: Applicability of Gratification Theory to Information-Seeking Behavior," *Journal of the American Society for Information Science* 42, no. 6 (1991):

438–49; Carol C. Kuhlthau, "Inside the Search Process: Information Seeking from the User's Perspective," *Journal of the American Society for Information Science* 42, no. 5 (1991): 361–71; Derek J. de Solla Price, "A General Theory of Bibliometric and Other Cumulative Advantage Processes," *Journal of the American Society for Information Science* 27 (1976): 292–306.

     21.   Peter Hernon and Charles R. McClure, "Unobtrusive Reference Testing: The 55 Percent Rule," *Library Journal* 111 (April 15, 1986): 37–41.

SUGGESTED READINGS

Sharon L. Baker and F. Wilfrid Lancaster, *The Measurement and Evaluation of Library Services*, 2nd ed. (Arlington, TX: Information Resources Press, 1991).

Douglas Cook and Lesley Farmer, eds., *Using Qualitative Methods in Action Research: How Librarians Can Get to the Why of Data* (Chicago, IL: Association of College and Research Libraries, 2011).

Peter Hernon and Charles R. McClure, *Evaluation and Library Decision Making* (Norwood, NJ: Ablex, 1990).

F. W. Lancaster, *If You Want to Evaluate Your Library . . .* 2nd ed. (Champaign: University of Illinois Graduate School of Library and Information Science, 1993).

"Qualitative Research," ed. Gillian M. McCombs and Theresa M. Maylone, special issue, *Library Trends* 46, no. 4 (Spring 1998).

"Research in Librarianship," ed. Mary Jo Lynch, special issue, *Library Trends* 32, no. 4 (Spring 1984).

Robert Swisher and Charles R. McClure, *Research for Decision Making: Methods for Librarians* (Chicago, IL: American Library Association, 1984).

Danny P. Wallace, and Connie Van Fleet, *Library Evaluation: A Casebook and Can-Do Guide* (Englewood, CO: Libraries Unlimited, 2001).

_2_

RESEARCH AND EVALUATION PROCESSES

Research is formalized curiosity. It is poking and prying with a purpose. It is a seeking that he who wishes may know the cosmic secrets of the world and that they dwell therein.

—*Zora Neale Hurston,* Dust Tracks on a Road, *1942*

You can't fatten a pig by weighing it.

—*Anonymous*

In This Chapter

Steps in conducting research and evaluation projects

Commonalities and differences of research and evaluation processes

Origins of ideas for research and evaluation

Strategies for defining an idea or need

Basic considerations in building an action plan

Principles of data gathering and analysis

Elements of reporting

Approaches to decision making

Opportunities for action

Some terms used in this chapter are more thoroughly defined in the Glossary and in subsequent chapters.

OUTLINE OF THE RESEARCH AND EVALUATION PROCESS

Research and evaluation are defined in Chapter 1, "Knowing, Research, and Evaluation." As a brief recap, research focuses on universal concerns and the search for new knowledge, while evaluation focuses on local needs and the development of effective solutions. The research and evaluation process can be effectively divided into the following more-or-less sequential elements:

1. Origination of a general idea or need
2. Preplanning to refine the initial understanding of the idea or need
3. Planning to build an approach to action
4. Data gathering
5. Data analysis
6. Processing of results
7. Reporting
8. Decision making
9. Action

The research and evaluation process is summarized visually in Figure 2.1. The model is deliberately one of integration and is intended to emphasize the extent to which research and evaluation are consistently and beneficially parallel. Although the remainder of this chapter and the flowcharts presented in Figures 2.2, 2.5, and 2.7 through 2.10, and 2.12 call attention to the differences between research and evaluation, the commonalities are extensive and important. Research informs and is informed by evaluation; evaluation informs and is informed by research. There really are no approaches to research that are not of use in

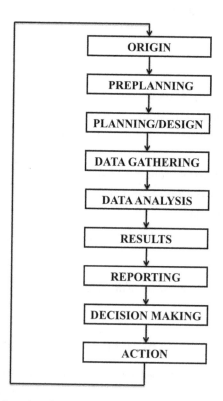

Figure 2.1   The research and evaluation process.

evaluation, and evaluation frequently becomes the basis for research. Even when the research and evaluation processes diverge, the distinctions are not hard and fast.

Origination of a General Idea or Need

Origins of Research and Evaluation Ideas

Understanding where research and evaluation ideas come from is a very common problem for people who have not previously been involved in research and evaluation activities. Reading and understanding the research literature can in and of itself be quite intimidating. Stepping beyond being a consumer of research or a beneficiary of evaluation and thinking about becoming a researcher or conducting an evaluation project can be overwhelming.

As indicated in Figure 2.2, the perception of a need for evaluation generally arises from the mission, goals, and objectives of a specific institution. The emphasis given to shaping mission statements, general goals, and specific objectives that pervades the library and information world has in large part to do with facilitating evaluation and understanding the extent to which goals and objectives are being met in the interest of fulfilling the institutional mission. In action, evaluation begins with the identification of a specific operational problem to be solved or need to be met.

Research ideas—and to some extent evaluation ideas—frequently have their origin in personal or professional curiosity. That curiosity leads to the identification of a previously unanswered question that becomes a target for research. A researcher is greatly benefited by a well-developed and continuously nourished sense of wonder. The role of curiosity in research and evaluation is a manifestation of what Donald Schön referred to as *reflective practice*.[1] The essence of reflective practice lies in the practitioner who, rather than simply following rules, applying standard tools, or adopting so-called best practices, is constantly questioning rules, tools, and practices. This is the process of asking not only "what should I do in this situation?" but accompanying that fundamental question with the equally important question "why?" Although the expression idle curiosity is a common part of general parlance, curiosity in research and evaluation is anything but idle. It is an active, systematic, and essential component in effective thinking about solving problems and answering questions.

For the most part, specific research and evaluation ideas arise from very understandable and fairly commonplace origins such as those summarized in Figure 2.3.

1. Experience. Many research ideas and probably most evaluation ideas arise directly from experience, particularly in an area of professional practice such as library and information science. Many of the most important findings in these fields have come directly from the efforts of professionals to improve the services they provide to their clienteles. Practitioners can be viewed as having a "privileged discourse with reality" that makes them particularly adept in and adapted to applying the benefits of their expertise and experience. Research and evaluation questions that arise from experience most frequently take the form of "how can we do this better?"

2. Literature. Reading the existing professional and research literature with a critical view is a second important source of research and evaluation ideas. Research and evaluation ideas that arise in response to critical reading often take the form of "why didn't the author do that in a different way?" or "what would happen if that were done in a

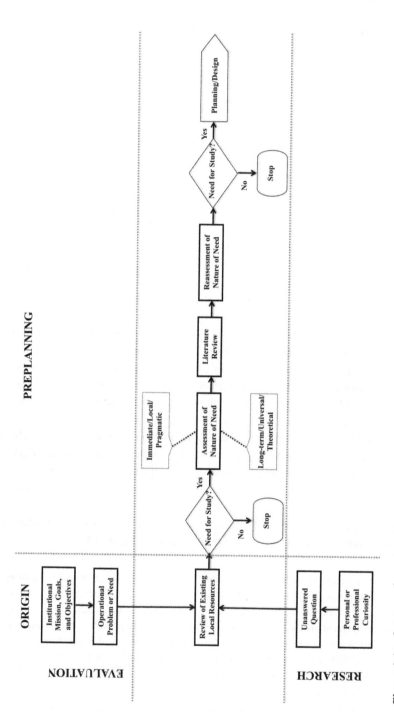

Figure 2.2 Origin and preplanning.

> Experience
> Literature
> Discussion
> External influence
> Theory

Figure 2.3 Origins of research and evaluation ideas.

different environment?" or "I just can't believe that; the author must have done something wrong!" Approaches to evaluating the professional literature are presented in Chapter 5, "The Project Plan or Proposal."

3. Discussion. Interaction with other professionals at conferences and workshops, at staff meetings, in a break room, or in any other setting is another useful source of research and evaluation ideas. Even if the discussion doesn't lead to collaboration in the research or evaluation process, exploiting the opportunity to discuss shared experiences or to conduct a reality check of an emerging research or evaluation idea is a clear benefit of professional interaction. Conferences and other professional meetings frequently include sessions that present results of research or evaluation projects or that are designed to teach evaluation methods and tools. Attending such sessions with a critical eye can be a good way to generate new ideas.

4. External influence. Sometimes the need to conduct research or carry out an evaluation project is imposed. The idea may take the form of an administrator saying, "Why doesn't this work better?" "Do we really need to be doing this anymore?" or "That other library is doing this; shouldn't we?" Sometimes the external influence is essentially political in nature: local evaluation or generalizable research may arise from perceived threats to funding or basic operations. All types of libraries and information centers are charged with accountability to their constituents and governing bodies that may have their origins in legal or statutory requirements. For some types of libraries, accreditation, certification, and similar compliance needs form the impetus for research or evaluation.

5. Theory. A theory is a body of interrelated assumptions, laws, and hypotheses that can, as a whole, be interpreted as a summary of a particular area of interest. One of the accepted characteristics of a mature field of interest is the existence of an established, recognized, general body of theory. There is at present no generally accepted unified theory for library and information science, although there are theories that can be used to understand specific subareas within the field. Information Theory plays an important role in understanding the factors involved in transmitting information from one location to another. Theories of information seeking behavior operate at the nexus of information transmittal and human information use. The Cumulative Advantage Principle provides a base for explaining why use of library materials tends to be concentrated in a small portion of a collection. Most research and essentially all evaluation in library and information science can be classified as empirical in nature, meaning that it is based primarily or entirely on experience and observation rather than having its origin in a body of theory.

Preplanning to Refine the Initial Understanding of the Idea or Need

Review of Existing Local Resources

Research and evaluation are deliberative acts that require not only careful methodological design but also benefit from planning to plan, as illustrated in Figure 2.2. A first step in preplanning is examination of the local knowledge repository to determine if a solution or answer already exists. This is particularly important in the context of evaluation. Library and information science problems tend to be cyclical. The problem at hand may have been examined in the past. The research question that seems novel and original may have been studied before. Review of institutional history or personal information files may reveal that there is no immediate need for the research or evaluation study being considered or may help in formulating the question or designing the project.

Assessment of the Nature of the Need

A meaningful difference between evaluation and research is that evaluation needs tend to be immediate, local, and pragmatic, while research needs tend to be long term, universal, and theoretical. This is, of course, not a fixed or absolute distinction, but understanding the nature of the need is essential in formulating a general problem statement. Although the nature of the problem statement may not vary greatly between a research project and an evaluation, understanding and articulating the nature of the need is essential.

Problems that have not yet been answered and problems that have not yet been solved—and in fact may never be answered or solved—are encountered by people in all walks of life. That perception is frequently vague and inchoate—a nagging, seemingly abstract feeling that corresponds to Taylor's conception of a *visceral* information need.[2] Research and evaluation require advancement to a state of thorough awareness of the problem or question that is understood at a level that can be subjected to action. Only when this step has been completed is it possible to make a positive move toward a solution or an answer.

The General Problem Statement

Research and evaluation are about asking questions and seeking answers. The research process always begins with a problem statement or basic question. The problem statement identifies the general subject area and context for the research or evaluation project and serves as a guide to initial action. Many of the most interesting and most important questions are so big and general that they cannot be directly answered through either research or evaluation. The problem statement may be relatively vague but must provide enough detail to serve as a starting point. The problem itself may be modified as the process is carried forward, but it is important to retain a clear sense of the origin of the problem or question and to be able to return to the original notion of what the project is intended to accomplish.

The Literature Search

The literature search and review serve to provide a specific context for the research or evaluation project. The literature search serves five fundamental purposes, which are summarized in Figure 2.4.

1. Confirmation of need. A beginning purpose of the literature search is establishing that there is indeed a need for the proposed research or evaluation activity. This is in

Confirmation of need

Establishment of focus

Identification of specific subject and context

Identification of theoretical base

Identification of methodological base

Figure 2.4   Purposes of the literature review.

part a matter of avoiding reinvention of the wheel. If the proposed work has already been done, there may be no point in repeating it. That doesn't mean that finding that a similar project has been completed by someone else necessarily makes the envisioned project moot. Replication may very well be merited to extend the project into a new environment or domain, explore aspects of the problem not previously examined, or simply to determine whether new results will confirm prior findings.

2. Establishment of focus. Examining prior work is an excellent way to add definition and specificity to the problem statement. If there is a useful body of prior work related to the problem, studying the literature can provide a basis for setting direction for new research.

3. Identification of specific subject and context. Problems that arise from specific local or personal experience may benefit from the added context base of prior work. Knowing that other research or evaluation activities have been carried out helps provide definition of the location of the problem area within the broader body of knowledge and serves to differentiate subareas or subproblems.

4. Identification of theoretical base. Although the literature of library and information science is largely empirical rather than theoretical, if there is a body of theory related to the problem, learning about that body of theory and its implications is essential.

5. Identification of methodological base. Knowledge of previous approaches to addressing the problem can be a great benefit to developing a specific methodology. It should be possible to determine which approaches have worked and which have not. Successful methodologies merit adoption or adaptation; unsuccessful ones should be avoided.

What If There Is No Directly Related Literature?

Although it is somewhat unlikely that there will be no directly related literature, it sometimes happens. When that appears to be true, the literature search may need to be expanded into cognate areas outside the library and information science literature to determine if similar problems have been encountered in other disciplines or professions. Library and information science is inherently a synthetic discipline—the adoption of ideas, theories, and methodologies from other fields is appropriate and beneficial.

Sometimes a researcher finds that he or she really is addressing a problem for the very first time and as a result can locate no directly related literature. Similarly, a practitioner seeking an effective approach to a specific evaluation need may find no evidence of a standard or widely accepted approach to addressing that need. The investigator is still charged with finding the best possible relationship to the existing literature. Additionally, the investigator who finds little or no pertinent literature has an intense obligation to document the search process as a means of demonstrating that there is no prior literature related to the study.

Reassessment of the Nature of the Need

Examination of the literature related to a need for research or evaluation nearly always leads to some analysis and reassessment of the nature of the need. A problem initially perceived as being relevant only to a specific kind of library environment may be found to be more universal. A problem conceptualized as very common may be poorly represented in the literature. A methodological approach previously unknown may be revealed as a potentially useful tool for the need at hand.

Although it may be difficult to abandon an idea once it has been conceived and explored, it is sometimes the case that abandonment is the most appropriate action given what has already been done and presented in the literature. Being attuned to the possibility that the envisioned work does not need to be done is essential for honesty and integrity in research and evaluation. Even when the core idea still merits exploration, the literature review may suggest a variation in the direction the project will be pursue. Sticking slavishly or stubbornly to a research or evaluation project when there is no evident need for the project is of benefit to no one except perhaps as a learning experience.

Planning to Build an Approach to Action

Once the need for the specific research or evaluation project has been confirmed, it is necessary to build a precise, actionable plan for actually gathering and analyzing data. The action plan is the equivalent to a blueprint. At its very best, the plan should be sufficiently detailed, specific, and understandable that the person or team responsible for development of the plan could simply hand it off to someone else with confidence that the plan would be executed in an appropriate manner and yield useful results. The planning process is presented graphically in Figure 2.5.

The Specific Problem Statement and Study Objectives

The literature search should yield results that will help refine and narrow the general problem statement to form a much more specific statement that will provide the actual focus for the research or evaluation project. The specific problem statement is a narrower, more concrete statement of the fundamental questions than the general problem statement. The fundamental characteristic of the specific problem statement is that it presents the question in a form that is amenable to using research or evaluation tools to seek an answer. The specific problem statement should include the following categories of study objectives:

1. A statement of *boundaries* that encompass the problem. Identifying boundaries serves to ensure that an appropriate focus is maintained throughout the research project. The statement of boundaries can also act as a disclaimer by explicitly stating those factors that have been defined as lying outside the realm of the project.

2. Division of the main problem into *subproblems* (if appropriate). Some problems are by their very nature too large or too complex to be addressed in a single research effort. In other circumstances, limited resources or time constraints may dictate that a problem

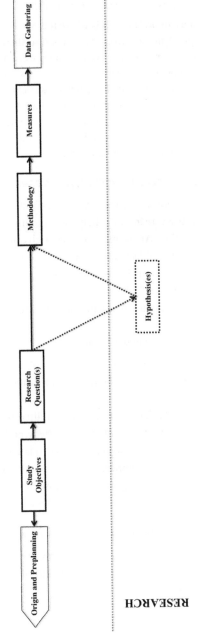

Figure 2.5 Planning.

be addressed in a serial manner by breaking it into manageable chunks. Leedy and Ormrod identified the following characteristics of subproblems:

a. Each subproblem should be a completely researchable unit.

b. Each subproblem must be clearly tied to the interpretation of the data.

c. The subproblems must add up to the totality of the problem.

d. Subproblems should be small in number.[3]

3. Implications for *action*. This is where the "so what?" question is addressed. Even if the research problem is relatively pure in nature, there needs to be some compelling reason to carry out the research or evaluation project. The specific problem statement should posit some potential outcome or action that will result from the successful completion of the research. A good investigator is always looking beyond the current project to its impact on practice or on future exploration. An evaluation of a perceived decrease in the circulation of DVDs in a public library implies the potential for reducing, eliminating, or modifying the nature of DVD collections, taking action to promote circulation of DVDs, or some other positive action.

Research Questions and Hypotheses

A research question is a general query that guides research but does not necessarily establish a formal structure for an anticipated outcome. A research question is normally stated explicitly as a question. An example of a research question for an evaluation project is "Why has circulation of DVDs decreased at the Anytown Public Library?" The question might be reframed for a research project as "what factors are associated with circulation volume of DVDs in public libraries?"

A hypothesis is a statement of a problem area that

a. builds upon existing understanding

b. states an expectation regarding the unknown

c. can be tested in a manner conducive to replication

A researcher might, based on the existing literature regarding the influence of the Internet on consumption of video, formulate the hypothesis that "Circulation of DVDs from public library collections will be negatively correlated with availability of video products via the Internet." A parallel hypothesis for an evaluation might be "Circulation of DVDs from Anytown Public Library will go down as more movies are made available by downloading but overall circulation (access) of videos in all formats will increase."

Design of the Research Methodology

Once the general problem statement has been reduced to a more specific, directly actionable problem statement, the next step is to design and define the specific methodology. Methodology design is discussed in further detail in Chapter 5, "The Project Plan or Proposal." The design and definition statement should include the five elements summarized in Figure 2.6.

1. A statement of the *general methodological area* (historical, descriptive, experimental, as discussed in Chapter 1, "Knowing, Research, and Evaluation") to provide an overall understanding of the focus of the project. A tool, such as a questionnaire or an interview, can serve multiple methodological purposes and does not in and of itself suffice to state

> Statement of the general methodological area
>
> Identification of the population to be studied
>
> Selection of a sample
>
> Definition of terms
>
> Delineation of assumptions

Figure 2.6 Methodology definition.

the methodological focus. An explicit statement such as "This project will map the history of the circulation of DVDs at the Anytown Public Library," "This project will explore the history of the circulation of DVDs in public libraries," "This study will assess the current status of DVD circulation in public libraries," or "This project will measure the impact of programs to promote DVD circulation in public libraries" is necessary to provide appropriate context and to guide refinement of the specific methodology.

2. Identification of the *population* to be studied. The population for a research or evaluation study consists of all those entities that are by definition of interest to the researcher. For the question, "Why has circulation of DVDs decreased at the Anytown Public Library?" the population of interest is the entire DVD collection of the Anytown Public Library, the service population of the Anytown Public Library, or both. For the question, "What factors are associated with circulation volume of DVDs in public libraries?" the population is the DVD collections of all public libraries.

3. Selection of a *sample*. A sample is a subset of the population that is identified as being a useful representation of the population for purposes of a specific research endeavor. A sample is a tool of convenience—although it is probably possible to track the circulation of the entire DVD collection of an individual library, examining the circulation records of all public libraries would be a difficult (to the point of impossible) and wasteful task. Selecting an appropriate sample that is to a reliable extent representative of the population makes it possible to draw inferences about the population as a whole without gathering data from the population as a whole. Populations, samples, and sampling are explored in depth in Chapter 6, "Measurement, Populations, Samples, and Sampling."

4. Definition of *terms*, including both conceptual and operational definitions. Even concepts that are at first glance seemingly self-evident frequently require refinement for purposes of research. Circulation of DVDs, for instance, is conceptually pretty clear, but closer examination reveals some potential problems. Some books, for instance, have companion DVDs that may be shelved with the books themselves rather than housed in the main DVD collection. Tracking the circulation of those DVDs may be difficult. Further issues arise from the need to decide whether children's DVDs will be tracked or whether nonfiction as well as popular DVDs are of interest. The process of reducing a concept to an actionable definition is known as *operationalization*.

5. Delineation of *assumptions* related to the project. Any analytical or decision-making process relies heavily on the extent to which assumptions about the process are identified and the reliability of those assumptions. An assumption is an assertion or

statement that is taken on faith and is not subject to data gathering and analysis. In many cases, it would be possible to gather data related to assumptions, but a decision is made that doing so will not substantively advance the objectives of the research or evaluation process. In some cases, gathering data to confirm or support an assumption would simply be impractical. A study of circulation of DVDs in public libraries, for instance, is dependent on the accuracy of the assumption that circulation data gathered by different libraries are comparable.

Identification of Measures

Measures are approaches to describing, summarizing, and representing the entities that have been defined as the focus of a research or evaluation activity. Although the term *measure* is frequently interpreted as requiring quantification, a more generic definition is inclusive of both quantitative and qualitative data. The number of DVD titles held by the Anytown Public Library, circulation figures for the DVD collection, and user assessments of the quality of the DVD collection are all measures. The first two are fundamentally quantitative, but the third is qualitative and can only be indirectly represented in quantitative terms. Quantitative and qualitative measures are discussed in detail in later chapters. Identification of measures entails two essential planning processes:

1. Description of a *data gathering plan.* Data, whether quantitative or qualitative, are the core building blocks of any research or evaluation undertaking. Research and evaluation may be based on previously existing data, such as routine records of library activities, or may require identification of new data sources, such as the results of a survey or experiment. Even when data are from existing sources, it may be necessary to refine the data for use in research or evaluation.

2. Description of a *data analysis plan.* Although the availability of sophisticated data analysis software makes it possible to in essence toss the data into a blender and see what comes out, indiscriminate or poorly planned use of analytical tools can lead to unreliable results and invalid conclusions. A basic principle of systematic research is "don't gather data unless you know in advance what you will do with them."

Data Gathering

Data gathering is typically the most time-consuming part of the research process. The goal is to gather those data that truly reflect the nature of the phenomenon being studied and to gather them in a manner that retains as much integrity and usability as possible. Data, whether quantitative or qualitative, must be gathered in a manner that

1. preserves the relationship between the ways in which data are defined and the data that are actually gathered

2. ensures the integrity of the data in their raw form and following any transformations or calculations to which they are subjected

3. ensures the reliability and validity of conclusions drawn from the data

Data can be thought of as falling into two major categories:

1. *Primary data* are those data that are truly of interest to the researcher. A researcher or practitioner exploring success in answering factual reference questions is primarily

interested in binary (yes or no; true or false; correct or incorrect) analysis of whether questions were answered correctly.

2. *Context data* are those data that provide a framework to understand the primary data. Context data for a study of success in answering factual reference questions might address factors such as whether the question was answered by a professional or support staff employee, the subject area of the question, the time of day when the question was asked, the length of the queue of patrons waiting to ask questions, or other factors.

Both primary and context data must be carefully defined in advance. The relationship between primary and context data has greatest validity when the two categories of data can be gathered through a single process. In an unobtrusive study of success in answering reference questions, for instance, it would be ideal for the person asking the question to be able to capture both the answer provided, which is the source of the primary data, and the employment status of the person answering the question simultaneously. Although it would be possible to capture only the time at which the question was answered and compare it to the desk assignment calendar to determine who would have been available to answer the question, that approach adds a greater potential for error.

Data gathering is presented graphically in Figure 2.7 and includes the following components.

1. Selection of data sources. Data sources may be internal to a particular library or other institution or external. Data used for evaluation purposes are frequently internal and commonly employ preexisting data or a combination of preexisting data and data gathered specifically for evaluation purposes. Research data may be drawn from internal or preexisting sources, but are frequently gathered from sources external to the institution. Even when internal sources are used, questions arise as to the quality and consistency of the data, where within the institution the data exist, who is allowed access to the data, the forms the data take, and other administrative and pragmatic issues. Use of external data sources usually requires approval through an Institutional Review Board. Approval processes and research ethics are addressed in Chapter 3, "Ethics and Politics in Library and Information Science Research and Evaluation."

2. Selection of tools and instruments for data gathering. Any mechanism or approach to gathering data can be considered a tool or instrument. Frequently used tools for research and evaluation include library records, questionnaires, interviews focus groups, texts, government databases or publications, and many more possibilities. The essential quality of any tool or instrument used in research or evaluation is that the tool must be capable of being used to gather the data necessary for the project. The accuracy and reliability of a tool drive the accuracy and reliability of the data gathered via use of the tool.

3. Implementation of data gathering processes. Putting the data gathering phase of a project into action is not as simple as simply bringing data gathering tools into contact with sources of data. There are issues of staffing the data gathering, training staff in data gathering processes, timing, monitoring data gathering errors, resolving problems, consolidating data, and preparing data for analysis. Implementation processes are revisited in greater detail in Chapter 5, "The Project Plan or Proposal."

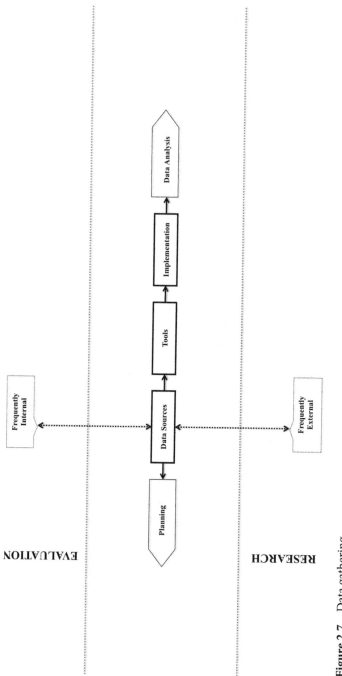

Figure 2.7 Data gathering.

Data Analysis

Regardless of whether the research is quantitative or qualitative in nature, some process of making sense of the data must be carried out. Data analysis, presented graphically in Figure 2.8, is explored in Chapter 12, "Data Analysis and Presentation," and has five essential aspects:

1. Data validation and correction. It is an exceptionally rare for a research project to yield exactly the data sought in exactly the form sought. Respondents to a questionnaire may fail to understand a question. A key witness in a historical study may decline to be interviewed. There may be reason to believe that an interviewee deliberately provided false information. The impact of missing or flawed data must be assessed and an approach to excluding or accommodating such data determined prior to proceeding with data analysis. It may be necessary to exclude entire cases or variables from the analysis. Alternatively, it may be possible to exclude only those data items that are missing or obviously flawed.

2. Data consolidation. Data drawn from multiple sources through use of single data-gathering tool or multiple tools must be coordinated and aggregated to facilitate application of analytical tools. This may involve creation of a database or spreadsheet for quantitative data, categorization of qualitative data drawn from field notes, or other approaches to reducing data to a manageable, understandable form. Data gathered through use of a questionnaire, for instance, may be recorded in a spreadsheet in which each column represents a response to a question and each row represents a respondent. Data consolidation techniques are presented in Chapter 9, "Descriptive Methods—Observation."

3. Application of analytical tools. Tools for conducting data analysis can be as simple as manual counts of data in different categories and as sophisticated as the calculation of complex statistical analyses using statistical analysis software. Specific categories of quantitative and qualitative analytical tools are presented in Chapter 12, "Data Analysis and Presentation."

4. Exploration of relationships between research questions and data. The essential purpose of data analysis is to determine whether the data support, refute, or have no relationship to the project's research questions and, if appropriate, hypotheses. This includes determining the extent to which the primary data are related to the research questions and hypotheses and exploring the ways in which context data contribute to understanding the nature of the primary data.

5. Application of interpretive tools to add understanding to data. Data are virtually never self-explanatory. It is always necessary to apply appropriate tools for interpreting the meanings and implications of data. For quantitative data, this may include estimation of statistical and/or practical significance. For qualitative data, the tools may focus on sense making or other nonquantitative interpretations. Evaluation studies frequently employ externally derived and authorized standards or guidelines or internally derived and authorized policies as interpretive tools.

Processing of Results

Data analysis is a highly technical process that relies on systematic examination of data and the application of appropriate tools for assuring the validity and reliability of the data. As noted in Chapter 1, "Knowing, Research, and Evaluation," validity is a measure of the extent to which conclusions accurately reflect reality and reliability is a measure of the extent to which conclusions are repeatable or replicable. Processing results includes those actions and tools that help to make analyzed data understandable. This includes five fundamental phases of processing results, which are presented in Figure 2.9.

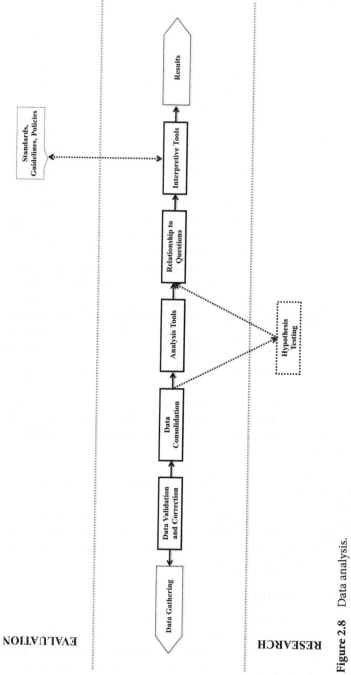

Figure 2.8 Data analysis.

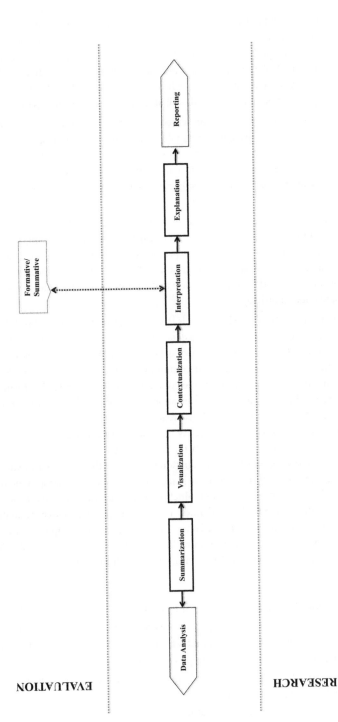

Figure 2.9 Processing results.

1. Summarization. Raw data, even data already subjected to sophisticated analytical tools, is not necessarily easily understood, particularly if the audience includes individuals who are not themselves familiar with those analytical tools. The responsibility of the investigator is to produce summarizations of analyzed data that are readily understood by lay practitioners and perhaps by the general public. For quantitative data, summarization may focus on calculation of statistical indicators such as means, medians, and the output of more sophisticated statistical procedures. For qualitative data, the summarization may focus on division in nameable, describable categories or groupings of results.

2. Visualization. Some results are readily presented in visual or graphic form. Quantitative data are amenable to visual presentation as tables that show the relationships between various categories of data. Quantitative data can also be visualized using line charts, bar graphs, pie charts, time series graphs, and related numeric presentations. Qualitative data can be presented visually in relationship clusters, thematic maps, and related non-numeric presentations.

3. Contextualization. Contextualization takes two primary forms. The first is description, through appropriate summarization and visualization, of relationships within the primary data, relationships between the primary data and the secondary data, and relationships between data and research questions. The second is the process of tying results to the outcomes of the literature review to demonstrate how the study has or has not contributed new knowledge.

4. Interpretation. An investigator whose goal is to see results put to use is responsible for careful and complete interpretation of the data. The contention that the data are what they are or that the data stand on their own is facile and unhelpful. The investigator is directly and inherently responsible for communicating the meaning of the results, using the summarization, visualization, and contextualization generated by the investigator. For research, this is largely a matter of building the case for validity and reliability through careful description and discussion of the design of the methodology and the processes of ensuring data integrity and establishing significance of results. The evaluator may also have responsibility for determining the summative and formative impacts of the results. Summative evaluation has to do with assessing the extent to which existing targets for performance are being met—if there are existing standards, guidelines, or benchmarks, summative evaluation places current performance within the context of those standards, guidelines, or benchmarks. Formative evaluation emphasizes improvement and is focused on assessing the adequacy or appropriateness of existing performance targets, determining the necessity of desirability of establishing new targets, and identifying methods or mechanisms for meeting new targets.

Reporting

However interesting the results of a research or evaluation project may be, they are of little value if they are not reported. If the project was motivated by a request from an administrator to find a solution to a problem, that administrator is likely to expect some kind of report, which may be fairly informal. If the project was funded by a government agency or nonprofit foundation, that agency will undoubtedly expect to receive a formal report. Reporting is presented visually in Figure 2.10.

The essential elements of a research or evaluation report include:

1. A thorough description of the research or evaluation process, beginning with the origin of the problem statement, including a summary and discussion of the literature review, explaining the methodology, presenting the manner in which data were gathered, and ending with a description of the data analysis.

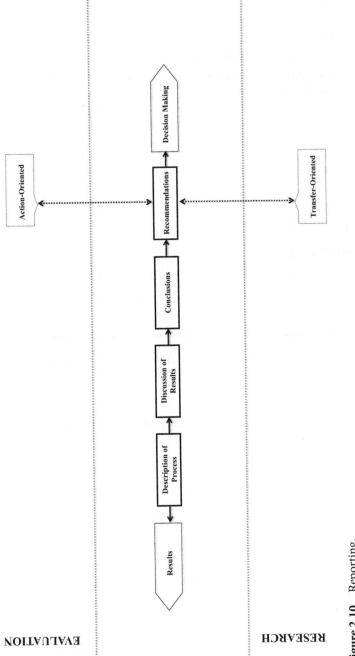

Figure 2.10   Reporting.

2. A description and discussion of the results with appropriate references to data analysis.

3. One or more conclusions based on understanding of:

   a. the significance of results, both statistical and practical

   b. any limitations of results, including the influence of missing or faulty data

   c. the implications of results for understanding the phenomenon of interest and for influencing action

   d. the relationships of the results to previous work

4. The report should end with recommendations that can be provided for further study or action. Providing such recommendations supports the cumulative benefit of research by linking the study not only to prior work but also to targets for the future. Recommendations drawn from evaluations tend to be action oriented, in keeping with the focus of evaluation on solving immediate, local problems. Recommendations drawn from research tend to be focused on the potential for transfer to the broader knowledge base and to research conducted in other settings.

Figure 2.11 provides a summary of an article from *College & Research Libraries* with tips on preparing a report for publication.

Decision Making

Both evaluation and research are input for decision-making processes. Decision making is presented graphically in Figure 2.12. The decisions to be made as a result of research tend

---

Study: Tschera Harkness Connell, "Writing the Research Paper: A Review," *College & Research Libraries* 71, no. 1 (2010): 6–7.

Question/Purpose: This guest editorial provides tips on writing a research report for publication.

Summary: The author emphasizes essential components of a publishable research report: (1) inclusion of a clear problem statement that provides context, establishes focus, explains the need for the research, and emphasizes the importance of the results for the field; (2) a literature review that effectively grounds the reader in the topic, relates the research to earlier work, and locates the research within the domain of related research; (3) a thorough and understandable exposition of the methods used to gather and analyze data; (4) a description of the means that were employed to ensure and document the quality of results; and (5) a conclusion is derived directly from the results and is tied to data and analysis.

Figure 2.11   From the professional literature—components of a research report.

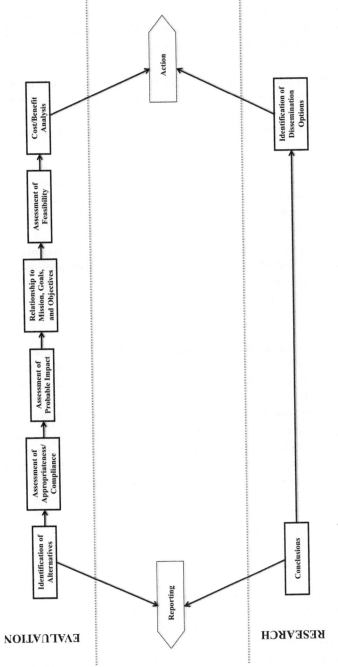

Figure 2.12 Decision making.

to be grounded in the conclusions that can be drawn from the research endeavor and have largely to do with how the outcomes of the research project will be disseminated for broad consumption. The general assumption of research is that useful results will appear as articles, reports, conference presentations, or in other widely available forms.

Decision making for evaluation usually is based in assessing the usefulness of the outcomes of the evaluation process for the institution in which the evaluation takes place. Decision making for evaluation may entail the following:

1. Identification of alternative approaches, strategies, or actions. Evaluation results are frequently part of a process of weighing and assessing multiple competing ways of achieving goals and objectives. At a minimum, the decision-making process must be capable of identifying and giving shape to those alternatives to ensure decision-making efficacy.

2. Assessment of appropriateness or compliance. Some alternatives, although technically feasible and even perhaps technically superior, may be found wanting in terms of appropriateness to the environment of the library or compliance with societal or governmental norms. Alternatives that violate standards of public acceptability or legislative or administrative rules must be eliminated from consideration.

3. Assessment of probable impact. The pragmatic nature of evaluation makes assessing impact essential. Each alternative that has passed the tests of appropriateness and compliance must be assessed in terms of its potential for improvement within the context of institutional goals and objectives. The basic question for each alternative is "to what extent will this lead to improvement is services, programs, collections, or other activities of the library?"

4. Relationship to institutional mission, goals, and objectives. Those alternatives that survive the test of anticipatable impact must be examined to determine the extent to which they support the institution mission, goals, and objectives statements. In some cases, objectives, goals, or even the institutional mission may need to be reassessed in the interest of improvements to be gained as the result of evaluation activities.

5. Determination of feasibility. Feasibility has two critical components. Technical feasibility has to do with the physical and technological worlds and the ease with which a solution to a problem can be implemented. Organizational feasibility is a function of the impact of the solution on the organizational structure and operational capacity of the institutions. Many technologically viable solutions go through periods when, from the point of view of an individual institution, they are organizationally unfeasible.

6. Cost/benefit analysis. The final phase in the decision-making process for any proposed solution to a problem is determination of the relationship between the cost of implementation and maintenance of the solution and the value of the solution to the institution. Cost/benefit analysis is not always grounded in the principle that the benefit must outweigh the cost. Two comparable approaches to providing bookmobile services to a large rural area, for example, both carry monetary costs that exceed the comparable cost of a books-by-mail program. The human factors benefit of contact between bookmobile staff and community members may, however, necessitate that the less costly of the two bookmobile approaches take precedence over the even less costly books-by-mail program. The relationship between the cost and the benefit must be assessed as appropriate within the framework of the mission, goals, and objectives of the institution.

Action

The final phase of the process is action. It is difficult to conceive a meaningful research or evaluation project that fails to result in some form of action, at least at a small level. The action might take the form of implementation of a new approach or technique to accomplishing an essential task, lead to elimination or modification of existing wasteful acts, or contribute to the professional literature by generating a publication. The action phase of research and evaluation is presented in Figure 2.13.

Action and Research

Although successful and beneficial research can have a meaningful impact entirely through its contribution to local policy development or practice, publication of the results of the research is almost always an appropriate goal and is one of the most significant actions that can result from a research project.

The action component of research includes four phases:

1. Selection of a dissemination outlet. There are three prominent forms of dissemination for the results of research. Traditional publication outlets include periodical and book publishers who assume responsibility for working with an author to produce a work in a carefully edited and produced form, usually focusing on print on paper but increasingly including a digital version. Conferences and other meetings serve as opportunities to share the researcher's work with an audience in a physical or digital meeting environment. Conference presentations may or may not be peer reviewed and may or may not be accompanied by published conference proceedings that are in some cases considered comparable to publications. Traditionally, research has focused on publication in peer-reviewed journals, but there have always been other alternatives and new alternatives have appeared in the Internet era. Web publication includes opportunities for self-publication by the author, inclusion in an institutional repository, or inclusion in a peer-reviewed digital journal that has no print equivalent.

2. Preparation of the results in the selected dissemination outlet. This may take the form of a manuscript formatted to meet the needs of a journal, a proposal for a conference presentation, or preparation of a web publication. Regardless of the format, the product must be prepared carefully and appropriately. Journals have varying publication requirements and use differing style manuals. A manuscript that does not conform to the required style manual is unlikely to be treated kindly in the editorial review process. Conference proposals are expected to adhere to stated content and length requirements. A good web publication typically emulates a journal article in style, content, and length.

3. Editorial review. Most research moves into the action mode through some sort of editorial review process. This may be a matter of interaction and negotiation between the author and a single editor, but the editor is frequently supported by and responsible to an editorial board charged with making decisions about the appropriateness of research outcomes for dissemination. In some cases, there may be an additional peer review in which members of a panel of experts are recruited to advise on the quality and suitability for publication of a researcher's work.

4. Identification of targets for further research. Research is at its best when it grows and becomes a cyclical process. For many researchers, the greatest delight in the entire research endeavor comes from the questions that were not answered, perhaps because

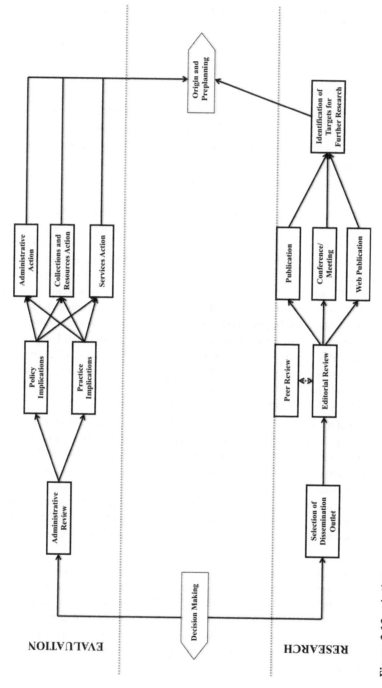

Figure 2.13 Action.

they were not asked, and the hypotheses that were neither supported nor refuted. These are the invitations to ask more and different questions, to reformulate hypotheses, and to do more. This is the re-entry into the research process that keeps the process cycling.

Action and Evaluation

Evaluation results are more closely associated with pragmatic forms of action that are anticipated to have direct impacts on library policy or practice. The three essential phases of initiating action based on evaluation are:

1. Administrative review. Action based on the results of evaluation can rarely be implemented directly and immediately without some sort of managerial or administrative review. Greater implications of action imply higher levels of review. It is essential in implementing the results of any evaluation project to be thoroughly cognizant of the nature of the library as a system, with multiple subsystems, administrative units, functional units, and processes that inherently interact with each other. Implementation of the results of an evaluation in any given area of library processes must be assumed to have implications for other areas.

2. Assessment of policy and practice implications. Although evaluation activities are most frequently undertaken to address perceived problems in practice, technique, method, or tools, results of evaluation inherently have implications for review and revision of policy as well as practice. In general, policy decisions must precede practice revisions; at a minimum, actions related to policy and practice must be closely coordinated if the results of evaluation are to be truly beneficial.

3. Action. The final stage is action, which may affect administrative practices, collections and resources practices, service practices, or all three in an integrated and inseparable manner. In many cases, implementation is not the direct responsibility of the evaluator.

An important fourth activity, although frequently not required for an evaluation project, is dissemination. Although sharing results with library staff members and other constituents may not be a requirement of the administrator who initiated or authorized the project, disseminating results is a means for providing recognition for contributions made to the project, informing staff and constituents of actions taken as a result of the evaluation activity, and establishing buy-in for evaluation through building toward what Wallace and Van Fleet have referred to as a "Culture of Evaluation."[4]

RESEARCH AND EVALUATION: LINKED BUILDING BLOCKS FOR KNOWLEDGE AND ACTION

The parallel natures of research and evaluation—from general idea or need to preplanning, planning, data gathering, analysis, processing results, reporting, decision making, and action—emphasize how closely linked the two areas of exploration and study truly are. These are the tools of understanding and of knowledge. The interests of research and evaluation in a tightly related professional field such as library and information science are functionally coterminous. Regardless of whether a library and information professional is an academic librarian facing the research demands of tenure or a truly reflective practitioner interested solely in applying efficient tools to effective problem solving, the professional has a need and an obligation to be familiar with the nature, processes, techniques, and tools of both research and evaluation and to be aware of which are most appropriate to a particular need or issue. It is through the effective linkage of research and evaluation and the development of a collective professional commitment to both that professions gain and sustain public accountability, credibility, and excellence.

 THINK ABOUT IT!

1. How might the origin of an idea for a project differ for an evaluation project and a research project?
2. Circulation of downloadable e-books for use on handheld readers can be addressed as either a research project or an evaluation project? How might the preplanning and planning phases of a research project exploring the issue differ from those of an evaluation project?
3. Circulation of materials held by academic libraries has been declining for several years. To what extent does examination of this issue lend itself to quantitative methods? To what extent does examination of the issue lend itself to qualitative methods?

 DO IT!

1. Use *Library Literature and Information Science* or a similar database to identify a research article dealing with information literacy. What does the report tell you about the origin of the research idea and the author's decision to conduct the project?
2. Use *Library Literature and Information Science* or a similar database to identify a research article dealing with readers' advisory services in public libraries. What does the report tell you about the outcomes and potentials for action of the project?
3. Identify a real library and information science problem and outline the steps in addressing the problem based on the model presented in this chapter.

NOTES

1. Donald A. Schön, *The Reflective Practitioner: How Professionals Think in Action* (New York: Basic Books, 1983).

2. Robert S. Taylor, "Question-Negotiation and Information Seeking in Libraries," *College & Research Libraries* 29 (May 1968): 178–94.

3. Paul D. Leedy and Jeanne Ormrod, *Practical Research: Planning and Design* (Upper Saddle River, NJ: Pearson, 2005), 57–58.

4. Danny P. Wallace and Connie Van Fleet, *Library Evaluation: A Casebook and Can-Do Guide* (Englewood, CO: Libraries Unlimited, 2001).

SUGGESTED READINGS

Emily Stier Adler and Roger Clark, *An Invitation to Social Research: How It's Done* (Belmont, CA: Cengage, 2011).

Earl Babbie, *The Practice of Social Research*, 12th ed. (Belmont, CA: Cengage, 2010).

Lynn Silipigni Connaway and Ronald R. Powell, *Basic Research Methods for Librarians*, 5th ed. (Santa Barbara, CA: Libraries Unlimited, 2010).

Herbert Goldhor, *An Introduction to Scientific Research in Librarianship* (Washington: U.S. Department of Education Bureau of Research, 1969).

David R. Krathwohl, *Methods of Educational and Social Science Research: An Integrated Approach*, 2nd ed. (New York: Harlow, 1998).

Lawrence T. Orcher, *Conducting Research* (Glendale, CA: Pyrczak, 2005).

Julian L. Simon and Paul Burstein, *Basic Research Methods in Social Science: The Art of Empirical Investigation*, 3rd ed. (New York: McGraw-Hill, 1985).

Royce A. Singleton, Jr. and Bruce C. Straits, *Approaches to Social Research*, 5th ed. (New York: Oxford University Press, 2010).

3

ETHICS AND POLITICS IN LIBRARY AND INFORMATION SCIENCE RESEARCH AND EVALUATION

It is not cruel to inflict on a few criminals sufferings which may benefit multitudes of innocent people through all centuries.

> —*Celsus,* De Medicina, *Prooemium 26, 1st century AD*

Ethics, too, are nothing but reverence for life.

> —*Albert Schweitzer,* Civilization and Ethics, *1923*

In this Chapter

Definitions of ethics

Professional values related to ethics

Ethics in research and evaluation

Research ethics concerns

The Belmont Report and other important research ethics documents

Federal oversight of human subjects research

Confidentiality and anonymity

Deception

Research conduct

Politics in library and information science research and evaluation

ETHICS DEFINED

The *Encyclopedia of Philosophy* identifies three approaches to defining the term *ethics:* "(1) a general pattern or 'way of life,' (2) a set of rules of conduct or 'moral code,' and (3) inquiry about ways of life and rules of conduct."[1] The first definition is one of the most commonly used in everyday life. The study of ethics as an academic or philosophical area of interest has tended to focus on the third definition. Traditional approaches to the study of ethics concentrate on defining value systems by distinguishing between good and bad at a broad level based in principles of fundamental issues of morality and judgment.

Professional ethics, codes of ethics, and judgments of ethical or unethical behavior fall under the second definition. This is the definition of greatest pertinence in the ethical environment of research and evaluation. In contrast to the highly moralistic traditions of traditional ethics, Sidgwick proposed a more utilitarian view of ethics that he termed practical ethics.[2] Practical ethics is also known as applied ethics. The *Encyclopedia of Philosophy* defines applied ethics as "the application of general ethical theories to moral problems with the objective of solving the problems."[3] According to O'Neill, "practical ethics can go beyond the consideration of principles and the types of situations in which they could or should be applied by saying more about the institutional structures and cultural support needed if respect for significant ethical and other principles is to be adequately achieved in public, professional and private life."[4]

FUNDAMENTAL PROFESSIONAL VALUES RELATED TO ETHICS

Considerations of ethics for research and evaluation in library and information science have their origin in the nature of professions. Professions can be viewed as aligned with a set of highly intertwined fundamental responsibilities that have a close bearing on ethical behavior: self-regulation, advancement of knowledge, social goals and advancing the public good, and avoidance of harm.

Self-Regulation

Self-regulation is the basic principle that the members of a professional community such as library and information science are charged with collectively setting boundaries, standards, and codes of practice for the profession. Where generalized standards for behavior exist, they are adopted by the profession from within rather than being imposed upon the profession by an external agency. Self-regulation requires a substantial amount of shared self-awareness, ongoing dialog about the need for and nature of self-regulation, and meaningful collective scanning of the internal and external environments of the profession.

Advancement of Knowledge

A second professional principle related to ethics in research and evaluation is a dedication to the advancement of knowledge. This includes both the internal knowledge and tools that benefit the advancement of the profession and the promulgation and distribution of knowledge that benefits the external world. Professions tend to be open about their knowledge bases rather than jealous or protective of them. Professionals understand that failure to move the knowledge base forward inevitably leads to stagnation, loss of relevance to the external community, and ethical lapses.

Social Goals and Advancing the Public Good

Dedication to the inherently social role of the profession is a third tenet of ethical professionalism. A profession exists not to support and exalt itself, but to serve the needs and purposes of the publics that support and are supported by the profession. When professions or institutions become insular, self-absorbed, or overly focused on activities that benefit the profession rather than the public, they tend to sink into reliance on inflexible rules and practices, acts that distance the profession from the public, and ultimately loss of public understanding, public trust, or even public awareness.

Avoidance of Harm

Perhaps the most important manifestation of the role of a profession in advancing the public good is the principle of avoidance of harm. Although the words "first do no harm" don't actually appear in the Hippocratic Oath, they are a succinct and appropriate statement of the paramount principle that research and evaluation are of most value when they yield useful and positive outcomes, of marginal value when they fail to yield useful and positive outcomes, and of least value when they produce results that are counterproductive, negative, or directly harmful. Although Celsus's comment at the beginning of this chapter on the expendable nature of prisoners may have been appropriate to the research ethics of the first century, it has no relevance to and—it is to be hoped—no support in the 21st century.

The need to observe ethical policies, practices, and procedures in research and evaluation is not a recent concern. Court cases related to issues such as informed consent and treatment of special research populations arose in the 18th century and led to the development of codes of ethical conduct, first in medicine and later in other professional areas.

ETHICS IN RESEARCH AND EVALUATION

Ethical behavior is essential to the appropriate application of research to revealing new knowledge and evaluation to solving specific problems. Ethical behavior is not tied to any particular family of research and evaluation methods, to any particular situation, or to any specific phase of the research or evaluation process. Ethical principles must be applied throughout the research or evaluation lifecycle, from conceptualization of the need for the project to any and all actions taken on the basis of results and decision making.

The role of ethics in research and evaluation is to ensure honesty and to protect the rights of all individuals and groups affected by the research or evaluation initiative. Identifying constituents and carefully analyzing the probabilities of benefits and harms are potentially intimidating but absolutely essential components in research and evaluation. Although the investigator may be inclined to minimize or trivialize the potential for risk or undue benefit, nearly every research or evaluation project opens the door to risk and favoritism. Figure 3.1 identifies the individuals and groups who may be inappropriately favored or harmed by failure to engage in ethical practices in research and evaluation.

RESEARCH ETHICS CONCERNS

Humane Treatment

Respect for life, health, and well-being are fundamental precepts of research ethics for projects involving human or animal subjects. Although animal subjects are rare to the point of unlikely in library and information science research and evaluation, investigation involving human subjects is commonplace.

The researcher or evaluator

Individuals who report to the researcher or evaluator

Individuals to whom the research or evaluator reports

Coworkers

Functional units of the institution

Administrative units of the institution

Governing bodies

Local, state, or federal governments

Professional bodies

Consumers of published reports

Patrons of the local library

Patrons of other libraries

The general public

Figure 3.1   Beneficiaries of ethical practices in research and evaluation.

Humane Treatment and Medical Research

Medical research involving human subjects has been carried out on a limited basis for several centuries, but did not assume a prominent role until the late 19th century. According to Shamoo, the medical profession prior to World War II was fundamentally "ambivalent" toward the humane treatment of human research subjects.[5]

The Nuremberg Medical Trials

The Nuremberg Medical Trials that followed World War II revealed a horrifying pattern of human experimentation carried out under the auspices of the Third Reich. Twenty-three individuals, including 20 physicians, were charged and subsequently sentenced for a variety of acts that varied from questionable to genuinely atrocious. The Nuremberg Code, adopted by the American Medical Association in 1947 and subsequently published in 1949, although never incorporated into law, was the first generally accepted core statement on humane principles in research. The Nuremberg Code is reproduced in Figure 3.2.[6]

The Tuskegee Syphilis Study

Unfortunately, inhumane treatment of human subjects in research was not confined to the horrors of World War II. The U.S. Public Health Service initiated a study of the effects of untreated syphilis in 1932, drawing on a population of impoverished and uneducated sharecroppers living in southern Alabama. The study was designed to test the cardiovascular and neurological impacts of syphilis and to explore whether there was a differential effect between white and black subjects. Six hundred subjects were involved in the study,

1. The voluntary consent of the human subject is absolutely essential. This means that the person involved should have legal capacity to give consent; should be so situated as to be able to exercise free power of choice, without the intervention of any element of force, fraud, deceit, duress, over-reaching, or other ulterior form of constraint or coercion; and should have sufficient knowledge and comprehension of the elements of the subject matter involved as to enable him to make an understanding and enlightened decision. This latter element requires that before the acceptance of an affirmative decision by the experimental subject there should be made known to him the nature, duration, and purpose of the experiment; the method and means by which it is to be conducted; all inconveniences and hazards reasonable to be expected; and the effects upon his health or person which may possibly come from his participation in the experiment.

   The duty and responsibility for ascertaining the quality of the consent rests upon each individual who initiates, directs, or engages in the experiment. It is a personal duty and responsibility which may not be delegated to another with impunity.

2. The experiment should be such as to yield fruitful results for the good of society, unprocurable by other methods or means of study, and not random and unnecessary in nature.

3. The experiment should be so designed and based on the results of animal experimentation and a knowledge of the natural history of the disease or other problem under study that the anticipated results will justify the performance of the experiment.

4. The experiment should be so conducted as to avoid all unnecessary physical and mental suffering and injury.

5. No experiment should be conducted where there is an a priori reason to believe that death or disabling injury will occur; except, perhaps, in those experiments where the experimental physicians also serve as subjects.

6. The degree of risk to be taken should never exceed that determined by the humanitarian importance of the problem to be solved by the experiment.

7. Proper preparations should be made and adequate facilities provided to protect the experimental subject against even remote possibilities of injury, disability, or death.

8. The experiment should be conducted only by scientifically qualified persons. The highest degree of skill and care should be required through all stages of the experiment of those who conduct or engage in the experiment.

9. During the course of the experiment the human subject should be at liberty to bring the experiment to an end if he has reached the physical or mental state where continuation of the experiment seems to him to be impossible.

10. During the course of the experiment the scientist in charge must be prepared to terminate the experiment at any stage, if he has probable cause to believe, in the exercise of the good faith, superior skill and careful judgment required of him that a continuation of the experiment is likely to result in injury, disability, or death to the experimental subject.

Figure 3.2 The Nuremberg Code.

two-thirds of whom were infected. Infected subjects were not informed of their infected status nor educated about the nature of the disease. The study was originally intended to last only a few months. Even after penicillin was identified as being effective as a treatment for syphilis in the 1940s, the subjects in the study were not treated, even though failing to do so was directly in violation of federal law. It is estimated that at least a hundred subjects died of untreated syphilis. The study was not exposed to the public until the publication of an article in the *Washington Star* in 1972. A class-action suit against the federal government regarding the study was settled out of court in 1974. The National Research Act was passed in response to the study and the ensuing court action. The National Research Act mandated the creation of the National Commission for the Protection of Human Subjects of Biomedical and Behavioral Research. President Bill Clinton formally apologized for the Tuskegee Syphilis Study in 1997.

Human Radiation Studies

During the three decades following World War II the U.S. Government and several universities carried out tests of the impact of radiation and radioactive materials on human subjects, most of whom were unaware of the nature of the research. The studies, which affected more than 4,000 U.S. citizens, included injection of weapons-grade nuclear materials, radio-isotope tracing materials, experiments on the effects of radioactive materials on children, total body radiation for therapeutic purposes, and testicular radiation experiments carried out on prisoners.[7] The experiments were investigated by a presidential advisory committee beginning in 1994, following a 1993 expose published in the *Albuquerque Tribune*. President Clinton formally apologized to the victims of the radiation studies in 1995.

Humane Treatment and Social Sciences Research

Although social sciences research is rarely accompanied by the risk of physical harm characteristic of medical research, physical harm in social sciences research is not an impossibility. Psychological harm, however, is a frequent risk in social sciences research, including research in library and information science, and has potential for being a risk in evaluation. Although library and information science studies with the potential for psychological harm have been infrequent and relatively innocuous, other social sciences studies invoking fears of psychological harm have been fairly frequent and sometimes infamous. Two in particular—Milgram's obedience studies and the Stanford Prison Experiment—are frequently cited as ethical dilemmas in social sciences research.

Milgram's Obedience Studies

Stanley Milgram conducted a series of laboratory studies during the 1960s and 1970s designed to explore the concept of obedience in the context of the willingness of subjects to harm others in the interest of following instructions from a perceived authority figure.[8] In the most widely known of these experiments, Experiment 5, 40 men with diverse backgrounds were recruited for what was described to them as a study of "the relation between punishment and learning."[9] Each participant was told that he was to be a member of a research team consisting of a researcher, a learner, and a teacher. The researcher and the learner were in fact trained research assistants. The experiment began with the participant and a research assistant drawing slips of paper to determine who would be teacher and who would be learner. In fact, the researcher always manipulated the results so that the participant would be in the role of teacher. The researcher then strapped the learner to a chair and attached electrodes to the learner's arm. The teacher's task was to first read a series of word pairs to the learner, then read the first word of each pair followed by a series of four words. The learner's task was to identify the word among the four that had originally been paired with the first word. The learner indicated his choice by pressing a button that caused a light to be displayed on the teacher's console.

The teacher's console, known as the shock generator, consisted of 30 levers labeled from 15 to 450 volts. The switches were arranged in groups of four, with the groups labeled "Slight Shock, Moderate Shock, Strong Shock, Very Strong Shock, Intense Shock, Extreme Intensity Shock, and Danger: Severe Shock."[10] Although the shock generator was not in fact real, each teacher was administered a mild shock, supposedly by the shock generator, to gain a sense of how it would feel to be shocked and to lend authenticity to the experiment. The teacher's task was to administer a shock each time the learner incorrectly identified the paired word, with explicit instructions to increase the voltage of the shock with each wrong answer. When the teacher reached the 150-volt switch, the learner began to protest, complain of pain, and report heart problems. The learner's reaction became more extreme as the experiment progressed. At the 300-volt point the learner ceased to answer, which the teacher had been instructed to treat as a wrong answer. The experimenter encouraged the teacher to continue to administer the test even after the learner had stopped responding. Ultimately, 65 percent of participants continued to administer shocks until the maximum voltage indicated on the console had been reached.

Milgram was primarily interested in the role of authority and the phenomenon of obedience. Although Milgram and others have defended the experiments as a major contribution to the study of response to authoritarian demands in a stressful situation, the studies were widely criticized both at the time and during the intervening decades for the intense stress and potential psychological harm inflicted on the participants. Slater et al. replicated Milgram's study in a virtual environment in 2006, noting that, although Milgram's "line of research is no longer amenable to direct experimental studies," the impact of a simulated Milgram-like experiment might have less potential for harm.[11] Although their research produced promising results, they found that even participants in a virtual experiment in which they knew the "learner" was not real produced substantial physiological and psychological stress.

The Stanford Prison Experiment

In 1971, an experiment was carried out at Stanford University to study "interpersonal dynamics in a prison-like setting" using a "functional simulation of a prison."[12] A team of researchers under Philip G. Zimbardo recruited a deliberately homogenous sample of 24 male university students—the "best and brightest"—for a two-week study of prison life. Half the participants were randomly assigned to play the role of guards, while half were assigned to the role of prisoners.[13] Zimbardo played the role of the superintendent of the prison. Verisimilitude was introduced by having the mock prisoners actually arrested without notice by the local police, processed and briefly detained at the police station, and then transported to the mock prison.

A variety of data-gathering methods were employed, including audiotaping, videotaping, questionnaires, self-reporting instruments, and interviews. The first day of the experiment was uneventful, but by the morning of the second day the prisoners staged a rebellion by barricading the doors of the cells. The guards retaliated in an attempt to assert authority over the prisoners. As the experiment progressed, the guards became increasingly abusive. Although they were not allowed to be directly physically aggressive, they invented psychological punishments such as depriving prisoners of clothing, placing prisoners' heads in nylon stockings to simulate shaved heads, chaining prisoners' legs, and other humiliating experiences. By the fifth day of the experiment, five of the prisoners had experienced sufficient stress that they were released from the prison and excused from the study. Zimbardo himself was actually co-opted by his role as superintendent and had to be jolted back to reality by a colleague. The study was terminated after the sixth day. Zimbardo later described the experiment as being "more akin to Greek drama than to university psychology study."[14] The outcomes of the Stanford Prison Experiment were mimicked in real life to a startling extent by the events at Abu Ghraib Prison in Iraq during the Second Gulf War in 2003 and 2004.[15]

Informed Consent

Informed consent is the fundamental principle that human participants in research projects should know and understand that they are research subjects and should be aware of the nature, extent, and likelihood of any risks to them as a result of their participation. The Nuremberg Code addressed informed consent in the context of medical research.

Although the Nuremberg Code was undoubtedly influential, the failure to widely adopt its principles into law and the Code's origin in a military court rather than a professional environment led to uncertain acceptance of its principles and incomplete adoption of the Code. In 1964, the World Medical Association published the first version of the Declaration of Helsinki as an internationally agreed upon set of ethical principles related to experimentation with human subjects. Like the Nuremberg Code, the Declaration of Helsinki has no legal weight, but is generally credited with heightening attention to ethical principles related to human subjects and has been extremely influential in the development of national codes of ethical conduct in research. The Declaration was revised in 1975, 1983, 1989, 1996, 2000, and 2008.[16]

Neither the Nuremberg Code nor the Declaration of Helsinki addressed informed consent outside the context of medical research. A prominent social sciences informed consent controversy arose from a 1953 study carried out by researchers from the University of Chicago. As part of the study, a concealed microphone was placed in the jury room during federal court jury trial in Wichita Kansas, with the knowledge of the judge and attorneys involved in the case, but without the knowledge of the jury. The study, widely condemned in the press, resulted in a Senate committee investigation and the subsequent passage and adoption of a federal law explicitly forbidding recording, observing, or listening to the proceedings of a federal court jury.[17]

Informed consent is not a guarantee of participant protection. Participants in the Stanford Prison Experiment, with consultation from university legal counsel, drew up an informed consent document that "specified that there would be an invasion of privacy, loss of civil rights and harassment;" the document was signed by all participants.[18]

THE BELMONT REPORT

During 1975 and 1976, the National Commission for the Protection of Human Subjects of Biomedical and Behavioral Research reviewed existing laws, regulations, and procedures for ensuring humane treatment and informed consent in federally funded research. The Commission's deliberations were directly influenced by the Tuskegee Syphilis Study and other questionable research activities. The Commission's review was intensified by a four-day session held at the Smithsonian Institution's Belmont Conference Center in February 1976 and monthly meetings that continued for nearly four years following the Belmont meeting. In 1979 the Commission issued the Belmont Report, a statement of fundamental ethical principles related to research involving human subjects.[19] The Belmont Report focused primarily on biomedical and behavioral research, but has specific implications for social sciences research and for evaluation activities.

Basic Ethical Principles

Three basic ethical principles are enumerated and defined in the Belmont Report: (1) respect for persons, (2) beneficence, and (3) justice. These principles are summarized in Figure 3.3.[20]

Respect for Persons

Respect for persons, as defined in the Belmont Report, has two fundamental aspects: "first, that individuals should be treated as autonomous agents, and second, that persons with diminished autonomy are entitled to protection."[21] As an autonomous agent, any individual has the right and responsibility to guide his or her judgments, decisions, opinions, and actions. Acting as an autonomous agent requires access to appropriate and complete information on which to base judgments, decisions, opinions, and actions. The most critical impact of the principle of respect for persons on research and evaluation is the individual right to enter into any research or evaluation process voluntarily and with access to appropriate information on which to make the decision to participate or not participate.

Some people, however, lack the ability to act autonomously due to factors of maturity, disability, or status. Members of such vulnerable populations require special protections to ensure that they are not unduly subjected to harmful situations nor denied the benefits of participation in research or evaluation activities. The information needs and information-seeking behaviors of children are of great interest to library and information science research and evaluation. Children are by definition a protected group who require special protections. McKechnie noted that little empirical research regarding library programming for babies and toddlers has been done, in part because of the difficulty of working with very young human subjects.[22]

1. Respect for persons
   a. Individuals as autonomous agents
   b. Protection for individuals with diminished autonomy
2. Beneficence
   a. Avoidance of harm
   b. Maximization of benefits and minimization of harms
3. Justice
   a. Equitable treatment of human research subjects

Figure 3.3   Fundamental principles of the Belmont Report.

Beneficence

The Belmont Report addresses the fundamental professional responsibilities of social goals and avoidance of harm both at the collective level and at the individual level. Beneficence, which "is often understood to cover acts of kindness or charity that go beyond strict obligation," is defined in the Report as an absolute obligation.[23] This obligation leads to two explicit rules for beneficence in research: (1) "do not harm" and (2) "maximize possible benefits and minimize possible harms."[24]

Justice

The principle of justice has to do with equitable distribution of the benefits and burdens of research: "An injustice occurs when some benefit to which a person is entitled is denied without good reason or when some burden is imposed unduly."[25] The critical feature of justice in this context is equitable treatment of human research subjects. According to the principle of justice, "the selection of research subjects needs to be scrutinized in order to determine whether some classes . . . are being systematically selected simply because of their easy availability, their compromised position, or their manipulability, rather than for reasons directly related to the problem being studied."[26]

Applications to Research

The Belmont Report extends from the three basic ethical principles to three specific areas in which the principles influence the actual conduct of research. These three applications are (1) informed consent, (2) assessment of risks and benefits, and (3) selection of subjects.

Informed Consent

Grounded in the principle of respect for persons, the principle of informed consent as presented in the Belmont Report requires that "subjects, to the degree that they are capable, be given the opportunity to choose what shall or shall not happen to them."[27] Informed consent requires that the prospective research subject be properly informed regarding the purpose of the research activity, the nature of research procedures and alternatives, possible risks, and anticipated benefits. Additionally, the prospective subject must have the opportunity to ask questions, request additional information, and withdraw from the study at any time and for any reason.

Making appropriate information available to prospective subjects is not in and of itself an adequate approach to ensuring respect for persons. There is an additional requirement that the information be made available in a form and manner that are comprehensible to the prospective subject as an individual and that the researcher has established that such comprehension has in fact taken place.

Finally, agreement to participate in a research project constitutes valid informed consent only to the extent that participation is truly voluntary. This means that there must be no element of coercion, either explicit or implied, or of undue influence. Undue influence occurs when the reward the prospective subject perceives as being associated with participation is excessive, inappropriate, or otherwise viewed as being irresistible. Faculty members in schools of library and information science, as well as in other disciplinary and professional areas, must exercise great care in creating special rewards such as extra credit for student participation in research projects.

Assessment of Risks and Benefits

Ethical research or evaluation requires careful examination of the risks and benefits of the proposed project and effective assessment of the balance of risks and benefits as they will affect the outcomes of the project, society as a whole, and particularly individual research subjects. Risk is a comparative factor for which it is necessary to establish a level of probability of harm and the severity of harm. Benefit, in the terms of the Belmont Report, is an absolute: the results of research or evaluation either carry some benefit at some level or they do not.

Assessing the risks and benefits of a proposed project serves to provide a judgment of the extent to which the project can be justified. Such justification is grounded in five fundamental principles of warrant for human subject research:

1. Brutal or inhumane treatment of human subjects is never morally justified.
2. Risks should be reduced to those necessary to achieve the research objective.
3. When research involves significant risk of serious impairment, review committees should be extraordinarily insistent on the justification of the risk.
4. When vulnerable populations are involved in research, the appropriateness of involving them should itself be demonstrated.
5. Relevant risks and benefits must be thoroughly arrayed in documents and procedures used in the informed consent process.[28]

Selection of Subjects

Just as the principle of respect for persons requires careful attention to informed consent and the principle of beneficence requires systematic and effective assessment of risks and benefits, the principle of justice requires that the selection of subjects be carried out in a fair and equitable manner. Equitable selection of subjects has both individual and societal consequences. The principle of individual fairness dictates that subjects should not be selected either because they are perceived as especially good or explicitly poor subjects for the research project at hand. Individual fairness can be effectively addressed through random selection of participants and random assignment to groups. The societal impact is based on the principle that "injustice arises from social, racial, sexual and cultural biases institutionalized in society."[29]

FEDERAL OVERSIGHT OF RESEARCH INVOLVING HUMAN SUBJECTS

Federal oversight for human subjects research is provided in the U.S. Code of Federal Regulations under Title 45, Public Welfare Department of Health And Human Services, Part 46, Protection of Human Subjects, originally issued in 1991 and subsequently revised in 2005, known as 45 CFR 46 or the "Common Rule."[30] The general principles and legal requirements of 45 CFR 46 are based heavily on the Belmont Report. All research involving human subjects that is in any way funded or supported by any federal agency must comply with the policy guidelines provided in Title 45 CFR 46. This includes research carried out by federal agencies and research carried out by other institutions but in any way supported by federal funding. Oversight responsibility for 45 CFR 46 is provided by the Office of Human Subjects Research (OHSR) of the National Institutes of Health, but the responsibility of OHSR effectively extends far beyond health sciences research.

Institutional Review Boards

One of the key provisions of 45 CFR 46 is the establishment of a requirement that research involving human subjects be carried out under the auspices and approval of an Institutional Review Board (IRB). An IRB is an administrative and oversight body of a specific institution that has comprehensive responsibility for ensuring the protection and ethical treatment of human research subjects. All universities and research institutions have established IRBs that work within the context of local policies and government regulations to oversee human subjects research compliance. Although 45 CFR 46 technically applies only to federally funded research, in practice many universities apply the same standards and processes to all human subjects research, regardless of funding source. IRB membership is required under 45 CFR 46 to include at least five members that include both men and women, at least one of whom has a scientific background, at least one of whom does not have a scientific background, and at least one of whom is not otherwise affiliated with the institution. The fundamental responsibilities of IRBs, as defined in 45 CFR 46, are presented in Figure 3.4.[31]

In some situations there may be no formally established IRB. A public library, for instance, may operate in an environment in which formal research is not a common activity and in which the constitution of an IRB is unlikely. The responsibility for oversight for research or evaluation projects involving human subjects is not moot in such circumstances. The need for care in oversight for projects may in fact be greatly heightened by the lack of routine policies or practices for ensuring protection of human subjects.

In the absence of an IRB or a formally established equivalent, the responsibility for ensuring oversight falls on the investigator. The most typical approach to ensuring such oversight is to appoint and consult a panel of community members and individuals with expertise related to the research or evaluation project to review the conceptualization, design, and implementation of the project. Ideally, responsibility for appointing and convening the review panel should lie with someone other than the project director, such as a library administrator or a governance board. The typical expectation is that the local panel will be dismissed at the culmination of the project.

Vulnerable Populations

The library and information professions have a long, if varied, history of dedication to serving the needs of diverse populations. The commitment to address the needs of diverse clienteles instills a particular necessity of sensitivity to vulnerable populations in library and information science research and evaluation. Three specific vulnerable populations requiring special protections are identified in 45 CFR 46:

1. pregnant women, human fetuses, and neonates
2. prisoners
3. children

Pregnant women, human fetuses, and neonates are vulnerable primarily but not exclusively in the context of medical research involving physical or drug-related interventions. Psychological harm may also be a significant factor. The primary consideration of 45 CFR 46 is minimization of risk. The general principles of informed consent are greatly intensified when research involves these populations.

(a) In order to approve research covered by this policy the IRB shall determine that all of the following requirements are satisfied:

(1) Risks to subjects are minimized: (i) By using procedures which are consistent with sound research design and which do not unnecessarily expose subjects to risk, and (ii) whenever appropriate, by using procedures already being performed on the subjects for diagnostic or treatment purposes.

(2) Risks to subjects are reasonable in relation to anticipated benefits, if any, to subjects, and the importance of the knowledge that may reasonably be expected to result. In evaluating risks and benefits, the IRB should consider only those risks and benefits that may result from the research (as distinguished from risks and benefits of therapies subjects would receive even if not participating in the research). The IRB should not consider possible long-range effects of applying knowledge gained in the research (for example, the possible effects of the research on public policy) as among those research risks that fall within the purview of its responsibility.

(3) Selection of subjects is equitable. In making this assessment the IRB should take into account the purposes of the research and the setting in which the research will be conducted and should be particularly cognizant of the special problems of research involving vulnerable populations, such as children, prisoners, pregnant women, mentally disabled persons, or economically or educationally disadvantaged persons.

(4) Informed consent will be sought from each prospective subject or the subject's legally authorized representative, in accordance with, and to the extent required by §46.116.

(5) Informed consent will be appropriately documented, in accordance with, and to the extent required by §46.117.

(6) When appropriate, the research plan makes adequate provision for monitoring the data collected to ensure the safety of subjects.

(7) When appropriate, there are adequate provisions to protect the privacy of subjects and to maintain the confidentiality of data.

(b) When some or all of the subjects are likely to be vulnerable to coercion or undue influence, such as children, prisoners, pregnant women, mentally disabled persons, or economically or educationally disadvantaged persons, additional safeguards have been included in the study to protect the rights and welfare of these subjects.

Figure 3.4   Criteria for IRB approval of research.

Prisoners have historically been unwilling or unwitting subjects of a substantial array of research initiatives. The primary risk to prisoners as research subjects is related to the restricted extent to which they may have the ability to make truly voluntary and informed consent to participate in research projects. Additional IRB requirements for studies involving prisoners include ensuring that a majority of IRB members have no other affiliation with the prison where research is to take place and that at least one member of the IRB be a prisoner. IRBs for research involving prisoners as subjects also have additional responsibilities for ensuring that subjects do not accrue unfair advantages in comparison to prisoners who are not subjects, that risks are comparable to those encountered by subjects who are not prisoners, that selection of subjects is fair to all prisoners in the research environment, and that parole boards will not give undue consideration to prisoner participation in research.

Children are the identified vulnerable group most frequently of interest in library and information science research and evaluation. Young people are an obvious subject for library and information science research and evaluation, and a large proportion of research and evaluation in librarianship revolves around services to young people.

Children are defined in 45 CFR 46 as individuals who have not yet attained the age of consent for research procedures. Children are particularly vulnerable in that they are not usually viewed as capable of granting full consent on their own; permission for children to act as research subjects is generally confirmed by their parents or legal guardians. There is, however, a critical distinction between parental permission and the child's *assent* to participate in the project. Assent is defined as "a child's affirmative agreement to participate in research."[32] IRB responsibility for ensuring the protection of children as research subjects is paramount; strict definitions of risk and requirements for IRB review of proposed research projects involving children as subjects are strongly emphasized in 45 CFR 46.

Also addressed in 45 CFR 46, although not in detail commensurate with that provided for pregnant women, human fetuses, neonates, prisoners, and children, are requirements for protection of mentally or developmentally disabled subjects and economically or educationally disadvantaged individuals. Mentally or developmentally disabled subjects may be vulnerable due to a lack of effective ability to provide informed consent. Either group may be subject to unintentional or purposeful coercion or undue influence. These individuals may also be excluded from research or evaluation due to the perceived difficulty of working with them and thus, as a group, be excluded from the benefits of research or evaluation.

Exemption from IRB Review

Some categories of research and evaluation are exempt from normal IRB review, although in practice IRBs generally conduct an expedited review of any proposal that potentially qualifies for exemption. The grounds for exemption, as identified in 45 CFR 46 are presented in Figure 3.5. Many evaluation projects, especially those that concentrate on analysis of data gathered for routine purposes such as maintenance of common library statistics are exempt from human subjects review. Surveys of patron satisfaction with library services, collections, and programs, for instances, do not normally require any semblance to human subjects approval.

CONFIDENTIALITY AND ANONYMITY

In addition to directly protecting human subjects from physical or psychological harm through effective research design and informed consent, investigators have an obligation to appropriately protect the identities of human subjects. Issues of identity protection and identity theft have been of heightened concern in the public sphere and in the news media for some time. In research and evaluation, protection of subject identities is a means of protecting subjects from potential physical or psychological harm.

(1) Research conducted in established or commonly accepted educational settings, involving normal educational practices, such as (i) research on regular and special education instructional strategies, or (ii) research on the effectiveness of or the comparison among instructional techniques, curricula, or classroom management methods.

(2) Research involving the use of educational tests (cognitive, diagnostic, aptitude, achievement), survey procedures, interview procedures or observation of public behavior, unless:

(i) information obtained is recorded in such a manner that human subjects can be identified, directly or through identifiers linked to the subjects; and (ii) any disclosure of the human subjects' responses outside the research could reasonably place the subjects at risk of criminal or civil liability or be damaging to the subjects' financial standing, employability, or reputation.

(3) Research involving the use of educational tests (cognitive, diagnostic, aptitude, achievement), survey procedures, interview procedures, or observation of public behavior that is not exempt under paragraph (b)(2) of this section, if:

(i) the human subjects are elected or appointed public officials or candidates for public office; or (ii) federal statute(s) require(s) without exception that the confidentiality of the personally identifiable information will be maintained throughout the research and thereafter.

(4) Research involving the collection or study of existing data, documents, records, pathological specimens, or diagnostic specimens, if these sources are publicly available or if the information is recorded by the investigator in such a manner that subjects cannot be identified, directly or through identifiers linked to the subjects.

(5) Research and demonstration projects which are conducted by or subject to the approval of department or agency heads, and which are designed to study, evaluate, or otherwise examine:

(i) Public benefit or service programs; (ii) procedures for obtaining benefits or services under those programs; (iii) possible changes in or alternatives to those programs or procedures; or (iv) possible changes in methods or levels of payment for benefits or services under those programs.

(6) Taste and food quality evaluation and consumer acceptance studies, (i) if wholesome foods without additives are consumed or (ii) if a food is consumed that contains a food ingredient at or below the level and for a use found to be safe, or agricultural chemical or environmental contaminant at or below the level found to be safe by the Food and Drug Administration or approved by the Environmental Protection Agency or the Food Safety and Inspection Service of the U.S. Department of Agriculture.

Figure 3.5 Grounds for exemption from IRB review.

Confidentiality

Confidentiality in research and evaluation, as in news reporting, is a matter of an agreement between the investigator and human subjects that, although the identities of subjects will be known, those identities will not be revealed. True informed consent requires that the identities of subjects must be known, but not that data regarding subject identities be made known outside the context of the relationship between the investigator and the subjects.

Unfortunately, researchers, evaluators, and news reporters do not have access to the legal status of privileged communication conferred on physicians, attorneys, and members of the clergy. As a result, simply claiming confidentiality may not be a viable tactic in the unlikely event that a court or other legal body demands that an investigator reveal the identities of subjects. There are, however, tools available to investigators for use in the protection of confidentiality of subject identities.

1. A first principle of the protection of subject identities is to gather no more personal data than is necessary for purposes of the research or evaluation effort. Data that have not been gathered and recorded are not amenable to revealing subject identities.

2. A second effective tool for protecting subject identities is to eliminate links between other data and personal data as soon as they are no longer needed. It may, for instance, be necessary to initially maintain a link between a respondent's identity and the respondent's data related directly to the research or evaluation project for purposes of respondent follow-up, correction of data, or clarification of data. When those needs have been addressed, there may be no further need to retain the link between primary data and respondent identity data.

Anonymity

Where confidentiality requires ensuring that the identity of the subject, although known, will be protected, anonymity requires that the investigator will never know the identity of the subject. In some ways, anonymity is easier to ensure than confidentiality. Although mail and Internet surveys make assurance of anonymity difficult, an onsite survey can easily be made truly anonymous. An easy approach to an anonymous onsite survey involves placing questionnaires at service desks in a library and asking respondents to place completed questionnaires in locked drop boxes located at the library's exits.

Some research and evaluation methods can never be made truly anonymous. Even if the interviewer in a face-to-face interview setting never asks the identities of respondents, the transaction cannot be considered anonymous. The basic test of anonymity in such situations is the question, "could the interviewer pick the respondent out in a police lineup?" If the answer is even provisionally yes, anonymity has not been achieved.

DECEPTION

Milgram's obedience studies, in addition to possibly causing psychological harm, introduced an element of deliberate deception of research subjects. The purpose of the study presented to subjects differed substantially from the real purpose of the study. Additionally, subjects were led to believe that the "learners" in the study were really being subjected to electrical shocks. Although deception in research is not inherently unethical, deception does carry with it the potential for harm and must be handled carefully and with thorough oversight.

"Deception research is research in which subjects are purposely allowed to or caused to have false beliefs or assumptions or to accept as false that which is true, and in which the researcher studies their reactions; the reactions and the study of those reactions are made possible by the incorrect beliefs or assumptions of the subject."[33] Deception techniques in research are sometimes referred to as covert methods. Sieber identified five core motivations for deception in research:

1. avoiding sensitization to the true nature of the research
2. ensuring adequate stimulus control or ensuring random assignment to groups
3. economic viability when observing social phenomena in their natural state would be impractical
4. reducing risk to subjects
5. obtaining data that would otherwise be unavailable due to embarrassment, defensiveness, or fear of reprisal[34]

Sieber distinguished between the process of observation of deception as it exists in the natural world—studying subjects who are self-deceived or deceived by a third party for reasons unrelated to the research project—and deception introduced by the researcher. Deception introduced by the researcher falls into a continuum with five levels:

1. In the first and weakest form of deception, informed consent is obtained but it is understood by both the researcher and the subject that some form of deception will take place; the subject knows in general the conditions under which deception may take place, but is not informed of the specific form the deception will take.
2. In the second form of deception, informed consent is obtained and the subject agrees to be deceived with no prior knowledge of the conditions under which the deception may take place.
3. The third form of deception requires an explicit waiver of the right to be informed. The subject gives up the right to be fully informed about the research procedure and has no prior knowledge that deception may be involved.
4. In the fourth category of deception, informed consent is obtained and the subject is deliberately misled regarding the nature of the research project.
5. In the fifth and most extreme form of deception, the subject is not informed, has no opportunity to consent, and is unaware that he or she is part of a research project.[35]

In practice, it is extremely difficult to obtain IRB approval for any form of research that involves deception. The conditions set forth in 45 CFR 46 under which an IRB can waive or alter informed consent are limited and strict:

1. The research involves no more than minimal risk to the subjects.
2. The waiver or alteration will not adversely affect the rights and welfare of the subjects.
3. The research could not practicably be carried out without the waiver or alteration.
4. Whenever appropriate, the subjects will be provided with additional pertinent information after participation.[36]

The final stipulation regarding debriefing is generally held to be an essential substitute for full informed consent in advance of participation. Generally speaking, the researcher has a responsibility once participation has ended to inform the subject of the existence and nature of the deception, to describe and explain in detail the true nature and methodology of the study, to allow the subject to comment on his or her reaction to the deception, and possibly to disallow use of data gathered through deception of the subject. The process of dehoax-ing is in and of itself complex and sometimes difficult—once deceived by the researcher, a subject may be disinclined to believe that he or she has been deceived and may be reluctant to believe anything further the researcher says. In addition to the direct act of revealing the truth, the debriefing is also an opportunity to desensitize the subject and provide him or her with an opportunity to return to the mental state he or she would normally have had prior to involvement in the deceptive situation.

Debriefing almost always takes the form of a face-to-face interview. The personal nature subjects tend to assign to deception makes in-person contact necessary and allows for the subject to express feelings, thoughts, and concerns about the research project and the decep-tive act. The debriefing is not so much an apology as it is compensation for participating in a process in which the subject has been deceived. Debriefing by means of distributing a docu-ment or sending an e-mail containing information about the research project may be viewed as impersonal, insensitive, and demeaning.

RESEARCH CONDUCT

In addition to the protections researchers must provide to the subjects of research, inves-tigators have ethical obligations to the general public related to appropriate conduct of re-search. Although evidence of inappropriate conduct or misconduct in research has emerged periodically for as long as there has been scholarly publishing, the impact of misconduct in the United States was highlighted by the 1981 hearings of the Investigations and Oversight Subcommittee of the House Science and Technology Committee, "prompted by the public disclosure of research misconduct cases at four major research centers in 1980."[37] In 1985, Congress passed the Health Research Extension Act, which required administrative over-sight to minimize fraud in scientific research. Final guidelines for federally funded research were published as "Responsibilities of Awardee and Applicant Institutions for Dealing With and Reporting Possible Misconduct in Science" in 1989.[38] The Act required that the Public Health Service establish a process for reviewing and responding to reports of misconduct; the Office of Research Integrity was established in 1989 to deal with research misconduct. The Act also mandated creation of a Commission on Research Integrity to review and pro-vide guidance on procedures and policies in place to prevent research misconduct. The Commission issued its final report in 1995.[39] The report defined misconduct as "significant misbehavior that improperly appropriates intellectual property or contributions of others, that intentionally impedes the progress of research, or that risks corrupting the scientific record or compromising the integrity of scientific practices."

Although the Commission's report and the Office of Research Integrity focus primarily on deliberate acts of dishonesty in research, research misconduct is a much larger and more complex concept than dishonesty alone. In addition to dishonesty, this chapter will review conflicts arising from collaboration in research and conflicts of interest.

Dishonesty

Dishonesty in research can take place at the design stage, at the data analysis stage, or at the data reporting stage. Dishonesty in research design falls into the category the National

Academies of Science have termed "questionable research practices": "actions that violate traditional values of the research enterprise and that may be detrimental to the research process."[40] Bias in selection of subjects, phrasing of questions to lead respondents to a desired answer, and modification of data as they are being collected are examples of dishonesty in design.

Dishonesty in analysis includes fabrication of data, falsification of data, and misrepresentation of the outcomes of analysis. Fabrication is the creation of data or results without a legitimate research process. Data, whether numeric, qualitative, or historical, are simply made up. Although evidence of fabrication is fairly rare, some examples have been quite spectacular. In 1983, for instance, the German weekly news magazine *Stern* announced that 60 volumes of Adolf Hitler's diaries, written between 1932 and 1945, had been discovered by a *Stern* reporter. The find created an international sensation for approximately a month, but chemical analysis of the diaries revealed them to be a colossal hoax.[41]

Falsification is the alteration of data to achieve a desired effect. It can be very tempting, for instance, to complete incomplete data by filling in missing values with educated guesses. Falsification can include cooking or cherry picking the data by carefully selecting data to be included or not included in analysis as a means of influencing the outcome of analysis and trimming, the process of modifying data by incorrect rounding or other data-altering techniques. Misrepresentation is falsification of results—real data are presented in a misleading manner through inappropriate use of analytical tools or misstatements regarding the meaning of results.

The most obvious manifestation of dishonesty in reporting is plagiarism: nonexistent, inadequate, or inappropriate attribution of sources, word, or ideas. The Commission on Research Integrity report used the term "misappropriation" to include both plagiarism and dishonest use of information in violation of the confidentiality principles of peer review of manuscripts or grant proposals. A characteristic of plagiarism that makes it different from other forms of dishonesty is that, while fabrication, falsification, and misrepresentation are conspicuously conscious and deliberate acts, there are aspects of plagiarism that can be interpreted as accidental or unknowing. Some fairly famous accusations of plagiarism include criticism of Stephen Ambrose's book *The Wild Blue* and the 1978 suit charging that Alex Haley plagiarized substantial portions of his best-selling biographical novel *Roots: The Saga of an American Family,* which Haley contended was based on extensive research.[42]

A concern of fairly recent origin is that of self-plagiarism. This issue made the news in 2010 in response to accusations that a researcher at a university in Canada had duplicated as much as 20 percent of the content in his publications from previous publications. The accusations against the researcher prompted an investigation by the Natural Sciences and Engineering Research Council and retraction of some of the researcher's papers by scholarly journals.[43] Although self-citation is accompanied by a number of issues, self-plagiarism has been explored to only a very limited extent in the literature. As Samuelson has pointed out, there is a fine line between self-plagiarism and the principle of fair use of ones' own intellectual property. The only legal case in which a copyright decision found a copyright infringement in an instance of self-plagiarism was decided in 1914.[44] The fundamental concern in self-plagiarism is not so much the mere failure to provide appropriate attribution as it is the expectation in scholarly publishing that a manuscript will represent new and original work. David argued that, as long as there is acknowledgement that the author's previous work has been incorporated into the current work, the previous work is at least minimally cited, and there is no copyright violation, self-plagiarism is harmless. "If duplication of content within these constraints helps the author to reach a new or larger readership, and/or if text recycling within these constraints helps to present the same idea more accurately across several publications, they become legitimate conduct."[45] Roig, in a comprehensive and very well reasoned discussion of the pros and cons of self-plagiarism, concluded that self-plagiarism is, after all, a form of plagiarism and is not to be tolerated.[46] The topic of self-plagiarism has been a topic for the online discussion list of the Library & Information Science Editors group and is the subject of the group's "A Statement of Ethics for Editors of Library and Information Science Journals," in which it is described as "redundant publication."[47]

Collaboration

Increasing collaboration in research has been a major trend for several decades. Research was at one time a primarily solitary endeavor and most research publications were the products of solo authors. Larger research teams and inter-institutional research collaborations are encouraged by federal agencies that provide funding support for research. The model for research that includes faculty members as research team leaders and graduate students as collaborators that has prevailed in the empirical sciences for several decades has more recently come to play a role in the social sciences, including library and information science.

Credit for effort or authorship is not an issue when there is only one author, but may become an issue when the effort becomes a collaborative one. Although it may seem counterintuitive, increased collaboration is frequently associated with increased conflict and competition. In academic environments, authorship is both "the coin of the realm" and "the source of complaints."[48] Endersby found that by 1996 nearly half of all social science research publications had multiple authors.[49]

Understanding the roles and responsibilities of authorship requires distinguishing between those activities that constitute true authorship and those that do not. Activities essential to authorship include

1. involvement in conceptualization, design, conduct, analysis, or interpretation of research
2. development and creation of intellectual content in the form of reports or manuscripts for publication
3. participation in editorial processes related to publication

Activities that do not constitute authorship, but which may be essential to research or evaluation include

1. obtaining funding for research or evaluation activities without direct involvement in research or evaluation processes
2. providing oversight for research or evaluation activities without direct involvement in research or evaluation processes
3. authority or seniority, also referred to as honorary authorship

Avoidance of Collaboration-Related Disputes

Although it might seem safe to assume that individuals would not choose to collaborate unless they were sufficiently comfortable working together to prevent conflict or disputes, disputes do happen. Conflicts in collaboration can range from disagreement regarding who should be the first author of a publication to who should present an evaluation report to a library administration to disagreements about ownership of intellectual or physical property. Steneck reported that more than 10 percent of applicants for medical research fellowships inflated their resumes to claim more publication credit than was due.[50] Steneck's analysis found that estimates of honorary authorship, in which the contribution of a named individual was insufficient to warrant authorship credit, ranged from nine to sixty percent in the medical literature.[51] Ultimately, honesty in collaboration and authorship comes down to the vagaries of interpersonal communication and what are in most cases informal or implied agreements as to responsibility. In some cases, but probably not many, a formal agreement may be formulated before a research or evaluation project begins. In the most extreme conflict situations, some form of mediation may be required through a formal body such as an ombudsperson's office. In the very worst situations, conflicts of collaboration may lead to disciplinary or even legal action.

Conflicts of Interest

Many ethical dilemmas in research and evaluation arise because the interests of the investigator are in conflict with the interests of honesty, integrity, and ethical behavior. "Although the most obvious conflicts are those that have to do with money or status, conflicts of interest also involve individual friendships (and hostilities), national, political, or religious differences, or an apparently innocent desire to further the aims of a particular pressure group that the author or reviewer considers beneficial to society."[52]

Many professional associations have statements on conflicts of interest incorporated into their codes of professional ethics. The statement from the American Library Association's Code of Ethics is quite terse: "We do not advance private interests at the expense of library users, colleagues, or our employing institutions."[53] The statement from the American Society for Information Science & Technology is also brief; members are encouraged to adhere to the standards of "not knowingly making false statements or providing erroneous or misleading information, informing their employers, clients or sponsors of any circumstances that create a conflict of interest, not using their position beyond their authorized limits or by not using their credentials to misrepresent themselves."[54]

In 1965, the American Council on Education and the American Association of University Professors issued a joint statement on Preventing Conflicts of Interest in Government Sponsored Research at Universities that presents a comprehensive overview of potential conflict situations:

1. Favoring of outside interests. When a University staff member (administrator, faculty member, professional staff member, or employee) undertaking or engaging in Government-sponsored work has a significant financial interest in or a consulting arrangement with a private business concern, it is important to avoid actual or apparent conflicts of interest between his Government-sponsored university research obligations and his outside interests and other obligations. Situations in or from which conflicts of interest may arise are the:

   a. Undertaking or orientation of the staff member's university research to serve the research or other needs of the private firm without disclosure of such undertaking or orientation to the university and to the sponsoring agency;

   b. Purchase of major equipment, instruments, materials, or other items for university research from the private firm in which the staff member has the interest without disclosure of such interest;

c. Transmission to the private firm or other use for personal gain of Government-sponsored work products, results, materials, records, or information that are not made generally available. (This would not necessarily preclude appropriate licensing arrangements for inventions, or consulting on the basis of Government-sponsored research results where there is significant additional work by the staff member independent of his or her Government-sponsored research);

d. Use for personal gain or other unauthorized use of privileged information acquired in connection with the staff member's Government-sponsored activities. (The term "privileged information" includes, but is not limited to, medical, personnel, or security records of individuals; anticipated material requirements or price actions; possible new sites for Government operations; and knowledge of forthcoming programs or of selection of contractors or subcontractors in advance of official announcements);

e. Negotiation or influence upon the negotiation of contracts relating to the staff member's government-sponsored research between the university and private organizations with which he has consulting or other significant relationships;

f. Acceptance of gratuities or special favors from private organizations with which the University does or may conduct business in connection with a Government-sponsored research project, or extension of gratuities or special favors to employees of the sponsoring Government agency, under circumstances which might reasonably be interpreted as an attempt to influence the recipients in the conduct of their duties.[55]

The ACE/AAUP joint statement also provides guidance regarding the responsibilities of universities for ensuring that conflicts of interest are minimized and that effective communication with funding agencies takes place.

Each university participating in Government-sponsored research should make known to the sponsoring Government agencies:

1. The steps it is taking to assure an understanding on the part of the university administration and staff members of the possible conflicts of interest or other problems that may develop in the foregoing types of situations, and:

2. The organizational and administrative actions it has taken or is taking to avoid such problems, including:

a. Accounting procedures to be used to assure that Government funds are expended for the purposes for which they have been provided, and that all services which are required in return for these funds are supplied;

b. Procedures that enable it to be aware of the outside professional work of staff members participating in Government-sponsored research, if such outside work relates in any way to the Government sponsored research;

c. The formulation of standards to guide the individual university staff members in governing their conduct in relation to outside interests that might raise questions of conflicts of interests;

d. The provision within the university of an informed source of advice and guidance to its staff members for advance consultation on questions they wish to raise concerning the problems that may or do develop as a result of their outside financial or consulting interests, as they relate to their participation in Government-sponsored university research. The university may wish to discuss such problems with the contracting officer or other appropriate Government official in those cases that appear to raise questions regarding conflicts of interest.[56]

POLITICS IN LIBRARY AND INFORMATION SCIENCE EDUCATION AND RESEARCH AND EVALUATION

Although research and evaluation are generally thought of as open and objective processes intended to yield knowledge and solve problems, research and evaluation are, like most human activities, subject to influences that can be thought of as fundamentally political. "Regardless of approach, all research is political in nature and is affected, to some degree, by the social, political, and economic climates that surround the research community."[57] The axiom that "information is power" applies to the information world of research and evaluation just as it does in other environments. Politics influence what can be studied, where it can be studied, who can be studied, who can conduct studies, and the decisions investigators make regarding what they choose to study.

Politics and What Can Be Studied

Library and information science, like other disciplinary and professional areas, operates in the context of certain accepted standards and norms that are viewed as defining the profession. In any discipline or profession there are certain practices, policies, rules, and tools that are so ingrained into the professional consciousness that they tend to defy reflection, examination, or analysis. In a 1915 article in the *Boston Evening Transcript*, Pearson wrote "would it not be the best the most fortunate thing that could happen to all the libraries in the world if their catalogues should be utterly consumed by fire this very night?"[58] Grose and Line argued more seriously in 1968 that catalogs are made necessary primarily by decisions made by librarians, not by any universal principle.[59] Although it could be argued that the federated search systems implemented in many libraries to a considerable extent negate the ongoing need for library catalogs, it doesn't appear to be the case that libraries have seriously considered abandoning the catalog as a fundamental tool. As a result, there really hasn't been any effective research into the need for library catalogs, although there has been much research and evaluation regarding the nature and use of catalogs.

Politics and the Locales for Study

Community Acceptance

Communities of all kinds—nations, states, municipalities, neighborhoods, and institutions—make decisions about who will be welcomed into the community and what behaviors are acceptable within the community. Research and evaluation may be looked on with skepticism by the members of any community, particularly when the fundamental nature of research and evaluation is not understood or when there is the perception of risk to members of the community. Lack of understanding in fact frequently leads to fear of risk. Gaining access to a community can be a tricky and trying process that involves both formal and casual introductions to members of the community.

Entrée into a community for purposes of research or evaluation can be particularly difficult when there is fear that the community will be called upon to change as a result of the outcomes of research or evaluation. Employees in many environments, including libraries, frequently fear that projects that are presented as evaluations of the library and its operations are really evaluations of their performance as employees in disguise. Professionals may fear that research into a new process or technique will mean that they must learn that process or technique in order to remain professionally viable.

Fear of Disruption

Another common fear that can limit options for where research or evaluation can be carried out is concern that the process may and in and of itself be disruptive. Research and evaluation frequently require time and effort not only from the individuals with principal responsibility for the project but also from others. Some projects require that physical space be rearranged or that employees do things in different ways. This may lead to administrative concern that the project is interfering with efficiency or effectiveness. It can also lead to the employee grumble "we have to spend so much time evaluating what we do that we don't have time to do it." Real disruption can occur when patrons feel that the burden of completing satisfaction surveys or other questionnaires is onerous or when evaluation activities intended to be unobtrusive intrude on the relationship between patron and library.

Politics and Who Can Be Studied

The concern about vulnerable populations discussed in the section of this chapter on human subjects research can sometimes take on a life of its own, with communities potentially viewing themselves as being vulnerable to all research or evaluation, regardless of purpose or potential for negative impact.

Ideology has historically imposed political constraints on which groups of people can be studied and the ways in which they can be studied. Research involving populations such as racial or ethnic minorities, economically or socially deprived groups, the homeless, or gay, bisexual, lesbian, or transgendered (GBLT) communities risks conflict with prevailing ideological norms and convictions. This is frequently a product of fear that research or evaluation will challenge those norms and convictions. Myrdal's extensive study of race relations in the United States undoubtedly did challenge norms and convictions and is widely believed to have had a direct influence on race relations.[60] Lyons noted that, in addition to the impact of Myrdal's conclusions on the civil rights movement in the United States, his work has lasting methodological implications.[61]

Politics and Who Can Conduct Studies
Big Science and Small Projects

There are many ways in which politics influences who can enter into research and evaluation projects. The emphasis on big science that has prevailed in many arenas since the beginning of the Cold War era has tended to confer status on large projects with substantial external funding and has particularly favored projects with major government agency funding. Such projects generally require that the researcher have an academic background and the support of an academic institution or a major nonacademic research institution. Big projects require big research teams, big budgets, and long timeframes for completion. There is frequently also an emphasis on interinstitutional collaboration, which further complicates and enlarges the research endeavor. Practitioners in library and information science, particularly those in nonacademic environments, may feel disenfranchised.

Practitioners may also feel that the demands of their jobs exclude them from carrying out voluntary research or evaluation projects. A librarian who works 40 hours a week simply meeting defined responsibilities can find the prospect of adding on to that a research or evaluation project just too intimidating. Furthermore, library administrators have sometimes discouraged elective research and evaluation projects out of fear that essential tasks will not be done.

There is, though, a need for small research and small evaluation. A research or evaluation project doesn't have to be universal or large scale to be useful. Even very small projects can have large impacts. Baker's study of the display phenomenon in public libraries was not a huge project, but has had a major influence on library practice.[62]

The Insider/Outsider Phenomenon

Merton, in describing the insider/outsider phenomenon in research, distinguished between groups that have monopolistic access to knowledge and groups that have privileged access to knowledge.[63] Historically, researchers have been members of the majority population who had a monopolistic hold on research processes and research knowledge. One of the impressive aspects of Myrdal's study of race relations in the United States is that he was in every way an outsider—a white Swedish researcher who was not even a U.S. citizen. Minority researchers were historically expected to study only minority group members and minority group interests, which members of the majority could also do. Merton noted a "doctrinal" shift in research in the last third of the 20th century in which it was argued that only minority group members could study minority group members and minority group interests because only a member of the minority group could understand its history, its culture, its needs, and the ways in which it differs from the majority. Merton feared the "the balkanization of social science, with separate baronies kept exclusively in the hands of Insiders bearing their credentials in the shape of one or another ascribed status."[64] Asselin has pointed out that "when the researcher works in the setting and is a peer of the group under study, there is often a tendency to believe one knows the culture."[65] He recommended that the researcher assume that he or she knows nothing about the phenomenon under study and start gathering data from a fresh perspective with his or her "eyes open."[66] Dwyer and Buckle described their experiences as being both in insider and outsider roles for different research projects. They suggested that it is possible for an effective researcher to be either and that presenting "these concepts in a dualistic manner is overly simplistic."[67] They contend that the researcher more properly occupies a "space between" insider and outsider and that the time has come to abandon these constructed dichotomies and embrace and explore the complexity and richness of the space between entrenched perspectives.[68]

Nonetheless, the insider/outsider dichotomy continues to be a concern. In library and information science, questions arise as to whether research and evaluation can cross over institutional lines. Can an information scientist understand reference services in public libraries? Is it appropriate for a university librarian to explore library services to children? Can a library and information science faculty member, who has no direct daily contact with libraries and their patrons, understand libraries at all? These examples of the "siloization" of the profession have a political impact on research and evaluation. All too frequently, research and evaluation projects carried out in one environment are simply assumed not to be relevant to other environments. There are, however, many issues of concern to library and information science that cut across all institutional lines. Information literacy, for instance, is properly a topic to be studied along a lifelong continuum; the similarities among information literacy solutions for children, young adults, adults, and older adults, are very likely more meaningful than the differences.

Politics and Who Must Conduct Studies

There are some political influences that dictate research and evaluation roles. Although the extent to which academic tenure in college and university settings is or is not a political phenomenon is subject to debate, there are aspects that are inherently political. It is not unusual for members of the professorate to be told which are the best journals in which to publish, which are the right conferences to attend, or with whom they need to collaborate to get ahead. The insider/outsider controversy reappears in the context of the politics of academic tenure—a faculty member who does the right things can become an accepted insider, while the faculty member who goes his or her own way risks becoming an outsider within his or her own faculty.

A second form of prescribed involvement in research and evaluation occurs when libraries are required to comply with data gathering, reporting, and structured planning activities. Some state library agencies have required that public libraries complete the Public Library Association's planning process or a parallel state process to qualify for Library Services and Technology Act funding. School library media centers have felt the impact of the No Child Left Behind Act, and are generally subject to state and/or local performance standards as well. Any situation that requires that libraries, librarians, and the institutions they serve engage in prescribed evaluation processes is likely to carry with it a political component.

That does not mean that standards and prescribed evaluation programs are bad. When the motive for them is overly political, though, there is a tendency for such planning, data gathering, and planning processes to take on a cynical nature that has to do not with improving effectiveness but solely with ensuring the appearance of compliance. A principle pursued throughout this book is that ethical and professional practice, research, and evaluation require a dedication to ethics and professionalism that is sincere and to the greatest extent possible free from political influences.

ETHICS AND REVERENCE FOR LIFE

Reverence for life is the central theme of the writings of Albert Schweitzer as discussed in *Civilization and Ethics* and other works.[69] Although reverence for life isn't typically taught directly in schools of library and information science and is a rare topic of discussion for professional meetings or conferences, in a very real sense reverence for life is at the heart of the philosophy of providing the highest levels of service to the greatest numbers of people that is at the core of library and information science ethics.

The discussion in Chapter 1, "Knowing, Research, and Evaluation," of the benefits of research and evaluation emphasized three benefits to society: improvement of the quality of life, reduction of expense, and removal of danger. In a professional field such as library and information science, these benefits define a sense of reverence for life that permeates the research and evaluation process and its outcomes. Ultimately, the motivations for expanding the knowledge base of the profession and evaluating library products, programs, and services have to do with maximizing the benefits of the institutions that define and are served by the profession. Doing so in an ethical manner is truly no more and no less than an expression of reverence for the lives and well-being of the communities served by the library and information professions.

THINK ABOUT IT!

1. How do the problems that characterize the research of Milgram and Zimbardo relate to research and evaluation in library and information science?
2. In what ways is confidentiality an issue in an evaluation project related to library staff performance?
3. How does the concept of reverence for life as a core ethical principle relate to the Library Bill of Rights?

DO IT!

1. Read the Library Bill of Rights and the American Library Association Code of Ethics. What do these documents imply about research and evaluation in library and information science?
2. Identify the codes of ethics of professional associations both in library and information science and in other professional areas. What are the commonalities and differences across professional areas?
3. Confidentiality of patron use of the Internet is of great concern to the library and information professions. What ethical considerations are likely to apply to patron confidentiality and the Internet?

NOTES

1. *Encyclopedia of Philosophy*, 2nd ed. (New York: Macmillan, 2006), s.v. "Ethics, History of."

2. Henry Sidgwick, *Practical Ethics: A Collection of Addresses and Essays* (New York: Macmillan, 1898).

3. *Encyclopedia of Philosophy*, 2nd ed. (New York: Macmillan, 2006), s.v. "Applied Ethics."

4. Onora O'Neill, "Applied Ethics: Naturalism, Normativity and Public Policy," *Journal of Applied Philosophy* 26, no. 3 (2009): 229.

5. Adil E. Shamoo, *Responsible Conduct of Research* (New York: Oxford University Press, 2002), 184.

6. National Institutes of Health, Office of Human Subjects Research, Regulations and Ethical Guidelines, "Nuremberg Code," http://ohsr.od.nih.gov/guidelines/nuremberg.html (accessed May 30, 2011).

7. Anna Mastroianni and Jeffery Kahn, "Remedies for Human Subjects of Cold War Research: Recommendations of the Advisory Committee," *Journal of Law, Medicine, and Ethics* 24 (1996): 119.

8. Stanley Milgram, "Behavioral Study of Obedience," *Journal of Abnormal and Social Psychology* 67, no. 4 (1963): 371–78; Stanley Milgram, "Some Conditions of Obedience and Disobedience to Authority," *Human Relations* 18 (1965): 57–76; Stanley Milgram, *Obedience to Authority: An Experimental View* (New York: Harper and Row, 1974).

9. Milgram, "Behavioral Study of Obedience," 373.

10. Ibid.

11. Mel Slater, Angus Antley, Adam Davison, David Swapp, Christopher Guger, Chris Barker, Nancy Pistrang, and Maria V. Sanchez-Vives, "A Virtual Reprise of the Stanley Milgram Obedience Experiments," *PLoS ONE*, no. 1 (2006), doi: 10.1371/journal.pone.0000039.

12. Philip G. Zimbardo, "On the Ethics of Intervention in Human Psychological Research: With Special Reference to the Stanford Prison Experiment," *Cognition* 2, no. 2 (1974): 244.

13. Philip G. Zimbardo, "Revisiting the Stanford Prison Experiment: A Lesson in the Power of Situation," *The Chronicle of Higher Education* 53, no. 30 (2007): B6.

14. Ibid.

15. Mohamad G. Alkadry, and Matthew T. Witt, "Abu Ghraib and the Normalization of Torture and Hate," *Public Integrity* 11, no. 2 (2009): 135–53.

16. World Medical Association, "WMA Declaration of Helsinki—Ethical Principles for Medical Research Involving Human Subjects, http://www.wma.net/en/30publications/10policies/b3/index.html (accessed August 19, 2011).

17. Waldo W. Burchard, "Lawyers, Political Scientists, Sociologists—and Concealed Microphones," *American Sociological Review* 23, no. 6 (1958): 686–91.

18. Zimbardo, "On the Ethics of Intervention in Human Psychological Research," 254.

19. "The Belmont Report: Ethical Principles and Guidelines for the Protection of Human Subjects of Research." National Commission for the Protection of Human Subjects of Biomedical and Behavioral Research. Washington: Government Printing Office, 1979.

20. National Institutes of Health, Office of Human Subjects Research, Regulations and Ethical Guidelines, "The Belmont Report: Ethical Principles and Guidelines for the Protection of Human Subjects of Research," http://ohsr.od.nih.gov/guidelines/belmont.html (accessed May 30, 2011).

21. Ibid.

22. Lynne McKechnie, "Observations of Babies and Toddlers in Library Settings," *Library Trends* 55, no. 1 (2006): 190–201.

23. Ibid.

24. Ibid.

25. Ibid.

26. Ibid.

27. Ibid.

28. Ibid.

29. Ibid.

30. "Protection of Human Subjects," Department of Health and Human Services (Washington: Government Printing Office, 2005).

31. National Institutes of Health, Office of Human Subjects Research, Regulations and Ethical Guidelines, "§46.111 Criteria for IRB approval of research," http://ohsr.od.nih.gov/guidelines/45cfr46.html#46.101 (accessed May 30, 2011).

32. Ibid.

33. Joan E. Sieber, "Deception in Social Research I: Kinds of Deception and the Wrongs They May Involve," *IRB: Ethics and Human Research* 4, no. 9 (1982): 2.

34. Ibid.

35. Ibid., 3.

36. "Protection of Human Subjects."

37. "About ORI—History," Office of Research Integrity, U.S. Department of Health and Human Services, http://ori.dhhs.gov/about/history.shtml (accessed March 28, 2011).

38. "Responsibilities of Awardee and Applicant Institutions for Dealing with and Reporting Possible Misconduct in Science," Department of Health and Human Services. Washington: Government Printing Office, 1989.

39. "Integrity and Misconduct in Research: Report of the Commission on Research Integrity," Washington: U.S. Government Printing Office 1995.

40. "Responsible Science: Ensuring the Integrity of the Research Process," Washington: Committee on Science Engineering and Public Policy, Panel on Scientific Responsibility and the Conduct of Research, National Academies of Science, 1992, 28.

41. Eric Rentschler, "The Fascination of a Fake: The Hitler Diaries," *New German Critique*, no. 90 (2003): 177–92.

42. David Kirkpatrick, "2 Say Stephen Ambrose, Popular Historian, Copied Passages," *New York Times*, January 5, 2002, A8; Phil Stanford, "Roots and Grafts on the Haley Story," *Washington Star*, April 8, 1979, F4.

43. Eugenie Samuel Reich, "Self-Plagiarism Case Prompts Calls for Agencies to Tighten Rules," *Nature* 468, no. 7325 (2010): 745.

44. Pamela Samuelson, "Self-Plagiarism of Fair Use?" *Communications of the ACM* 37, no. 8 (1994): 21–25.

45. Daniel David, "Letter to the Editor: Duplication Spreads the Word to a Wider Audience," *Nature* 452, no. 7183 (2008): 29.

46. Miguel Roig, "The Debate on Self-Plagiarism: Inquisitional Science or High Standards of Scholarship?" *Journal of Cognitive and Behavioral Psychotherapies* 8, no. 2 (2008): 245–58.

47. Library and Information Science Educators, "A Statement of Ethics for Editors of Library and Information Science Journals," http://www.lis-editors.org/ethics/2009section2.shtml (accessed May 30, 2011).

48. Linda J. Wilcox, "Authorship: The Coin of the Realm, the Source of Complaints," *Journal of the American Medical Association* 280, no. 3 (1998): 216–17.

49. James W. Endersby, "Collaborative Research in the Social Sciences: Multiple Authors and Publication Credit," *Social Science Quarterly* 77, no. 2 (1996): 375–92.

50. Nicholas H. Steneck, "Fostering Integrity in Research: Definitions, Current Knowledge, and Future Directions," *Science and Engineering Ethics* 12, no. 1 (2006): 59.

51. Ibid., 60.

52. Harvey Marcovitch, "Coping with Publication Misconduct," *Serials Librarian* 57, no. 4 (2009): 334–41.

53. "Code of Ethics of the American Library Association." Chicago: American Library Association, 2008, http://www.ala.org/ala/issuesadvocacy/proethics/codeofethics/codeethics.cfm (accessed March 31, 2011).

54. "ASIS&T Professional Guidelines." Washington: American Society for Information Science & Technology, 1992, http://www.asis.org/professionalguidelines.html (accessed March 31, 2011).

55. *On Preventing Conflicts of Interest in Government Sponsored Research at Universities*. Washington: American Council on Education, 1964.

56. Ibid.

57. Emily Stier Adler and Roger Clark, *An Invitation to Social Research: How It's Done* (Belmont, CA: Cengage, 2011). 403.

58. Edmund Lester Pearson, in *The Librarian: Selections from the Column of That Name*, ed. Jane B. Durnell and Norman B. Stevens (Metuchen, NJ: Scarecrow, 1976), 427.

59. M. W. Grose and M. B. Line, "On the Construction and Care of White Elephants," *Library Association Record* 70 (January 1968): 2–5.

60. Gunnar Myrdal, *An American Dilemma: The Negro Problem and Modern Democracy* (New York: Harper, 1944).

61. Stina Lyons, E. "Researching Race Relations: Myrdal's American Dilemma from a Methodological Perspective," *Acta Sociologica* 47, no. 3 (2004): 203–17.

62. S. L. Baker, "The Display Phenomenon: An Exploration into the Factors Causing the Increased Circulation of Displayed Books," *Library Quarterly* 56, no. 3 (1986): 237–57.

63. Robert K. Merton, "Insiders and Outsiders: A Chapter in the Sociology of Knowledge," *American Journal of Sociology* 78, no. 1 (1972): 9–47.

64. Ibid., 32.

65. Marilyn E. Asselin, "Insider Research: Issues to Consider When Doing Qualitative Research in Your Own Setting," *Journal for Nurses in Staff Development* 19, no. 2 (2003): 100.

66. Ibid.

67. Sonya Corbin Dwyer and Jennifer L. Buckle, "The Space Between: On Being an Insider–Outsider in Qualitative Research," *International Journal of Qualitative Methods* 8, no. 1 (2009): 60.

68. Ibid., 62.

69. Albert Schweitzer, *Civilization and Ethics* (London: A & C Black, 1923).

SUGGESTED READINGS

Ellen Altman and Peter Hernon, eds., *Research Misconduct: Issues, Implications, and Strategies* (Greenwich, CT: Ablex, 1997).

Thomas Blass, ed. *Obedience to Authority: Current Perspectives on the Milgram Paradigm* (Mahwah, NJ: Lawrence Erlbaum Associates, 2000).

Ian Gregory, *Ethics in Research* (New York: Continuum, 2003).

Richard Hauptman, *Ethics and Librarianship* (Jefferson, NC: McFarland, 2003).

Mark Israel and Iain Hay, *Research Ethics for Social Scientists: Between Ethical Conduct and Regulatory Compliance* (Thousand Oaks, CA: Sage, 2006).

James H. Korn, *Illusion of Reality: A History of Deception in Social Psychology* (Albany: State University of New York Press, 1997).

Donna M. Mertens and Pauline E. Ginsberg, eds., *The Handbook of Social Research Ethics* (Thousand Oaks, CA: Sage, 2009).

Susan M. Reverby, *Examining Tuskegee: The Infamous Syphilis Study and Its Legacy* (Chapel Hill: University of North Carolina Press, 2009).

Bruce D. Sales and Susan Folkman, eds., *Ethics in Research with Human Participants* (Washington: American Psychological Association, 2000).

Philip Zimbardo, *The Lucifer Effect: Understanding How Good People Turn Evil* (New York: Random House, 2007).

PUBLISHED REPORTS AND THE PROFESSIONAL AS CONSUMER

Almost all scholarly research carries practical and political implications.

—*Stephanie Coontz,* Chronicle of Higher Education, *October 21, 1992*

In science one tries to tell people, in such a way as to be understood by everyone, something that no one ever knew before. But in poetry, it's the exact opposite.

—*Paul Dirac, quoted in Howard W. Eves,* Mathematical Circles Adieu, *1977*

In This Chapter

The nature of publication in library and information science

Essential elements of published reports

Criteria for evaluation of published reports

THE NATURE OF PUBLICATION IN LIBRARY AND INFORMATION SCIENCE

The literature of library and information science is plentiful. As of April 2012, *Ulrich's International Periodicals Directory* listed 4,816 serials under the subject heading Library and Information Sciences, 942 of which were identified as being peer-reviewed journals. *Books in Print* contained nearly 118,340 entries with subject headings that included the word "library" or the word "information," and 38,143 that included both words. Those subject headings are far from inclusive in that they do not include those areas of interest that are best described with other words or phrases.

Peer-reviewed journals, whether in print-on-paper or digital format, have long been the standard for scholarly publication. The *Journal of the American Society for Information Science & Technology* and *Library Quarterly* are examples of peer-reviewed journals in library and information science. The fundamental nature of peer review is that the contributions of scholars are reviewed by other scholars prior to acceptance for publication and dissemination. Acceptance of a manuscript for publication in a peer-reviewed outlet may require that the author revise and resubmit his or her work more than one time prior to a positive decision to publish. The number of peer scholars varies by journal, but is almost never fewer than two and rarely more than five. The rigor of the peer review process is at least a provisional assurance of the quality and rigor of the research process that led to the publication.

Some journals that are not peer reviewed nonetheless serve a serious scholarly purpose. *Library Trends,* published by the Graduate School of Library and Information Science at the University of Illinois and the *Annual Review of Information Science & Technology,* published by the American Society for Information Science & Technology, are examples of high-quality publications that are based on rigorous editorial processes that do not involve peer reviewing as such.

Other periodicals serve nonresearch or mixed purposes. *Library Journal* and *American Libraries* are professional publications oriented toward practitioners that sometimes publish articles based on research or systematic evaluation. *College & Research Libraries* is primarily an outlet for peer-reviewed articles but includes other content as well. *Reference & User Services Quarterly* publishes a mixture of peer-reviewed scholarly articles, columns, and commentaries. The *Journal of the American Society for Information Science & Technology* publishes only articles that are refereed, but also publishes book reviews.

Books in scholarly disciplines serve primarily as syntheses of important topics, compilations of the collected works of important or carefully selected authors, or textbooks. Although books undergo appropriately rigorous editorial reviews, which may include commentary by scholars in the field, they are rarely subject to any true peer review.

It is important for the informed consumer of the professional literature of library and information science to be aware of and work within the confines of the fundamental intent and nature of any given publication. News reports should not be given the credence of research reports, while research and evaluation reports should not be expected to present the zingy editorial style of news reports or the pithy commentary of editorials. Books, whatever their purpose, rarely operate at the cutting edge of innovation or the forefront of research or evaluation methodology. A publication must be understood and assessed for what it is, for no more and no less.

THE INFORMED CONSUMER AND PUBLISHED REPORTS IN LIBRARY AND INFORMATION SCIENCE

Assessing published reports in any professional field can be difficult for even a very informed and experienced practitioner. The novice practitioner may find reading and understanding published reports, especially research reports, intimidating to the point of daunting. O'Connor and Park found that 62 percent of American Library Association-accredited library and information science programs did not require a research methods course.[1] No comparable study of the availability of evaluation courses in schools of library and information science appears to have been published, but the implication is clear. Many students of library and information science are not directly prepared to act as effective consumers of library and information science research and evaluation reports. That doesn't mean graduates of the field's professional programs are totally unprepared. Nearly every master's student is responsible for analyzing and synthesizing the professional literature at least to the extent of completing one or more term papers or related products, but this often entails accepting published research at face value rather than through a critical lens.

The guidelines that are presented in this chapter are designed to serve as an outline guide to the ways in which this book as a whole can contribute to understanding the professional literature. The relationship between functioning as an informed consumer of professional reports and being prepared to carry out research and evaluation projects has some of the aspects of the chicken and egg dilemma. Being able to read and understand published reports is surely beneficial to understanding research and evaluation processes, but the reader cannot be a completely capable consumer of research and evaluation reports without some fundamental understanding of the research and evaluation process. The discussion of the elements of published reports and how to assess them presented in this chapter is best viewed as guidance on how to understand the fundamental nature of the research and evaluation process presented throughout the book.

BEALS ON THE LITERATURE OF LIBRARY AND INFORMATION SCIENCE

Beals took an early critical, and somewhat scathing, look at the literature of librarianship and concluded that it fell into three categories:

1. glad tidings
2. testimonial
3. research[2]

Beals observed that the third category was by far the least well represented in the literature and called for librarians to draw on communication studies as a model for building a body of professional literature with a more substantial basis in research.

A more detailed analysis of the current periodical literature in library and information science suggests the following categories, in decreasing order of frequency.

1. News. Some library and information science publications, such as *Library Hotline*, are entirely devoted to news. Others, such as *Library Journal, American Libraries*, and many regional or state publications, have very substantive news sections. Most professional associations and many individual organizations issue newsletters on a regular basis. It is only fair to note that these publications present no pretense of being scholarly in nature or of emphasizing research.

2. Authoritative commentary. Columns and regular features such as the "Internet Librarian" column in *American Libraries* and the "How Do You Manage?" column in *Library Journal* are examples of authoritative commentary. The views expressed in these commentaries are assumed to be valid and useful based primarily on the credentials of the authors. The authors are generally well known and are frequently employed in positions of prominence and power.

3. Summaries of practice. Summaries of professional practice are frequently referred to in a disparaging manner as "how we have done it good in our library" accounts. *Knowledge Quest*, the journal of the American Association of School Librarians, and *Public Libraries*, the journal of the Public Library Association, both tend to emphasize summaries of practice. These journals generally publish articles of high quality that are close approxi-

mations of case studies. What is generally missing from summaries of practice is the evidence that the tools or techniques described are in fact good or beneficial.

4. Case studies and descriptions. Case studies are more analytical and provide greater depth than summaries of practice. They may emphasize detailed description of current environments or current practices or may provide a historical context. The emphasis is on thorough explication approaching research. Published reports of evaluation projects typically fall into this category.

5. Listings and explications of rules. Listings of rules, guidelines, standards, and related documents are less prevalent in the library and information science literature than was once true. They still play a role, however. *Reference & User Services Quarterly,* for instance, is the publication of official record for standards and guidelines generated by the Reference & User Services Association.

6. Informed commentary. Informed commentary is found in outlets such as the "On My Mind" column in *American Libraries.* O'Connor and Park's column "On My Mind: Research Methods as Essential Knowledge," is an example of informed commentary.[3] The authors are in a position to be knowledgeable regarding the topic under consideration and have reinforced their opinions with some informal research.

7. Speculation. Speculation is closely related to both authoritative commentary and informed commentary and is frequently an aspect of commentary-oriented columns in the professional literature. Dougherty's "The Google Books Project: Will It Make Libraries Obsolete?" is an example of a speculative commentary.[4] New technological developments and social upheavals tend to result in substantial speculation that finds its way into the professional literature. Speculative articles and columns therefore tend to be episodic rather than regular.

8. Research. Still last in frequency, research is unquestionably more prominent than it was in Beals's time. O'Connor and Park provided a compelling argument for a strategy for increasing the volume of library and information science research produced and presumably increasing the publication of research results as well. Some journals in the field are exclusively devoted to research (*Journal of the American Society for Information Science and Technology, Library Quarterly, Journal of Library and Information Science Research*), while others have a significant research emphasis but include content that is not research centered (*Information Technology & Libraries, Library Trends, Reference & User Services Quarterly*).

ESSENTIAL ELEMENTS OF PUBLISHED REPORTS

Research and evaluation can be understood both as a process and as a product. The outcome of the investigative process (described in Chapter 2, "Research and Evaluation Processes") is a report that can be used to convey results to those individuals or groups who are the intended consumers of the results.

The essential elements of a published report include the following:

1. A thorough description of the research or evaluation process, beginning with the origin of the problem statement, including a summary and discussion of the literature review, explaining the methodology, presenting the manner in which data were gathered, and ending with a description of the data analysis.

2. A description of the results with appropriate references to data analysis.

3. One or more conclusions based on the author's understanding of
   a. the significance of results, both statistical and practical
   b. any limitations of results, including the influence of missing or faulty data
   c. the implications of results for understanding the phenomenon of interest and for influencing action
   d. the relationships of the results to previous work
4. Any suggestions for further study or recommendations for action the author can provide. By providing such direction the author helps fulfill the cumulative benefit of research by linking the study not only to prior research or practice but also to targets for the future.

The process of evaluating reports of research and evaluation activities is in a sense a matter of reverse engineering the research process itself. The author's goal is to carry out a project that adheres to the basic rules of research or evaluation and produces results that are valid and reliable and that will be found useful or interesting to the consumers of the research. The consumer's goal is to determine whether the author adequately met the author's goal and conveyed the results in a manner that is accessible, engaging, and useful.

CRITERIA FOR EVALUATING PUBLISHED REPORTS

The essential factors or criteria for evaluating published research and evaluation reports are summarized in Figure 4.1.

Relevance of the topic to an identifiable need

Adherence to the research or evaluation process

Completeness and thoroughness of the description of the research or evaluation process

Evidence of bias or dishonesty

Evidence of error

Comparison to similar studies

Qualifications of the authors

The general literary qualities of the report: logic, clarity, economy, simplicity, and so on

Figure 4.1   Criteria for evaluating published reports.

Relevance of Topic to the Reader's Needs

The reader should be able, as he or she reads a published report, to answer the question "what does this mean to me?" "What does this mean to me?" is a question that can be addressed and answered at many levels: personal versus professional, practical versus enlightening, immediate impact versus delayed benefit, and others. If the reader reaches the end of the report with no concrete answer to the question, the ultimate answer is probably "this means nothing to me."

Practitioners read the professional literature for a purpose. That purpose may focus on improving local practice, setting local policy, maintaining professional awareness and competence, or developing proficiency as a researcher. No published report is of either immediate or enduring value if the reader cannot relate it to some personal or professional need. The process of determining the relevance of the topic to the consumer's needs requires analysis and understanding of the nature of those needs.

Perhaps the most obvious form of need in a field of professional practice is improvement of practice. Improvement of practice can be reflected in comparative evaluation of alternative approaches to providing service, reduction of error, achieving optimal effectiveness, achieving optimal efficiency or cost-effectiveness, avoidance of duplication of effort, development or improvement of policy, and documentation and communication of performance.

A second area of need is that of the consumer who is also a researcher. The cumulative advantage of research is in part in the links formed among research reports. Every researcher has an obligation to tie his or her research to pertinent preexisting research efforts through a careful and appropriately thorough search for related literature and effective analysis and synthesis of what that literature reveals about the topic.

A third area of need has to do with ensuring the quality of the professional literature through the process of refereeing manuscripts prior to their acceptance for publication. The process and structure of peer reviews of manuscripts require that there be some body of professionals who are both willing to and capable of providing expert assessments of reports prepared by others. Although manuscript referees may most frequently be drawn from the ranks of researchers, there is a need in any field of professional practice for referees who can provide the context of direct involvement in practice.

Regardless of the specific motivating need to evaluate the published report, the first task for the consumer is to determine the extent to which the reported project is relevant to his or her specific short-term or long-term needs. It is tempting, particularly for the consumer who is interested in improvement of practice, to make judgments based on superficial characteristics of the report rather than focused assessment of the qualities of the reported outcomes. A reference librarian in a research university, for instance, may reject out-of-hand a study conducted in a school library media center as being irrelevant due to the differences in working environments. Professionals working in the for-profit sector frequently view public sector research as irrelevant. Librarians may reject works focused on theory building and testing because they as professionals are pressed for solutions to immediate tangible problems. Literature reviews in published reports frequently display a noticeable bias in favor of more recent publications, possibly based on the assumption that older works are inherently obsolete and therefore irrelevant.

An important task for the consumer of published reports is to go beyond such superficial decision points and make judgments based on meaningful aspects of the relationship of the report to the reader's needs. If the process of searching for pertinent literature produced a reference to the report it can be assumed as an initial point of assessment that there is some potential relevance of usefulness that transcends the superficial. There are many commonalities in professional practice—such as the fundamental professional focuses on identifying, assessing, organizing, and providing both physical and intellectual access to information—that inherently link and traverse diverse environments. Theories, concepts, and models can be applied across contexts and populations to enhance understanding and promote innovation. There are problems, practices, and policy issues that have been of concern for as long as the profession has existed. The careful consumer has an obligation not only to avoid rejecting research on the basis of superficial factors but also to actually seek out those reports that expand knowledge by crossing boundaries.

Adherence to the Research or Evaluation Process

In addition to being relevant to the reader's needs, an acceptable research report must demonstrate adherence to some acceptable research process as described in Chapter 2, "Research and Evaluation Processes." The outline described in Chapter 2 is one model for understanding and presenting adherence to the research or evaluation process. The primary access point to understanding and assessing adherence to the research process is the author's description of the research or evaluation process. In the absence of a thorough and compelling description of the process, the careful consumer must reject the report as failing to adhere to an appropriate process. The credentials of the author, the prestige of the author's institutional affiliation, the status of the journal in which the report is published, and the appeal of the results and conclusions are individually and collectively inadequate to overcome failure to describe the process as it was carried out. The critical questions are "does the investigator present adequate and convincing evidence that an acceptable approach to the research or evaluation process was implemented?" and "did the author provide enough detail for me to form my own assessment of the process?"

Even when the length of the report is constricted by available space, as in the case of an article published in a nonrefereed general readership periodical such as *American Libraries* or *Library Journal,* the author has an obligation to offer at least enough discussion to provide some level of confidence that an appropriate model of the process was followed. The availability of the World Wide Web affords an unprecedented opportunity for authors to augment their published research with digital appendices to provide the reader with access to additional information about every aspect of the reported project, including expanded access to details regarding the process and methodology.

Logic and Sense of the Problem Statement

The basic initial question related to the description of the research or evaluation process is "is the problem statement understandable?" The consumer may have little appreciation for or prior understanding of the project itself; even so, it should be possible for a consumer who has some basic level of understanding of the field to interpret the underlying logic and general sense of the problem statement. The author who writes exclusively for other authors knowledgeable within the specific domain of the project inherently restricts the scope of usefulness of the results of the research effort.

One of the essential functions of the literature review portion of a published report is explication of the problem statement. The literature review should provide a confirmation of the need for exploration, establish a focus for the research or evaluation effort, identify the specific subject domain and context, identify the project's theoretical base, and establish the project's methodological base. In the process of accomplishing those tasks, the literature review should solidify the consumer's understanding of the fundamental problem that was studied.

Completeness, Thoroughness, and Adequacy of the General Methodology

The author's obligation to the consumer includes demonstrating the appropriateness of the general methodological base for the project, documenting the author's understanding of the methodology, and establishing that the general methodology is appropriate as an approach to addressing the problem. That is, "does this approach to gathering evidence seem an appropriate way to address the problem?" In the best research reports, the author explicitly describes and explains the pertinence of the general methodological base to the specific research question. This does not necessarily need to be part of a section of the report labeled methodology, although many research reports include such a section; the description of the methodology may alternatively be distributed across the report as an approach to improving readability and sustaining reader interest.

Most methodological areas—historical, descriptive, or experimental—can be divided into nameable subcategories. Any such identifiable subcategory should be named, defined, and described to an extent sufficient to provide precise placement of the problem in the domain of the general methodology. If the subcategory has its origin in a specific prior project, a reference to some source of information regarding that project is appropriate. Eponyms— theories, processes, tools, or other entities associated with named individuals—should be linked to their sources.

In addition to describing and justifying the general methodology, the author should provide guidance regarding the limitations of that methodology. The need to document such limitations increases as the impact of the limitations increases.

Soundness of the Specific Methodology

Demonstration of the appropriateness of the general methodological area must be accompanied by a thorough and understandable description of the specific methodology employed in the study. Has the general method been appropriately implemented as evidenced in the description of the specifics of the project methodology? This should include details regarding the identification and definition of the population, the sampling process and the nature of the sample, substantial detail describing the data-gathering techniques employed in the project, definition and explication of any tests and measurements employed in analyzing the data, and an overview of data analysis techniques and tools.

Validity and reliability were introduced in Chapter 1, "Knowing, Research, and Evaluation," and revisited in Chapter 2, "Research and Evaluation Processes." Validity and reliability are recurring topics throughout the book. The basic questions to be asked with regard to the soundness of the specific methodology address validity and reliability. One form of the basic question is "could another researcher follow the description of the specific methodology in carrying out an exact duplicate of the project?" "Replicability is a basic premise of research and is frequently essential to evaluation; it is the duty of the author to explain what was done in sufficient detail that others could repeat the study."[5] Even if the consumer does not possess the technical prowess to directly replicate the project, it should be possible for the consumer to understand the fundamental concepts and the ways in which they have been operationalized and to correctly assess the potential for replication.

Integrity of Data

The question here is "can I have confidence that the data have been carefully gathered and appropriately prepared for analysis?" Correct application of the specific methodology should yield data that support valid and reliable conclusions. Any flaws, gaps, or errors in the data should be described and explained. The author's obligation is to demonstrate that any problems in the data as gathered present no threat to the integrity of the data as a whole, to the analysis of the data, or to the conclusions drawn from the data. If there are no such flaws, gaps, or errors, the author should emphasize their absence and the resulting quality of the data. It is, of course, rarely the case that there are no data problems. The careful consumer should be especially cautious in assessing the results and implications of a published report in which no discussion of the integrity of the data is provided.

In some cases, problems with the data as gathered are sufficient to cause the author to engage in extraordinary efforts to correct those problems. The author may find, for instance, that there is a systematic difference between the desired sample and the returned data for some meaningful variable. If there is a need to compensate for some such problem, the author has a particular obligation to document the problem and to explain and justify the approach taken to correcting for the problem. If no particular action has been taken to correct the problem, the author should provide a detailed and explainable rationale for not taking action and should additionally provide substantial detail regarding the impact of the problem on the results and their interpretation.

Appropriateness of Analysis

There are many possible tools and techniques for analyzing any body of data. The author should answer the question "has the analysis process resulted in an accurate and revealing understanding of the evidence?" The investigator's task is to identify the best possible tools and techniques and to explain how they are employed in the process of analyzing the data gathered for a particular body of data. Assessing the appropriateness of the analysis requires some basic understanding of approaches to analysis, but does not necessarily require that the consumer be capable of employing the analytical tools and techniques used by the author. It is relatively easy in a quantitative study to assess the levels of measurement used (nominal, ordinal, interval, ratio) and to compare the level of measurement to any statistical tests used in the analysis. Qualitative research is potentially less easy to evaluate, which increases the responsibility of the author to explain and document the appropriateness of the analysis and the tools used in carrying it out.

Clarity of the Relationship of Conclusions to Results

Do the conclusions follow clearly and logically from the results? An author should never operate on the assumption that conclusions drawn follow naturally from the results reported. The author's obligation to explain the relationship between the results and the conclusions is absolute and paramount. As Drott has pointed out, "analysis is not some abstract objective activity, but an active argument for the authors' point of view."[6] Formulating conclusions is in part interpretation of the output of analysis and in part informed conjecture. That conjecture is informed by a combination of results, knowledge of prior studies, and the author's worldview. If the author has not adequately explained how and to what extent the results lead to the conclusions, the conclusions cannot be trusted.

Strength of the Relationship of the Results and Conclusions to the Problem Statement

Do the results and conclusions clearly and compellingly address the question as presented in the problem statement? An important role of the section of a published report frequently titled "Conclusions" is the process of tying the results and conclusions to the problem statement itself. The role of the problem statement is to define and guide the research or evaluation effort. Failure to adequately and insightfully relate the initial problem statement to the results and conclusions results in a report that is inherently unsatisfying to the careful consumer, like a story that has a climax but no denouement. The consumer needs to know how the question was answered; the author needs to explicitly provide an assessment of how the question was answered and the nature of the answer within the context of the question.

The conclusion of a published report is frequently the most difficult portion to write and is not infrequently the most difficult to read and assess. The author must condense a great deal of content into what is usually a rather brief segment of the research report. In an especially skillful report, the conclusion can be read and understood in and of itself, with the body of the report available as a source of expansion and clarification.

Analysis of the Relationship of Results and Conclusions to the Literature Review

The key question here is "has the outcome of the project been effectively contextualized?" Because the literature review serves in part as a source of support and explication for the problem statement, there is a need for the author to tie the results and conclusions to the literature review. It is important for the consumer to know whether the results of the project reinforce the results of prior research efforts. It is especially important for the consumer to know whether the results contradict prior results or reveal truly new knowledge. The concept and implications of new knowledge can be understood only in the context of prior knowledge.

Evidence of Bias or Dishonesty

Does the author present the project with absolute honesty and objectivity? Bias in reporting can with fair frequency be detected through analysis of stated, implied, or unstated assumptions regarding any aspect of the project as reflected in the published report. If, for instance, the author has artificially rejected prior results because they do not reflect the place or time of the author's home environment, having done so may reflect a bias that could influence the study at hand. Some forms of bias, such as those related to the gender, ethnicity, or age of population groups, may be fairly conspicuous. Other forms of bias are more subtle and may be found in the literature review or the description of the methodology. Evidence of bias is not necessarily a condemnation of the research or evaluation process, results, or conclusions, but may influence the consumer's approach to interpretation and assessment of the report.

Dishonesty is much more difficult to detect in that the author will necessarily attempt to hide evidence of any dishonesty. Dishonesty in analysis or reporting of results may be suggested by discrepancies between the results and conclusions and those of other studies of the same phenomenon. Unfortunately, the consumer of published reports rarely has direct access to evidence of explicit dishonesty.

Closely related to the ethical requirement to minimize bias and avoid dishonesty is the author's obligation to inform the reader of fundamental limitations of the study that may influence interpretation of results. If for instance, the sample for a report is based purely on the convenience of the investigator, the author of the published report is obliged to explain the ways in which the convenience approach to sampling could have had an impact on results. Approaches to sampling and their advantages and disadvantages are discussed in Chapter 6, "Measurement, Populations, Samples, and Sampling."

It is particularly important for the author to avoid implying that results can be generalized in a manner that is not justified. Students in schools of library and information science are often used as research subjects or as surrogate "secret shoppers" in unobtrusive studies of the quality of library services. The Library Visit Study at the University of Western Ontario is an example of a "secret shopper" study.[7] The author of a research report based on this kind of study has an obligation to address the limitations of generalizing from results obtained from student subjects or student surrogates for patrons and the population of actual library patrons.

Evidence of Error

Is the report carefully presented to avoid inadvertently suggesting unjustified conclusions or implications? Any source of apparent error in the results or conclusions of a published report should raise concern regarding the accuracy of the report as a whole. Sometimes small errors are included in a report as a result of carelessness on the part of the author or through errors inserted as part of the editorial process. A frequent source of minor errors in research reports results from incorrect use of bibliographic style. Bibliographic style issues are addressed in Chapter 5, "The Project Plan or Proposal." Even such small and easily explained errors may be just cause for skepticism regarding results and conclusions. When a more substantial discrepancy is detected, the consumer should deliberately seek and evaluate other sources of error.

Some useful approaches to assessing error include comparing discussions of data in the text of the report to presentations of the same data in tables, graphs, or appendices and comparing discussions at one point in the text to reiterations elsewhere in the text. The logic of any nontextual presentation of data should be relatively obvious. Numeric data broken into subcategories should be accompanied by accurate totals; percentages should always total to 100. Reporting percentages rather than absolute counts for small samples may yield a distorted impression of the magnitude of the results.

Comparison to Similar Studies

How does the article relate to the larger of context of studies of similar or related problems or questions? The author should provide explicit comparisons to similar studies as part of the literature review, the discussion of results, and the presentation of conclusions. The consumer may want to examine some of the studies referenced in the report and will definitely want to relate the report to any similar studies known to the consumer but not referenced in the report. If important studies have been overlooked there may be reason to suspect the origins, biases, and results of the study. If the results of the project contradict or refute the results of prior studies, the author has an explicit responsibility to explain how and why.

Qualifications of Authors

Although it is nice to know as much about the author's qualifications as possible, the extent to which the qualifications of the author are described in the report is quite variable. There is more often than not some indication of the qualifications of the author, although it may be very brief. Some journals include a brief biographical sketch, while others carry nothing more than the author's name and institutional affiliation; some general readership periodicals provide no indication of the author's qualifications. Some universities require master's theses and doctoral dissertations to include a page-length biographical statement, but others require only a listing of the student's degrees and institutions on the title page.

The consumer should avoid making unfounded assumptions based on any statement of the author's qualifications or affiliation. Being on the faculty of a prestigious research university is not inherently evidence of either general research ability or specific capability within the context of a specific project. An apparent mismatch between the author's institutional affiliation and the topical area of the research or evaluation effort is not necessarily evidence of a lack of qualification.

In some cases, it may be possible for the reader to undertake independent research into the qualifications of the researcher. A simple search engine inquiry may be enough to reveal some additional information. This will generally work better for acquiring information about academics and practitioners who have risen into positions of visibility than for front-line practitioners or student authors. Care should be taken in assessing information from social networking sites or from sources that lack the imprimatur of an institutional host. In any case, independent biographical research can to some extent confirm the credentials of an author for whom additional information can be found, but cannot refute the credentials for an author for whom no additional information can be located.

In general, the qualifications of authors are probably of little interest if the consumer has no other reason to be concerned about the research report. If the consumer has established some degree of confidence in the content of the report itself, there is little reason to explore the author's background or affiliation. Many refereed journals employ a double-blind manuscript review process to minimize any negative or extraneous influence of the author's identity in the evaluation of manuscripts. The author of a manuscript almost never has access to the identities of those individuals responsible for evaluation of the manuscript; in a double-blind evaluation, the referee has no access to information regarding the identity of the author, thereby eliminating any undue influence of prior knowledge of the author or the institution with which the author is affiliated.

General Literary Qualities: Logic, Clarity, Economy, Simplicity

Last but extremely far from least, any published report should be readable. Is the report written and structured with the reader in mind? A research or evaluation report is a very specific and specialized form of literature, but is nonetheless a form of literature and requires attention to basic literary qualities. Although a research or evaluation report is not intended to be entertaining, the best published reports are compelling and written in such a way that the consumer wants to read and understand. A good report is a cohesive essay that has a beginning, middle, and end. Much like a newspaper or news magazine article, a research or evaluation report must combine elements of exposition and persuasion. When the appropriate balance of exposition and persuasion is difficult to establish, a report should err on the side of exposition, but no effective research report is completely expository. The need to present and support—sometimes even to defend—conclusions and recommendations makes the persuasive aspect of a published report an essential component. The author who neglects the persuasive emphasis of a published report does so at the risk of failing to provide the consumer with a complete picture of the research endeavor. The most persuasive report is one that addresses all the components of the research process fully and explains decisions, results, and conclusions with clarity.

Style is in part a personal matter and in part a matter of connecting the report with its audience to achieve a specific purpose. Considerations of style in writing research and evaluation reports are a matter of finding balance. The author wants the report to be readable, and so does the reader, but there must be sufficient formality in the style of research and evaluation reports to avoid any sense of trivialization of the results. That element of formality, however, can easily produce a product that is sterile and wooden. There are some style considerations that can be considered general rules; other considerations of style can be found in sources such as William Strunk and E. B. White's classic work *The Elements of Style*.[8]

1. Simplicity is one of the most desirable and most difficult to attain of all elements of style. There is something about writing about research and evaluation that seems to encourage compound sentences, inverted sentence structures, use of the passive voice, adoption of the regal "we," and other needless complexities. It is possible to present research and evaluation results primarily in the form of simple declarative sentences. Doing so is also highly desirable.

2. Economy is another principle that is often violated. Even in a thesis or dissertation, which is expected to be a comprehensive exploration of a research and evaluation problem, there is a need to say only what needs to be said.

3. Jargon should be used very selectively, both to avoid confusion for current readers and to anticipate the potential for obsolescence of current usage. One of the most difficult writing tasks for a professional insider is the recognition of jargon as jargon. When the use of jargonistic terms is unavoidable, they should be carefully defined for the initiated reader. Acronyms are a special form of jargon that demand definition. An acronym, unless it can reasonably be assumed to be universal, such as TV, AAA, or NASA, should be spelled out the first time it is used.

4. One of the difficulties in finding balance in style revolves around the avoidance of colloquialisms, particularly in an increasingly colloquial media environment. A very few years ago, for instance, one would never have heard the expression "looking to" as a synonym for "intending to" or "planning to" in a television news report. The problem with colloquialisms is that they are by their very nature not universal. Residents of northeast Ohio are intimately familiar with the concept of "tree snow," a term that has no meaning in many other locations. Everyone in New Orleans knows what the expression neutral ground means. Tree lawn and devil strip are terms used to describe the strip of grass between a street and a sidewalk. The area next to a highway that is known as the shoulder in some locations is called the berm in other places. Even some formal terms are lacking in universality. The intensity of storm reporting in the midwest means that most residents of the area probably know what a wall cloud is, but the term is never used in weather reporting in other locations.

The author of any report is, of course, writing for a specific audience and must shape the text accordingly. The expectations and style requirements of *American Libraries, Reference & User Services Quarterly, The Library Quarterly,* the *Journal of the American Society for Information Science and Technology,* the *Journal of Documentation, Science, Scientific American, Discovery,* Scarecrow Press, Libraries Unlimited, and a university press are all tailored to the needs of those publication outlets and therefore differ in substantive ways. Requirements for master's theses and doctoral dissertations are established and in most cases rigorously enforced by colleges and universities. There is, however, no report venue that explicitly requires that the presentation be boring, unintelligible, or unintelligent.

THE PROFESSIONAL LITERATURE AS TEXT AND CONTEXT

The literature of any discipline or profession constitutes the major recorded content of that discipline or profession. That content is fluid over time and across boundaries such as the practices of specific subgroups within the profession, geographic locations such as differing countries, and the functional policies and accepted best practices of the profession. The literature is in a very real sense the message the profession shares within itself and with the world at large regarding the nature, focus, and concerns of the profession.

In addition to constituting the text or content of the profession, the professional literature identifies the context for the profession. The literature exemplifies and codifies the ways in which the profession addresses its problems, codifies its practices, and reflects on the profession and its relationship to the universe of disciplines and profession. Taken as a whole, the literature defines not only what the profession has to say about its own nature and interests, but also the ways in which it chooses to examine itself as an entity. The content of the professional literature constitutes the cognitive processing and institutional memory of the profession. The context of the professional literature is the profession's heart and soul. Working together, the content and the context function as both the internal focus of the profession and as the profession's external image.

 THINK ABOUT IT!

1. How do the ethical and political principles discussed in Chapter 3, "Ethics and Politics in Library and Information Science Research and Evaluation," relate to assessing publications from the professional literature of library and information science?

2. What can a novice to the professional literature of library and information science do to enhance his or her ability to be an effective consumer of the literature?

3. How can being a conscious consumer of the professional literature enhance the on-the-job competence of a library and information science professional?

DO IT!

1. Conduct a search in *Library Literature and Information Science Fulltext* on a topic of interest to you. How do the results compare to the categorization of the library and information science literature as (a) news, (b) authoritative commentary, (c) summaries of practice, (d) case studies and descriptions, (e) informed commentary, (f) speculation, (g) listings and explications of rules, and (h) research?

2. Identify a real library and information science problem. Locate three published reports that relate to the problem and describe the ways in which the publications help define approaches to research and/or evaluation of the problem.

3. Identify a research article from the professional literature of library and information science and analyze it using the outline presented in this chapter.

NOTES

1. Dan O'Connor and Soyeon Park, "On My Mind: Research Methods as Essential Knowledge," *American Libraries* 33, no. 1 (2002): 50.

2. Ralph A. Beals, "Implications of Communications Research for the Public Library," in *Print, Radio, and Film in a Democracy*, ed. Douglas Waples, 159–81 (Chicago: University of Chicago Press, 1942).

3. O'Connor and Park, "On My Mind: Research Methods as Essential Knowledge."

4. William C. Dougherty, "The Google Books Project: Will It Make Libraries Obsolete?" *Journal of Academic Librarianship* 36, no. 1 (January 2010): 86–89.

5. M. Carl Drott, "How to Read Research: An Approach to the Literature for Practitioners," *School Library Media Quarterly* 12 (Fall 1984): 446.

6. Ibid.

7. Kirsti Nilsen and Catherine Ross, "Evaluating Virtual Reference from the Users' Perspective," *The Reference Librarian* no. 95/96 (2006): 53–79.

8. William Strunk and E. B. White, *The Elements of Style* (Ithaca, NY: Thrift Press, 1958).

SUGGESTED READINGS

Shirley L. Aaron, "Apply Drott's Criteria for Reading Research," *School Library Media Quarterly* 13 (Winter 1985): 64–68.

Elke Greifeneder and Michael S. Seadle, "Research for Practice: Avoiding Useless Results," *Library Hi Tech* 28, no. 1 (2010): 5–7.

Peter Hernon and Candy Schwartz, "Research by Default," *Library and Information Science Research* 31, no. 3 (2009): 137.

Peter Hernon and Candy Schwartz, "What Is a Problem Statement?" *Library and Information Science Research* 29, no. 3 (2007): 307–09.

Ray Lyons, "Statistical Correctness," *Library and Information Science Research* 33, no. 1 (2011): 92–95.

Fred Pyrczak, *Evaluating Research in Academic Journals*, 4th ed. (Glendale, CA: Pyrczak, 2008).

Doug Suarez, "Evaluating Qualitative Research Studies for Evidence Based Library and Information Practice," *Evidence Based Library and Information Practice* 5, no. 2 (2010), http://ejournals.library.ualberta.ca/index.php/EBLIP/article/view/7418.

THE PROJECT PLAN
OR PROPOSAL

I have always found that plans are useless, but planning is indispensible.

—Dwight D. Eisenhower, quoted in Richard Nixon, Six Crises, *1962*

I keep six honest serving-men
(They taught me all I knew);
Their names are What and Why and When
And How and Where and Who.

—Rudyard Kipling, "The Elephant's Child," Just So Stories, *1902*

In This Chapter

Purposes of research and evaluation project plans and proposals

Elements of plans and proposals

Writing plans and proposals

PURPOSES OF PLANS AND PROPOSALS

The research or evaluation process frequently begins with preparation, submission, and approval of a project plan or proposal. A plan or proposal is a form of persuasive writing that is intended to influence the reader in a specific and carefully designed manner. The sole determiner of the quality of a plan proposal is the extent to which the reader is successfully persuaded. Even those projects that are not subject to external review or internal approval benefit from a clearly articulated plan that follows the model presented in this chapter. In these cases, the plan clarifies the investigator's thinking, forces attention to detail, and ensures that the project is completed in an effective manner. Plans and proposals serve many purposes, the four most prominent of which are summarized in Figure 5.1.

```
To guide research or evaluation

To justify research or evaluation

To explain research or evaluation

To obtain funding for research or evaluation
```

Figure 5.1   Purposes of plans and proposals.

To Guide Research or Evaluation

The project plan or proposal is a blueprint for a set of tasks to be accomplished. A plan or proposal frequently takes on the role of a formal agreement or contract between the investigator and some other entity. If the researcher is a student working on a thesis or dissertation, the proposal is an agreement that completion of the proposed project in the manner specified will result in conferral of a graduate degree. If the investigator has received a grant from a foundation or governmental agency, the proposal is a contract that specifies the tasks that will be completed in exchange for funding. If an evaluator is seeking permission from an administrator or supervisor to carry out an internal project, the plan may be a memo describing the nature of the project and the commitments of time, effort, and resources expected of the institution.

In any case, a project plan or proposal sets the direction for the research or evaluation process and is available as a constant reminder of the investigator's intentions and plans. Every investigator should periodically return to the proposal as a means of ensuring that the project is being carried out as it was intended. This is especially important for lengthy or complex projects. An important goal of every research or evaluation project is to achieve the results predicted by the proposal. That doesn't imply that there is no room for careful and deliberate deviation from the plan or proposal when the project necessitates an alteration in the course of project activities, but any such variation requires a systematic reevaluation of the plan or proposal.

To Justify Research or Evaluation

For some individuals, such as college and university faculty members, research is an expectation and a requirement of employment. For many library and information professionals however, research—and especially evaluation—is a direct means to an end: a problem exists and it is perceived that conducting a research or evaluation project is a viable and appropriate approach to solving the problem. The institutional setting in which such a professional is employed may be enthusiastically supportive of research and evaluation, cautiously accepting of research and evaluation, or directly skeptical of research and evaluation as a legitimate professional activity. One role a carefully structured plan or proposal can serve is to provide justification for why a research or evaluation project needs to be carried out.

An administrator who is not innately inclined to accept formal research or evaluation as an approach to problem solving may be swayed by an effectively presented plan. In some cases, an administrator may respond to an apparently good idea by explicitly requesting a plan. In other instances, the administrator may be providing his or her own justification in the event that the research or evaluation endeavor is questioned by an even higher authority.

Justification is also a factor in thesis and dissertation proposals. In most colleges and universities, a requirement of a thesis or dissertation is that it produces new knowledge or original understanding in a meaningful domain. A fundamental purpose of a proposal (sometimes called a prospectus) for a thesis or dissertation is to demonstrate that the proposed research or evaluation merits being done because it has not been done before. An additional justification element in academic proposals is demonstration that the student is prepared to carry out the research or evaluation process without further coursework.

A final form of justification relates to the risks associated with research and evaluation. Research or evaluation projects that involve human or animal subjects, that require manipulation of hazardous materials, or that entail fiscal obligations for an institution carry an obvious and sometimes substantial potential for producing harmful results. When there is any risk of harm associated with a research or evaluation project it is necessary to provide adequate and compelling justification that the potential for harm has been minimized by design and that there are probable benefits that outweigh the impact of any harm that may be done.

To Explain Research or Evaluation

Project plans and proposals are not intended to be thrilling reading but should be understandable explanations of the proposed project. The easiest way to describe and explain a research or evaluation project while it is under way is to share the plan or proposal with colleagues, fellow researchers, members of the practitioner community, or other interested parties. The role of the plan or proposal in explaining the research or evaluation project suggests that understandability is an important characteristic of plans and proposals. Although plans and proposals are prepared for a wide variety of audiences, it is usually appropriate and frequently essential to write the plan or proposal such that it can be understood, at least in general terms, by a reader who is intelligent but has no prior understanding of the domain, discipline, or profession of the author of the plan or proposal. It is almost always possible to provide jargon and technical content for the more sophisticated reader within a context that can be read and understood by a naive reader.

To Obtain Funding

Support for internal evaluation activities may or may not be built into administrative budgets, just as those activities may or may not be specified in job descriptions. Although there are some institutional settings in which research is an expected or required condition of employment, there are few environments in which funding for research is built into the institutional budget process at a level suitable to support a broad range of research or evaluation initiatives. Even in colleges and universities, where research is an expectation and a criterion for tenure, access to institutional funds is usually competitive and frequently very limited. Some of these internal sources are intentionally designed to play a role in leveraging external funding from foundations, government agencies, or other sources.

In the early 1960s Derek J. de Solla Price wrote *Little Science, Big Science,* in which he described forces transforming the nature of research in the Western world.[1] One of those forces was and is the increasing availability of external sources of funding and the accompanying increased reliance on external funding to support the research missions of colleges, universities, and other research institutions. It is not at all uncommon for researchers in the physical and biological sciences to hold faculty or graduate student appointments that are funded entirely by grants.

A carefully and competently written proposal is an essential requirement for obtaining funding for research or evaluation. It will influence internal resource allocation for evaluation activities as well as determine whether external funding for research is obtained. Funding agencies, regardless of whether they are governmental or private in nature, are almost never interested in funding projects just because they see an opportunity to do something good for an educational institution, museum, library, or other public entity. Funding agencies are rarely interested in funding projects related to for-profit organizations. Funders want results that are broad in scope and applicable across a range of institutional settings. Obtaining funding for research or evaluation (or for any other project) from a government or foundation source requires careful research to tailor the proposal to the needs and preferences of the funding source. Funding for research and evaluation is addressed in detail in Chapter 14, "Funding for Research and Evaluation."

PROPOSAL ELEMENTS

Although requirements for proposals vary according to the specific purpose of the proposal and the environment in which the proposal is prepared, the following elements are typical. It is almost always best to include each of these elements unless stated requirements explicitly indicate that the element should not be part of the proposal. Some funding agencies, for instance, may explicitly indicate that no attachments or appendices are allowed. As mentioned earlier, a proposal is a form of *persuasive* writing; every element of every proposal should be structured and tailored to maximize its persuasive impact. The proposal outline presented here, which is summarized in Figure 5.2, is predicated on a proposal for funding from an external source such as a government agency or a foundation, but most of the proposal elements are applicable to any project proposal.

Title

Every project needs a title. The title provides a convenient means of identifying, explaining, and communicating the nature of the project. The title of a special evaluation project distinguishes it from other activities and establishes both links to and distinctions from the routine functions of the setting in which the project is to be carried out. A title for a research or evaluation project needs to possess three fundamental characteristics.

1. The title must be succinct. In some cases, such as a proposal for external funding, this is a matter of designing a title that will fit into a compressed space on a required form. In every case, the title should be brief enough that it is easily read and remembered.

2. The title must be indicative. The title must provide a preview of the nature and focus of the proposed project. Regardless of what else is provided in the plan or proposal in the way of an abstract or executive summary, the title serves as a single-phrase summary of the focus of the project.

3. The title must be expressive. One role of the title is to catch the reader's attention. The title is typically the first element of a proposal or plan encountered by a reader, administrator,

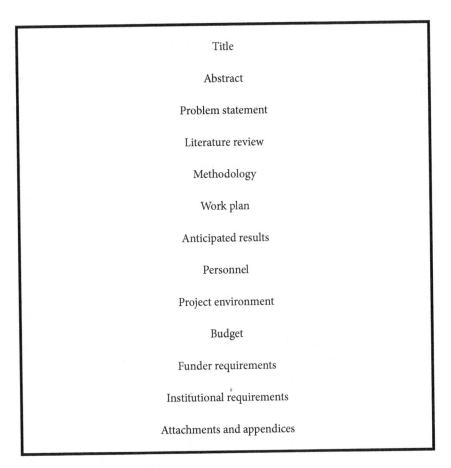

Title

Abstract

Problem statement

Literature review

Methodology

Work plan

Anticipated results

Personnel

Project environment

Budget

Funder requirements

Institutional requirements

Attachments and appendices

Figure 5.2 Typical proposal elements.

or evaluator. The reader should get an immediate impression of the purpose of the project—the project's hook—just from reading the title. Although there are risks in emphasizing catchiness, designing a title that has verbal appeal is usually desirable.

The trick in selecting a title for a research or evaluation project is balancing these three characteristics. A title must be long enough to be indicative but brief enough to be memorable. A research or evaluation proposal is a formal document, so expressiveness should not be stretched to the point of silliness or excessive cuteness. Acronyms are sometimes useful ways to express project titles, but acronyms and initialisms should be used with care to avoid presenting a sense of excessive cleverness.

Abstract or Executive Summary

An abstract or executive summary forms a bridge between the brevity of the title and the depth of the body of the plan proposal. Abstracts and executive summaries serve slightly different purposes. Abstracts are more frequently associated with research proposals and usually emphasize the research question or hypothesis of the proposed study, the design of the methodology, and the anticipated nature of the results. Plans for evaluation projects more typically include an executive summary that focuses on the origin and pragmatic implications of the problem to be addressed, the projected benefits of the proposed evaluation project, the resources necessary to carry out the project, and the impact of the project on the normal operations of the institution.

The fundamental characteristics of an abstract or executive summary are very much like those of a title:

1. The abstract or executive summary must be brief. The goal is to summarize and synthesize the entirety of the plan proposal in a small space. Five hundred words is a good rule of thumb for the length of an abstract for research proposal. An executive summary is usually one page in length.

2. The abstract or executive summary must be to an appropriate degree complete and self-contained. The essential purpose of an abstract or executive summary is to attract the reader's attention and encourage the reader to read the remainder of the plan or proposal. Although it is clearly impossible for an abstract or executive summary to state everything that is in the body of the proposal narrative, it is essential to address the fundamental aspects of the plan or proposal. The abstract component of a research proposal generally concentrates on the need for new knowledge and the appropriateness of the proposed methodology. An executive summary attempts to condense all the elements of the project plan into a brief—usually no more than one page—digest that can be read and understood quickly.

The abstract or executive summary must indicate the nature of the problem that underlies the proposed project, the basic question or questions to be addressed, the essential elements of the methodology, and the anticipated outcomes of the project. An abstract or executive summary does not normally address the literature review component of the plan or proposal. Although a research proposal rarely addresses the budgetary and managerial aspects of the project, budget and project management are essential components of an executive summary. The abstract should stand on its own as a representation of the project; readers of plans and proposals frequently return to the abstract or executive summary as a resource for a quick reminder of the nature of the project.

Problem Statement

The problem statement defines the boundaries that encompass the problem, identifies subproblems, delineates questions and hypotheses, and states implications for action. The problem statement doesn't necessarily have to explicitly address all of the components identified in the Chapter 2 discussion of the research and evaluation processes, but needs to convey a sense that all those components have been considered. The problem statement is the domain of two of Kipling's six honest serving-men. It must address *what* is to be studied and *why.* The problem statement of a project proposal serves the following purposes:

1. The problem statement demonstrates the *importance* of the proposed project. No funder or administrator is interested in supporting a project that is not perceived as being important. Importance is never self-evident and must be explained. The problem statement portion of the proposal presents the case for attaching importance to the project by demonstrating that there is indeed a problem and that there is a compelling need to solve the problem.

2. The problem statement demonstrates the *generality* of the proposed project. Although a library administrator may be primarily interested in the local impact of the project, the public and external relations potential for demonstrating the success of an internal evaluation project may have appeal to an administrator. Master's theses and doctoral dissertations are inherently expected to address broadly generalizable research problems. If the goal is external funding, projects are typically looked upon as models that can be emulated or adapted to solve similar problems in other environments; few funding agencies are interested in supporting efforts to solve problems of a purely local or idiosyncratic nature. Even though the impetus for the project may be the need to solve an immediate problem in a specific setting, the proposal writer's task is to establish that solving that problem in that setting will help solve similar problems in other settings.

3. The problem statement defines the *scope* of the proposed project. It is very frequently the case that the core problem to be addressed by a project is too large or too complex to be solved by a single study. The problem statement defines the scope of the proposed project both inclusively by carefully stating those aspects of the problem the project will address and exclusively by stating those aspects of the problem that explicitly and by design will not be addressed. The scope of the project should be stated with absolute clarity and total honesty. There should never be any occasion for the investigator to have to explain his or her perception of the scope of the project was different from that of the entity responsible for approving the project.

4. The problem statement demonstrates the *uniqueness* of the proposed project. The problem statement establishes that the specific approach to solving the problem is sufficiently unique to merit support. This is the essence of academic proposals for thesis or dissertation projects, for which the student's research effort is expected to reveal new knowledge. It is also important for proposals for evaluation projects or for funding. It is frequently the case that the general problem area has already been studied, perhaps extensively, and that explanations or solutions have already been presented. The task of the proposal writer is to demonstrate that the approach taken in the proposed project is different from any attempt that has been previously made. For evaluation projects this may be as simple as testing the applicability of best practices or general theories in a local setting. In other evaluation projects, such as those mandated by government bodies and undertaken on a regular cyclical basis, uniqueness is a less critical factor.

5. The problem statement demonstrates the *appropriateness* of the proposed project. A project can be important, generalizable, of an appropriate scope, and truly unique but still not be appropriate for the interests or programs of a particular funding agency or of interest to a library administrator. The problem statement must establish the ways in which the project is a good match for the funding agency or local institution. It is frequently possible to do so by directly relating the problem and approach to an official statement of the funding agency or library's mission, goals, objectives, or priorities. The need to establish such a match means that there really are no generic plans or proposals—every plan or proposal must be carefully tailored to the targeted approving agency.

Literature Review

The role of the literature review was delineated in the discussion in Chapter 2, "Research and Evaluation Processes"; the literature review of a plan or proposal must address the fundamental purposes of confirmation of need, establishment of focus, identification of the specific subject and context, identification of the theoretical base, and identification of the methodological base. The literature review for a proposal is additionally characterized by two potentially conflicting factors:

1. Completeness. One of the purposes of the literature review is to establish and confirm the need for the proposed project. The literature review must suggest to the reader that the author has examined the preexisting literature thoroughly enough and completely enough to form a full and effective understanding of the problem and its context. The literature review for an academic proposal for a thesis or dissertation is expected to be comprehensive. One way in which an author can suggest completeness is by systematically categorizing the ways in which the problem has been addressed in the literature and discussing each category or approach to categorization.

2. Selectivity. The literature review for a project plan or proposal other than a thesis or dissertation proposal is rarely comprehensive. When length is a consideration, the literature review must provide a sense of completeness while simultaneously being deliberately selective. The impression to be given is that the author is familiar with the relevant literature in its entirety and has chosen the best and most exemplary items to include in the literature review.

Methodology

The most important and lengthiest section of a project plan or proposal is description of the methodology. The methodology is the responsibility of one of Kipling's six honest serving-men. The methodology must describe in detail *how* the project will be carried out. The methodology section should include the following:

1. A statement of the general methodological area. This aspect doesn't need to be belabored, but it is essential to convey a clear understanding of the general domain (historical, descriptive, or experimental) within which the project lies. This may be a simple statement such as "An experiment will be conducted to determine whether structured training in the use of Internet search engines is associated with the quality of resources chosen for research papers in a freshman-level English composition book." The statement of the methodological area (experiment) is closely tied to the specific nature of the project and provides a preview of the remainder of the methodology.

2. Identification of the population to be studied. The population for a study consists of all those entities that are actually of interest to the project. The population is defined primarily by the nature of the problem, but requires specific definition within the plan or proposal. If the problem is poor choice of resources for research papers, there are several possible populations that can be studied, including the students who write the papers, the faculty members who teach the courses for which the papers are written, the searches that produce the resources, the tools used to conduct the searches, the research papers, and the resources themselves. Given the array of possible populations that can be studied, the plan or proposal must precisely define the population to be studied to avoid confusion.

3. Selection of a sample. The sample for a study consists of those members of the population that will actually be studied. The sample is defined primarily by the project designer in an effort to establish a manageable approach to studying a population. The essential goal of the sample selection process is to identify a sample that is adequately representative of the population. Populations and samples are addressed in detail in Chapter 6, "Measurement, Populations, Samples, and Sampling."

4. Definition of terms, including both conceptual and operational definitions. Operational definitions need to be carefully and explicitly stated. Some terms can be assumed to be generally understood and not in need of definition, but the author should reach that conclusion carefully, not casually. The term *circulation* is library jargon that is generally

well understood by practitioners in the field but may not be understood by the public or by institutional managers and administrators. If the meaning of a term is in any way modified for purposes of the project, the operational definition of that term must be stated. A study of circulation of reserved readings in an academic library, for instance, may need an explicit definition of the meaning of *circulation*.

5. Delineation of assumptions related to the project. The fundamental principle of quality research or evaluation is that assumptions are known, articulated, and justified. The author has an explicit duty to share key assumptions with the reader of the plan or proposal as a means of conveying a shared understanding of the nature of the proposed project. The delineation of assumptions should not be overemphasized, though. Some assumptions are so fundamental and obvious that they don't really merit mention. In a study of patterns of circulation of library materials, for instance, the assumption that circulation in some way implies use needs to be stated only if use or usefulness of the materials is a focus of inquiry.

6. Description of a data-gathering plan. The data-gathering plan describes in detail the ways in which data will be acquired for the project. This includes definition of the primary and secondary data to be gathered, a description of the origin and nature of the tools used to gather data (observation, interview, questionnaire, etc.), anticipation of any barriers to effective data gathering, and discussion of the ways in which data will be measured.

7. Description of a data analysis plan. The data analysis plan describes in detail the impact of missing or faulty data, the approach that will be taken to exploring the relationship of the primary data to context data and to exploring relationships within the primary data, and the ways in which significance will be assessed. The data analysis plan addresses both statistical and qualitative analyses and describes the analytical tools that will be used in the project.

Work Plan

The work plan, also known as a schedule of completion or project timeline, describes in detail the sequence and flow of the tasks necessary to carry out the project and the timing of the project. The work plan should be clear and understandable and should account for all events from the beginning to the end of the project. The work plan must also identify personnel and organizational units involved in or affected by the project and assignment of responsibility for project oversight and project activities. The work plan is the domain of three of Kipling's six honest serving-men. The work plan answers the questions "*Who* will be involved? and "*Where* and *when* will they be involved?" The work plan may be in the form of a step-by-step chronological narrative, a Gantt chart, or both. Figure 5.3 provides an example of a Gantt chart for a library project.[2]

Anticipated Results

What are the anticipated outcomes of the proposed project? The element of prediction is inherent and explicit in the concept of a directional hypothesis, but even projects for which a directional hypothesis is inappropriate are subject to prediction. A plan or proposal has little appeal if the author cannot to some extent anticipate the results of the project and their implications for action. The plan or proposal should also emphasize:

1. Dissemination of results. Results are of interest only to the extent that they are made available for use by those institutions, groups, or individuals who will benefit from them.

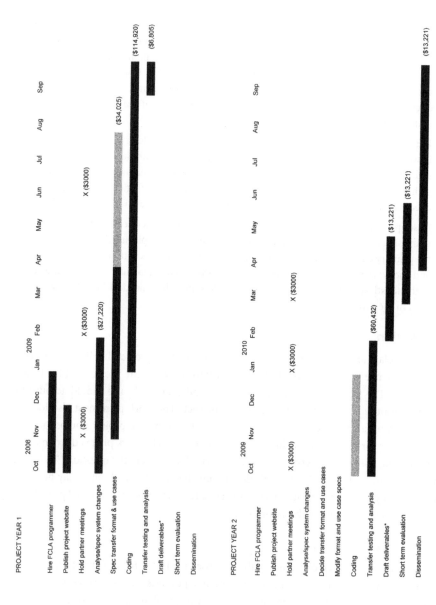

Figure 5.3 Project Gantt chart..

Although theses and dissertations may garner only limited use, thesis and dissertation defenses are frequently at least nominally public presentations and dissemination takes place at least at the level of the thesis or dissertation committee and the required filing requirements of the university, which usually involves a copy that becomes a permanent part of the university library's collection. Funding agencies, in keeping with their usual emphasis on supporting projects that are broadly generalizable, tend to expect grant recipients to actively seek to disseminate results beyond the required final report to the funding agency. Research projects don't always lead to publications as methods of dissemination, but publication is a frequent goal of a research project. Leaders of internal evaluation projects must plan for dissemination of results to administrators, decision makers, and other essential stakeholders.

2. Byproducts. In addition to reports of results, research and evaluation projects sometimes generate tangible, useful byproducts. Bibliometric studies frequently require compilation of comprehensive bibliographies. A historical study may be accompanied by creation of a unique collection of primary and secondary resources. An experimental study may involve an innovative approach to measuring an important phenomenon. Any research or evaluation project has the potential for yielding a new methodology that can be emulated or adapted for other purposes. Evaluation results may be used in public relations or advocacy efforts. On fairly rare occasions, a research or evaluation project may result in a byproduct with tangible monetary value, such as a book, an implementation manual, a software product, or a patent. Such byproducts should be anticipated in the plan or proposal.

3. Ownership. A shared understanding of issues related to ownership of data, results, reports, and byproducts must be established at the time the plan or proposal is prepared. Librarians may find that they need explicit administrative or managerial permission to share results of evaluation projects beyond—or even within—the local institution. The same permissions may be required for results of research projects. Most external funding agencies assume that copyright for publications derived from a funded project lies with the grant recipient, but there are exceptions. Issues of ownership arise most frequently in the context of tangible byproducts. Byproducts for which patents can be sought are especially subject to conflicts regarding ownership. Ownership issues are frequently but not always addressed in the documentation provided by a funding agency regarding its grant programs. When such documentation does not exist, the investigator is well served to inquire and to establish a clear, written agreement regarding what is owned by all parties involved.

Personnel

The personnel section of a project plan or proposal serves the following basic purposes:

1. It describes the responsibilities of the individuals who will be involved in the project. These individuals may include the project director(s), other permanent employees who will be involved in the project, temporary employees who will be hired for the project, paid consultants or advisers who will work with project personnel, and unpaid consultants or advisers. Research or evaluation projects for which there is no external funding or additional internal funding represent a reallocation of staff time and responsibility. The number of staff and the extent of staff involvement are key elements in determining the feasibility of a project to which no new resources will be allocated.

2. It documents the expertise of the individuals who will be involved in the project. Pertinent expertise involves a combination of research or evaluation experience and

expertise and professional experience and expertise. The goal is to demonstrate that an appropriate and effective combination of knowledge and abilities is possessed by the research or evaluation team in the aggregate. The project director may not possess certain abilities in areas required for the success of the project, such as computer programming, advanced questionnaire design, construction of equipment, or statistical analysis. When the project director is not capable of carrying out all project activities, it is appropriate and desirable to bring expertise into the project environment by identifying other staff with the desired knowledge, hiring new permanent of temporary employees, seeking the services of unpaid advisors, or allocating funding for consultants.

3. It establishes formal permission for involvement of project personnel. Regardless of whether the project is entirely internal or based on external funding, establishing the chain of approval for the project is essential. In the case of an internal evaluation, supervisors give their tacit approval for allocating staff time to the project when the proposal is accepted. For a thesis or dissertation, the student's committee agrees to commit appropriate time and effort to the project and usually some higher office of the university such as a graduate college approves the roles of the committee members. In the case of an externally funded project, a grant is normally an agreement between the funding agency and the institution that employs the project director, with careful and precise definition of the roles of the project director and other project personnel.

Project Environment

Just as it is important to document the expertise of the research or evaluation team, it is essential to document adequacy of the infrastructure in which the research or evaluation project will take place. This section of the plan or proposal includes the following:

1. Identification and location of the research or evaluation site. Where will the research or evaluation project actually take place? How is that location appropriate to the project? What are the characteristics of the location? How is the institution positioned within its environment?

2. Support facilities. This section describes the basic facilities available for supporting the research or evaluation project, including office space, furniture, computer hardware and software, access to telephone services, and any other aspect of the physical environment that is essential to the success of the project.

3. Institutional support. In addition to physical facilities, the institution hosting the project may provide other support, such as secretarial assistance, student workers, research or evaluation consulting services, bookkeeping support, or other services that are primarily matters of support via the existing infrastructure of the institution.

In the case of a local evaluation project in which it can be anticipated that the supervisor or administrator is familiar with the environment, the project director may nevertheless want to describe the ways in which the institution will be called upon to support the completion of the project and justify any aspects of the project that may have a temporarily disruptive impact on the institutional setting.

Budget

A carefully prepared and documented budget is perhaps the most obvious element of any proposal or plan. The budget explains to those individuals responsible for approving the project exactly what monetary and nonmonetary investments will be necessary for completion of the project and how those investments will be funded. Every project, whether internally supported or dependent on external funding, is associated with costs that require appropriate and complete accounting. In the case of an internal evaluation or research project with no anticipation of special funding, the budget must account for reallocation of funds to support the project. Applications for external funding must describe the need for funding in explicit and thorough terms and detail either all costs of the project or only those costs for which funding is actually sought. For either internally or externally funded projects, it is important for internal purposes to carefully analyze, document, and budget all costs associated with the project. The following are prominent budget lines for research or evaluation proposals:

1. Personnel. Project personnel fall into three categories:

   a. Permanent employees of the host institution who will devote some portion of their time to the project. It is typically the case that permanent employees devote only a portion of their time to the project and spend the remainder of their time in fulfillment of their normal duties. The grant budget may request funding to recover the employee's wages for time devoted to the project. For projects that do not require external funding, it is still wise to show the actual cost by including employee time as an indirect cost. This practice demonstrates to administrators that the project director is cognizant of the efforts and resources the organization must commit to the activity. For an hourly employee, this is a simple matter of determining the number of hours that will be spent on the project during its lifetime. The norm for a salaried employee is to calculate the percentage of the employee's time that will be spent on the project and budget that percentage of the salary for the project period. In addition to wages, it may be necessary to include a budget line for benefits for either permanent or temporary employees. Benefits are typically budgeted as a percentage of wages, but may be determined more precisely by calculating the actual costs of insurance, retirement, worker's compensation, and related benefits.

   b. Temporary employees who will be hired for the project. Depending on the nature of the project, it may be necessary to hire clerical staff, computer staff, or student employees whose sole employment responsibility is to the project. Regardless of whether these employees are paid on an hourly or a salaried basis, determination of the rate of pay should be realistic and reasonable based on the nature of the job and typical rates of pay for the institution or the community in which the research or evaluation project is to be carried out.

   c. Consultants who will be paid on a contractual basis to perform specific tasks. Consultants are typically paid a flat fee negotiated individually with each consultant. Consultants are not normally paid benefits. As an alternative to paid consultants, a project may involve unpaid advisors whose time and effort are either contributed voluntarily or are provided as part of their normal responsibilities for agencies other than the local institution. A university faculty member, for instance, may be willing to advise on project design or analysis of results as a voluntary act of public or professional service. State library agencies frequently provide consultant services to libraries for a variety of project support activities. Students may be available on a volunteer basis or as part of service learning activities for which they earn academic credit.

2. Facilities. Every project has to happen somewhere. Although a research or evaluation project may require only minimal use of facilities, it is inevitably the case that facilities cannot simultaneously be used for a research or evaluation project and other purposes.

A realistic assessment of the need to budget for facilities is an essential component of the process of developing a research or evaluation proposal. The most prominent facilities issues have to do with space, furnishings, and equipment.

a. Space. Space is frequently a cost absorbed by the host institution, although long-term complex projects may require rental of office, laboratory, or other space. Security of the space is an issue for some projects. It may be necessary to set aside space for the project that will not be accessible for other purposes. Since unallocated space is rarely readily available in libraries and information centers, setting aside significant space for a research or evaluation project can be a difficult issue. Budgeting for dedicated use of existing space can also be difficult, but can be accomplished by determining typical rental rates in the community.

b. Furnishings. Access to furnishings is often overlooked in the preparations of research or evaluation proposals. It is a rare research or evaluation project that does not require filing cabinet space, shelving, secure storage, or other basic office furniture. Even a small research or evaluation project can generate a substantial amount of paper that must be kept somewhere. If a questionnaire is distributed as part of the research or evaluation project, there will be a need for table space to support collating, assembling, and preparing the questionnaire for mailing.

c. Equipment. The most frequent need for equipment involves computer hardware and software. For some projects the need for access to a computer will be sufficiently intense that no solution other than a dedicated computer will be adequate. Even when the volume of demand doesn't merit a dedicated computer, issues of data security may make using a shared computer undesirable.

d. Evaluation project plans for which no external funding is sought typically do not include an explicit budget for space allocation or utilization, furnishings, or equipment, unless purchase of specialized equipment or software to support the project is required. Even so, assessment of available and needed facilities is an essential planning activity.

3. Materials, supplies, and services. Paper, pencils, envelopes, file folders, paper clips, USB drives, backup drives, and other basic office supplies are part of every research or evaluation project. Postage for distributing questionnaires, shipping costs, voice and data telecommunications, and other services are also common. It is generally fairly easy to determine the volume of materials, supplies, and services required for a research or evaluation project. Unit costs for materials, supplies, and services are usually fairly easy to determine, but doing so can be time consuming and should not be left until the last moment or simply assigned generically to a department with in the organization.

4. Travel. Some research or evaluation projects require travel to gather data or for other purposes related to successful completion of the project. Many institutions have established policies and procedures to govern employee travel; those policies and procedures typically prevail even when the institution is not paying for the travel. Determining the impact of local policies and procedures is an essential part of budgeting for travel related to a research or evaluation project. Institutions supported by local, state, or federal government usually have standard rates for housing, meals, and mileage. One of the difficulties of budgeting for travel is that some components, such as airfare, may change between the time when the proposal is developed and the time when the travel actually takes place. There is no direct solution other than using the best cost information available. Some funding agencies also allow for travel to present the results of research or evaluation at professional association conferences. Budgeting for travel to present research or evaluation results is a very positive indicator of a plan for active dissemination of the results.

Proper citation of sources consulted or used in preparing a proposal or report serves the dual purposes of appropriately and honestly attributing the origins of ideas and expressions and making it possible for the reader to find and use the cited source. Using a standard style manual both ensures accurate attribution and eases the task of the reader who chooses to find the cited source.

A style manual is a guide to preparing a proposal, report, or other document for a specified purpose. Style manuals are probably most frequently consulted for guidance on structuring bibliographic references, but typically also include guidance on preparing the text, editing and proofreading, formatting tables, presenting information graphically, and other structural features. Examples of commonly used style manuals include

- *The Chicago Manual of Style*. 16th ed. Chicago: University of Chicago Press, 2010.
- *Publication Manual of the American Psychological Association*. 6th ed. Washington: American Psychological Association, 2009.
- Turabian, Kate L. *A Manual for Writers of Research Papers, Theses, and Dissertations*. 7th ed. Revised by Wayne C. Booth, Gregory G. Colomb, Joseph M. Williams, and University of Chicago Press Editorial Staff. Chicago: University of Chicago Press, 2007.

Choice of a style manual is frequently dictated by specific needs. Most universities designate one or more style manuals that are acceptable for use in preparing theses or dissertations. In some cases, the choice of a style manual for a thesis or dissertation may be a function of the subject area or discipline of the student. Publishers of journals and books typically have requirements or preferences for style manuals. *Reference & User Services Quarterly*, the official journal of the Reference & User Services Association, a division of the American Library Association, requires that manuscripts submitted for publication be prepared according to the provisions of the *Chicago Manual of Style*. The *Journal of the American Society for Information Science & Technology* requires that manuscripts be prepared using the *Publication Manual of the American Psychological Association*.

Style manuals are frequently referred to using a form of shorthand. The *Chicago Manual of Style* is referred to simply as Chicago, A *Manual for Writers of Research Papers, Theses, and Dissertations* is reduced to Turabian, and the *Publication Manual of the American Psychological Association* is known as APA Style or APA.

Figure 5.4   Research and evaluation checknote: Bibliographic style.

5. Support services. Some research or evaluation projects require contractual support services, such as special custodial services, transcription of audio recordings, use of centralized computing facilities, meeting room space, food and beverage services, housing, or other services essential to the project. Budgeting for such services is generally fairly easy when the institution has routine arrangements in place and more difficult when the project director must identify and determine rates for services independently.

6. Overhead/indirect costs. Indirect costs are the overhead items that are necessary to support the institution in which the project is to take place. These include heat, air

conditioning, electricity, routine custodial services, basic maintenance, and all the infrastructure costs that are necessary to support any business or service activity. The principle underlying indirect cost calculation is that some portion of the cost of maintaining the infrastructure is associated with the research project and requires that the institution be reimbursed by the funding agency for those costs. Such costs are rarely included in plans for research or evaluation projects that do not involve external funding. Indirect cost calculation for externally funded projects is addressed in Chapter 14, "Funding for Research and Evaluation."

7. Evaluation. An essential component in any research or evaluation project is assessment of the quality and success of the completed project. Although a line item for project evaluation may not be included in the budget, it is essential to recognize and acknowledge that evaluation does incur costs. The most frequent budget item for project evaluation is support for the time spent by project personnel in activities directly related to project evaluation rather than project completion.

8. Justification of budget items. Many funding agencies require, in addition to a budget presented in a line-by-line format, a narrative discussion of the need for and nature of the items included in the budget. Even when an explicit justification is not required, a brief explanation of how specific budget items will contribute to the success of the project may serve to heighten interest on the part of individuals responsible for project approval and make the project more understandable. Internal research or evaluation plans should include a detailed budget with a well-written, persuasive, and documented narrative explaining each line item.

Technical Requirements

Institutional policies or the requirements of external funding agencies may impose the need to address specific administrative requirements that are not inherent components of the project plan or proposal. Some institutions have specific requirements, forms, and approval processes for internal projects. Even though a library may internally have no such technical requirements, the institutional context of the library—a local government, a school district, a college or university—may impose such requirements. Being aware of and in compliance with such requirements is an essential to project success and institutional harmony.

Colleges, universities, and school districts almost always have formal structures for assuring that grant proposals adhere to institutional policies and procedures. Other institutions may not have formal policies and procedures, but the same concerns apply regardless of the institutional setting. Some typical institutional requirements include the following:

- Routing forms used to obtain signatures of individuals responsible for approving various aspects of the institution's commitment to the proposed project.

- Institutional reviews designed to ensure that risks are minimized, that costs are covered appropriately, and that there is adequate compliance with institutional policies and procedures.

- Human-subject reviews to ensure that the principles of concern for research involving human subjects discussed in Chapter 3, "Ethics and Politics in Library and Information Science Research and Evaluation," are addressed.

Style manuals such as the *Chicago Manual of Style* and the *Publication Manual of the American Psychological Association* provide guidance on how to describe the elements of a bibliographic reference for purposes of documenting the origins of ideas and expressions other than those of the author of a report or publication. Although the specific way in which bibliographic elements are presented varies among style manuals, the elements themselves tend to have a great deal of commonality. The following references show how a single article is represented by three different style manuals.

- *Chicago Manual of Style* (Numbered Footnote or Endnote)

1. Kathy Lehman, "Teaching Information Ethics to High School Students," *Library Media Connection* 27, no. 6 (May 2009): 28–30.

- *Chicago Manual of Style* (Bibliography Entry)

Lehman, Kathy. "Teaching Information Ethics to High School Students." *Library Media Connection* 27, no. 6 (May 2009): 28–30.

- *Chicago Manual of Style* (Author-Date)

Lehman, Kathy. 2009. "Teaching Information Ethics to High School Students." *Library Media Connection* 27 (6): 28–30.

- *A Manual for Writers of Research Papers, Theses, and Dissertations* (Note)

2. Kathy Lehman, "Teaching Information Ethics to High School Students," *Library Media Connection* 27, no. 6 (May 2009): 28–30.

- *A Manual for Writers of Research Papers, Theses, and Dissertations* (Bibliography)

Lehman, Kathy. "Teaching Information Ethics to High School Students." *Library Media Connection* 27, no. 6 (May 2009): 28–30.

- *A Manual for Writers of Research Papers, Theses, and Dissertations* (Reference List)

Lehman, Kathy. 2009. "Teaching Information Ethics to High School Students." *Library Media Connection* 27: 28–30.

- *Publication Manual of the American Psychological Association*

Lehman, K. (2009). Teaching information ethics to high school students. *Library Media Connection, 27,* 28–30.

Note that the *Chicago Manual of Style* and *A Manual for Writers of Research Papers, Theses, and Dissertations* share a common origin, which accounts for the similarities between the two style manuals; these style manuals are frequently used in the humanities and social sciences.. The *Publication Manual of the American Psychological Association* is more closely associated with the sciences and technology.

Figure 5.5   Research and evaluation checknote: Citing sources 1—style manual variations.

Attachments and Appendices

Anything that cannot be presented in the body of the plan or proposal that is viewed as important by the proposal writer and is not expressly forbidden by an approving body is a potential candidate for inclusion as an appendix. This might include a complete vita for the project director, letters of support from interested parties who are not directly part of the research or evaluation team, documents that provide support for the appropriateness of the institutional base for the project, or anything else that lends support to the proposal. Attachments and appendices should be included judiciously and with a clear and understandable purpose. Readers of plans and proposals tend to feel responsible for reading every aspect of every proposal for which they have responsibility. It is essential for the investigator not to alienate the reader with the burden of examining extraneous materials.

WRITING THE PROPOSAL

A plan or proposal for a research or evaluation project is an explicitly persuasive document that is prepared to achieve some combination of the multiple purposes of guiding, justifying, explaining, and gaining funding or other support for the proposed project. The essential ways in which to be persuasive in writing a proposal are to

- be thorough and straightforward and to make a sincere effort
- address the needs, wants, and requirements of the funding agency
- be absolutely honest in every aspect of the proposal

Some things a proposal does not need to be, and in most cases shouldn't be, are

- fun
- cute
- preachy
- colloquial

Project plans and proposals are technical documents. Like other technical documents, they should be written in a business-like manner. The structure should be clear, headings should be used effectively to separate sections of the proposal, pages should be numbered, and the language should emphasize simple declarative sentences.

Plans and proposals should generally be written in the third person. The first person tends to make the plan or proposal seem personal and local rather than professional and universal. A proposal written in the first person implies a primary relationship between the approving administrator or agency and the author of the proposal rather than a relationship with the project itself. In the case of an internal project, writing in the first person implies that the project is primarily an initiative intended to benefit the project director rather than the institution. For a proposal for external funding, writing in the first person suggests that the project is primarily local and personal rather than universal and generalizable.

Plans and proposals are written primarily in the future tense. The basic purpose of a proposal is to explain a sequence of events that, if the plan or proposal is approved, will happen. Writing in an active voice and using action-oriented words, phrases, sentences, and paragraphs is essential to effective plan or proposal preparation. Grantproposal.com provides a list of 145 active verbs that are effective in preparing plans or proposals for research or evaluation projects.[3] Speculative words such as *would, should, could, might,* or *may* must be avoided. The technical term for such words is *weasel words,* words that allow the author to avoid making a commitment to an assertion or plan.

A project plan proposal is very much analogous to a blueprint for construction of a building. The plan or proposal, like a blueprint, is a structured plan of action that is stated in highly formalized and structured terms. It is therefore essential that the design be presented in a manner that can be executed by others. The best project plans and proposals are written in a clear, step-by-step manner that inspires confidence that the reader could actually carry out the project. When writing the plan or proposal it is helpful to think of it as instructions for someone else to use in completing the project.

A final consideration for a research or evaluation project plan or proposal that makes it very different from most other forms of writing is that, pursuant of the essential persuasive nature of a plan or proposal, a proposal does not and cannot reach a conclusion. The fundamental implication of a project proposal is that no conclusion can be reached without carrying out the proposed project. The plan or proposal may and should address anticipated outcome and their impact.

Using a standard style manual such as the *Chicago Manual of Style or the Publication Manual of the American Psychological Association* provides a means of consistent communication of bibliographic content. The availability of online databases from sources such as EBSCOhost and WilsonWeb provide ready access to bibliographic data and the full texts of articles and other publications. The bibliographic formats used in databases, however, serve purposes other than compliance with standard manuals of style. The following examples show an article as represented by the *Chicago Manual of Style,* EBSCOhost, and WilsonWeb:

- *Chicago Manual of Style* (Bibliography Entry)

Lehman, Kathy. "Teaching Information Ethics to High School Students." *Library Media Connection* 27, no. 6 (May 2009): 28–30.

- EBSCOhost

Teaching Information Ethics to High School Students. Full Text Available By: **Lehman, Kathy.** Library Media Connection, May 2009, Vol. 27 Issue 6, p28–30, 3p, 1 Chart

- WilsonWeb

Lehman, K. Teaching Information Ethics to High School Students. Library Media Connection v. 27 no. 6 (May/June 2009) p. 28–30

Neither EBSCOhost nor WilsonWeb is a good approximation of the *Chicago Manual of Style* or any other standard style manual. The bottom line is that copying and pasting bibliographic references from databases or other online sources is generally not a good idea.

Figure 5.6   Research and evaluation checknote: Citing sources 2—the dangers of copy and paste.

PLAN OR PROPOSAL REVIEW AND APPROVAL

Most authors of project plans and proposals have in mind an important project that will yield meaningful and useful results. A project director who is fully engaged in the proposed project will have a natural sense of eagerness and perhaps even impatience to begin work. There is almost always, however, a lesser or greater potential for delay in the approval process for the project.

For a project requiring only internal approval, there may be a need for the project director's supervisor to seek approval at a higher level. This may even mean seeking authorization from an advisory or governing board, a higher office of the institution, or an oversight committee or panel. Some projects, such as those involving human subjects approval in an institution that has no standing Institutional Review Board, may require review by legal counsel. Administrators and governing bodies tend to be conservative with regard to projects that have the potential for incurring risk. Although it may seem reasonable to anticipate that the approval and authorization processes for an internal project will involve minimal time, some delay is inevitable.

External funding agencies typically, although not always, operate within the confines of set schedules for proposal submission, review, decision making, and notification. The decision process typically involves initial analysis by agency staff of compliance with technical requirements, one or more rounds of peer review of the proposal, and final decision making by agency program officers and/or administrators. The review and notification processes can easily require a few months or even as much as a year.

NEGOTIATION AND REVISION

Every project director responsible for preparing a plan or proposal for a research or evaluation project should be prepared in advance for the possibility that some negotiation and revision will be necessary prior to final approval and initiation of the project. A library administrator may conclude that the project timeline is sufficiently aggressive that an excessive amount of disruption will occur and ask that the timeline be extended to ameliorate potential negative effects of the project. It is not at all unusual for a funding agency to request revisions in the budget and accompanying scope of a project prior to approval and distribution of funds. Although such a request typically asks for a reduction in the proposed budget, it is not unheard of for a funding agency to ask what more could be done for an incremental increase in project funding.

The essential task for the author of a project plan or proposal is to plan for possible negotiation and necessary revision by considering in advance the aspects of the project that have built-in flexibility or innate rigidity. Some project activities may be so fundamental to the success of the project that they cannot be altered with any reasonable expectation of project success. Other activities or project components may be subject to modification with only a limited negative impact on the project's outcomes. The proactive author of a project plan or proposal assesses the extent to which the project can or cannot be modified as the project design unfolds and as the plan or proposal is prepared for approval.

THE PROJECT PROPOSAL AS INVESTMENT

It is easy to view the proposal for a research or evaluation project as being a cost that may not be recovered. If an administrator rejects a plan for an evaluation initiative, the impact on the individual or team who prepared the plan may be discouragement and a reluctance to propose future ideas. Even if the plan is accepted, but only with major modifications, the investigator or investigative team may feel that the ideas presented in the plan weren't quite good enough. It is frequently a matter of months before a major funding agency reaches a decision on a proposal for external funding. Although a negative funding decision may be accompanied by explicit or implied encouragement to resubmit the proposal in a future round, the passage of time itself can be a discouraging factor. When an investigator submits a proposal, receives a negative review, revises and resubmits, and still gets a negative review, the impetus to continue with the project may wane substantially.

Preparation and review of a proposal or plan also entails costs to the institution. The investigator or team's time and effort devoted to drafting, revising, finalizing, and submitting the proposal are time and effort not spent on other activities. The time and effort of administration required to review and reach a decision to support an evaluation project or endorse a proposal for external funding are additional costs. In the case of a proposal for external funding there is a factor of uncertainty with regard to the ongoing commitment of resources expected of administration.

As potentially discouraging as the process of preparing and gaining approval for a project proposal or plan can be, though, there are almost always benefits even if the project is ultimately not supported. Thinking about, discussing, and dissecting a problem in the manner necessary for preparing a quality proposal or plan calls attention to the need to think about the problem area or conceptual question that underlies the proposal. Detailing the resources necessary for carrying out the problem focuses attention on existing resource allocation and the ways in which the problem impinges on deployment of resources. Ultimately, the project proposal or plan is a conscious, structured consideration of a problem or question that has implications for the institution, the profession, or society at large. Focusing attention on the problem or question can add to the knowledge base of the profession or the functional base of the institution even when a decision is made not to pursue the project. When the decision is to approve the project or fund the proposal, the investment of a carefully prepared plan or proposal pays off in the form of an efficiently implemented and effectively monitored project.

 THINK ABOUT IT!

1. Preparing a project proposal or plan requires time and effort and in some ways may delay the initiation of the project. How does the benefit of the proposal or plan balance with the disadvantage of delaying the beginning of the project?

2. How can preparation of an evaluation project plan influence administrative and staff perceptions of the problem area to be evaluated?

3. How does a proposal for a master's thesis or doctoral dissertation differ from a proposal for an evaluation project?

DO IT!

1. Identify a real library and information science problem. Outline a proposal for conducting a research project to address the problem.
2. Identify a real library and information science problem. Outline a plan for conducting an evaluation project to assess the problem in a specific institutional setting.
3. Identify a real library and information science problem for which an evaluation project is appropriate. Prepare a draft budget of the costs to the institution of carrying out the project.
4. Select a research article or evaluation report form the library and information science literature. Create the project plan or proposal that would have preceded the project.

NOTES

1. Derek J. de Solla Price, *Little Science, Big Science* (New York: Columbia University Press, 1963).

2. "Grant Applicants: Program Guidelines," http://www.imls.gov/applicants/schedule_of_completion.aspx (accessed April 8, 2011).

3. "Proposals>Active Verbs," Grant Proposal.com, http://www.grantproposal.com/tips.html (accessed June 3, 2011).

SUGGESTED READINGS

Yvonne L. Bui, *How to Write a Master's Thesis* (Thousand Oaks, CA: Sage, 2009).

Raymond L. Calabrese, *The Dissertation Desk Reference: The Doctoral Student's Manual to Writing the Dissertation* (Lanham, MD: Rowman and Littlefield Education, 2009).

David R. Krathwohl, *How to Prepare a Dissertation Proposal: Suggestions for Students in Education and the Social and Behavioral Sciences* (Syracuse, NY: Syracuse University Press, 2005).

Lawrence F. Locke, Waneen Wyrick Spirduso, and Stephen J. Silverman, *Proposals that Work: A Guide for Planning Dissertations and Grant Proposals*, 5th ed. (Thousand Oaks, CA: Sage, 2007).

Susan Louise Peterson, *The Research Writer's Phrase Book: A Guide to Proposal Writing and Research Phraseology* (San Francisco, CA: International Scholars Publications, 1998).

Elizabeth Thody, *Writing and Presenting Research* (Thousand Oaks, CA: Sage, 2006).

MEASUREMENT, POPULATIONS, SAMPLES, AND SAMPLING

It is much easier to make measurements than to know exactly what you are measuring.

—*Attributed to J. W. N. Sullivan in Robert L. Weber,* More Random Walks in Science, *1982*

The tendency of the casual mind is to pick out or stumble upon a sample which supports or defies its prejudices, and then to make it the representative of a whole class.

—*Walter Lippmann,* Public Opinion, *1929*

In This Chapter

Definitions of measurement

The nature of measurement

Populations, samples, and sampling

MEASUREMENT

Measurement Defined

A typical dictionary definition of measurement is "The action or an act of measuring or calculating a length, quantity, value, etc.," which is not a particularly satisfying definition.[1] The corresponding definition for the verb form of "measure" is "to ascertain or determine (a magnitude or quantity)."[2] The central feature of dictionary definitions of measurement tends to be a nearly complete emphasis on quantification. One of the limiting aspects of the dictionary definition is the need to include "etc." to indicate that the list of qualities to be ascertained is incomplete. Not only is the list incomplete, it cannot be complete—no list of possible measurable characteristics can hope to be exhaustive.

Babbie defined measurement as "deliberate observations of the real world for the purpose of describing objects and events in terms of the attributes composing a variable."[3] In the context of research and evaluation this is both a simpler and a more complete definition than the dictionary definition. It is also more satisfying in that it concentrates attention on the object or event to be observed rather than on the mechanics of observation. A notable feature of Babbie's definition is that it does not directly address numbers in any way. Although measurement does very often take on a quantitative form, measurement can be either quantitative or qualitative. The central and essential element in measurement is the emphasis on understanding the fundamental characteristics or qualities of the object of the observation.

The Nature of Measurement

Description versus Measurement

Description and measurement are very closely related in that both are approaches to summarizing the characteristics of some object of interest. As noted in Chapter 1, "Knowing, Research, and Evaluation," description is a fundamental component of all research and evaluation. In general, though, description tends to be impressionistic and informal. Description in its role in daily life is a tool of conceptualization. It is perfectly possible in a casual conversation to share ideas, concepts, and representations of the real world without any process of ascertaining that images of those ideas, concepts, and representations are accurately shared by all participants in the conversation. The byplay between Sherlock Holmes and Dr. Watson in Conan Doyle's stories is an excellent example of the distinction between observation for purposes of conceptualization and observation as it contributes to Babbie's definition of measurement. Where Watson's descriptions of people, things, and events tended to be vague and based largely on his own personal view of the world, Holmes concentrated on deliberate, objective analysis based on systematic and to some extent scientific examination of the world. Watson's conclusions were arrived out in a primarily deductive manner, but Holmes developed measurements based on inductive analysis. Although measurement can and does contribute to conceptualization and description, measurement adds the elements of system and the deliberate intent of effectively characterizing the object of interest. In many cases, measurement involves the introduction and application of tools other than those of the human senses.

Directly versus Indirectly Measurable Data

The concept of measurement is most readily understood in the context of objects that can be measured directly. Heights, lengths, weights, extents, and any kind of countable unit are directly measurable, assuming some reasonably accurate measurement tool is available. Libraries engage in many kinds of routine direct measurements. Spines of books have historically been measured in centimeters. Door counts, reference question counts, circulation counts, and other simple numeric measures are standard library management and planning tools. Even these apparently obvious measures require definition. Do renewals count as circulations? Does a two-disk CD set count as one circulation or two? How can varying circulation periods be accounted for when comparing circulation among libraries, or even among formats? There is a very direct relationship between such measures and the concepts they represent. As long as these measures are interpreted as being conceptually no more than what they are, they constitute direct counts of library-related activities.

Many interesting and meaningful characteristics are not amenable to direct measurement. Public opinion polls, student evaluations of teacher performance, and many other tools and processes attempt to provide indirect measurements for objects of interest that are conceptually easy to understand but which challenge or defy direct measure. A fundamental challenge in library and information science is the concept of use. The volume, nature, and patterns of use of libraries and information systems are of paramount interest, but are very difficult to assess in a direct manner. Circulation of library materials is surely in some way an indicator of use, but is confounding as a direct measure of use. Has a book that was checked out but never opened while checked out been used? If a book is checked out and read by multiple people, does that constitute one use or many? Must a book, once checked out, be read from beginning to end to constitute use? At best, circulation is an indirect measure of use and may be a very distant measure of use.

The role of measurement, particularly but not exclusively with regard to indirectly measurable data, is that of operationalization. Operationalization is the process of formulating a usable representation of a concept for purposes of measurement. Although circulation is clearly not a direct measure of use, it can be operationalized as an indirect measure of use. Similarly, although circulation counts are at an operational level a direct indicator of circulation desk activity, they are not a perfect representation of the concept of circulation desk activity, which normally includes many kinds of transactions, of which direct circulation of materials is only one.

Qualification versus Quantification: Data Reduction

Qualification and quantification are both manifestations of measurement, with a fundamental distinction that has to do with the application of numeric or quantitative methods. Both qualitative and quantitative methods are tools for exploring and categorizing the fundamental characteristic, attributes, or qualities of phenomena of interest. Both paradigms require the process known as data reduction, in which conceptual information is transformed into operationalized data.

Almost all objects of interest to research or evaluation are too large, too vague, too complex, or too extensive to be observed and understood in their entirety. The role of the investigator is to identify those qualities of the object of interest that will actually be observed. The inevitable counterpart to the process of determining what will be observed is determining what will not be observed. The raw data that define the concept of interest must be reduced to a body of operational data that are capable of being observed. The operational data may be words, phrases, or interpretive notes in a field journal, or may be counts, calculations, or the output of statistical testing.

Manifestations of Measurement

Directly measurable manifestations of data include anything that can be counted or calculated—distances, lengths, heights, thicknesses, weights, durations, extents, variations, and so on—but also include things that can't be counted in the same manner—such as color, gender, race, ethnicity, or country of origin. Indirect measures include attitudes, opinions, beliefs, assessments, projections, and other less tangible objects of interest. Ultimately, although it may seem counterintuitive, anything can be measured in some way of another.

Measurement Scales

There are four standard scales for defining levels of complexity in measurement. Those levels of measurement include nominal, ordinal, interval, and ratio. The distinctions among the four measurement scales are defined by two different fundamental characteristics of measurable variables.

Characteristics of Variables: Quantity within Values and Quantity across Values

Quantity within values addresses the basic questions of "how much?" or "to what extent?" Lengths, heights, weights, durations, and other measures of count or extent, when measured numerically, exhibit the characteristic of measurable quantity differentiations within a single variable. There is a numerically measurable difference between the values of two or more different lengths that can be expressed both absolutely (a publication date of 2004 versus a publication date of 2007) or relatively (a difference of three years) within the basic nature of the variable. The relative difference is a measure of extent: one book is three years newer than the other.

Quantity across values addresses the fundamental and simple question of "how many?" If objects of interest can be divided into categories, it is easy and convenient to count the number of entities in each category. If a library holds 300 titles published by the Great Books Company and 150 published by the Pretty Good Books Company, the number of titles from Great Books is twice the number from Pretty Good Books, but that doesn't mean that Great Books is twice the publisher as Pretty Good Books. The differences in numbers of holdings can be expressed absolutely, but the basic nature of the variable doesn't allow for expression of extent. These two manifestations of quantity define the four levels of measurement. Levels of measurement are summarized in Figure 6.1.

Measurement Scale 1: Nominal

The nominal measurement scale allows for the division of the object of interest into nameable categories. The categories must be mutually exclusive: any given entity cannot fall into more than one category. Quantity is a characteristic across values but is not a characteristic within values. Some obvious examples of nominal level variables are color, gender, type, status, location, or class. Although color-related variables such as hue and saturation are measurable on a numeric scale, named color such as red, blue, green, and yellow are not. Items of differing colors can be grouped, and the numbers of items in each group can be counted, but there is no underlying "colorness" scale that distinguishes among the colors. Figure 6.2 illustrates the nominal level variable *genre* for three categories, mystery, science fiction, and romance. Although there are varying numbers of books in each genre classification,

Scale	Nature	Quantity within Values	Quantity across Values
Nominal	Division into categories	No	Yes
Ordinal	Division into categories + Order across categories	Maybe	Yes
Interval	Division into categories + Order across categories + Equal distances between categories	Yes	Yes
Ratio	Division into categories + Order across categories + Equal distances between categories + True zero	Yes	Yes

Figure 6.1   Measurement scales.

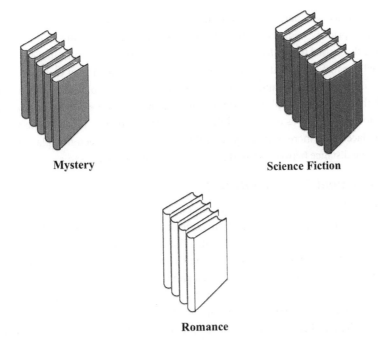

Figure 6.2   Nominal measurement scale.

a manifestation of quantity across values, genre itself is simply a family of categories, not a scale that addresses quantification within categories. The extent to which a romance novel is a romance novel, for instance, is not a factor and isn't even particularly meaningful.

Nominal level variables may be dichotomous or multinomial. Color is a multinomial nominal level variable in which the number of categories is driven by the imagination and the marketers of crayon sets. Genre is a multinomial nominal level variable based on loose standards for classification based on content, subject, or theme. Gender is a dichotomous or binomial variable that is usually allowed to take on one of two values. For some library and publishing purposes, fiction versus nonfiction is a useful dichotomous nominal level variable.

Measurement Scale 2: Ordinal

In addition to division into discrete categories, the ordinal level of measurement adds an element of order among the categories. Any variable that represents a pure order ranking is an ordinal level variable. Educational achievement as measured by completion of diplomas or degrees is an example of an ordinal measurement scale. It is clear that completion of a doctoral degree is a higher level of achievement than completion of a master's degree, which is higher than completion of a bachelor's degree, which is higher than achievement of an associate's degree, which is higher than completion of a high-school diploma. The question that cannot be answered with regard to any of these comparisons is "how much higher?" Because the distances between the different levels of achievement are not equal, there is really no basis for comparison other than the rank order itself. Quantity is a characteristic across values—the numbers of individuals who fall into each category can certainly be counted—and is an implied characteristic within values, but there is no scale for assessing the degree to which quantity is a characteristic within values. Examples of ordinal level characteristics include rank, priority, sequence, and some units of time, such as month of the year. Rating scales such those used in satisfaction studies (1 = very unsatisfied, 2 = unsatisfied, 3 = neither unsatisfied or satisfied, 4 = satisfied, 5 = very satisfied) are ordinal level variables.

Figure 6.3 illustrates the rank variable represented by winners of a book award. Although the book that received first place clearly was judged through some evaluation process to be superior to the second place book and the second place book was judged to be superior to the third place book, there is no suggestion that the distance between first place and second place and the distance between second place and third place are the same.

Measurement Scale 3: Interval

The interval level measurement scale adds equal distances among categories to the division into categories and the ordering of categories, but without a true zero, which is the basic characteristic of the final measurement scale. The most obvious examples of interval level measurement are temperature as measured on the Fahrenheit or Celsius scales. The differences between temperature readings are equal and meaningful, but the zero degree designation for both scales is arbitrary. Quantity is a characteristic both across values and within values. There are few interesting interval level variables related to library and information science or to the social sciences in general. Standardized test scores such as intelligence quotients and academic achievement tests are frequently interpreted as being interval level measures, but even that is subject to interpretation and argument. One of the most frequently used interval level variables is year expressed as a standard number. The difference between the year 2000 and the year 2005 can be conceptualized as being the same as the difference between the year 2005 and the year 2010, but the Gregorian calendar does not have a year zero.

Figure 6.4 shows the mean annual ambient temperatures for three different library collections. The mean ambient temperature for Collection A was 10° higher than that for

Figure 6.3   Ordinal measurement scale.

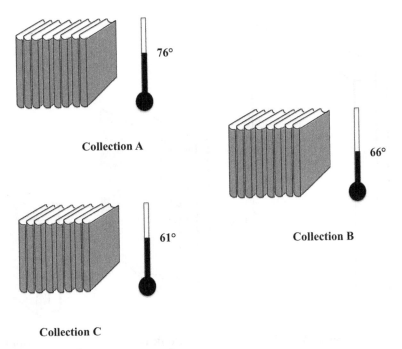

Collection A

Collection B

Collection C

Figure 6.4   Interval measurement scale.

Collection B, which was in turn 5° higher than the mean ambient temperature for Collection C. Although it is accurate to say that the difference in temperatures between Collection A and Collection B was twice the difference between Collection B and Collection C, there is little else to be said other than to comment on the extent to which any of the three collections maintains a mean annual ambient temperature that is within accepted preservation guidelines, which generally recommend a temperature of 65° at 40 percent relative humidity.

Measurement Scale 4: Ratio

The ratio level of measurement is the most complex and in many ways the most interesting of the four measurement scales. In addition to division into discrete categories, order among categories, and equal distances between categories, the ratio measurement scale adds a true zero. A true zero means that an observed value of zero denotes the complete absence of the characteristic of interest. In other words, a value of zero for a particular variable means that the specific observed instance of the object of interest lacks any value for that variable. Quantity for any ratio level variable is a characteristic both across values and within values. Examples of ratio level characteristics include anything that can be interpreted as a measure of degree or extent, including height, depth, width, length, weight, number, and passage of time. Although it is tempting to think that an object that has zero height must not exist, issues of accuracy and calibration allow for at least the possibility that the object exists but that its height cannot be measured using available tools. As a conceptual construct, the presence of any of these characteristics must, due to the existence of a true zero on the measurement scale, allow for the complete absence of the characteristic as well.

Figure 6.5 shows the heights in centimeters of three books. The spine of Book A is 26 cm tall, compared to 19.5 cm for Book B and 13 cm for Book C. Not only is Book A 6.5 cm taller

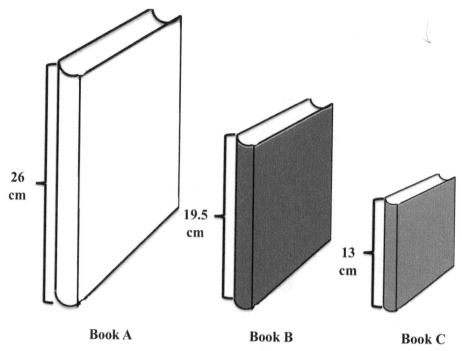

Book A   **Book B**   **Book C**

Figure 6.5 Ratio measurement scale.

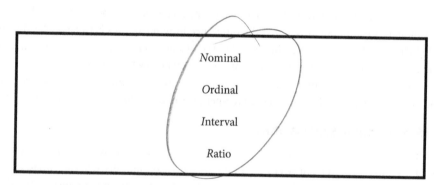

Figure 6.6 The NOIR mnemonic.

than Book B, Book A is one-and-one-third the height of Book B, which means the height of Book B is 75 percent the height of Book A. Book A is twice the height of Book C, which means Book C is half as tall as Book A. The mean (or average) height of the three books is 19.5 cm, which is also the median height (means, medians, and other statistical calculations are discussed Chapter 13, "Descriptive and Inferential Statistics").

NOIR: Nominal, Ordinal, Interval, Ratio

The four measurement scales or levels of measurement can be remembered using the acronym *NOIR*, for *nominal, ordinal, interval,* and *ratio*. The *NOIR* mnemonic is illustrated in Figure 6.6.

MEASUREMENT CONCERNS

Implications of the Four Measurement Scales

The importance of the differing levels of stringency and complexity of the four measurement scales lies in the ability to represent data in a quantitative manner. The differences between categories of a nominal level variable have no quantitative meaning at all, although the numbers of entities in each category can be counted; in many cases, though, such counts add little to understanding of the phenomenon of interest. The differences between categories of an ordinal level variable rarely have true quantitative meaning. More quantitative analysis can be done with interval level data than with nominal or ordinal level data, but it is only with ratio level data that truly sophisticated quantitative analysis can be done. This is a function of the inclusion of a true zero. Only with a true zero is it possible to make really meaningful comparisons. The value of the year 2000, an interval level measure, is not by any means twice the value of the year 1000, and there is no possible meaning to be derived from calculating an average for a set of discrete years. As a measure of the passage of time, however, a value of 2,000 years is indeed twice a value of 1,000 years, and an average elapsed time or time difference is quite meaningful.

Discrete versus Continuous Measures

The implications of the four measurement scales are in part a function of the distinction between discrete and continuous measures. Discrete measures can be equated to integers; the measure can be used to count objects, but cannot be used to draw precise comparisons at a fine level. The number of values possible may be very large, but is finite. The precision of the measure is not dependent on calibration. Continuous measures are those that, at least theoretically, can be measured with an infinite level of precision; the degree of precision that can actually be achieved is a function of the nature of the instrument and its calibration. The number of values is theoretically infinite. Ratio scale variables are inherently continuous variables in that, at least conceptually, the precision of measurement is entirely a function of the accuracy of available measurement tools. The essential characteristic of a measurement of length, such as inches, is a matter of how finely the measurement can be made. All measures of central tendency and dispersion can be used with ratio level variables (central tendency and dispersion are discussed in Chapter 12, "Data Analysis and Presentation"). Nominal and ordinal scale variables are inherently discrete variables—the categories are not separated by intervening steps or stages with quantitative meaning. The only measure of centrality that can be ascribed to a discrete variable is the mode, the most frequently occurring value; measures of dispersion are meaningless for discrete variables. Interval scale variables are a hybrid—although an interval scale variable lacks a true zero, the presence of equal intervals allows for some opportunity to assign limited characteristics of ratio scale measurement to interval scale variables. The mode and median (the central point of a distribution of values), for instance, can be used as measures of centrality for interval scale variables, but the mean (also known informally as the average), which measures distance from zero, cannot. Measures of centrality are explored in detail in Chapter 13, "Descriptive and Inferential Statistics."

Calibration

The recordable values of any variable are a function of the extent to which the variables characteristics can be accurately and precisely defined and observed. Calibration is dependent on the ability of the observer to define and record the observable characteristics of the phenomenon of interest. Even variables that seem relatively simple can be complex. Assigning a color category to a collection of objects such as the covers of books may seem very straightforward, but the Pantone color-coding scheme, which is widely used in graphics and fashion design, includes thousands of color categories. The number of questions fielded at a reference desk can be measured by the month, by the week, by the hour, or even conceivably by the minute.

Calibration then, is in part a matter of the availability of measurement tools and in part a matter of decisions made regarding the use of tools. Although the Pantone scheme allows for thousands of color specifications, a study of library patrons' opinions or perceptions of the use of color in a library logo probably doesn't demand that level of precision. Measuring reference question volume by hour may assist in decisions related to reference desk staffing, but measuring at the level of questions per minute is unlikely to be useful in staffing and may result in the record-keeping process becoming an intrusion into the reference process.

Measurement Scales and Deception: A Caveat

When the measurement scale fails to accurately reflect the phenomenon being measured, or inappropriate tools are used for analyzing the results of measurement, or the concerns or discrete versus continuous measurement or calibration are not adequately addressed, there is the potential for deceptive results and conclusions and inappropriate decisions and actions. Such deception is frequently not intentional, but the impact is much the same whether the intent was to deceive or the research or evaluator simply made a major mistake. Figure 6.7 introduces a recurring feature of this book. The "How to Lie" comments included in this

---

1. Choose an inappropriate measurement scale. Heights, weights, distances, and other characteristics that are inherently ratio-level measures can be easily expressed as low, medium, and high, but an actual ratio measurement is more appropriate.

2. Treat nominal level measures as if they have numeric meaning. In a typical rating scale, based on categories such as 1 = strongly agree, 2 = agree, 3 = neutral, 4 = disagree, 5 = strongly disagree, the numbers are merely placeholders for the textual statements of agreement or disagreement. Although it is easy to base mathematical calculations on the numeric placeholders, doing so doesn't give them real numeric meaning. In this case, the placement of 1 as high and 5 as low makes any such calculation particularly suspect.

3. Use overly lax or overly precise calibration. A scale for reporting respondent ages based on the system "20 or younger, 20–30, 30–40, 40–50, 50 or older" combines overlapping categories with uneven ranges. A scale that reports respondent ages to the nearest day rather than the commonly used year is overly discriminating and implies a false level of precision.

Figure 6.7 How to lie with measurement scales.

book are an homage to Darrell Huff's *How to Lie With Statistics* (New York: W. W. Norton), first published in 1954 and continuously in print since. "How to Lie" is not intended as a proactive guide to dishonest behavior, but as a set of considerations for reviewing the appropriateness of research and evaluation decisions and designs. The intent behind inappropriate decisions and designs is rarely deliberate deception, but the impact of poor analysis may be much the same as conscious dishonesty. The "How to Lie" boxes provide selected examples and should not be interpreted as comprehensive lists of the caveats that apply to research and evaluation.

POPULATIONS, SAMPLES, AND SAMPLING

Population

A fundamental early step in any research project is identification of the population of interest and selection of a subgroup—a sample—that will be used to represent that population for purposes of the study.

A population is all those entities (persons, organizations, things, events, etc.) that are the focus of interest of the research or evaluation study. The population is defined by the research question and/or hypothesis. The emphasis on the word *all* is critical. If the study is to address the impact of the Accelerated Reader program on elective school library media center use by middle school students enrolled in public schools, the population is by definition all middle school students enrolled in all public schools everywhere. In an ideal situation, the study will be designed to reach that broad population and data will be gathered regarding the impact of the Accelerated Reader program on school library media use among that population. Some members of the population will automatically drop out as a result of having no exposure to the Accelerated Reader program, reducing the volume of data to be gathered. More problematically, many members of the population will simply not be reachable within the scope of limited time and a reasonable budget.

For some research or evaluation projects, particularly those conducted exclusively as a guide to local action, the population may be defined more narrowly. A study conducted to determine whether Accelerated Reader will have an impact on elective school library media center use by middle school students in a particular public school district, for instance, effectively narrows the definition of the population. It is essential to understand, however, that narrowing the definition of the population also narrows the implications of the study. The school district may be able to make some effective internal decisions, but limits its opportunity to present its actions as a model for other districts.

Census

A descriptive study of an entire population is a census. There are some circumstances under which conducting a census is desirable or even necessary. The U.S. Decennial Census of Populations is mandated under Article I, section 2 of the Constitution, which establishes an "enumeration" of the population as the basis for apportioning seats in the House of Representatives. Efforts to alter the definition of enumeration to allow for some approach other than a census have been introduced for many decades, but have consistently failed to gain Congressional approval.

The federal government, most state library agencies, and some professional associations conduct periodic censuses of libraries, their resources, and their activities. The Institute of

Museum and Library Services (IMLS) administers the annual Public Library Survey and State Library Agency Survey, which were overseen by the National Center for Education Statistics (NCES) from 1989 through 2007. NCES continues to administer the annual Academic Libraries Survey and School Library Media Center Survey. The Association of Research Libraries (ARL) publishes an annual compilation of census data regarding its member libraries. The Association for Library and Information Science Education (ALISE) conducts an annual census characterizing schools that offer professional education in the field.

These activities document the importance of and viability of a census as an approach to gathering fundamental data, many of which are very directly usable in research and evaluation activities. As a research or evaluation tool, however, a census tends to present problems. A census of any large population tends to be complex, time consuming, and costly. State and federal censuses are made possible via the resources of governmental budgets. Furthermore, many of those censuses are mandated by the government agencies that sponsor them. When the population is small, a census is easier to conduct and a logical choice for gathering data: the Association of Research Libraries has 123 members; the Association for Library and Information Science Education has 58 member institutions. When the study takes place at the level of a single library, a census may be possible, but still may not be the best approach to data gathering.

Ultimately, the investment in conducting a census is justified only when there is a compelling reason to study the entire population. Such compelling reasons rarely occur, meaning that it is almost always more appropriate to choose an alternative to a census.

Sample

The alternative to studying an entire population is studying a carefully identified *sample* that is representative of the population. A sample is a subset of a population selected to represent that population for purposes of a particular research or evaluation project. The sample in and of itself is of absolutely no interest and is not the focus of the research or evaluation project. A sample is a tool for understanding the population; the population is the true focus of research or evaluation activity.

Survey

A survey is a descriptive study of a sample conducted as an approach to understanding the qualities of a population. This is a correct technical definition, but the term survey is actually quite ambiguous and is used in many other ways both in research and evaluation and in general parlance. It is important to understand the technical definition as a means of distinguishing a survey from a census.

Sampling Frame

A sampling frame is a source of information about a population used to make it possible to select a sample. The simplest approach to selecting a sample from any population is to list the members of the population and then determine an approach to selecting members of the population for inclusion in the sample. Many populations, however, have very fluid memberships, which can complicate identification of a representative sample. A list of middle school students enrolled in a specific school district at the beginning of the academic year, for instance, is likely to be an inaccurate indicator of the identities of the students enrolled at the end of the first quarter. Some populations are easily defined in conceptual terms but are difficult to enumerate. How, for instance, can a researcher go about generating a list of all middle school students enrolled in all public school districts in the United States?

A sampling frame, then, is a representation of the population of interest that is suitably comprehensive to be useful as a source for selecting a sample. This is almost always a matter of compromise and requires understanding that many sampling frames are inherently imperfect representations of their corresponding populations.

Certain commonly used sampling frames have recently fallen into question. Telephone surveys of all kinds, for instance, were historically based first on printed telephone directories and later on automated telephone listings. These listings are based almost entirely on the voluntary inclusion of subscriber information in directories of conventional line-based telephone services. For many years, the demographics of telephone subscribers were extremely well understood, allowing for very sophisticated approaches to reaching potential survey respondents. As an increasing number of individuals and even businesses are abandoning traditional telephone services in favor of wireless-only services, those listings are potentially increasingly flawed. Wireless subscribers additionally have a greater tendency than traditional subscribers to be protective with regard to listings of their numbers. At present, neither the demographics of subscribers who continue to maintain landlines nor of those who choose wireless only are adequately understood.

In public library environments, registration records are frequently used as sampling frames. Not all libraries, however, have active policies or effective procedures for updating registration roles. Registered public library patrons are unlikely to actively notify the library when they move away from the community. That and other factors can result in registration roles including names of individuals who are no longer members of the population. Furthermore, most public libraries have regular, dedicated patrons who for whatever reason do not choose to register and limit their use of the library to those materials and services that are available on the premises.

It should be noted that these difficulties in identifying a source to use as a tool for selecting a sample to represent a population apply equally to identifying a source for conducting a census of the entire population. The key to making effective use of any sampling frame is gaining an understanding of the limitations of the sampling frame and taking those limitations into account during the design and implementation of the research project.

The Purpose of Sampling

Convenience. That's it. The purpose of sampling is convenience. It has no other purpose whatsoever.

Convenience, however, can have a great many dimensions. Saying that the purpose of sampling is convenience does not in any way differentiate convenience from that which is right and proper or that which is desirable. The inconveniences associated with conducting a census rather than a survey are complex and in many cases overwhelming.

Perhaps the most obvious manifestations of convenience in sampling are those having to do with economics—conducting a census of any large population is an expensive undertaking in terms of money, time, effort, or any other economic measure. A survey of a representative population can obviously be conducted less expensively.

Another economic convenience factor in sampling is avoidance of waste. Large populations tend to be highly redundant. For many research purposes, a census will produce far more data than are actually needed for understanding the population. In such circumstances, the additional resources required to conduct a census rather than a survey are effectively wasted.

A third convenience factor in sampling is reduction of error. A simple rule for any project involving gathering data is that the greater the scope of the data gathering effort, the greater will be the volume of error in data gathering. An advantage of studying a sample rather than a population is that effort that will otherwise go into the processes of gathering data can be shifted to controlling the quality of the data that are gathered. One of the arguments presented in favor of using sampling rather than a true census approach for the Decennial Census of Populations is improvement of the quality of the data gathered.

A fourth convenience factor in sampling is simplified data handling. Data don't create themselves and, once created, are not self-regulating. Any research or evaluation project requires some approach to soliciting data, gathering data, storing data, cleaning data, and generating output. As the scope of the data-gathering effort increases, so does the scope of the data-handling effort. A smaller body of data is easier to manage, consumes less space, and is frequently easier to describe and understand.

A fifth convenience factor has to do with timeliness. Larger bodies of data take longer to collect, process, and analyze than smaller bodies of data. Most critically, the larger the body of data to be gathered, the longer it will be from initial data gathering to the generation of a final report. Particularly when the research or evaluation effort is action oriented, any delay in reaching the reporting stage is a potential delay in taking appropriate action or avoiding inappropriate action.

A final but far from negligible convenience advantage of sampling has to do with analysis. Smaller bodies of data are fundamentally easier to analyze. More importantly, many statistical analysis procedures are predicated on the principle that the data being analyzed are drawn from a sample and are being used to draw inferences about the nature of a corresponding population (inference in research is just that—the use of data gathered from a sample to draw conclusions about a population). The range of statistical tools designed for describing populations is narrow and restricted. Some statistical tools are extremely sensitive to large bodies of data and become useless when the size of the dataset is too large. Overall, statistical analysis rarely benefits from overly large bodies of data and in many cases a large body of data does more to make analysis difficult than to add precision to understanding of the population.

Sampling

Sampling and Sample Quality

Sampling is the process of extracting a representative sample from a population of interest. Sample quality is fundamentally and entirely an indicator of the extent to which a sample is truly representative of a population. The central guiding factor in designing a sampling process is determining that the sample is sufficiently representative of the population to be useful as the foundation on which to build a research project. The greatest sampling-related danger to research validity is a sample for which representativeness of the population is not known or is misestimated. Ultimately, if the quality of the sample is not adequately established, there is no basis for establishing the validity of results.

Sample Size

One of the components of sample size that frequently seems mysterious to the uninitiated is the process of determining the necessary size of a sample. Three basic factors influence sample size:

Population Size

Reasonably enough, the size of the population plays a role in determining the size of a sample capable of adequately representing the population. That role is not as great as most people unfamiliar with the techniques of sampling for research and evaluation purposes tend to expect. Although a larger population may require a larger sample, it is not necessarily the case that it will. The relationship between population size and sample size is not direct and is greatly influenced by population homogeneity.

Population Homogeneity

Homogeneity is a measure of how similar the members of a population are. Homogeneity is to a considerable extent a more important factor in determining sample size than is population size. Homogeneity is typically represented by its opposite, which is variability. Variability can conceptually be viewed as a value between 0 and 1, where 0 represents complete population homogeneity (no variability) and 1 represents complete population heterogeneity (total variability).

Imagine a population whose members, for some trait absolutely critical to the research interest at hand, share no commonality at all—variability is 1. How many members of that population need to be studied to achieve a fully representative sample with regard to understanding that trait? The answer is that no sample can be truly representative; if variability is absolute, nothing short of a census will yield completely accurate results.

Imagine a population whose members, for some trait absolutely critical to the research interest at hand, are completely alike with no variation at all—variability is 0. How many members of that population need to be studied to achieve a fully representative sample with regard to understanding that trait? In this case, when there is no variability, any one member of the population constitutes a valid sample.

Both of these scenarios are, of course, extremely unlikely. Absolute heterogeneity and absolute homogeneity are unusual circumstances for any quality of a population of interest, and neither situation is likely to constitute an interesting target for research or evaluation.

In the first case, that in which variability is 1, there is no possible sample that can be truly representative of the population, and even if data are gathered for the entire population, there is nothing that can be done to summarize the population with regard to the specified trait. The only way to present data related to that trait is to list all the individual, nonoverlapping characteristics of the population.

In the second case, that in which variability is 0, there is no need to study more than one member of the population. If all members of the population are truly identical with regard to that trait, studying one will substitute for studying all. What can be said about the population with regard to that trait, though, is extremely limited, since there is no variability.

The reality is that population variability for any trait truly of interest will lie somewhere between 0 and 1 and is a factor that can be determined or at least estimated for purposes of determining an appropriate sample size.

Economics

In nearly any research project, a factor that will inevitably emerge as an influence in determining sample size is economics. Few research or evaluation projects operate in an environment of limitless funding, personnel, time, or other resources. One of the decisions an investigator frequently has to make has to do with determining what can actually be done within the limits of available resources, understanding that more could be done with more resources. This is not an invitation to compromise sample quality—it is instead an imperative to include an understanding of resources in the earliest stages of the project design and to design the study such that scaling down the entire project doesn't take precedence over ensuring project quality. The best-designed research study, if compromised by a sample of inadequate quality, will fail to yield valid and reliable results.

Approaches to Determining Sample Size

Five basic approaches to determining sample size are presented here, but there are many more. The first four presented here are essentially computational; the fifth is logical and pragmatic.

1. Statistical. Most statistical approaches are in some way based on calculating the standard error of the mean for a critical trait that will be used to determine sample size. The formula for the standard error of the mean is:

$$SE_{\bar{x}} = \frac{s}{\sqrt{n}}$$

    where s is the sample standard deviation, an indication of the variability of the sample data (the nature and calculation of the standard deviation are addressed in Chapter 13, "Descriptive and Inferential Statistics") and n is the sample size.

    Solving for n based on an observed or estimated value of s yields the necessary sample size. Note that the size of the population doesn't enter into this simplest form of the standard error of the mean, although it does enter into more sophisticated versions.

2. Sample size calculators. Many free sample size calculators are available on the World Wide Web. Most interactive sample size calculators are based directly on solving for n in the formula for the standard error of the mean. The Social Psychology Network maintains a list of sample size calculators.[4]

3. Standard tables. There are many sources of standard tables for determining sample sizes. These are precalculated tools based on solving for n in the formula for the standard error of the mean. The table presented in Figure 6.8 is based on 50 percent variabil-

If the population size is:	Then the sample size should be:
10	10
15	14
20	19
50	44
75	63
100	80
200	132
500	217
1,000	278
5,000	357
10,000	385
25,000	394
50,000	397
100,000	398

Figure 6.8   Sample size table.

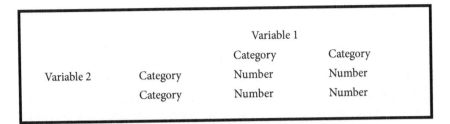

Figure 6.9   Contingency table model.

ity, meaning that the population is estimated to be about halfway between completely heterogeneous and completely homogeneous, and a 95 percent level of confidence in the adequacy of the sample. Note that there is little advantage in sampling for small populations, but as the population grows larger, there is a substantial advantage.

4. Cell size. Some statistical tests require that, when two variables are being related to each other, as in the table below, the numbers in the cells that represent the categories of one variable and those that represent the categories of the other variable not fall below an allowable minimum. One approach to selecting a sample when it is known that such tests will be used focuses on ensuring that each cell in the table (known as a contingency table) has at least the allowable minimum number of observations. A contingency table model is presented in Figure 6.9. A caveat related to this approach to sample selection is that some of the same statistical tests are void if the numbers of observations in the cells are too large.

5. Examination of similar studies. A less precise but sometimes useful approach to determining a sample size is to look for other studies that have addressed questions similar to that of the project at hand in similar population environments and adapt the process of selecting a sample used in one or more of those studies. The potential problem with this approach is that it is necessary to have some reason for believing that the researchers conducting the previous study or studies did things correctly.

Nonprobability Samples

Sampling techniques fall into two basic categories: probability samples, in which the probability of any member of the population being included in the sample is a factor, and nonprobability samples, in which the probability of any given member of the population being included in the sample is irrelevant. Nonprobability samples are potentially easier to conceptualize and work with and will be discussed first.

1. Accidental/convenience sample. This is a particularly easy and commonly used approach to sampling in which members of the population are selected because they are readily or easily available. One of the most frequent applications of the convenience sampling approach involves the selection of students as subjects based on enrollment in a course. The problem with any convenience sample is that there is no meaningful basis for determining the extent to which the sample is representative of the population. It may be possible to draw some inferences about representativeness by comparing known data about the sample, such as standardized test scores, to known data about the population, but in practice that is rarely done. It is more typically the case that the researcher simply assumes that the sample is representative of the population, an assumption that is frequently not justified. Students in freshman college psychology courses really cannot be

reasonably assumed to be typical of the population of the United States, or even of those members of the population within certain age parameters, but they are among the most prominent subjects in psychological research. Similarly, library and information science students are frequently involved in research projects such as "secret shopper" unobtrusive studies, but library and information science students are not typical library patrons.

2. Quota sample. In quota sampling, subcategories within the population are identified and subsample sizes determined. Data are then gathered until each subsample size has been reached. To a considerable extent, each subsample constitutes a convenience sample in which some key characteristic of the population has been used to identify subsample members, but overall representativeness remains unknown. This approach is very commonly used in product and marketing research, in which subcategories represent demographic characteristics, and subsample data are gathered sequentially until the subsamples are filled. If you've ever wondered why you were approached by a product researcher or marketer while walking through a shopping mall while people around you were not, it is probably because you were an apparent match for an unfilled subsample.

3. Saturation sample. Saturation sampling is a form of theoretical sampling frequently used in qualitative research and sometimes in quantitative research. Theoretical sampling is an approach to data gathering in which the nature of the sample emerges as data are gathered rather than being predetermined prior to data gathering. In saturation sampling, subcategories within the population are identified in the same manner as in quota sampling. Data are gathered until each subsample is determined to have been saturated, meaning that no new data are being gathered that are not already represented in the subsample. Saturation sampling has rarely been used in evaluation, but may have some applicability for evaluation purposes.

4. Purposive sample. In purposive sampling, members are selected from the population to serve some specific, presumably logical purpose. A study designed to solicit the views of library leaders regarding the future of libraries and librarianship, for instance, might identify the elected officers of national and state library associations as being a sample of individuals who should be in a position to be aware of trends, issues, and emerging concerns. An evaluation project focused on the views of community leaders toward a public library might focus on the opinions of elected and appointed officials, board members, and the officers of prominent community organizations.

Probability Samples

Probability sampling is based on the principle that, if the distribution of an overall population is reasonably well understood, it is possible to select a sample systematically from that population based on the probability that any given member of the population will be identified as a member of the sample.

1. Random sample. In random sampling, selection is by chance; each member of the population has a known (but not necessarily equal) probability of being included in the sample. That probability becomes the basis on which membership in the sample is determined.

2. Simple random sample. The most straightforward category of random sample is a simple random sample. For a simple random sample, selection is by chance and each member of the population has a known, equal probability of being chosen. The procedure for selecting a simple random sample is basically very straightforward:

   a. A sequential number is assigned to each member of the population.

   b. The needed sample size is determined.

c. Random numbers are selected; the number of random numbers needed is equal to the needed sample size.

d. Data are gathered from the sample.

Sources of random numbers. Since random sampling requires selection of random numbers, some source of random numbers is needed. Randomness is not a naturally occurring phenomenon, so some means of producing random numbers is necessary. The following are useful sources of random numbers; note that none of them is truly random, although the Rand Corporation tables are very, very close.

a. Rand Corporation, *A Million Random Digits with 100,000 Normal Deviates* (Glencoe, IL: Free Press, 1955). Rand's *A Million Random Digits* was one of the earliest useful large-scale products of the computer age. Developing the production algorithms for *A Million Random Digits* was a multistage iterative process that required generating tables, testing the tables for randomness, and modifying the algorithms until an acceptable level of randomness had been achieved. One of the tests involved treating five-digit blocks of numbers as if they were cards in a poker deck. Results indicated that the tables are in excess of 90 percent random. A sample section from *A Million Random Digits* is presented in Figure 6.10. The key to *A Million Random Digits* is its simplicity. As long as the researcher makes no effort to subvert the tables, there is no wrong way to use them. The leftmost column is a sequential number that, logically enough, runs from 0 through 99,999. Each line consists of 10 groups of five numbers. Let's say a sample of 278 is needed. A typical use of the tables is to start with the second column of the first line, examine the rightmost three digits of that group, and determine if it is needed. In this case, if the number is 278 or less, it is needed, so the first random number drawn will be 97. The last three digits of the second group are 533, which is too large, so that group is skipped. The next useful

Rand Corporation, *A Million Random Digits with 100,000 Normal Deviates* (Glencoe, IL: Free Press, 1955).

```
00000  10097  32533  76520  13586  34673 54876  80959 09117  39292 74945
00001  37542  04805  64894  74296  24805 24037  20636 10402  00822 91665
00002  08422  68953  19645  09303  23209 02560  15953 34764  35080 33606
00003  99019  02529  09376  70715  38311 31165  88676 74397  04436 27659
00004  12807  99970  80157  36147  64032 36653  98951 16877  12171 76833

00005  66065  74717  34072 76850  36697 36170  65813 39885  11199 29170
00006  31060  10805  45571 82406  35303 42614  86799 07439  23403 09732
00007  85269  77602  02051 65692  68665 74818  73053 85247  18623 88579
00008  63573  32135  05325 47048  90553 57548  28468 28709  83491 25624
00009  73796  45753  03529 64778  35808 34282  60935 20344  35273 88435

00010  98520  17767  14905 68607  22109 40558  60970 93433  50500 73998
00011  11805  05431  39808 27732  50725 68248  29405 24201  52775 67851
00012  83452  99634  06288 98083  13746 70078  18475 40610  68711 77817
00013  88685  40200  86507 58401  36766 67951  90364 76493  29609 11062
```

Figure 6.10   Table of random digits.

number is 117, which is found in the eighth group. In most, but not all research, once a number has been selected that number is no longer available for selection.

b. Specialized software. There are a number of free random number generators available on the World Wide Web. These tend not to be as random as the Rand tables. An example is the Research Randomizer sponsored by the Social Psychology Network.

c. Productivity software. Many standard productivity software suites offer tools for generating random numbers. For example, the Microsoft Excel Analysis ToolPak is an add-on packaged with but not automatically enabled in every version of the Microsoft Office Suite. The ToolPak includes a number of numerical analysis tools, including a simple random number generator.

d. Statistical software. Most specialized statistical software packages, such as the Statistical Package for the Social Sciences (SPSS), the Statistical Analysis System (SAS), StatPac, and Statistica include random number generators.

e. Telephone directories. In a pinch, the white pages from a large metropolitan telephone directory can be used in same manner as the Rand tables. It is generally necessary to discard prefixes and work only with the final four digits of the telephone numbers.

3. Systematic sample. For some populations, assigning numbers to the members of the population is difficult or even impossible. A systematic sample is an alternative to random sampling that doesn't require explicit assignment of numbers to the population, although it does require some useful sampling frame as a listing of the population and knowledge of the number of entities in the listing.

The formula for a systematic sample is:

$$I = N/n$$

where I is the interval; N the size of sampling frame; and n is the size of desired sample.

Beginning with the first entry in the sampling frame, every Ith member of the population is selected for inclusion in the sample. This will work as long as there is no systematic organization of the listing that undermines the process. Imagine for instance, what would happen if the listing identifies male–female couples, with the male always listed first. What will happen if the interval is an even number? An alphabetical listing is normally not a problem, although in some cases in can be.

4. Stratified sample. Stratified random sampling is a variation in which subcategories within the population are identified and subsamples are drawn randomly from within the subcategories. Stratified sampling is an appropriate tool when there is a naturally occurring structure to the population that is suggestive of the need for representation across subcategories that cannot be ensured using simple random sampling. Imagine, for instance, a study of the public libraries in a given state designed to address the core question "what services are provided by typical public libraries in the state?" It is desirable to ensure that all sizes of public libraries are properly represented and a standardized categorization of population groups already exists. A simple random sample is likely to overrepresent libraries from groups that have substantial numbers of members and underrepresent those groups that have few members. A majority of libraries fall into the 1,000–2,499, 2,500–4,999, 5,000–9,999, and 10,000–24,999 population groups and could be expected to dominate a simple random sample. A possible solution is a stratified random sample. A stratified random sample is shown in Figure 6.11.

5. Proportional sample. In a proportional random sample, subcategories within the population are identified and subsamples are drawn randomly from within the subcategories to reflect the proportional representation of subcategories within the population.

Population Group	Number of Libraries	Number of Libraries in Sample
Fewer than 1,000	993	44
1,000–2,499	1,644	73
2,500–4,999	1,339	60
5,000–9,999	1,508	67
10,000–24,999	1,657	74
25,000–49,999	863	38
50,000–99,999	509	23
100,000–249,999	306	14
250,000–499,999	92	4
500,000–999,999	50	2
1,000,000 or more	20	1
Total	8,981	400

Figure 6.11 Stratified random sample.

Population Group	Population Served	Number of Libraries in Sample
Fewer than 1,000	496,500	1
1,000–2,499	2,464,356	5
2,500–4,999	3,346,161	7
5,000–9,999	7,538,492	16
10,000–24,999	24,853,343	53
25,000–49,999	21,574,137	46
50,000–99,999	25,449,491	54
100,000–249,999	45,899,694	97
250,000–499,999	22,999,908	49
500,000–999,999	24,999,950	53
1,000,000 or more	80,000,000	20
Total	259,622,032	401

Figure 6.12 Proportional random sample.

1. Identify a population that isn't really a population. Although the service base of a particular library is an appropriate population for an evaluation study, the population for a research study is generally a much more broadly conceived entity. Even for an evaluation study, the members of the service base who actually make use of the library may be a questionable definition of a population.

2. Don't report the method that was used to select a sample. Simply stating that a sample of x size was selected from a population of y size doesn't provide enough information about the nature of the sample.

3. Select an inappropriate sample size. Although a larger sample may seem to be inherently better than a smaller sample, an excessive sample size is at best wasteful and at worst has the potential for skewing the results of statistical analyses.

Figure 6.13 How to lie with populations and samples.   (*Continued*)

4. Don't report the response rate. Some methods, such as questionnaires, rarely yield a perfect response rate. The quality of the data gathered can only be understood within the context of not only the desired sample size but also the actual rate of response.

5. Randomly sample from a sampling frame that doesn't ensure equal representation of all members of the population. Published telephone directories were once a standard and reliable sampling frame, but the increasing number of people who have only wireless phones places the continuing usability of telephone directories as sampling frames in serious question.

Figure 6.13   (*Cont.*)

Imagine this time a study of the public library patrons in a given state designed to address the core question "what services are received by the typical public library patron in the state?" Although the typical library in the above example serves a population of between 1,000 and 24,999, the typical patron is served by a library serving a population of 100,000 or more. A proportional sample deliberately emphasizes the distribution of the population of the state rather than the distribution of public libraries in the state. A proportional sample is shown in Figure 6.12.

MEASUREMENT, POPULATIONS, SAMPLES, AND SAMPLING

Measurement, populations, samples, and sampling are the fundamental building blocks of research and evaluation. No meaningful assessment can be conducted if measures are not chosen and applied appropriately and accurately. Understanding the nature of the population to be studied and effectively distinguishing between the population and sample are essential to communicating the nature and meaningfulness of any research or evaluation project. The investigator must be able to explain to the audiences for results and conclusions the ways in which a sample was drawn from its population and instill confidence that the sample is truly and appropriately representative. In the absence of adequate attention to the nature of measurement, population definition, and sampling, none of the methods or tools presented in subsequent chapters of this book are of any meaningful value.

 THINK ABOUT IT!

1. How can use of a library or information center be measured? What are the challenges of measuring use?
2. What are the challenges of random sampling for a local evaluation project?
3. How might the results of simple random sampling differ from the results of systematic sampling?

DO IT!

1. Identify a real phenomenon of interest to library and information science. How does describing that phenomenon differ from measuring it?
2. Identify five possible measures for a real phenomenon of interest to library and information science.
3. Identify a real library and information science problem. What is the population to be studied? How can a sample be selected that will effectively represent the population?
4. Select a published research or evaluation report. Identify the population and the sample. Does the sample seem representative of the population? Is the sampling technique clearly described and explained? How do the description of sampling and the sample chosen affect your confidence in the results?

NOTES

1. *Oxford English Dictionary.*, s.v. "Measurement."
2. Ibid., s.v. "Measure."
3. Earl Babbie, *The Practice of Social Research*, 12th ed. (Belmont, CA: Cengage, 2010), 125.
4. Social Psychology Network. http://www.socialpsychology.org/ (accessed February, 2011).

SUGGESTED READINGS

Paul P. Biemer and Lars E. Lyberg, *Introduction to Survey Quality* (Hoboken, NJ: Wiley, 2003).

Bert R. Boyce, Charles T. Meadow, and Donald H. Kraft, *Measurement in Information Science* (San Diego, CA: Academic Press, 1994).

Patrick Dattalo, *Strategies to Approximate Random Sampling and Assignment* (New York: Oxford University Press, 2010).

Jeffrey M. Edwardy and Jeffrey S. Pontius, "Monitoring Book Reshelving in Libraries Using Statistical Sampling and Control Charts," *Library Resources & Technical Services* 45, no. 2 (April 2001): 90–94.

A. K. Gupta, *Theory of Survey Sampling* (New York: World Scientific, 2011).

Edward T. O'Neill, Patrick D. McClain, and Brian F. Lavoie, "A Methodology for Sampling the World Wide Web," *Journal of Library Administration* 34, no. 3/4 (2001): 279–71.

Neil J. Salkind, *Tests and Measurement for People Who (Think They) Hate Tests and Measurement* (Thousand Oaks, CA: Sage 2006).

Jean Tague-Sutcliffe, *Measuring Information: An Information Services Perspective* (San Diego, CA: Academic Press, 1995).

7

HISTORICAL METHODS

History. An account, mostly false, of events, mostly unimportant, which are brought about by rulers, mostly knaves, and soldiers, mostly fools.

—Ambrose Bierce, The Devil's Dictionary, *1948*

Past and present are as one.

—John Greenleaf Whittier, "To William Lloyd Garrison," 1879

In This Chapter

Definitions of history

Primary and secondary sources in history

Criteria for assessing historical sources

Approaches to evaluating historical sources

Traditional historical analysis

Less traditional approaches to historical analysis

Interpreting historical data

Research questions and historical research

Concluding a historical research project

Historical methods and evaluation

DEFINITIONS OF HISTORY

The *Oxford English Dictionary* defines history as "A written narrative constituting a continuous methodical record, in order of time, of important or public events, esp. those connected with a particular country, people, individual, etc." or as "That branch of knowledge which deals with past events, as recorded in writings or otherwise ascertained; the formal record of the past, esp. of human affairs or actions; the study of the formation and growth of communities and nations."[1] History can be broadly defined as explanation of the past based on available evidence. The fundamental definitional characteristic of historical research is the focus on the past. Regardless of the purposes, goals, or outcomes of a particular historical exploration, to qualify as history the project must focus not on the present or future but on events that have already occurred. Although there is frequently a pragmatic expectation that a historical study will reveal understanding that can be applied in the present or in the future, history is necessarily about the past and no direct practical outcome or impact is essential to a good historical study. In some ways, the best historical research may be pure historical research in that pure research is relatively free of the bias and desires of applied research.

There is sometimes an emphasis in historical research on establishing an appropriate distance from the events being studied. Although there is and can be no fixed definition of the span of time that must elapse before an event can be studied from a historical point of view, the theme of establishing objectivity by creating a temporal distance between the events and the researcher is common in discussions of historical research. Some researchers and some research methods, however, consciously reject the need for historical distance. Oral history and related approaches to social history require that data be gathered directly from participants in events. This may argue against the need to establish distance in favor of the immediacy of gathering data while those participants are available to provide data.

History can be defined in a number of ways:

1. The word history has its origin in the Greek word *historia*, which is derived from the word *histor*, which can be translated as "one who knows or sees." Historia, then, can be translated as "learning or knowing by inquiry." By extension, historia means any account of natural phenomenon, as in natural history.

2. History frequently refers explicitly to past events related to humanity. This definition allows for the concept of prehistory, which refers to human history from the era before recorded knowledge. This distinguishes history from archaeology, anthropology, and paleontology.

3. History is sometimes understood as referring to a body of ascertained evidence about the past. This interpretation implies that there is a body of fixed truth regarding the past and that the goal of historical research is to uncover that truth. As noted in Chapter 1, "Knowing, Research, and Evaluation," truth is a very ambiguous concept that is subject to interpretation and disagreement, which makes this definition of history questionable.

4. A contrasting definition casts history as a carefully interpreted examination of the past. This interpretation ascribes a more mutable definition to history and implies that the past can be understood only in the context of human interpretation.

5. The view is sometimes presented that history is any research that is not explicitly experimental. This quasi-facetious point of view suggests that description of the present isn't really possible, since the present is very soon the past.

6. Another quasi-facetious definition of history is the activities of people who identify themselves as historians. There is some legitimacy to this definition, particularly as historians have adopted a variety of creative approaches to gathering and analyzing data that transcend the traditional structure of a chronological narrative based largely on primary sources.

7. History can also be understood as the process of gathering and analyzing data regarding the past. This is obviously very close to the previous definition of history as "being what

historians do," but allows for the possibility that historical research may be carried out by individuals other than historians.[2]

PRIMARY VERSUS SECONDARY SOURCES

Historical research, more than any other family of research methodologies, ascribes critical importance to the distinction between primary and secondary sources of data.

A primary source is an account of an event by a witness to the event. There is a fundamental assumption in traditional historical research that the most definitively knowledgeable source of information about any event lies in the memories of those individuals who witnessed the event.

Any source of historical data that is not an account of an event by a witness to an event is a secondary source. The term secondary source is most frequently used to refer to synthetic works, such as reports on previous historical projects based on primary sources.

The distinction between primary and secondary sources is not necessarily fixed or obvious. Traditional approaches to historical research concentrate in great depth and detail on the distinction between primary and secondary sources, with substantial room for debate as to what constitutes a primary source. It seems fairly obvious that an interview conducted by a researcher with a witness to some event is intended to produce primary source data. Do the interviewer's field notes then constitute a primary source? Is there a distinction between the field notes as used by the original researcher and that researcher's field notes used at a later time by a different researcher? Do census records constitute a primary source of historical data? If so, are reports compiled from census records primary sources?

Although these questions and their answers are interesting and informative, the ultimate truth about primary and secondary sources is that the role of any particular source of information is a function of its use in a specific historical project. History textbooks have typically been regarded as no more than secondary source data, and are frequently viewed as being inherently flawed and inferior sources of historical data. A historian exploring the root causes of the persecution of labor organizers in early 20th century California may find a great deal of useful data in published scholarly histories but is unlikely to find published history textbooks of much use at all. A researcher who is exploring the history of the ways in which history has been portrayed in textbooks will necessarily view history textbooks as the central, essential primary source.

GENERAL CRITERIA FOR ASSESSING HISTORICAL SOURCES

Validity and reliability in historical research are very closely intertwined. Primary sources of data cannot be assumed to be either valid or reliable. There are three essential criteria for validity and reliability that must be considered in assigning value to primary sources:

1. The lapse of time between the event and the account. It is generally assumed that an account recorded soon after the event is more reliable than an account recorded at a later time. As the amount of time between the event and the account increases, the potential for error in the account also increases. This may be a function of the natural decay of human memory, personal assessment and interpretation of the event, contamination from exposure to other accounts, contamination from exposure to secondary sources, or any combination of these and other causes. In any case, any substantial

passage of time between the event and the account should be carefully examined and assessed to estimate its impact on the validity of the account. At the other extreme, accounts recorded immediately after the event may be subject to undue influence from emotional, physical, or situational factors, particularly if the event was in any way traumatic for the witness. It may be necessary for some time to pass to allow the witness to assess and organize his or her perceptions of the event.

2. The purpose of the account. There are many reasons for a witness to an event to provide an account of the event. Some people keep regular diaries or journals in which they record all those events that seem meaningful (and maybe even some that don't). There may be something in the nature of the event itself that prompts an individual to describe his or her experience. The event may be recorded as part of an act of communication, such as a letter, between the witness and some other individual. The account may be the result of an interview between the witness and a researcher or between the witness and a news reporter. Understanding the purpose behind the recording of the account provides a historical researcher with an approach to assessing issues of validity, accuracy, completeness, and bias.

3. The confidentiality of the account. It can to some extent be assumed that confidential accounts are likely to be more reliable than accounts recorded in a nonconfidential manner. A diary entry or a letter to a friend is a fundamentally confidential document in which the witness can be expected to make an effort to provide an open and honest account of the event. An interview with a news reporter, even if the witness is promised confidentiality, is likely to be less open.

The sources Young used in his account of American Library Association activities during World War I meet all of these criteria. Internal correspondence among ALA officials, the War Service Committee members, and the Library War Service are contemporaneous with the events, used only for planning and organizational purposes, and written with no anticipation of dissemination beyond the immediate group.[3]

APPROACHES TO EVALUATING HISTORICAL SOURCES

Factors in evaluating and interpreting sources of historical data fall into two major categories: factors that are essentially external to the content of the source and internal factors related directly to the content of the source item. In practice, there is substantial interaction between external and internal factors in evaluating historical sources. Authenticity, for instance, can be evaluated both in terms of a document as a whole and in terms of specific content within the document.

External Factors

1. Authenticity. A key factor in determining the validity of any document is the question of whether the document is in fact *real*. There have been several instances in the past few years of the discovery of documents that, if authentic, would be significant contributions to the body of historical documents but which have proven to be deliberate fakes. The Hitler diaries described in Chapter 3, "Ethics and Politics in Library and Information Science Research and Evaluation," are an example of fakery in historical research.[4] Similarly, there have been instances of accounts that were intended as works of fiction but were interpreted as being historical and factual. Alex Haley's 1976 book *Roots* was originally marketed as a nonfiction work but was later rebranded as a novel.[5]

In some cases, establishing authenticity may require substantial expertise and true forensic examination.

2. Corroboration from other sources. If observations can be corroborated by multiple witnesses, the historical researcher can build a case for validity that is difficult to impeach. This is especially true if the researcher can establish corroboration both from a number of accounts of the same nature and from different kinds of accounts. The reaction of the popular press to an event can be assessed through examination of multiple newspaper articles covering the event. Interviews with participants in the event can be used to explore the extent to which participants agree on their experiences of the event and to determine the ways in which participant accounts corroborate media coverage. Examination of multiple sources of historical data not only builds the case for the reliability of the data but also adds richness to the historical account. In *A Book for a Sixpence*, Kaser examined newspaper and magazine accounts, library catalogs and ledgers, city directories, personal papers, and published memoirs to trace the history of circulating libraries in America. With wit and style, he wove the information and varying perspectives into an engaging narrative of events as well as a logical and compelling argument for his conclusions.[6]

3. Meaning. At the external level, *meaning* has to do with interpretation of the purpose and nature of the source. Apparently similar documents can have very different meanings related to the times or places at which they were produced. The statistical compilations of the Association of Research Libraries and the National Center for Education Statistics (NCES) show noticeable declines over time in circulation and reference transactions in college and university libraries. Given the historical prominence of circulation and reference as indicators of the volume of library use, it is tempting to interpret these declining counts as evidence of the decreased viability of academic libraries. An alternative interpretation is that the nature of use of academic libraries has changed. Although the *ARL Statistics* indicate a 56 percent drop in reference transactions and a 19 percent decline in total circulation between 1991 and 2009, interlibrary borrowing increased 171 percent, the number of participants in group presentations increased 110 percent, and the number of group presentations provided to patrons by library staff rose 73 percent.[7]

Internal Factors

1. Accuracy. Accuracy of the account is an obviously critical factor in evaluating and interpreting historical sources. Establishing accuracy requires some combination of corroboration from other sources and determining that assessment of other factors establishes a high likelihood of accuracy. Accuracy does not have to be absolute for historical research to be valid; there is almost always some element of inaccuracy in any account of a historical event.

2. Witness credibility. Confidence in the honesty and accuracy of an account is increased if the witness is viewed as being credible. The fundamental question to be asked with regard to credibility is "was the witness in a position to provide an accurate account of the event?" Credibility in historical research is conferred primarily by assessment of the potential for providing an accurate account as a result of having had a meaningful relationship to the event of interest. Credibility is not automatically conferred or challenged by superficial factors such as the educational, employment, or socioeconomic status of the witness. There is no obvious reason to believe that an adult is innately more credible than a child or that an administrator is innately more credible than an employee. In all

likelihood, there are some events to which the child or employee is more likely than the adult or administrator to be a credible witness.

3. Witness competence. Competence is closely related to credibility. One of the motives for emphasizing the lapse of time between the event and the account has to do with fears of declining witness competence to remember what actually happened. Where credibility is a matter of whether the witness was in a position to observe and provide an account of the event in question, competence has to do with the witness's ability to understand and interpret the observed event. Even though an individual may have had close contact with the event, if the witness did not have the prior understanding necessary to understand the event, the witness may not be a competent source of data. A student employed as a shelver in a public library may be able to describe a period of time during which a declining number of items was being returned to the shelves but have no understanding that the underlying cause was the introduction of a systematic weeding program.

4. Level of detail. Assessing the meaning of the level of detail provided in an account of an event can be very difficult. Lack of detail may imply a lack of witness credibility but may equally imply that the witness simply was not appreciative of the event at the time it occurred or that the witness is not by nature inclined to observe and remember details. An excess of detail may suggest that the witness has added embroidery to the account by filling in fabricated details.

5. Bias. Bias can be deliberate or wholly unconscious. A fundamental precept with regard to bias in historical research is that individuals' perceptions of events are influenced by their perceptions of and reactions to the environments in which those events occur in addition to their perceptions of and reactions to the specific events. A researcher studying the transition from card catalogs to online catalogs by interviewing librarians who were involved in conversion projects needs to account for those human reactions that may produce either rosy positive accounts of the successes of automation or glowing reminiscences of the wonders of the card catalog.

6. Style. The elements of style imbedded in a historical account can be a source of confusion and misinformation in historical research. Style has to do largely with the context within which the account was produced and may encompass variations attributable to era, geography, understanding and use of language, and discipline or vocation. A witness who left school at age 10 may provide an account that is stylistically very different from that of an account of the same event by a witness who is a psychiatrist. The fundamental evolution of language over time is associated with changes in the style of language that can be especially important in understanding documents produced at different times. The meaning of an apparently simple word or phrase can vary considerably over time. What does it mean when a diary from the year 1877 refers to having traveled by car? Does it have the same meaning as a reference to traveling by car in 1957 or 2007? What sort of lewd behavior is involved in a description of two young people making love on the front porch of a prosperous Indianapolis home in Booth Tarkington's 1916 novel *Seventeen*? These are matters of changes in the use of language over time that must be considered in evaluating and understanding the sources of historical data.

TRADITIONAL HISTORICAL ANALYSIS

A somewhat simplistic description of the end product of a traditional historical analysis is that it is a narrative account

  that begins with a discussion of the data, interpretations, and conclusions presented in
    appropriate secondary sources

  that progresses to the data, interpretations, and conclusions the researcher has drawn from
    primary sources

The use of secondary sources in historical analysis is to some extent similar to the literature review expected of any report on the results of a research or evaluation project. It is different from a literature review in that the role of the analysis of secondary sources for historical research is to raise questions that can be answered through examination and analysis of primary sources. The analysis of secondary sources for a traditional historical analysis requires extensive and intensive examination of the processes, analyses, and conclusions of existing secondary accounts to determine the extent to which they can be considered definitive and exhaustive. When an event has been explored at some length in secondary sources, the focus of the assessment of secondary sources is the identification of unanswered questions for which analysis of primary sources may lead to further understanding of the event.

The emphasis on the historical narrative is frequently viewed as being the defining characteristic of traditional reports of historical project results. The importance of the narrative presentation of results has given historical research a presence in literature that other forms of research cannot begin to match. There are many individuals who choose to read history for personal enlightenment and entertainment purposes. No other approach to research can claim such a popular readership. The potential for reaching a popular audience, combined with other factors such as the level of detail expected in scholarly historical research, has resulted in a distinct emphasis on "The Book" as the preferred format for reports on historical projects. In many academic history departments, success in reaching tenure is closely tied to completion of the book, which is frequently a publishable version of the faculty member's doctoral dissertation.

A historical narrative doesn't have to be presented in a chronological manner, and there is a clear distinction between chronology per se and history. It is difficult, though, to envision a historical narrative in which chronology does not play a role, since history is closely tied to sequences of events. The essential nature of the historical narrative is found not in its structure but in its purpose, which is interpretation of historical events. For instance, Kaser concluded his history by noting that circulating libraries grew and prospered through innovation, offering services for a fee that public libraries would not provide for free, then moving on to new services when public libraries adopted the innovations. He suggested that the commercial services offered today are reflective of "the boundless ingenuity inspired by the profit motive." Alternatively he suggested that the lesson focuses on "the inexorable absorbtive character of library services in a democracy . . . that any service, once its social utility has been proven, must of necessity be made available to all citizens."[8] Construction and presentation of a chronological sequence of events is not historical research or at least is not a very high level of historical research. The fundamental task of the historical researcher, as of any researcher, is determining the meaning of the data, particularly when the researcher's understanding of the meaning of the data differs from the understandings or interpretations of previous researchers. This should not be construed as implying that the historical researcher's role is to prove that his or her interpretation is the right one or is better than those presented by other researchers. A more honest and more direct goal of historical research is to expand the ways in which events can be interpreted and understood.

LESS TRADITIONAL APPROACHES
TO HISTORICAL ANALYSIS

The traditional approach to historical research seems likely to continue to be a significant force in understanding the past. There are many less traditional approaches, a few of which are presented here:

1. Literary analysis is the examination of literature as a source of social history. The basic principle of literary analysis is that the literature, particularly the popular literature, of a historical period can serve as a primary source of data for understanding that period. Cuseo explored the characterization of homosexuality in young adult novels as an approach to understand cultural changes at the midpoint of the 20th century.[9]

2. Image analysis is the examination of imagery and its impact on society, politics, or other factors. The image of the *frontier* has been examined extensively. There have been rather tentative attempts to examine the images of specific societal groups such as librarians. Zboray examined the industrialization of the publishing industry in the antebellum United States and the role print as "the primary avenue of national enculturation" and the image of a homogeneous American culture.[10]

3. Ideological analysis involves tracing an idea through literature. Literary analysis, image analysis, and ideological analysis are very closely linked and are all very closely related to content analysis, which is the search for patterns in recorded information sources. The major distinction between image analysis or ideological analysis and content analysis is that image and ideological analysis usually work within the framework of a predetermined image or idea, where content analysis focuses on identification of themes. Divelko studied the literature on digital reference service models, concluding that librarianship has developed an ideological conflict regarding the relative value of "subject knowledge of a diverse array of topics" and "ready acceptance of any form of technological innovation."[11] He concluded that this conflict had created a "competition to lay claim to the field of reference librarianship."[12]

4. Psychohistory is the use of psychological methods to examine historical events. Psychohistory usually focuses on the states of mind of participants in historical events. Psychohistory is distinct from psychobiography in that psychohistory focuses on psychological methods as an approach to understanding the events, not as an approach to understanding the participants.

5. Quantitative history encompasses a broad array of approaches to examination of numeric evidence related to historical events. Collective biography is a quantitative historical method that focuses on analysis of the demographic characteristics of carefully defined groups. Thomas examined the changing status and roles of African American children's librarians via a collective biography.[13]

INTERPRETING HISTORICAL DATA

As is true of every approach to research, historical research is of use only to the extent that it has been interpreted for use by the researcher. Regardless of the choice of the basic historical approach, the tools used in gathering and analyzing data, the establishment of a valid chronology of events, or the level of detail provided in descriptions of events, a historical project is incomplete if the researcher does not provide an interpretation. The basic question to be answered by the researcher is "what do the data mean?" In historical research, perhaps more than in any other family of research methods, it is especially important to emphasize the mutative and potentially transitory nature of the meaning of the data. The answer to the basic question may take the form of "this is what the data *may* mean."

Bias in Interpretation of Historical Data

Bias on the part of the researcher is a concern in all forms of research. Bias in historical research is of particular concern in that the researcher is frequently drawing interpretations from incomplete or questionable data sources. Some areas in which the researcher should be especially conscious of the potential for bias have to do with basic cultural assumptions, ideology, and historicism.

1. Basic cultural assumptions are those premises that are common to members of a particular culture, society, or societal group. These assumptions vary across time and space, sometimes radically. Very significant variations in basic cultural assumptions may be associated with relatively small variations in time and geography. There can be quite meaningful changes in basic cultural assumptions from one generation to the next. At the same time, the researcher should not assume that the popular view of changes in basic cultural assumptions is inherently accurate. Cultural assumptions cannot be understood in the form of stereotypes or truisms. The researcher's task then, is to explore the basic cultural assumptions of the time and place being studied and incorporate those assumptions into interpretation of data. The researcher must absolutely avoid imposing his or her own basic cultural assumptions as part of interpreting the time and place being studied.

2. Ideology is closely related to basic cultural assumptions but is more closely aligned with formal systems of belief or understanding. The basic concern is the same as that for basic cultural assumptions: any historical period, culture, or group is best understood within the framework to which it belongs historically, not from the point of view of the ideology to which the researcher ascribes. When the researcher's ideology is too prominent, there is the potential for revisionist history, in which the meanings of events are recast to reflect the belief system of the researcher rather than interpreted to reflect the ideology of the time and place that are the subject of the study.

3. Historicism has to do with the researcher's role in assigning current values to historical events. The term is used most frequently in a pejorative sense in that the investigator provides a negative depiction of events and people who have not had the benefit of lessons learned in intervening years to guide their actions. It is, for the most part, perceived as an intellectual exercise in hindsight. One prominent traditional view has been that assignment of values is not a legitimate role for a historical researcher, who is charged with presenting a neutral interpretation of past events. A conflicting view is that the researcher is inherently bound and controlled by his or her personal value system, is incapable of effecting a divorce from that system, and should be open and honest in representing the influence of that value system on the interpretation of results.

The central theme of concern for the role of bias in interpretation of historical research calls for a return to the basic definition of historical research as explanation of the past based on available evidence. When the interpretation presented by the researcher begins to take on elements of definition of the past based on the researcher's preferences, the basic definition has been abandoned and something other than historical research is taking place.

Context in Interpretation of Historical Research

Bias in historical research is essentially a special case of failure to provide proper consideration for the role of context in interpreting historical data. Because historical research has an inextricable link to understanding what actually happened and assessing the implications of what happened, the historical researcher has a somewhat limited ability to define the context to suit the study. This is an extreme contrast to power of the experimental researcher, who has absolute authority to define context.

It is a truism that history cannot be understood out of context. The historical researcher has a special and explicit obligation to explore, understand, and present the context within which the events of his or her study lies and to explain the influence of that context. The confounding factor in approaching the issue of context in historical research is that most historical phenomena exist within multiple contexts, each of which may be vastly complex. Describing and explaining the context of a historical study can be at best daunting and at worst impossible. The solution is careful formulation of a research question.

The articles by Harris and Dain summarized in Figures 7.1 and 7.2 provide an opportunity to explore the roles of context and interpretation in historical analysis.[14] Harris's "revisionist" history of the origin and early years of the Boston Public Library present a view of a small group of elitists who envisioned the public library as a resource for themselves and their peers and as a means of acculturating the working class by instilling elitist values. Ultimately, according to Harris, the emerging library profession became disenchanted with its inability to transform society. Dain examined the same time period, but worked within a broader context that included the establishment of other public libraries, including the New York Public Library, and other types of libraries. Dain's analysis suggests that Harris's sharp focus on the Boston Public Library and its leadership provides too limited a contextual framework for understanding the origins and evolution of public libraries in the United States.

Neither Harris nor Dain can be interpreted as being correct to the exclusion of the validity of the other's argument. The nature of historical interpretation is such that multiple interpretations not only are viable, but are typically considered healthy. No single historical analysis can ever really be considered to be the last word on the topic or event in question. It is through argument, counterargument, contention, and rebuttal that the historical record grows.

RESEARCH QUESTIONS AND HISTORICAL RESEARCH

Every good research or evaluation project has a research question. Historical projects are not an exception. Research projects generally don't begin with research questions. Instead, they begin with vague perceptions of problems to be solved or anomalous interests in broad topical areas. The broad topical area might be "working conditions for women in libraries." As is true of many interesting topical areas, this one could be explored using a large number of methodological approaches, including historical research. So, the broad topical area can be refined as "the history of working conditions for women in libraries." This is sufficiently precise to be understandable, but it fails to set a direction specific enough to guide a research project. *What about* "the history of working conditions for women in libraries?" What aspect of working conditions is of interest? Which women are of interest? Which libraries are of interest? What period of history is of interest? It is doubtful that a single finite study could

Study:	Michael H. Harris, "Purpose of the American Public Library: A Revisionist Interpretation of History," *Library Journal* 98, no. 16 (1973): 2509–14.
Question/Purpose:	The author sets about to question the public library myth and to discover the motives of those who founded, nurtured, and guided the public library movement in this country.
Personnel:	A single researcher
Data Sources:	Primarily secondary sources related to public library history.
Data Gathering:	Library-based research.
Summary:	The author traces the influences of important figures in the founding and development of the Boston Public Library, beginning with Edward Everett and George Ticknor, who are commonly looked upon as the visionaries for the library. The narrative proceeds to the era of the "technicians," who included Boston Public Library director Justin Winsor, William Frederick Poole, and Melvil Dewey. The role of philanthropist Andrew Carnegie in influencing library services to the general public is discussed. The major figures in the early history of the Boston Public Library and the public library movement in the United States are described using terms such as "intellectual class," "elitist," "patrician," and "authoritarian." The author questions the intent of these pioneers with regard to building a library system for the uneducated or undereducated public.
Conclusions:	The author concludes that public library pioneers failed to achieve the purposes they envisioned, which were for the most part far from egalitarian or humanitarian. He describes such pioneers as "beaten and demoralized" bureaucrats who were "convinced that most Americans were unappreciative and unreachable." According to the author, this pattern was not broken until the buildup to World War II and the Western reaction to the Axis Powers' suppression of freedom of information and knowledge. Ultimately, "the public library, conceived as a deterrent to irresponsibility, intemperance, and rampant democracy, and administered in an elitist and authoritarian fashion by librarians and trustees from the middle and upper classes, came in time to be viewed as librarians as a guardian of the people's right to know."

Figure 7.1 From the professional literature—historical method 1

Study:	Phyllis Dain, "Ambivalence and Paradox: The Social Bonds of the Public Library," *Library Journal* 100, no. 3 (1975): 261–66.
Question/Purpose:	The author's intent was to refute Michael H. Harris's "Purpose of the American Public Library: A Revisionist Interpretation of History" (Figure 7.1) by providing a "richer understanding of the course of the American public library."
Personnel:	A single researcher.
Data Sources:	Primarily secondary resources, but with reference to primary resources is cited in Phyllis Dain, *The New York Public Library: A History of Its Founding and Early Years* (New York: New York Public Library, 1972) and George S. Bobinksi, *Carnegie Libraries: Their History and Impact on American Public Library Development* (Chicago: American Library Association, 1969).
Data Gathering:	Library-based research.
Summary:	The author rejects Harris's contention that the historiography of librarianship is characterized by "too many facts and too little interpretation" in favor of the contention "that library history has had too few useful facts as well as too little interpretation and the sparsity of both is interrelated." Dain suggested that Harris's admittedly exploratory essay rested "on incomplete evidence" and was therefore "too emphatic." Dain's analysis emphasizes the range of libraries beyond the Boston Public Library that developed during the second half of the 19th century, including other public libraries, independent libraries such as mercantile libraries, mechanics and apprentices libraries, social libraries, libraries associated with charitable groups, endowed libraries, and others. Many of these libraries had lofty goals regarding the education and "uplifting" of the American public. The author also emphasizes the feminization of libraries in the last part of the 19th century, which Harris apparently overlooked.
Conclusions:	Dain questions Harris's assertion regarding a "crisis of confidence" among public librarians in the early 20th century, citing multiple factors that served both to challenge and strengthen library development. Dain concludes that, "partly by virtue of its own powerlessness and relative insignificance, the library can find room to maneuver, to experiment, to offer the chance for people to get from it the means to power."

Figure 7.2 From the professional literature—historical method 2

address all aspects of working conditions of all women working in all types of libraries in all locations throughout history. The researcher needs to add refinement and definition to achieve a research question that can lead to positive action. Here is one possible set of answers and a resulting research question:

1. aspect of working conditions: opportunities for advancement to managerial or administrative appointments
2. which women: professional librarians
3. which libraries: university libraries in the United States
4. what period of history: post-World War II

Research question: How successful were women professional librarians in advancing to managerial or administrative appointments in U.S. university libraries during the years 1945 to 1955?

There are aspects of this research question that are clearly arbitrary and the research question clearly cannot answer the big question of "what is the history of the working conditions for women in libraries?" It can, however, address a meaningful subset of that question in an achievable manner.

Note that this research question doesn't necessarily lead to any particular approach to gathering data. There is an implication of a quantitative element in the notion of "how successful," which implies assessment of some degree of success. This quantitative aspect could be addressed by searching for documentation of the number of female professional librarians employed during the postwar decade and calculating the percentage who held titles defined for purposes of the study as managerial or administrative. It might then be informative to calculate the same percentage for men and add other quantitative analyses. On the other hand, the researcher might go in a completely different direction and interview women who were employed as professional librarians during that decade to assess their perceptions of opportunities for success in seeking managerial or administrative appointments.

The central element here is defining the research question at a level of detail that makes it possible to understand every essential element of the question and also makes it possible to identify at least one approach to gathering data that will in some useful way provide at least part of the answer to the question.

CONCLUDING A HISTORICAL RESEARCH PROJECT

One of the most difficult aspects of conducting historical research is knowing when to stop. There is always the attractive possibility of turning up some as-yet-unexamined crucial document, arranging an interview with a key witness, or otherwise adding missing data. Anecdotal comments suggest that the failure to complete rate is higher for master's and doctoral students in history than in any other discipline.

There are many factors that assist the historical researcher in bringing the project to a conclusion. Two of the most important are setting and observing realistic deadlines and continuous data analysis.

1. Deadlines are essential to the success of any research project. Deadlines for historical projects tend to be less obvious in origin than deadlines for other types of research because historical research deadlines are less firmly tied to stages of task accomplishment. Historical research tends to take longer than other kinds of research (although it doesn't have to). Since stages of accomplishment may not be self-defining in historical research, it is important for a historical researcher to establish deadlines for completion of secondary source examination, completion of primary source examination, completion of data analysis, and completion of the final report and *stick to them.* A good resource for a historical researcher is someone who can answer the plaint, "I have to have that [document, book, interview, etc.]" by saying "No, you don't."

2. Continuous data analysis is a mechanism for helping determine when the researcher actually does have all the data needed to conduct the analysis and write the report. The traditional approach to data analysis in historical research is to gather all the data and then begin analysis, much as is the norm for descriptive and experimental research. Waiting until all the data are gathered to begin data analysis is an open invitation to keep looking for that one last bit of data. A historical researcher can greatly benefit from the qualitative researcher's approach, which is to continuously review and interpret the data, formulating revised interpretations as necessary. When further analysis of data has ceased to lead to revision of the interpretation of the data, it is time to stop gathering data and proceed to the final analysis and interpretation.

PRESERVING THE HISTORICAL RECORD: PROCEDURAL IMPERATIVES AND ETHICAL CONSIDERATIONS

Preserving the Research Record

Historical research is accompanied by a very special set of procedural and ethical concerns. Ultimately, the validity and reliability of any historical analysis are closely tied to the investigator's ability to document and verify his or her sources. The complex nature of primary and secondary sources for historical projects can make documentation and verification complex and tedious. The risk, however, of being unable to provide the documentary historical record that underlies the analyses can be devastating. In 2001, Michael A. Bellesiles received the prestigious Bancroft Prize for his book *Arming America: The Origins of a National Gun Culture.*[15] The book expanded on an earlier well-received article.[16] The book aroused immediate criticism, in part because of the politically charged nature of the topic of gun control. Much of the work was reportedly based on extensive examination of wills and probate inventories, but Bellesiles was unable to produce his records, citing a flood in his office that had destroyed his apparently rather informal records. Furthermore, it was contended that some of the records he reported having examined had been destroyed in the 1906 San Francisco earthquake and subsequent fire.[17] The Bancroft Prize was rescinded in 2002 and Bellesiles left his faculty position at Emory University. Although Bellesiles never admitted to any wrongdoing and the review panel at Emory didn't directly find him guilty of extensive falsification, the study was called into question and its validity and reliability remain inconclusive.

Ethics and Historical Sources

Many of the primary sources of most interest to historical analyses are generated by acts that are not intended to become part of the historical record. Diaries, journals, and correspondence are usually private communications with no designed public role. When such documents are made public, there is the risk of damage to the reputations of the authors of the documents, the recipients of correspondence, and the families, friends, coworkers, and acquaintances of the authors. The challenge for the historian is to find the appropriate balance of protecting privacy and even intimacy and expanding the historical record. Doing so requires tact and, in some cases, knowing when to consult those close to the author for guidance on what can or cannot be made explicit.

Oral history carries a specific ethical challenge in that the sources of data are known to the researcher through direct, sometimes frequent and intense, contact between the witness and the researcher. K'Meyer and Crothers summarized the obligation of the oral historian: "They must use their skills . . . to create as complete a document as possible, they should confront taboo topics and address them with open dialogue, and, finally, they must interpret the resulting information to the best of their abilities and knowledge."[18]

HISTORICAL METHODS AND EVALUATION

The preceding discussion of historical methods may give the impression that history plays no role in evaluation, but nothing could be further from the truth. Historical methods are among the most ingrained of evaluation tools in library and information science. The dominant form of numeric evaluation in libraries and many other information environments consists of gathering counts of various activities—circulation, reference questions asked, attendance at programs, income, expenditures, and others—and tracking those counts over time.

Time series studies can also be constructed using repeating surveys, interviews, focus groups, or other data gathering methods. The key to using any method for purposes of a time series study is that the data gathered must be comparable from year to year. That doesn't mean that the data collection model used for a time series study must be static; it simply requires sufficient consistency over time to facilitate making year-to-year comparisons.

The data collected by local libraries, state library agencies, professional associations, and governmental agencies can also be used to construct time series. The Association of Research Libraries annual Statistical Report emphasizes time series as well as library comparisons. Figure 7.3 reproduces a time series table from the *2007–2008 ARL Statistical Report.*[19]

A distinct advantage of time series data is that they are very amenable to presentation in graphic form. Figure 7.4 is a line graph based on data from the NCES biennial survey of academic libraries. This time series graph requires examining the annual NCES reports at four-year intervals from 1992 to 2008.

At a local level, time series data can be combined with the narrative history of a library to provide context for the library, its origins, its development over time, and its orientation toward the future. Many public libraries, sometimes through their friends groups, have conducted and published detailed library histories. The Library History Round Table of the American Library Association has compiled "*American Library History: A Comprehensive Guide to the Literature,*" a bibliography of sources related to the history of libraries in the United States.[20] Although the guide is somewhat out-of-date, it provides a starting point and

TABLE 1

Service Trends in ARL Libraries, 1991–2008
Median Values for Time-Series Trends

Year	ILL: Borrowed	Group Pres.	Participants In Pres.	Reference Trans.	Initial Circ.	Total Circ.	Ratio of Circ. Init./Tot.	Total Staff	Total Students
(Libraries)	(103)	(84)	(82)	(79)	(36)	(80)	(34)	(105)	(103)
1991	10,397	508	7,137	125,103	296,964	509,673	1.26	271	18,290
1992	11,362	526	7,154	132,549	342,989	554,579	1.27	265	18,273
1993	12,489	616	7,688	136,115	343,293	568,628	1.32	262	18,450
1994	14,007	568	7,831	147,582	369,996	572,749	1.31	264	18,305
1995	14,472	687	8,461	147,023	347,144	578,989	1.32	267	18,209
1996	15,278	719	8,410	155,336	336,481	560,244	1.39	264	18,320
1997	16,264	687	9,218	149,659	348,157	542,438	1.37	273	18,166
1998	17,656	698	9,462	132,850	354,924	514,574	1.37	273	18,335
1999	18,942	711	9,406	128,696	300,923	514,087	1.38	277	18,609
2000	20,475	722	9,596	115,636	273,231	482,542	1.42	267	18,908
2001	21,902	669	10,121	104,409	265,195	467,277	1.48	269	19,102
2002	21,339	776	11,350	95,910	251,146	462,223	1.51	279	19,925
2003	22,146	806	12,516	89,150	248,689	479,733	1.57	277	21,132
2004	25,737	757	12,864	84,546	261,526	496,369	1.60	273	21,562
2005	25,729	803	13,782	65,168	250,971	473,216	1.58	267	22,047
2006	27,412	833	13,051	67,697	267,213	466,403	1.52	267	22,618
2007	26,813	830	14,417	61,703	222,037	456,597	1.59	266	22,874
2008	27,822	803	15,480	58,763	221,144	429,626	1.59	260	22,762
Average annual % change	6.0%	2.7%	4.7%	-4.3%	-1.7	-1.0	1.4%	-0.2	1.3%

Figure 7.3   Time series table from *ARL Statistics* 2007–2008

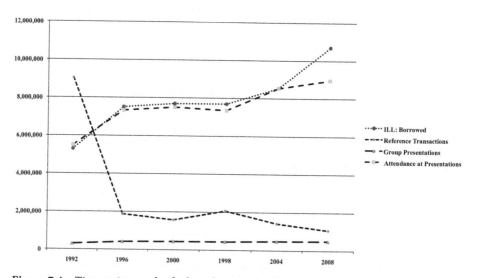

Figure 7.4   Time series graph of selected academic library indicators, 1992–2008

is useful for understanding the types of historical sources that exist at various levels from national to local. Changes in user groups over time or evolving institutional mission statements may explain where we have been but also provide predictions of where we are going. A good history may inspire confidence that libraries have successfully met challenges in the past. Historical analysis can reveal that changes that seem revolutionary at the time of their occurrence are in fact evolutionary in nature and reflective of the natural growth and maturation of the library.

THE DIGNITY AND PUZZLE OF HISTORY

History is a widely respected area of study that has its own deep and rich history. History has been recognized as an essential discipline throughout human history. There is probably no adult in the Western world who has not repeatedly studied history as part of basic public or private education. Examination of any standard dictionary of quotations is likely to yield dozens if not hundreds of entries related to history. History has a place alongside literature in the pantheon of the disciplines, as reflected in Scott's assertion that "A lawyer without history or literature is a mechanic, a mere working mason; if he possesses some knowledge of these, he may venture to call himself an architect."[21]

Not all quotations present history in a positive or dignified light. Ford may or may not have said "History is more or less bunk," but that and other quotations about history are suggestive that, at least to some people, history is not such a noble and dignified endeavor at all.[22] Santayana's often misquoted assertion that "Those who cannot remember the past are condemned to repeat it" echoes the anonymous "history repeats itself"; neither is a wholly positive view of the nature of history.[23] Bierce's quote at the beginning of this chapter certainly doesn't constitute a positive view, although that was of course Bierce's point.[24] Despite, or perhaps as a result of, having studied history throughout elementary and secondary school and in some cases college or university, many adults never read history after having completed their formal educations.

The puzzle and quandary of history is that, perhaps more than any other family of research methods, historical exploration almost always yields more new questions than definitive answers. To a considerable extent, only the most trivial of historical studies can be expected to produce a definitive and uncontestable interpretation of the past. Where, then, does the value of history lie? One answer is that, for any research or evaluation project, the question is as important as the answer. By questioning history, an investigator plumbs the depths of what is knowable about the past, seeking not necessarily questions, but indicative patterns that enhance understanding and may have practical implications as well. Even a time series analysis carried out for purposes of evaluating service trends in a library may not directly produce an answer to a question or a solution to a problem. Observation that the number of reference questions asked in Association of Research Libraries has been in decline while attendance at information literacy instruction sessions has been up doesn't automatically answer any question or solve any problem. It does, however, establish a concrete context in which to seek an answer or a solution. History in all its forms provides an essential context for assigning meaning to phenomena that cannot directly be defined as historical in nature. Through this process of contextualization answers may be found and solutions can be formulated.

THINK ABOUT IT!

1. What challenges might an investigator encounter in conducting a historical study of a local library?
2. How can historical analysis contribute to an evaluation project?
3. How do the distinctions between primary and secondary sources of historical data influence the difficulty of carrying out a historical study?

DO IT!

1. Locate a historical study, preferably book length, dealing with a topic related to library and information science. What types of sources are included? Which sources can be defined as primary and which as secondary sources in the context of the study?
2. Identify a target for a historical study and the likely primary and secondary sources necessary for such a study.
3. Visit an archive or historical collection. What kinds of historical studies could that collection support?
4. Locate a document that can be considered a primary source for historical purposes. Assess the validity and reliability of the source.
5. Compare the final chapters of Ditzion's *Arsenals of a Democratic Culture*, Kaser's *A Book for a Sixpence*, and Wiegand and Wiegand's *Books on Trial* (or any other three related historical studies).[25] How did each of these investigators interpret their findings?

NOTES

1. *Oxford English Dictionary*, s.v. "History."

2. Definitions courtesy of Dr. Robert S. Martin, course notes for guest lecture in research methods course, Louisiana State University School of Library and Information Science.

3. Arthur P. Young, *Books for Sammies: The American Library Association and World War I* (Pittsburgh: Beta Phi Mu, 1981).

4. Eric Rentschler, "The Fascination of a Fake: The Hitler Diaries," *New German Critique*, no. 90 (2003): 177–92.

5. Helen Taylor, "The Griot from Tennessee:' the Saga of Alex Haley's Roots," *Critical Quarterly* 37, no. 2 (Summer 1995): 46–62.

6. David Kaser, *A Book for a Sixpence: The Circulating Library in America* (Pittsburgh: Beta Phi Mu, 1980).

7. Martha Kyrillidou and Shaneka Morris, "ARL Statistics 2008–2009" (Washington: Association of Research Libraries, 2011).

8. Kaser, *A Book for a Sixpence*, 125.

9. Allan A. Cuseo, *Homosexual Characters in YA Novels: A Literary Analysis, 1969–1982* (Metuchen, NJ: Scarecrow, 1992).

10. Ronald J. Zboray, *A Fictive People: Antebellum Economic Development and the American Reading Public* (New York: Oxford University Press, 1993), xvi.

11. Juris Divelko, "An Ideological Analysis of Digital Reference Service Models," *Library Trends* 50, no. 2 (Fall 2001): 240.

12. Ibid., 241.

13. Fannette H. Thomas, "The Black Mother Goose: Collective Biography of African-American Children's Librarians," in *Culture Keepers: Enlightening and Empowering Our Communities, Proceedings of the First National Conference of African American Librarians, September 4–6, 1992, Columbus, Ohio*, ed. Stanton F. Biddle and Members of the BCALA NCAAL Conference Proceedings Committee (Chicago: American Library Association, 1992).

14. Michael H. Harris, "Purpose of the American Public Library: A Revisionist Interpretation of History," *Library Journal* 98, no. 16 (1973): 2509–14; Phyllis Dain, "Ambivalence and Paradox: The Social Bonds of the Public Library," *Library Journal* 100, no. 3 (1975): 261–66.

15. Michael A. Bellesiles, *Arming America: The Origins of a National Gun Culture* (New York: Alfred A. Knopf, 2000).

16. Michael A. Bellesiles, "The Origins of Gun Culture in the United States, 1760–1865." *Journal of American History* 83, no. 2 (September 1996): 425–55.

17. James Lindgren, "Fall from Grace: Arming America and the Bellesiles Scandal," *Yale Law Journal* 111, no. 8 (June 2002): 2195–249.

18. Tracy E. K'Meyer and A. Glenn Crothers, "'If I See Some of This in Writing, I'm Going to Shoot You:' Reluctant Narrators, Taboo Topics, and the Ethical Dilemmas of the Oral Historian," *Oral History Review* 34, no. 1 (2007): 71–93.

19. Martha Kyrillidou and Les Bland, "ARL Statistics 2007–2008" (Washington: Association of Research Libraries, 2009).

20. Library History Round Table, American Library Association, "American Library History: A Comprehensive Guide to the Literature," http://www.ala.org/ala/mgrps/rts/lhrt/popularresources/amerlibhis.cfm (accessed June 9, 2011).

21. Sir Walter Scott, *Guy Mannering* (Boston: West and Richardson, 1815).

22. Charles N. Wheeler, interview with Henry Ford, *Chicago Tribune*, May 25, 1916.

23. George Santayana, *The Life of Reason* (New York: Scribner's, 1922).

24. Ambrose Bierce, *The Devil's Dictionary* (Cleveland, OH: World Publishing Company, 1948), s.v. "History."

25. Sidney Ditzion, *Arsenals of a Democratic Culture: A Social History of the American Public Library Movement in New England and the Middle States from 1850 to 1900* (Chicago: American Library Association, 1947); Kaser, *A Book for a Sixpence*; Shirley A. Wiegand and Wayne A. Wiegand, *Books on Trial: Red Scare in the Heartland* (Norman: University of Oklahoma Press, 2007).

SUGGESTED READINGS

John E. Buschman and Gloria J. Leckie, eds., *The Library as Place: History, Community, and Culture* (Westport, CT: Libraries Unlimited, 2007).

Phyllis Dain, "The Historical Sensibility," *Libraries & Culture* 35, no. 1 (Winter 2000): 240–43.

Ronald E. Day, *The Modern Invention of Information: Discourse, History, and Power* (Carbondale: Southern Illinois University Press, 2001).

Charles A. Hamaker, "Time Series Circulation Data for Collection Development; Or, You Can't Intuit That," *Library Acquisitions* 19 (Summer 1995): 191–95.

Christine Pawley, "History in the Library and Information Science Curriculum: Outline of a Debate," *Libraries & Culture* 40, no. 3 (Summer 2005): 223–38.

Donald A. Ritchey, ed., *The Oxford Handbook of Oral History* (New York: Oxford University Press, 2011).

Scott Seaman, "Salary Compression: A Time Series Analysis of ARL Position Classifications," *portal: Libraries and the Academy* 7, no. 1 (January 2007): 7–24.

Lee Shiflett, "Clio's Claim: The Role of Historical Research in Library and Information Science," *Library Trends* 32 (Spring 1984): 385–406.

Lee Shiflett, "Louis Shores and Library History," *Libraries & Culture* 35, no. 1 (Winter 2000): 35–40.

John Mark Tucker, "Clio's Workshop: Resources for Historical Study in American Librarianship," *Libraries & Culture* 35, no. 1 (Winter 2000): 192–214.

Toni Weller, ed., *Information History in the Modern World: Histories of the Information Age* (New York: Palgrave Macmillan, 2011).

Andrew B. Wertheimer and Donald G. Davis, Jr., eds., *Library History Research in America: Essays Commemorating the Fiftieth Anniversary of the Library History Round Table, American Library Association* (Washington: Library of Congress Center for the Book, 2000).

Wayne A. Wiegand and Donald G. Davis, eds., *Encyclopedia of Library History* (New York: Garland, 1994).

8

DESCRIPTIVE METHODS— QUESTIONNAIRES AND INTERVIEWS

Description is revelation. It is not
The thing described, nor false facsimile.
It is an artificial thing that exists,
In its own seeming, plainly visible,
Yet not too closely the double of our lives,
Intenser than any actual life could be.

—*Wallace Stevens, "Description Without Place," 1945*

In This Chapter

- Definition of descriptive research and evaluation
- Categories of descriptive research and evaluation
- In-person interviews
- Telephone interviews
- Qualitative interview techniques
- Questionnaires
- Types of questions
- Wording of questions
- Arrangement of questions
- Questionnaire layout
- Questionnaire analysis
- Questionnaire administration

DEFINITION OF DESCRIPTIVE RESEARCH AND EVALUATION

The *Oxford English Dictionary* doesn't provide a definition for descriptive research, but the entry under "descriptive" provides a starting point for understanding descriptive research: "Having the quality or function of describing; serving to describe; characterized by description."[1]

A simple but somewhat circular definition of descriptive research and evaluation is that it describes some phenomenon of interest or concern. The emphasis is on description of the present in its natural state, based on systematic observation. Description can be either qualitative or quantitative in nature. The overview presented here focuses primarily on quantitative research and evaluation with some references to qualitative research and evaluation.

MAJOR CATEGORIES OF DESCRIPTIVE RESEARCH AND EVALUATION

Descriptive research and evaluations include a very large family of methodologies and tools. The five major categories discussed here are (1) in-person interviews, (2) telephone interviews, (3) questionnaires, (4) direct observation, and (5) case study. Interviews and questionnaires are included in this chapter; direct observation and case study are covered in Chapter 9, "Descriptive Methods—Observation."

IN-PERSON INTERVIEWS

An in-person interview is a question-and-answer exploration in which the investigator and a respondent or multiple respondents are in the same place. In some cases, this may involve multiple researchers or evaluators. The location can be the investigator's office, the respondent's office or home, a professional occasion such as a conference or workshop, a public place such as a street corner or a shopping mall, or any number of other environments. The interview may be highly structured, with a set of specific questions for which answer categories have been predetermined by the investigator. Alternatively, the interview may be an open-ended discussion from which the investigator hopes to gain a suggestive answer to a general question rather than precise answers to a series of specific questions.

The advantages and disadvantages of in-person interviews are best understood not as absolutes, but in comparison to telephone interviews and questionnaires, which are the major alternatives to in-person interviews.

Advantages of In-person Interviews

1. Interaction and explanation. To the extent that an in-person interview does allow for open-endedness and deviation from a preestablished set of questions with predetermined answer categories, there is substantial room for interaction between the questioner and respondent that can substantially improve the quality of the data gathered. The questioner can, for instance, include in the instructions to the respondent explicit authorization to ask for an explanation if the respondent doesn't understand the question. Conversely, the questioner can ask the respondent to define, explain, or expand upon an answer.

2. Depth and detail of information. Free-flowing, open-ended interviews are an excellent way to gather detailed information. The questioner can build new questions from respondent answers that take the interchange to the level of detail the investigator desires.

3. Potential for serendipity. If the interaction is reasonably open-ended, there is the potential for the respondent to provide answers that are unexpected.

4. Potential for low respondent stress. A skilled questioner can turn an interview into a conversation that has the appearance of a friendly chat, guiding the interaction so that it reveals essential information while having the appearance of being no more than a friendly chat. When that environment can be achieved, the potential for depth, detail, and serendipity is especially heightened.

5. Potential for eliciting beliefs, opinions, perceptions, experiences, etc. Carefully and skill-fully conducted in-person interviews are unparalleled in their ability to gather infor-mation that is oriented more toward the affective rather than the intellectual domain. Respondents are more likely to be open about their beliefs, concerns, actions, prefer-ences, and prejudices in an interview setting than in response to any other approach to gathering descriptive data.

Disadvantages of In-person Interviews

1. Unpredictability. Unpredictability is the dark side of serendipity. Just as the interview may take a useful direction the investigator didn't predict, the interview may strike off in an unproductive direction. In some cases it may be very difficult or even impossible to return the interview to the focus the investigator had intended.

2. Absence of anonymity. Although the investigator can and should offer interview respondents the protection of an appropriate guarantee of confidentiality, there is no potential for anonymity in in-person interviews. Even in a shopping mall setting where the interview is brief and the respondent's name isn't requested, the respondent has lost anonymity by participating in the interview and knows it. The lack of anonymity may introduce elements of respondent bias into the interview.

3. Potential for interviewer influence. Although a good interviewer makes a sincere effort to avoid influencing the respondent, there is always some potential for reactivity in interview research and evaluation. Even if the interview does not engage in acts that constitute "leading the witness," subtle factors such as nonverbal cues may serve as guides to the respondent. A smile from the interviewer can easily be interpreted as an indicator of a correct answer, while a knitting of the interviewer's brows or an uncon-scious shake of the head may be viewed as a signal that the answer was wrong.

4. Potential for respondent stress. Just as a really skilled interviewer can put a respon-dent at ease and encourage forthright answers, an incompetent interviewer can easily heighten the respondent's stress level. Questions that take on the form of "why did you do that" or "why didn't you do that?" can be intimidating or insulting. Just as an inter-viewer who registers too much facial reaction to the respondent can inadvertently influ-ence responses, an interviewer who shows no facial expression tends to be viewed as cold, aloof, and even threatening. An ill-at-ease respondent is frequently a poor source of information. A respondent who feels threatened will frequently refuse to contribute any information at all.

5. Variable potential for reliability. Reliability, introduced in Chapter 1, "Knowing, Research, and Evaluation," is a measure of the extent to which conclusions are repeat-able or replicable. Two different interviewers may elicit identical or comparable infor-mation from respondents, but may provide two very different reports or interpretations. A skilled interviewer is the essence of good interview-based research and evaluation. Reliability in interview research and evaluation is therefore a direct function of the skills of the interviewer(s). To the extent that such skills can be ensured there is some assurance of reliability. When those skills are absent or cannot be assessed, reliability is an unknown. When multiple interviewers are involved, and particularly when the

principal investigator is not the sole interviewer, training is necessary to ensure that all interviewers are presenting questions, interpreting answers, and recording responses in a comparable manner.

6. Uncertainty of accuracy. It can be very difficult to provide any crosscheck on responses to an interview, especially if the purpose of the interview is to elicit opinions or beliefs. Gathering data from a broad cross section of respondents will reveal a range of responses, but even a preponderance of expressions of a particular opinion does little to verify the accuracy of a particular opinion. A respondent may provide not the answer that is accurate, but the answer he or she feels to be socially acceptable or morally responsible. The investigator has little in the way of tools for assessing the accuracy of individual responses. It is hardly feasible to ask "do you really believe that?"

7. Variable potential for validity. Validity is a measure of the extent to which conclusions accurately reflect reality. Validity in interview research and evaluation, although it is certainly a function of research and evaluation design, is also largely dependent on the skills of the interviewer(s). Validity can sometimes be augmented by having multiple skilled interviewers work with multiple respondents to provide a basis for triangulation, but doing so requires extensive efforts to ensure that the interviewers have both comparable skills and compatible approaches. The more open-ended and flexible the interview process is, the greater are the threats to validity.

8. Intrusion of recording processes. It is difficult to create and maintain a sense that the interview is a friendly chat or even a polite conversation and also create a record of the interview. Taking notes, making marks on a checklist, or creating an audio- or video-recording are rarely part of an informal discussion. Audio recorders are frequently used in interviewing, but carry very specific challenges and risks. Some respondents will be indifferent to the presence of an audio recorder, others will be nervous at first and then essentially forget that the tape recorder is there, others will be nervous throughout the interview, and others will terminate the interview as soon as the tape recorder is mentioned. If the tape has to be turned over or replaced during the interview, the initial sense of unease may be immediately regenerated. At the present time, respondents are generally very reluctant to be videotaped for any purpose. It is almost never acceptable to make any kind of audio- or videorecording without the respondent's express, written permission.

The fact that the list of disadvantages or challenges is longer than the list of advantages or benefits should not be construed as a condemnation of in-person interviews. Every specific subcategory of any family of research methods is the right method to use under certain circumstances.

Interview Structure Principles

There are some techniques and principles that can be used effectively to enhance validity in interview research and evaluation:

1. Use of an interview schedule. An interview schedule is a guide to the direction the interview is expected to take or will be allowed to take. For a tightly structured interview made up entirely of closed-ended questions, an interview schedule is a list of questions and a checklist of predetermined answer categories. For a free-flowing discussion of a general topic, the interview schedule may be no more than a short list of questions on a note pad or in the interviewer's head. The basic principle is the same: the investigator needs to take some structured, systematic action prior to the interview to influence the direction the interview takes. In some cases, the investigator may even provide the

respondent with an advance copy of the interview schedule so that the respondent will have a means of anticipating and preparing for the interview.

2. Attention to purpose and maintenance of direction. Although an interview may superficially seem to be a freewheeling discussion, it is necessarily a discussion with a purpose and a direction. It is the interviewer's responsibility to maintain attention to the purpose and direction. Doing so requires active listening skills and the ability to shape questions that can lead the discussion in a new direction or return the discussion to a necessary direction from which it has deviated.

3. Neutrality. Although the interviewer must react to the respondent as a human being, there is almost always a need for the interview to react to answers and respondents in a neutral, nonjudgmental manner. Although it may be difficult to separate the respondent from the response, doing so is frequently critical. An interviewer reaction to an answer that is viewed by the respondent as judgmental will typically be treated not as a reaction to the answer but as a judgment of the respondent. This will at best require a rebuilding of trust between the interviewer and the respondent and at worst lead to termination of the interview and withdrawal of support for the research and evaluation project.

TELEPHONE INTERVIEWS

Telephone interviews were first used in the early part of the 20th century and rose to prominence in the post-World War II era. It seems likely that the only residents of the United States who have not been asked to participate in a telephone interview are those who do not have access to telephones.

Advantages of Telephone Interviews

1. Reduced expense. In comparison to in-person interviews, for which telephone interviews were initially a direct substitute, telephone interviews are very inexpensive to conduct. The interviewer can work from a centralized office or phone bank and has no need to travel to any particular location to conduct interviews. Agencies that conduct frequent telephone interviews are generally able to negotiate very low telephone rates.

2. Expanded range. Telephone interviewing extends the possible range of interview research and evaluation in two ways. First, respondents can be reached at any type of location, including in their homes. Second, geography becomes irrelevant. With inexpensive long distance rates, there is no effective restriction on the geographical area from which respondents can be drawn.

3. Ease of sampling. From the earliest efforts at telephone interviewing, ease of sample selection has been a major perceived benefit. Drawing a random sample of residential numbers from a community's telephone directory is an extremely simple process. Strategies for selecting an alternative number if a sampled number can't be reached or if the respondent declines to participate are easily planned and implemented. More recently, the use of autodialing systems makes sampling an essentially automatic process.

4. Ease of scheduling. If a prearranged time for the interview is part of the research and evaluation design, scheduling a telephone interview is frequently much easier than scheduling any form of in-person interview. Scheduling a telephone interview requires only that the respondent be available at a predetermined telephone number at a set time for an agreed-upon amount of time. Lengthy telephone interviews are usually unproductive due to respondent fatigue, so the prearranged amount of time is usually relatively brief. If calls are not prescheduled, the interviewer can easily ask the respondent if there is a better time to call back and recall at that time.

5. Reduced threats to reliability and validity. The same basic reliability and validity issues that apply to in-person interviews also apply to telephone interviews. Most telephone interviews are structured and closed-ended, though, which means that the threats to validity of open-ended discussions are absent. The benefits to validity of being able to explain questions or ask for expansion of answers, though, are frequently lost due to instructions to interviewers to closely follow an interview script.

6. Reduced impact of recording. Unauthorized electronic recording of telephone calls is both unethical and illegal. It is possible to introduce, however, to legally employ a variety of sophisticated tools for recording answers to telephone interview questions, with the provision that the respondent is aware of the recording process and has agreed to its use. Most telephone interviewers currently use computer-based equivalents to checksheets, which make it possible to readily record and aggregate responses without recording individual interviews in toto.

7. Reduced potential for interviewer influence. The ability of the interviewer to intentionally or unconsciously influence responses is greatly reduced when nonverbal cues are eliminated.

Disadvantages of Telephone Interviews

1. Loss of nonverbal cues. Although undue influence from nonverbal cues is eliminated in telephone interviews, so are all the benefits of nonverbal cues. A substantial portion of interpersonal communication is normally conveyed nonverbally. When nonverbal cues are removed from the communication process, the nature of the messages that can be communicated is limited in scope.

2. Compromise of verbal cues. In part because of the loss of nonverbal cues and in part because telephone technology does not convey the full range of sound, verbal cues in telephone interviews are compromised, sometimes severely. Tone of voice is conveyed and interpreted differently in a telephone interview than in face-to-face interaction. The telephone interviewer must be diligently careful to avoid conveying unwanted verbal cues and to avoid misinterpreting verbal cues supplied by the respondent.

3. Time limitations. The ubiquitous popularity of wireless phones tends to suggest that many people are willing to spend nearly all their time on the telephone. Few people, though, are willing to spend an extensive time responding to a telephone interview.

4. Maintaining direction and interest. Most respondents to telephone interviews are reached in their homes, places that are full of distractions and demands. Keeping a respondent focused on an interview when she is trying to monitor a toddler or eager to end the interview in time to watch a favorite TV show can be trying for even the most skilled telephone interviewer.

5. Product research and evaluation and solicitation. A threat to the viability of telephone interviews as an approach to conducting true research and evaluation is the proliferation of telephone-based product research and evaluation and telephone solicitation. In an environment in which many citizens view telephone sales as an extreme intrusion on dinnertime privacy and regard product research and evaluation as a thinly disguised form of solicitation, there is some reason for concern that telephone interviews with more serious research and evaluation purposes will be viewed in a similar manner. There is in fact some reason to believe that response rates for telephone interview-based research and evaluation are generally declining.

6. Compromised sampling due to migration away from landline telephones. Historically, ready access to telephone numbers has been widespread. Published telephone directories and commercial number sampling services have been widely used in all forms of

Study:	Donna M. Braquet, "Library Experiences of Hurricane Katrina and New Orleans Flood Survivors," LIBRES Library and Information Science Research Electronic Journal, no. 1 (2010), http://libres.curtin.edu.au/.
Question/Purpose:	Research Question 1: What was the prevalence of library use among survivors?
	Research Question 2: How did survivors use libraries?
	Research Question 3: What were survivors' thoughts and feelings related to their post-disaster library use?
Population:	Survivors of Hurricane Katrina
Sample:	Respondents to request to participate published in local newspaper and television discussion forums, blogs, and related online sources
Personnel:	One researcher
Data Sources:	Online survey; in-person and telephone interviews
Data Gathering:	Information about the online survey was posted on New Orleans area newspaper and television news discussion boards, blogs maintained by New Orleans area residents, national online forums and groups related to Hurricane Katrina, and neighborhood online discussion forums. Individuals were solicited for in-person interviews by posting flyers in the New Orleans area. Telephone interviews were arranged for individuals who were interested in the study but who did not live in the New Orleans area.
Summary:	Survivors of Hurricane Katrina used libraries in five prominent ways: (1) as a source of access to the Internet; (2) as a source of information and technology access related to immediate needs; (3) as a source of materials for escape reading; (4) as a trusted place of physical refuge; and (5) as a symbol of continuity and hope in the midst of loss.
Conclusions:	The researcher concludes that libraries play an important role in survivors of a natural disaster and that libraries have a meaningful impact on communities affected by natural disasters. Further study is needed to determine how post-disaster use of libraries differs from pre-disaster use.

Figure 8.1   From the professional literature—combined survey and interview method.

telephone interviewing. The migration to wireless telephone services has substantially undermined researcher and evaluator access to personal telephone numbers. Data from the National Center for Health Statistics indicate that as of June 2010, 26.6 percent of U.S. residences had wireless telephone access but no landline access.[2] Since many wireless telephone companies do not provide access to their customer's numbers, the use of telephone sampling services may no longer be a viable approach to reaching respondents.

QUALITATIVE INTERVIEW TECHNIQUES

The focus on in-person and telephone interviews in this chapter has been largely on interviews designed to capture quantifiable data. Interviews are also used extensively to gather qualitative data. Two interview approaches commonly used in the context of the qualitative paradigm are in-depth, open-ended interviews and group interviews.

1. In-depth, open-ended interviews are used to gain understanding of respondents and the groups to which they belong. These differ from interviews used in quantitative descriptive research in that qualitative interviews are more oriented toward understanding respondents than soliciting information from respondents. An additional difference is that data gathered through qualitative open-ended interviews are not synthesized or reduced, although they may be subject to thematic analysis, which is discussed further in Chapter 12, "Data Analysis and Presentation."

2. Group interviews are used to gather data in circumstances in which the group experience can be expected to yield data that are different from those gathered in individual interviews. Group interviews are especially useful for assessing shared understanding or common perspectives on a phenomenon of interest. Focus groups are a variety of group interview in which a discussion is used to assess shared perceptions of the phenomenon of interest. Successful focus groups must be simultaneously open-ended and directional. Application of a true focus group methodology requires that participant comments be reported verbatim, not paraphrased or synthesized.

QUESTIONNAIRES

The questionnaire, most usually distributed by mail in the past but increasingly distributed electronically, is probably the most frequently used approach to descriptive research and evaluation. Questionnaires abound, from brief customer service surveys found in hotel rooms or on restaurant tables to student evaluations of teaching to the Decennial Census of Populations.

Advantages of Questionnaires

1. Low cost. An effective questionnaire-based research and evaluation project can be conducted for the cost of stationery, postage, and the investigator's time. The real cost per targeted respondent can easily be less than one dollar, although it is frequently more than that. Web-based digital questionnaires have the potential for being even more cost-effective.

2. Low pressure on respondents. Individuals approached to participate in interview-based research and evaluation may feel a sense of pressure to respond. That pressure is greatly reduced in questionnaire research and evaluation. There is generally a sense that there is no specific urgency to respond.

3. Ease of preparation and administration. A questionnaire is relatively easy to design, prepare, and administer. The design and preparation process can typically be carried out in a short period of time. Administration is an essentially straightforward process involving identifying appropriate recipients, distributing the questionnaire, and processing returned questionnaires.

4. Ease of tabulation of responses. Assuring ease of tabulation is almost always a design objective in questionnaire research and evaluation. Questions can be selected and constructed such that tabulation is essentially automatic. When a questionnaire is presented as a Web form, results can be automatically recorded in a database.

5. Potential for confidentiality or anonymity. Questionnaires offer a high potential for ensuring respondent confidentiality and are the only descriptive research and evaluation tool that has any potential for ensuring respondent anonymity.

6. Ease of quantification. Questionnaire research and evaluation is closely associated with quantitative analysis based on returns from large samples. Assigning responses to categories, counting the numbers of responses in categories, and using statistical techniques to analyze results across categories are so frequently a part of questionnaire research and evaluation that they can be considered the normal approach to analyzing questionnaire results.

7. Potential for large response. The volume of response from other descriptive approaches is necessarily limited by factors of time and expense. It is quite feasible, however, to think in terms of distributing thousands of questionnaires and processing thousands of responses.

8. Limited variation in responses. The possible variability in responses to a questionnaire is a designed-in feature of the questionnaire. Although questions asked on questionnaires frequently allow for a response of "other," there is usually a substantial effort made to predict probable responses so that the need for respondents to select "other" is limited. Effective pretesting can significantly reduce the occurrence of other responses. Some questionnaires allow only for preformulated responses to closed-ended questions.

9. High potential for reliability. Questionnaire research and evaluation carries a high potential for replication, and therefore for reliability, in that the questionnaire stands as a tangible record of the research and evaluation design. Assuming that the questionnaire was designed appropriately, the respondent sample was chosen correctly, the actual response was representative of the sample, and the results were analyzed properly, a research and evaluation project based on a questionnaire should have a high degree of reliability.

10. High potential for validity. The questionnaire itself and the processes that surround it are also a major source of assessment for validity in questionnaire-based research and evaluation. Construct validity is of especially great concern in questionnaire design. Since respondents will usually not have an opportunity to ask for explanations of concepts presented in the questionnaire, it is of paramount importance that the questionnaire correctly and thoroughly defines the concepts that underlie critical variables.

Disadvantages of Questionnaires

1. Absence of personal contact. A questionnaire, whether distributed via regular mail, handed to patrons as they enter the library, posted to an e-mail discussion list, or mounted on a Web page, is a faceless and personality-devoid tool. Even though most researchers or evaluators prepare a cover letter designed to personalize the research and evaluation project, many recipients will not read the cover letter even if they complete and return the questionnaire. It is not unusual for the questionnaire to provide contact information so that recipients can ask questions of or request clarification from the investigator. It is, however, very unusual for recipients to make use of such contact information.

2. Low response rate. Questionnaire-based research and evaluation tends to yield relatively low response rates. There is at least anecdotal evidence to suggest that response rates are declining over time. For a questionnaire distributed to a very large sample, a response rate of 30 percent may be considered impressive, even though it means that two-thirds of the sample didn't respond.

3. Self-selecting sample. One of the greatest problems with questionnaire research is that, regardless of the response rate, respondents to any questionnaire constitute a self-selecting sample. The investigator inherently possesses information regarding respondents that is not available for nonrespondents. The problem is that the investigator cannot accurately know what difference in the two groups motivated one to respond and one to not respond.

4. Flaws in questionnaire design. The effectiveness of a questionnaire is found primarily in the wording of individual questions and the interactions among questions. Wording and arrangement are discussed later in this chapter.

5. Differentiation between fact and opinion. One of the most difficult aspects of questionnaire research and evaluation is that, even when questions are very carefully constructed to elicit a particular category of information, the investigator cannot definitely ascertain that answers to factual questions are not actually respondent opinions. This makes assessing respondent knowledge very difficult. For instance, a question may ask "what is the per capita amount of ad valorem tax support for the public library?" and provide five multiple-choice response categories. A respondent who feels that any amount is too much may choose the highest category in an attempt to express dissatisfaction with the tax rate. A respondent who feels that the public library needs all the funding it can get may choose the lowest category for exactly the same reason. In either case, the respondent was expressing an opinion when what was expected was an indication of the respondent's knowledge of the true tax rate.

6. Misinterpretation of questions. There are unfortunately almost no questions that are not subject to misinterpretation. A seemingly simple question such as "how many times in the past month have you used the Anytown Public Library?" can easily lead to confusion. What does it mean to use the public library (or any library)? Does consulting the library's website to determine operating hours constitute a use of the library? Is attendance at a library-sponsored event held at a site other than the library a use of the library? Is attendance at an event not sponsored by the library but held in the library's public meeting room a use of the library? The central problem is that the investigator may have no meaningful clues to indicate whether questions were correctly interpreted.

7. Misinterpretation of responses. Just as respondents can misinterpret questions, researchers or evaluators can easily misinterpret answers. If the question is "are you a registered borrower of the Anytown Public Library?" and the only possible answers are yes and no, the respondent who doesn't know has two basic choices: to guess or to not answer. The investigator can with some confidence assume that most respondents who didn't answer the question didn't know the answer, but some may have simply overlooked the question. The investigator therefore has no reliable way to know what failure to answer means. Worse, the investigator has absolutely no means of distinguishing between those respondents who guessed either yes or no and those who knew the correct answer and may have no perception that there is a distinction between the two respondent groups. The term "Native American" may be used by the investigator to mean a member of a recognized American Indian nation, but may easily be interpreted by a respondent as meaning nonimmigrant. The investigator can account for lack of knowledge by including a "don't know" category.

8. Deliberate sabotage. Some people, for reasons sometimes detectible but often not, choose to deliberately sabotage research or evaluation projects by knowingly providing incorrect answers. Some people, for instance, don't like being asked their ages. Regardless of the way in which age information is requested, they resent the question being

asked at all. Some of these people will simply decline to answer the question or discard the questionnaire. Others will be complete the questionnaire but deliberately falsify the answer to the question about age. Others will complete the questionnaire and deliberately falsify every answer to every question. It is hard to anticipate such direct sabotage, but the potential for it reinforces the general principle of not asking a question unless the answer is really needed.

Questionnaire Design Principles

A questionnaire is very easy to design, prepare, and administer but a good questionnaire requires expertise, care, and planning. The contention that a high volume of bad questionnaires is designed and distributed is almost undeniable. Nearly everyone can recount an experience with receiving a questionnaire that was poorly explained, poorly worded, difficult to understand, or personally offensive. The following guidelines are suggestions for ways to ensure quality questionnaire design and to enhance the success of questionnaire-based research and evaluation.

TYPES OF QUESTIONS BY PURPOSE

Questions can be categorized and understood in two major ways: by purpose and by structure. Questions can be categorized by their primary intent or purpose as being to gather respondents' perceptions of facts, knowledge, behaviors, or opinions.

1. Factual questions

The fundamental assumption underlying factual questions is that there is some body of data that could be reported by anyone with appropriate access to the answers; it is assumed that everyone with access to the answers would answer in an identical manner. In other words, factual questions are intended to gather verifiable data. Factual data address questions such as

- which?
- how many?
- how much?
- what kind?
- which type?
- when?
- how long?

and similar questions that can be answered by referring to concrete data. Demographic data such as the respondent's age, race, level of education, and related data are examples of factual data.

Answers to factual questions are limited by the respondent's ability to assess, record, and report factual data. When confronted by a factual question for which real or accurate date are not known, the respondent may choose to not answer, estimate an answer, or fabricate an answer. In many cases, the investigator will have no basis on which to judge the respondent's basis for the answer.

There are, however, some circumstances under which the investigator may be able to assess the probable accuracy or truth of the respondent's answers. If a series of questions includes the question, "what is the population base for your library?" the investigator may be able to compare the respondent's answer to an external source such as an annual state library statistical report. Assessment of the respondent's agreement with the data provided by the external source may provide some basis for judging the probable accuracy of answers to other questions on the questionnaire.

2. Knowledge-eliciting questions

Knowledge-eliciting questions are designed to gather data related to the respondent's understanding of knowledge of some focus of the questionnaire. Knowledge-eliciting questions are inherently more personal that factual questions. They are designed to assess the respondent's knowledge base rather than the respondent's access to data. Knowledge-eliciting questions address such areas as

- why?
- under what circumstances?
- according to what authority?
- what happened?

and similar questions that call for reference to person-embodied knowledge.

Answers to knowledge-eliciting questions are personal in nature, and the investigator generally has no means of verifying the accuracy or honesty of the answer. The investigator may be able to compare the answers to knowledge-eliciting questions to standards related to what a class of respondent in some sense should be expected to know.

The relationship between factual questions and knowledge-eliciting questions is not necessarily a hard line. The question "what professional association is responsible for the Library Bill of Rights?" is clearly a factual question for which the answer is the American Library Association. The question "what are the six provisions of the Library Bill of Rights?" calls for a more detailed memory of facts. The question "how do your library's policies support the Library Bill of Rights?" is a knowledge-based question that requires both memory of policies and an element of interpretation.

3. Behavioral questions

Behavioral questions address actual, perceived, or projected behaviors. Behavioral questions are very personal in nature, although answers may be compared to general guidelines for acceptable behavior. Behavioral questions take the form of

- what did you do?
- how frequently did you do it?
- when did you do it?
- where did you do it?
- who did you do it with?

and similar questions. Behavioral question are among the most frequently asked in library research and evaluation studies. The question "how frequently did you visit the library in the last year?" is a common example of a behavioral question.

Behavior questions are very value laden and have a very high potential for intimidation, irritation, exaggeration, subterfuge, and refusal. Answers to behavioral questions can be compared to external standards such as the American Library Association's Code of Ethics, but only with substantial care. Respondents may be reluctant to accurately or honestly report behavioral data for any number of reasons, including reluctance to report behaviors that the investigator would regard as negative.

4. Opinion questions

Opinion questions attempt to gather data regarding attitudes, self-assessments, or projections. A basic tenet of opinion-oriented research and evaluation is the possibility that opinions may be completely and inherently unrelated to facts about, knowledge of, or experience with the phenomenon about which an opinion is being sought. It is a more or less fundamental principle of a democracy that everyone is entitled to an opinion about anything and everything. Answers to opinion-oriented questions must be assessed in that context.

a. Attitude questions are oriented toward what respondents feel about the subject matter of the question. They assess what people think, feel, prefer, accept, or reject. Attitudes are very changeable over time and from place to place; they are both circumstantial and situational. Any questionnaire that attempts to assess attitudes must be designed to place those attitudes in the environments to which they belong.

b. Self-assessment questions are among the most personal of questions. They address questions such as

   i. what do you think about this?

   ii. how does this affect you?

   iii. what have you done about this?

   iv. what does this mean to you?

c. Projection questions take the respondent into the realm of speculation. They address question such as

   i. what would you do?

   ii. what would you think?

   iii. how would this affect you?

   iv. how should society react to this?

Answers to projection questions are among the most difficult to assess because respondents are explicitly being asked to make guesses. Respondents' answers to projection questions can never be expected to directly predict their actual actions regarding the concepts or principles about which they are asked to speculate. A fundamental principle of projection questions is that respondents cannot accurately predict the future.

TYPES OF QUESTIONS BY STRUCTURE

Questions can also be categorized by structure. The two fundamental structural categories of questions are open-ended and closed-ended.

1. Open-ended questions

Open-ended questions allow the respondent an opportunity to formulate an answer that has not been predicted, preformulated, or preformatted by the investigator. If, for instance, there is a legitimate and compelling reason to record the respondent's age to the nearest year, an appropriate open-ended question could be

How old are you?

or

In what year were you born?

Open-ended questions allow for honesty, openness, and serendipity, but tend to require a great deal of investigator effort in interpreting, categorizing, and assessing answers.

Some questions can be best answered only through open-ended questions. The question "where were you born" allows for a range of answers that cannot be predicted or anticipated. Most respondents are likely to answer with a geographic location that, while it may be ambiguous or not completely specific, may be highly useful in reflecting the respondent's assessment of place of birth.

In some cases, though, answers to open-ended questions will defy categorization. In response to the open-ended question, "how old are you?" a respondent may answer, "37," "adult," "middle-aged," or "old enough." The answers are not directly comparable and may lead to problems at the analysis stage.

2. Closed-ended questions

Closed-ended questions deliberately limit the respondent's range of possible answers. Instead of "where were you born?" the closed-ended question may provide a list of the 50 U.S. states and "outside the U.S." as mutually exclusive answer categories. The respondent is forced to choose an answer.

Closed-ended questions must be designed such that the respondent can choose a valid answer. In the above example, in which the choices for place of birth are the 50 U.S. states and "outside the U.S.," individuals born in the District of Columbia or the U.S. territories have no opportunity to provide an accurate answer.

Closed-ended questions fall into five prominent categories: multiple response list, single response forced choice, ranked list, and true/false. There are possible variations within each of these categories.

A. Multiple response list questions are generally accompanied by some instruction such as "check all that apply." The basic principle is that the respondent is allowed to identify more than one answer to the question and has no obligation to identify any answer as being more important or more prominent than any other. The question might be

Which of the following library materials have you used in the past month?

books

e-books

audiobooks (on disk)

audiobooks (downloaded)

movies (DVD)

movies (downloaded)

magazines

databases

The respondent has the opportunity to check as many of the items on the list as apply to his or her recent history of library use.

B. Single response forced choice questions require the respondent to select one and only one answer from a list. The question is frequently accompanied by an instruction such as "select the answer that best describes" whatever phenomenon is being addressed. The question might be

Which of the following library materials do you use most?

books

e-books

audiobooks (on disk)

audiobooks (downloaded)

movies (DVD)

movies (downloaded)

magazines

databases

Answering this question implies a higher degree of precision than answering a multiple response list question based on the same categories, but may create problems of interpretation. If a respondent finds two or more categories of materials to be of equal value and use, making a choice may be an artificial process.

C. Ranked list questions require the respondent to apply an ordinal value to preidentified categories. The question might be:

Rank the following library materials in the order of the frequency with which you use them; do not assign the same rank to any two materials.

books

e-books

audiobooks (on disk)

audiobooks (downloaded)

movies (DVD)

movies (downloaded)

magazines

databases

This example is a combination of ranked list and forced choice in that the respondent cannot assign the same rank to two categories. Other ranked list questions may allow for ties in the rankings. The fundamental characteristic of ranked list questions is that the respondent is expected to differentiate among categories on the basis of some factor that quantifies within a variable.

D. True/false questions require the respondent to supply a dichotomous answer. The answer may be true/false, yes/no, always/never, or any other response category that has only two possible answers. The key characteristic of such a question is that the response categories must be exhaustive and mutually exclusive.

An example of an exhaustive and mutually exclusive question is:

Did you personally, using the library card that bears your name, check out one or more books from the Anytown Public Library between January 1 and December 31 of last year?

There is almost no potential for ambiguity in answering this question. Compare this question to the following:

Did any member of your family use the collections or services of the Anytown Public Library last year?

The second question, although it can lead to a "yes" or "no" answer, isn't truly dichotomous because every aspect of the question is subject to interpretation.

The worst kind of true/false question is the "have you stopped beating your spouse question." This is most often asked in terms of opinion questions that force choices when there are other possible choices. An example might be:

How often did you check out books from the Anytown Public Library between January 1 and December 31 of last year?
Frequently

Never

The respondent who checked out books rarely or occasionally, or who doesn't understand what "frequently" means, is disenfranchised from answering.

The basic rule is that dichotomous-answer questions should be used only when the answer is inherently dichotomous. Multiple response questions should never be recast as true/false questions.

E. Likert scale questions—also known as rating scale questions—require the respondent to indicate a response on an explicit scale, such as

How often did you check out books from the Anytown Public Library between January 1 and December 31 of last year?

Never   Rarely   Occasionally   Frequently   Very Frequently

Likert scale questions are most frequently used to elicit behavioral or opinion data. Because the respondent is being asked to judge the appropriate position on the scale, Likert scale questions are rarely useful in gathering factual data; they may be used with care to assess knowledge.

The actual presentation of a Likert scale can vary substantially; there is no one prescribed format. Other questions might be associated with the following scales:

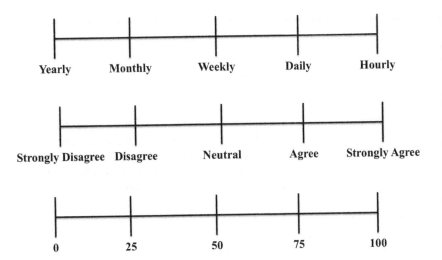

Research into the validity of Likert scales has found a tendency for respondents to generally choose the middle position when they are uncertain or have no opinion, even if the middle position is not defined as "neutral" or "no opinion." As a result, many investigators choose not to include a middle position, thereby forcing a choice:

Researchers and evaluators frequently add a number to each point on the scale to imply an interval scale and to add a sense of precision to the question:

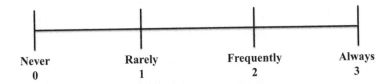

The scale with numbers added, however, is exactly the same conceptually as the scale without numbers.

The results for conceptual, nonnumeric scales are most appropriately reported as percentages of respondents who selected each response level, such as "70 percent of respondents agreed or strongly agreed that the university library is important to their education." A major perceived advantage of adding a numeric value to a Likert scale lies in the potential for performing statistical analyses using the numeric responses. It then becomes possible to calculate averages and perform comparative and relational statistical tests. Doing so must be done with caution and has the greatest validity when

1. the variable for which data are being gathered is truly quantitative in nature
2. there is a zero on the scale that indicates absence of the characteristic described by the variable
3. there is a logical basis for the numeric scale

Study:	Jessica Kayongo and Clarence Helm, "Graduate Students and the Library: A Survey of Research Practices and Library Use at the University of Notre Dame," *Reference & User Services Quarterly* 49, no. 4 (2010): 341–49.
Question/Purpose:	The study looked at the following types of questions: What were the information-seeking strategies graduate students employed in research and writing? How did they identify and acquire relevant research materials? What was their level of satisfaction with the library's collections?
Setting:	A medium sized private university library.
Personnel:	Two researchers, both university librarians.
Data Sources:	Online survey of graduate students.
Data Gathering:	Twenty-question questionnaire incorporating quantitative and qualitative questions; 53 percent response rate.
Summary:	Graduate students were found to use the library for a variety of purposes and in a variety of modes. Students used the library almost exclusively for their own purposes rather than on behalf of faculty members or others. A wide variety of library materials were used. Respondents ranked books, journals, online databases and indexes, online full text journals, and library hours as the five most important library resources. Graduate students reported limited contact with librarians.
Conclusions:	The study found that graduate students do make considerable use of the library and are satisfied with its resources and services. Results have implications for collection development and efforts to increase interaction between graduate students and librarians.

Figure 8.2   From the professional literature—survey method.

4. increasing numeric values are associated with a logically increasing characteristic such as frequency, value, quality, success, and so on. Statistics cannot be calculated when increasing numeric values are associated with a decreasing characteristic (for instance, when 1 means excellent and 5 means poor)

WORDING OF QUESTIONS

Wording of questions is of particular concern and calls for extreme care. Five essential factors related to wording of questions involve avoidance of unnecessary jargon, avoidance of implied value judgments, avoidance of unnecessary personal questions, maintaining independence of questions, and seeking parsimony in instructions, definitions, and directions.

Avoidance of Unnecessary Jargon

Every professional field has its own specialized language. Professional jargon evolves as a means by which members of the profession can easily communicate with each other. The danger of jargon is that individuals who are schooled in the specialized language of a profession can easily forget that other people don't speak or understand that language.

The language of library and information science is replete with jargon, including the expression library and information science and its synonyms. Other frequently used jargon includes circulation, monograph, serial, main entry, bibliographic record, database, reference question, and many, many more terms that either have no obvious meaning to the general public or have a meaning within the context of the profession that differs from the meaning applied in everyday usage.

The critical point about jargon is that its use can confound questionnaire respondents and produce invalid results. One of Herbert Goldhor's rules of thumb with regard to wording of questionnaires was "have you mother read it." The basic notion was that if someone not familiar with the professional jargon could read and understand the questionnaire, the questionnaire was probably sufficiently free of jargon to be useful. Of course, if your mother is a librarian or a researcher, she may not be the best choice as a reader.

Avoidance of Implied Value Judgments

One of the essential goals of questionnaire design is to avoid offending the respondent. In addition to sloppy, ambiguous, and repetitive design and presentation, two prominent ways of unintentionally offending respondents are implying negative value judgments and asking unnecessary personal questions. Avoiding value judgments requires thinking very carefully about how respondents might react to each question. A frequent structure that implies a value judgment is the unbalanced question

> Did you check any books out of the Anytown Public Library between January 1 and December 31 of last year? If not, why not?

The very clear implication of this question is that checking out books is good and not checking out books is bad. The respondent is directly encouraged to adopt a defensive attitude and may decline to answer the question or may conclude that it is both easier and more "correct" to answer "yes," which requires no explanation. Balancing the question by asking for explanations for both yes and no answers is one way to minimize the appearance of a value judgment.

The implied value judgment in this type of question is very problematic in that the desire to determine why people don't do something is a very frequent focus of research and evaluation in a field of practice such as library and information science. Ultimately, it is almost always best in questionnaire research and evaluation to seek to determine why people do something rather than why they do not.

Avoidance of Personal Questions

The fundamental rule of asking questions that are in any sense real is "don't ask if you don't need to know." Although it is difficult to predict exactly what questions any given respondent will consider excessively personal or intrusive, there are some categories that inherently have a high potential for being viewed as personal. These include questions that address age, gender, ethnicity, income, and personal relationships. Such questions should be asked only when they truly have a bearing on the phenomenon being studied, either as primary data or as context data.

In some cases, the intrusiveness of a question can be reduced by the structure of the question. Consider the following two questions:

1. What is your age? _____

2. What category best describes your age?

   20–29 _____ 30–39 _____ 40–49 _____ 50–59 ___ 60 or older _____

Both questions are designed to elicit information about the respondent's age. The second question may be interpreted as less intrusive, though, because it allows the respondent to report within a range rather than reporting a discrete value. Even this question, though, could be offensive to respondents in their 60s, who may feel that they have been included in a category that could be defined as "old." Unless necessary for restricting the sample, demographic questions should be placed at the end of the questionnaire. This helps minimize any reflexive negative reaction and lets the respondent make decisions about such questions after becoming familiar with the project.

Independence of Questions

One of the most difficult tasks in designing a questionnaire is building relationships among questions. A basic rule is that questions should be independent of one another unless there is a compelling reason to build a structure that links different questions. Interrelated questions have two major forms: redundant checks and if-then sequences.

A redundant check is a question designed to verify the answer to another question. Redundant checks form pairs of questions that, from the questionnaire designer's point of view, should have essentially the same answer. Redundant checks are sometimes built into a questionnaire to determine whether the respondent appears to have answered honestly or to lessen the impact of the sequence of questions on answers. A redundant check pair usually consists of two questions that are worded very differently but address the same content and which are positioned at a sufficient distance from each other in the question sequence to minimize the possibility of the respondent detecting the redundancy. The risk is that respondents will detect the redundancy and will be either be offended by being asked the same question twice or otherwise question either the motivation or the competence of the questionnaire.

If-then sequences build on answers to specific questions. The typical form of an if-then sequence is

If the answer to question 9 is "no," skip to question 26.

The presumption is that a respondent who answered "yes" to question 9 will answer questions 10 through 25 but a respondent who answered "no" will not. In practice, respondents often fail to read if-then instructions. The investigator is then forced to decide what to do with questionnaires for which (in the case of the example), the answer to question 9 was "no" but the respondent answered questions 10 through 25 anyway. The most typical decision is to discard the answers to questions that should not have been answered. The most valid decision, however, is usually to discard the entire questionnaire, since the respondent clearly did not understand what was expected. This is less of an issue with an online questionnaire, which may include technical strategies that render the "if-then" structure invisible to the respondent.

Avoidance of Excessively Lengthy Instructions, Definitions, and Directions

The basic principle underlying instructions, definitions, and directions is that respondents rarely read and follow any instruction that is longer than a relatively short sentence. Introductory paragraphs are therefore of limited value. The more complex the instruction, the greater the potential for misunderstanding and error. Dillman, Smyth, and Christian provide detailed guidance on inclusion of instructions, definitions, and directions in questionnaires.[3]

The best approach to incorporating directions or instructions into a questionnaire is to start by making questions as self-explanatory as possible. Provide instructions, directions, or definitions only when they are absolutely necessary to reduce confusion or ambiguity, or when the respondent group can be expected to have an inherent interest in reading and following directions. Instructions, directions, and definitions must be placed at the point of need and directly linked to the questions to which they apply. Separate instruction booklets or lengthy appendices with definitions are rarely good adjuncts to a questionnaire.

Another positive use of instructions or directions is in calling attention to transitions from one section of a questionnaire to another. This is especially important if the structure of the sections is similar but the nature of the questions is different. There may, for instance, be two Likert scale sections with different scales. If something isn't done to call attention to the transition, respondents will tend to continue to use the first scale.

ARRANGEMENT OF QUESTIONS

There are many possible ways in which a questionnaire can be sequenced. The following are some prominent approaches.

Accidental

In some cases there is no compelling reason to apply any particular sequence to a series of questions. If the questions are truly independent, all have the same purpose and structure, and do not lend themselves to division into subtopics, there may be no need to design a specific order. Even so, the investigator has an obligation to examine the order to ensure that there are no accidental factors that might interfere with the respondent's ability to or motivation to complete the questionnaire. Development of an explicit, designed structure should always be considered.

Grouped

Questions are frequently, perhaps even typically, grouped according to content, purpose, or structure. If the topic of the questionnaire is amenable to grouping into subtopics, it may be appropriate to group questions for each subtopic. For other designs, however, the investigator may choose to deliberately scatter questions on different subtopics throughout the sequence. It is not unusual for factual questions to be grouped separately from opinion questions or behavioral questions. It is almost always best to group questions that share both purpose and structure. If there is a set of Likert scale questions all designed to elicit projection data using a common scale, for instance, it clearly makes sense to group them rather than to scatter them across the questionnaire.

Logical Sequence

Sometimes there is a prevailing logic that naturally influences the sequence of questions. The fundamental logic of an if-then sequence, for instance, is fairly obvious. It is frequently the case that knowledge-eliciting questions are placed before opinion-based questions dealing with the same content. If there is a chronological nature or a step-by-step process related to the topic of the questionnaire, it may be logical to follow that order in developing the sequence of questions. A series of questions dealing with historical eras, for instance, can logically be ordered according to the chronological sequence of history.

Canonical Sequence

In some cases the logic of the sequence is dictated by the subject matter. A series of questions designed to assess familiarity with the content areas defined by Dewey Decimal Classification main class numbers, for instance, will probably be listed in the order of the classes.

Easy Questions First

Questions designed by the investigator to be easy to answer may be placed before questions that are designed in a manner that makes them more difficult to answer. The motivation for this approach is the expectation that the respondent will develop a commitment to completing the questionnaire and make a more sincere effort to answer the more difficult questions. If the difficult questions come first, the respondent may be discouraged and fail to even attempt to complete the questionnaire. Closed-ended questions are frequently grouped before open-ended questions on the assumption that closed-ended questions are inherently easier or at least less time consuming to answer.

Inoffensive Questions First

If questions that might be perceived by the respondent as offensive, intrusive, or excessively personal must be included in the questionnaire, it may make sense to include those questions last. A respondent who encounters such a question frequently responds by stopping the process of completing the questionnaire. If such questions are included at the end of questionnaire, there is some hope that the respondent will still make the effort of returning the questionnaire to the investigator, even though it is incomplete.

QUESTIONNAIRE LAYOUT

Size and Appearance

The two basic factors involved in questionnaire layout are brevity and page size and appearance. Although these factors are understandable as separate elements, they are in fact so closely linked that it is difficult to discuss them independently.

In many ways and for many purposes, the ideal mail questionnaire is one that consists of a single 8-1/2 inch by 11-inch sheet of white paper with 1-inch margins, printed in a normal business-purpose 12-point font with normal line spacing. This may change as the impact of digital publishing on print-on-paper products intensifies and as more questionnaires are presented as interactive Web pages, but at least for the short term the basic image of the questionnaire as a form of business correspondence is very compelling.

There is rarely any meaningful reason to use colored paper for a questionnaire. Matching the paper of the letterhead stationery on which the cover letter will be reproduced is probably the most legitimate motivation for using nonwhite paper for the questionnaire. Similarly, there is little reason to use colored ink. Using colored ink on colored paper has great potential for producing a disaster if the contrast between the colors is inadequate.

Using a smaller font, reducing the margins, and reducing the space between lines are all techniques that can be used to squeeze a questionnaire onto a single page. Used judiciously, these can combine to provide a means of accommodating a set of questions that otherwise almost fit. When these techniques are used to fit two pages worth of questions onto a single page, though, they tend to become conspicuous for what they are: economy at the expense of ease of respondent completion. Legal-sized paper may be used if necessary, but it is important to be aware that legal-sized paper is more difficult for respondents to handle than letter-sized paper.

There is more latitude in the format of questionnaires that are distributed in person. For instance, an early study of video use in libraries was printed on a threefold brochure size to fit inside the library's videocassette boxes along with an appropriately sized cover letter and return envelope. This format facilitated distribution and enhanced return rates.

Multiple-Page Questionnaires

There are, of course, inevitably topics that cannot adequately be addressed in the space of a single page. The investigator who must violate the principles of brevity and business correspondence appearance should do so from a position of awareness that anything that violates those principles is likely to reduce the rate of return of questionnaires. A one-sheet, front-and-back questionnaire is usually better than a questionnaire with an excessive amount of information compressed onto one side. A typical office photocopier can be used to reproduce professional-looking one-sheet questionnaires. Producing multiple-sheet questionnaires is more difficult. Stapled multiple-page questionnaires tend to look amateurish. Multifold and booklet questionnaires are more expensive to produce and usually cannot be reproduced on an office photocopier. When multiple pages are used it is useful to the respondent if each page is labeled "Page x of y" where x is the number of the current page and y is the total number of pages.

Answer Space

There is nothing as frustrating to a respondent as not having adequate space in which to provide an answer to a question. Ultimately, if the respondent can't easily provide an answer, the investigator won't have data to analyze. Answer space is most obviously an issue with open-ended questions, but can present problems in answering closed-ended questions as well. If, for instance, the respondent is expected to circle an answer in a list and can't easily do so because the list entries are too close together or too small, the respondent is likely to both be frustrated and to provide responses that are difficult to analyze. Many investigators make the mistake of providing a single line for filling in a mailing address on questionnaires sent to business addresses, which very frequently involve multiple lines. At a minimum, the investigator should include actually filling out a questionnaire as part of the process of testing the questionnaire prior to use.

Online Questionnaires

The advent of the Internet was accompanied by what many observers view as a revolution in descriptive research and evaluation: the online survey. Although interactive computer-based questionnaires have been in use since the 1960s, the limitations of access to computers placed significant restrictions on the extent to which such techniques could be implemented. E-mail surveys arose in the 1980s and Web-based surveys appeared very shortly after the widespread adoption of the World Wide Web in the 1990s. Early attempts were accompanied by both technological and methodological challenges. Despite the attraction of the ease of administration and tabulation presented by online surveys, many investigators in the social sciences were extremely skeptical about online surveys. The rapid adoption of online surveys for commercial market research and evaluation added to that skepticism. Although online surveys are still not universally accepted, they are clearly a part of the way in which survey research and evaluation is done in the 21st century.

Because online surveys are relatively new and have undergone a rather cautious adoption process, the research and evaluation literature on their use is fairly limited. Evans and Mathur enumerated the major advantages and disadvantages of online surveys.[4]

Advantages of Online Questionnaires

1. Global reach
2. Appeal in commercial applications
3. Flexibility
4. Speed and timeliness
5. Technological enhancements
6. Convenience
7. Ease of data entry and analysis
8. The ability to use a diverse range of question structures
9. Relatively low administration costs
10. Ease of follow-up
11. Ease of sampling
12. Ability to work with very large samples
13. Ease of constructing controlled path sequences
14. Ability to require that questions be answered
15. Ease of determining differences between respondents and nonrespondents

Disadvantages of Online Questionnaires

1. Perception of e-mail invitations to participate as junk mail
2. Atypical characteristics of population; lack of representativeness
3. Potential for unintended respondents
4. Respondent lack of experience/expertise
5. Technological inconsistency
6. Necessity for extreme clarity in instructions
7. Impersonal nature
8. Privacy and security issues
9. Generally low response rates

Glover and Bush compared online surveys to other survey techniques and suggested that online surveys are most valuable when the information sought by the survey is relatively simple and easily defined and described. Their results indicated that online surveys were substantially less useful in obtaining data on complex or highly structured topics.[5] Potential respondents to an online survey may be especially skeptical regarding assurances of confidentiality of responses. There may also be audiences for whom online surveys are either more or less appropriate. It seems obvious, for instance, that an online survey requires some preexisting familiarity with computers and the Internet.

Online Questionnaire Administration

Online questionnaires can be mounted and administered locally, using software such as PHP and Microsoft Access, although using that approach requires some technical expertise. Various software packages are available for local use; many statistical analysis software packages have questionnaire hosting and administration modules. There are also many free or low-cost sources for hosting online questionnaires, such as those provided by Survey Monkey and Google Docs. Issues of confidentiality and data security may argue against the use of such hosting sites for some questionnaires.

QUESTIONNAIRE ANALYSIS

Once the questionnaire has been drafted, it is important to engage in some process of assessing the quality of the questionnaire prior to questionnaire administration. There are two basic ways in which this can be done: expert advice and pretesting.

Expert advice involves consulting with some individual or group who can be expected to provide constructive comments on the questionnaire. Individuals with greater questionnaire expertise than the investigator may be sought to advise on structure, form, wording, and other technical matters. Individuals with greater subject expertise than the investigator may be called upon to advise on matters of subject, use of jargon, and general understandability to the target respondent population.

Regardless of whether such subject expertise is sought, it is almost always advisable to pretest the questionnaire. In a classic questionnaire pretest, the draft questionnaire is administered to a small sample drawn from the respondent population. The investigator then both assesses the apparent ease or difficulty respondents encountered in completing the questionnaire and analyzes the pretest data to determine whether they are likely to yield usable results. Pretest respondents are then excluded from the respondent sample for the administration of the final questionnaire.

In some cases, the classic questionnaire pretest can be modified to accommodate extenuating circumstances. If, for instance, the target population for the questionnaire is either very small or perceived as being easily sensitized, the investigator may choose to conduct the pretest using a sample drawn from a separate but similar population. If no changes are made to the questionnaire following the pretest, the investigator may with some validity incorporate the pretest results with the results of the main administration of the questionnaire.

Expert advice and pretesting are sometimes incorporated in a hybrid model in which a sample of respondents is asked both to complete the questionnaire and to comment on the questionnaire. When this model is used, it is almost never advisable to incorporate pretest data with final data, as the pretest respondents have been artificially sensitized to the potential for errors or problems in the questionnaire.

Study:	Shannon Walker, "Career Motivations of the Scientist-Turned-Librarian: A Secondary Analysis of WILIS Data," *Issues in Science and Technology Librarianship* no. 64 (Winter 2011), http://www.istl.org/11-winter/refereed4.html (accessed April 22, 2011).
Question/Purpose:	The study addressed two questions:
	What might motivate someone with a natural science degree to forgo the lab and pursue a nontraditional career in librarianship?
	Are there differences between LIS graduates with and without a science degree that might impact recruitment strategies?
Population:	Graduates of schools of library and information science.
Sample:	Data collected for a study of graduates of schools of library and information science in a single state.
Personnel:	One researcher.
Data Sources:	Longitudinal data gathered as part of the Workforce Issues in Library and Information Science (WILIS), a survey of graduates of five library and information science programs from 1964 to 2007.
Data Gathering:	Secondary analysis of existing data, including additional coding of the original data.
Summary:	Graduates with science backgrounds were demographically indistinguishable from other graduates. Science majors, like other graduates, cited prior work experience in libraries as a major motivational factor for pursuing a library career. Science majors were less likely than other graduates to report that they "always wanted to be a librarian." Science majors were attracted to careers in academic and special libraries—and particularly science libraries—than were other graduates.
Conclusions:	"Most current librarians became interested in the career at least in part due to experience in a library. Thus, perhaps the most promising recruiting practices might be to target science majors to serve as assistants in academic or special libraries, to develop close collaboration with science faculty or researchers, and to provide library assistants opportunities to do research in collaboration with practicing scientists. Such a strategy may boost recruitment of future professionals while providing enhanced service to patrons."

Figure 8.3 From the professional literature—secondary analysis.

QUESTIONNAIRE ADMINISTRATION

When the questionnaire has been finalized following input from experts or pretesting, it is ready to be administered. Questionnaire administration involves development of a cover letter, actual distribution of the questionnaire, and follow-up activities.

Cover Letters

Every questionnaire should be accompanied by a cover letter. The fundamental purpose of the cover letter is to provide a persuasive introduction that motivates the recipient to respond by completing and returning the questionnaire. The most persuasive elements of a cover letter are an explanation of the anticipated impact of the results of the questionnaire, evidence of the credentials of the investigator, and an expression of the value of the respondent's time and effort. Dillman, Smith, and Christian suggest that the cover letter is the essence of gift-exchange theory, in which the investigator demonstrates appreciation for the respondent by (1) being honest about what to expect and (2) letting the respondent know the value of his or her participation.[6]

Cover letters frequently consist of three concise paragraphs. A cover letter should never be more than one page in length. The opening sentence of the first paragraph should establish a need for the results of the research and evaluation by stating a problem in need of solution. The remainder of the first paragraph explains how the data gathered from returned questionnaire will be used to solve the problem. The second paragraph briefly states the investigator's qualifications, identifies the environment in which the research and evaluation is taking place, and describes any form of sponsorship of the research and evaluation that can be expected to have a positive influence on response. The final paragraph describes any incentives offered to the respondent and thanks the respondent for contributing to the research and evaluation endeavor. The cover letter should not provide instructions, directions, or definitions, although it may include the desired return or completion date.

The cover letter should ideally be on the letterhead of some institution that can be expected to make a positive impression on the recipient. The cover letter may be signed by the investigator, but may alternatively be signed by some official of the institution represented on the letterhead. A questionnaire distributed to the membership of a professional association, for instance, may accrue extra credibility if the cover letter is signed by the president or another officer of the association. In some cases, an Institutional Review Board may dictate the format for the cover letter.

Distribution

Most questionnaires are distributed by mail, although some paper questionnaires are distributed via other means and an increasing number are mounted on the World Wide Web. The questionnaire should be sent in an envelope bearing the same letterhead as the cover letter. It is essential to ascertain that adequate postage is affixed to the envelope. The best way to make sure postage is adequate is to take a filled envelope to a post office and ask what postage is needed.

Enclosing a self-addressed stamped envelope (an SASE) greatly increases the probability of return. It also, of course, increases the cost of the project. Very few respondents are likely to take the initiative of addressing and stamping an envelope in which to return a questionnaire and it is very likely that questionnaire recipients will be offended at being asked to do so. An offended recipient rarely becomes a respondent.

Other incentives for completing and returning the questionnaire are sometimes included in the mailing. If the respondents are members of a professional group who can be expected to be directly interested in the results of the study, a promise of a report at the end of the project may be an effective incentive. Bookmarks, calendars, gift certificates, and cash have all been used as incentives, sometimes with apparently beneficial results. Probably the greatest incentive, however, is an assurance that participation will contribute to some good outcome.

There are other forms of distribution in addition to mail and the Web. Forms can be distributed at a service point such as a reference desk or circulation desk, handed to library patrons as they enter or leave a service area, distributed at library programs, tucked into books, posted in racks on ends of course ranges, and distributed in a wide array of other creative ways. Many of these approaches have the paired advantages of very inexpensive distribution and the ability to ensure respondent anonymity by allowing unsigned questionnaires to be returned via a drop box.

Follow-Up

Researchers and evaluators frequently plan follow-up activities in an attempt to urge recipients to respond. Some issues related to follow-up activities have to do with follow-up methods, timing, data consistency, and confidentiality and anonymity.

The simplest method of follow-up is to send nonrespondents the complete questionnaire package, usually with a slightly different cover letter that serves as a reminder that this is the second time the recipient has received the questionnaire. This is also usually the most expensive method.

A less expensive alternative is to send a postcard reminder. The problem with a postcard reminder is that the recipient may not have received the original mailing or may have discarded the original mailing. The postcard reminder can provide instructions for requesting a new questionnaire, but that entails added delay and the possibility that the recipient still will not complete and return the questionnaire.

Another alternative is a direct telephone call to the recipient asking if the questionnaire was received and offering to send another one. The major problems with this approach are the difficulty of actually reaching the recipient by telephone and the expense of making telephone calls if there is significant geographic dispersion of recipients. An alternative that combines elements of the postcard and telephone follow-up methods is follow-up by e-mail, which is generally very inexpensive.

Ultimately, the decision to employ follow-up activities and the nature of the follow-up activities is dictated by the importance of increasing the return rate for the study. If a high rate of return is viewed as essential, a combination of all available follow-up methods may be used. If a low rate of return is acceptable, there may be no follow-up at all.

Another factor in follow-up is determining when to conduct the follow-up activities. This requires making an educated guess regarding when the typical recipient should have received the original distribution and how long it should take to complete and return the questionnaire. If the follow-up takes place too soon, the recipient may feel unnecessarily and unfairly nagged and decide not to complete the questionnaire. If the follow-up takes place too late, the data received in response to the initial distribution may begin to become stale or irrelevant.

A third important factor in planning and carrying out follow-up activities is consistency between initial and follow-up data. Those respondents who returned questionnaires in a timely manner and those who returned questionnaires only after having been reminded form two distinct subpopulations that differ in some manner. The actual nature of the difference may be both unknown and unknowable and may influence the overall results of the study. It is prudent to code questionnaire data such that any systematic differences between the two groups can be identified and assessed.

The confidentiality and anonymity issues associated with follow-up activities are easily stated. If the investigator is able to make a follow-up contact, the recipient clearly is not anonymous and should be offered no assurance of anonymity. The recipient may be offered an assurance of confidentiality if the investigator has structured the project such that confidentiality can be assured.

A typical method of identifying nonrespondents involves assigning a unique code number to each questionnaire recipient, maintaining a file tying the code number to recipient contact information, and recording the code number on the questionnaire. As questionnaires are received the recipient information record is destroyed and the code number on the questionnaire is obliterated. At the time that it is concluded that no more follow-up activities will be attempted, all remaining recipient contact information records are destroyed.

There are many other approaches to ensuring respondent confidentiality, all of which are designed to provide the recipient with a feeling of security. All of these methods provide the investigator with an assurance that the confidentiality of respondents is being maintained. All of them are flawed with regard to providing respondents with an accompanying assurance of confidentiality. The basic problem is that the recipient of a questionnaire *knows* beyond doubt that the investigator can determine whether recipient has or has not responded. A natural extension from that knowledge is the assumption that the investigator can associate the respondents' identities with their responses. There is nothing the investigator can do that will overcome recipient suspicion and allow for follow-up.

WHAT'S THE QUESTION?

One of the somewhat spurious attractions of interview and questionnaire methods of research and evaluation is that it is possible to frame nearly every need for data in terms of a series of questions. Questions can address many factors, from knowledge to behavior to opinion, and any combination of types and structures of questions can be incorporated into a single series. There are two caveats that apply to all approaches to basing a research or evaluation project on soliciting answers to series of questions.

The first caveat is that it is truly the case that "it is not every question that deserves an answer."[7] Questions should be asked because answers are needed and can be interpreted to the benefit of the project. It is rarely the case that there is an obvious question to be asked, and when there is such a question, the answer is generally also so obvious that the question doesn't need to be asked. Questions should never be wantonly tossed into the mix of an interview or questionnaire on the grounds that respondents will find it easy to answer the question. Again, easy questions tend to yield easy answers, and the easily answered question frequently produces uninteresting answers.

A second caveat is that, under the most favorable circumstances, respondents to an interview or questionnaire can be expected to answer to the best of their ability. Even seemingly unambiguous questions such as "in what county were you born?" don't necessarily have unambiguous answers. Some communities overlap counties; it is even possible that a hospital overlaps counties. The state of Louisiana has parishes rather than counties. In many cases such ambiguities can be anticipated, but overly aggressive attempts to anticipate and ameliorate ambiguity can lead to overly complex and difficult to read questions. In some cases, as has been noted, seemingly innocent and bland questions can be interpreted as intrusive or oblique. At the extreme, the principle present in Cooley's aphorism, "the question you're not supposed to ask is the important one" applies.[8]

For all the dangers and pitfalls that accompany interview and questionnaire research, there are some research questions and evaluation problems that can be addressed only by asking questions to human respondents. When care is taken in all aspects of designing and implementing the interview or questionnaire experience, there can be a great deal of justified confidence in the outcome of the process. When care is lacking, the answers an investigator gets may be very different from those he or she sought.

THINK ABOUT IT!

1. How can interviews and questionnaires be used together in a single research or evaluation project? What are the advantages and disadvantages of doing so?
2. Identify a real library and information science problem. To what extent are interview and questionnaire methods appropriate and inappropriate for studying the problem?
3. What ethical issues might arise from using a commercial survey service such as SurveyMonkey?

DO IT!

1. Identify a real library and information science problem for which interview or questionnaire research is appropriate. Develop three interview questions and three questionnaire questions for use in exploring the topic. How are the interview questions different from the questionnaire items?
2. Identify a real library and information science problem requiring input from the public. Interview a friend, colleague, or family member to assess that individual's ability to answer questions about the problem.
3. Identify a published article that used questionnaire research. Was the questionnaire reproduced as part of the article? If not, were the questions made clear and understandable? Can you identify any potential problems with the wording of the questions or the interpretation of the answers?

NOTES

1. *Oxford English Dictionary*, s.v. "Descriptive."
2. Stephen J. Blumberg and Julian V. Luke, "Wireless Substitution: Early Release of Estimates from the National Health Interview Survey, January–June 2010," (Washington: Centers for Disease Control and Prevention, 2010).
3. Don A. Dillman, Jolene D. Smyth, and Leah Melani Christian, *Internet, Mail, and Mixed-Mode Surveys: The Tailored Design Method*, 3rd ed. (Hoboken, NJ: Wiley, 2009).
4. Joel R. Evans and Anil Mathur, "The Value of Online Surveys," *Internet Research* 15, no. 2 (2005): 195–219.
5. Derek Glover and Tony Bush, "The Online or E-Survey: A Research and Evaluation Approach for the ICT Age," *International Journal of Research & Method in Education* 28 (October 2005): 135–46.
6. Dillman, Smyth, and Christian, *Internet, Mail, and Mixed-Mode Surveys*.
7. Publius Syrus, *Maxim 581*, 42 BC.
8. Mason Cooley, *City Aphorisms: Thirteenth Selection* (New York: Pascal, 1994).

SUGGESTED READINGS

John Carlo Bertot and Paul T. Jaeger, "Survey Research and Libraries: Not Necessarily Like in the Textbooks," *Library Quarterly* 78, no. 1 (January 2008): 99–105.

Bill Gillham, *Developing a Questionnaire* (New York: Continuum, 2007).

Judy T. Greenwood, Alex P. Watson, and Melissa Dennis, "Ten Years of LibQUAL: A Study of Quantitative and Qualitative Survey Results at the University of Mississippi 2001–2010," *Journal of Academic Librarianship* 37, no. 4 (July 2011): 312–18.

Patricia A. Gwartney, *The Telephone Interviewer's Handbook: How to Conduct Standardized Conversations* (San Francisco: Jossey-Bass, 2007).

James A. Holstein and Jaber F. Gubrium, eds., *Inside Interviewing: New Lenses, New Concerns* (Thousand Oaks, CA: Sage, 2003).

Deborah Lee, "Survey Research: Reliability and Validity," *Library Administration & Management* 18, no. 4 (Fall 2004): 211–12.

Peter M. Nardi, *Doing Survey Research: A Guide to Quantitative Methods* (Boston, MA: Allyn and Bacon, 2003).

Stephen R. Porter, ed., *Overcoming Survey Research Problems* (San Francisco, CA: Jossey-Bass, 2004).

Louis M. Rea and Richard A. Parker, *Designing and Conducting Survey Research: A Comprehensive Guide* (San Francisco, CA: Jossey-Bass, 2005).

Irving Seidman, *Interviewing as Qualitative Research: A Guide for Researchers in Education and the Social Sciences*, 3rd ed. (New York: Teachers College Press, 2006).

9

DESCRIPTIVE METHODS— OBSERVATION

Where observation is concerned, chance favors only the prepared mind.

—*Louis Pasteur, inaugural lecture as professor and dean of the faculty of science, University of Lille, Douai, France, December 7, 1854, in R. Valley-Redot*, La Vie de Pasteur, *1900*

Practitioners have a privileged discourse with empirical reality.

—*Mary Ann Swain, "Models of Collaboration & Competition: The University Expectation," Association for Library and Information Science Education Annual Conference, 1989*

In This Chapter

The nature of direct observation

Implementing direct observation

Advantages and disadvantages of direct observation

Descriptive case study

Qualitative approaches to direct observation

List checking

Transaction log analysis

Content analysis

THE NATURE OF DIRECT OBSERVATION

Direct observation includes any research or evaluation model in which the focus is on creating an environment in which it is possible to directly experience the phenomenon of interest. Suppose that the goal is to study the appropriateness of behaviors of staff members working at a library reference desk. A very simple and straightforward approach is to identify a set of observable behaviors that reflect the concept of *appropriate behaviors* and then to establish an approach to observing the extent to which those behaviors are exhibited by staff at the reference desk.

IMPLEMENTING DIRECT OBSERVATION

A good basis for such a set of observable appropriate behaviors for reference staff is the *Guidelines for Behavioral Performance of Reference and Information Service Providers* developed by the Reference & User Services Association. The *Guidelines* emphasizes five general behavioral areas and provide specific examples of behaviors within each of those areas.

The five areas are (1) approachability, (2) interest, (3) listening/inquiring, (4) searching, and (5) follow-up. The RUSA *Guidelines* can easily be adapted for an observation-based research or evaluation study, with the added advantage of grounding in an authoritative source. For purposes of simplicity and ease of observation, the design might be reduced to inclusion of a single behavior from each of the five areas. The approachability area can be represented by the behavior "acknowledges the presence of patrons through smiling and attentive and welcoming body language." Interest can be represented by "maintains or re-establishes eye contact with patrons throughout the transaction." "Uses a tone of voice and/or written language appropriate to the nature of the transaction" can represent listening/inquiring. "Asks the patrons if additional information is needed after an initial result is found" can be used as a key indicator for the searching area. "Asks patrons if their questions have been completely answered" can represent the follow-up category.

Following the first step of identifying five key behaviors, a next essential step is to identify a setting in which those behaviors can be observed. Direct observation requires that the observation process occur in a real-life rather than an artificial setting. The only appropriate setting for the study presented here, then, is one or more reference service outlets in libraries. The challenge, then, becomes to establish a situation in which the targeted behaviors can be accurately and reliably reserved. Additional professional standards and guidelines are identified in Figure 9.1.

The Reference & User Service Association's *Guidelines for Behavioral Performance of Reference and Information Service Providers* is one example of the professional association standards and guidelines that can serve as highly beneficial platforms for research and evaluation projects. Many professional associations in library and information science generate and continuously revise such standards and guidelines. A distinct advantage of these standards and guidelines statements is simply that they bear the official imprimatur of the associations that promulgate them. Although it is frequently necessary to use such standards and guidelines selectively in research and evaluation, and using them may require modification for specific purposes, they are a useful starting point for many research and evaluation processes.

A sampling of additional standards and guidelines statements includes:

- American Association of Law Libraries, *County Public Law Library Standards*, http://www.aallnet.org/about/policy_county_standards.asp
- Association for College and Research Libraries, *Standards for Distance Learning Library Services*, http://www.ala.org/ala/mgrps/divs/acrl/standards/guidelinesdistancelearning.cfm

---

Figure 9.1   Research and evaluation checknote: Using professional standards and guidelines.   (*Continued*)

- Association for Library Services to Children, *Competencies for Librarians Serving Children in Public Libraries*,
  http://www.ala.org/ala/mgrps/divs/alsc/edcareeers/alsccorecomps/index.cfm
- Medical Library Association, *Copyright Management Guidelines*,
  http://www.mlanet.org/government/positions/copyright_mgmt.html
- Reference & User Services Association, *Guidelines for Library and Information Services to Older Adults*,
  http://www.ala.org/ala/mgrps/divs/rusa/resources/guidelines/libraryservices.cfm
- Young Adult Library Services Association, *YALSA's Competencies for Librarians Serving Youth: Young Adults Deserve the Best*,
  http://www.ala.org/ala/mgrps/divs/yalsa/profdev/yacompetencies2010.cfm

Figure 9.1   *(Cont.)*

ADVANTAGES OF DIRECT OBSERVATION

Direct observation has two major advantages:

1. Direct contact with phenomena. Direct observation and case study are the only descriptive methods that bring the investigator into actual contact with the phenomenon being observed. In the study of behaviors at the reference desk, it is possible to observe and tally anticipated behaviors and also to assess the impact of behaviors not in the original set. A simple addition to the study is identification of a set of patron reactions to staff behavior, which may also be amenable to direct observation. The result is a sense of *reality* and *authenticity* difficult to obtain with other research designs.

2. High potential for reliability. Assuming that the phenomena to be observed can be accurately defined and categorized and that there is a dependable mechanism for recording observations, there is substantial potential for reliability in direct observation research. Those are, however, meaningful assumptions and great care needs to be taken to ensure the appropriateness of such assumptions. A seemingly simple concept such as smiling, for instance, is intensely subject to interpretation.

DISADVANTAGES OF DIRECT OBSERVATION

Despite having two potentially very strong advantages, direct observation is associated with a number of possible disadvantages:

1. Definition of "direct." What does it mean to directly observe something? In its purest form, direct observation involves a single investigator observing some interesting phenomenon in a nonreactive setting. A *nonreactive* setting is one in which the phenomenon being observed can reliably be expected not to react to the processes of observation. Good examples of nonreactive direct observation in the realm of natural history are found fairly frequently in articles in *National Geographic* and similar magazines.

In these studies, usually of animals, the investigator creates some sort of blind that carefully emulates the natural environment and from which observations can be made without the observed animals knowing the investigator is there. Such studies are difficult and expensive. In the social sciences, they are almost impossible to accomplish, since creating the equivalent to a blind is unlikely to be attainable. In the reference staff behavior example, if the observer is frequently seen in the reference area engaged in an unidentified activity that doesn't seem to be related to reference services, suspicions are likely to be aroused. If reference staff members know or suspect that something unusual is happening, they will inevitably react, perhaps in an unpredictable manner. Direct observation also carries distinct ethical implications—observation of patron behavior can make patrons feel uncomfortable and has the potential for constituting a violation of patron privacy.

2. Need for external verification of data. Descriptive research frequently draws support for validity from a process known as *triangulation* in which data are gathered in a variety of ways and results are examined to provide corroborative support for conclusions. It is very difficult in observational research to isolate and gather any source of verification for the observational data. The appeal of direct observation is that there really are no other viable approaches to gathering the same kind of data. As a result, the validity of direct observation usually rests entirely on the care with which the observational data are defined and gathered.

3. Determination of what to observe. Most societal actions and human behaviors are complex and difficult to define. Take a moment to reflect on those factors that constitute *attentive and welcoming body language*. There are standard techniques suggested for initiating any client–professional interchange that include such professional behaviors as smiling at the client, inclining the head and upper body slightly toward the client, using open rather than closed gestures, and other actions that are typically interpreted as open and inviting. How can the observer determine whether a particular staff member is employing such behaviors as an act of natural inclination as opposed to doing so in a rote manner because the staff member has been told to exhibit those behaviors? Is one approach in some way more *welcoming* than the other? Can patrons tell the difference? How well can a single observer assess each of a set of simultaneous, interwoven behaviors such as those that constitute the characteristics of *welcoming*? The observer has to make decisions regarding what will and will not be observed based on operational definitions of the phenomena of interest. It is almost inevitable that some aspects of the phenomenon of most interest will be excluded from the observational process.

4. Recording mechanisms. Direct observation as a descriptive tool is primarily a quantitative mechanism; the goal is to observe frequencies of manifestations of some phenomenon. It is essential to have some method for recording counts of what is observed. The simplest way to record data in a direct observation study is with the use of checklist. The checklist usually lists predetermined behaviors or actions to be observed; when such a behavior is observed, the observer makes some kind of tally mark on the checklist. This is a simple, reasonably reliable, and fundamentally conspicuous approach to gathering data. There are electronic counting devices that achieve the same results (it's possible to do this with a personal digital assistant or smart wireless phone), but they all carry that disadvantage of conspicuousness. It is difficult to imagine any such on-the-spot observation that can be carried out in a nonreactive manner. It is possible to think in terms of such devices as hidden video cameras and concealed microphones, but the ethics of recording observations of individuals who don't know they are being observed and recorded are questionable at best.

5. Calibration. Calibration is the process of determining where on a measurement scale a particular manifestation of a phenomenon lies. Some human behaviors are fairly easily calibrated. It should be possible, for instance, to count the number of exploratory questions a staff member asks as part of a reference interview on an absolute scale with a minimum of zero and a theoretically infinite maximum. Other behaviors are very difficult to calibrate. Although most observers can probably identify a smile as having occurred, judging the sincerity of an apparent smile is difficult. A behavior such as smiling is difficult to calibrate even for one staff member; calibrating across staff members could be a truly intimidating task.

6. Accuracy. Even if a behavior can be effectively defined and calibrated, it is difficult to ensure the accuracy of data gathered through observation. A patron sitting at a public computer workstation in a library is surely in some sense using the library's resources, but unobtrusively determining with any accuracy that the patron is using the workstation for library-related purposes is difficult.

7. Control. Although control of the observed environment is not a typical goal in direct observation, the observer's inability to influence the environment can create problems. Even if past records have been examined to predict typical patterns of use and observation times have been based on those patterns, the actual volume of activity at the reference desk may deviate from the norm in a manner that interferes with the opportunity to gather observational data.

8. Comparability. If the volume of data desired is such that multiple observers are necessary, comparability of observations made by different observers becomes an issue. Although the likelihood of comparability can be increased through careful training of observers, doing so adds complexity to the project and cannot provide an absolute assurance of comparability. Intercoder reliability, explored in Chapter 1, "Knowing, Research, and Evaluation," is particularly problematic in direct observation involving multiple observers. Furthermore, observations recorded by a single individual may vary according to the characteristics of the observer as well as the characteristics of the phenomenon being observed. An observer who is personally in a good mood may be predisposed to interpret the actions of others as being positive.

9. The Hawthorne effect. The Hawthorne effect is a particular kind of reactivity in which individuals perform better than usual because they know they are being observed. The phenomenon is named for a series of studies carried out at the Hawthorne plant of the Western Electric Company from 1927 to 1933. The concept of the Hawthorne effect is intended "to account for unexpected outcomes which are believed to depend on the fact that the subjects in a study have been aware that they are part of an experiment and are receiving extra attention as a result."[1] There are many variations on the general issue of reactivity, including the tendency to exhibit the behavior the observed individual thinks the observer wants to see, resentment of the observational process, and many other reactive behaviors, all of which contaminate the validity of conclusions drawn from the research.

10. Challenges to validity. The overall tendency in direct observation is toward a relatively limited potential for documentable validity. There are so many confounding factors at work simultaneously in direct observation that accounting for all the threats to validity is nearly impossible.

Despite this extensive list of disadvantages, there are circumstances under which direct observation is the only research or evaluation approach that will yield the desired data. When that is the case, it is the obligation of the investigator both to work to minimize the impact of these limitations and to be actively aware of them throughout the process.

Study:	Lynne (E. F.) McKechnie, "Observations of Babies and Toddlers in Library Settings," *Library Trends* 55 (Summer 2006): 190–201.
Question/Purpose:	To discover what happens at library baby storytime programs and if and how these programs benefit the children who take part.
Setting:	Babies and toddlers attending public library storytimes.
Sample:	Babies and toddlers attending 11 storytimes at two branches of a large public library system.
Personnel:	Two researchers and one research assistant.
Data Sources:	Observation of child behavior at 11 30-min storytimes; interviews and focus groups with adult participants.
Data Gathering:	Field observation notes; audio recording.
Summary:	Children and family members attending baby storytimes were observed from the point of entry to the library through the conclusion of each storytime session. Room layout and materials provided or displayed were also observed. Multiple observers were used to address challenges presented by physical activity and volume of noise. Observers acted as participant–observers, sitting on the floor with adult and child participants, to minimize the intrusiveness of observation. Audiotapes were transcribed and transcriptions were used to augment observer field notes.
Conclusions:	Direct observation is an appropriate and useful method for examining the behaviors of very young children in public library storytime settings. The author provides thirteen explicit guidelines for ensuring successful observation in group situations involving children.

Figure 9.2   From the professional literature—direct observation.

CASE STUDY

Although the term *case study* has recently become most closely aligned with qualitative research, case studies have been used as an approach to descriptive research for many years. The fundamental characteristic of case study research of any kind is that the investigator, rather than studying many instances of some phenomenon to reach an inductive conclusion about the phenomenon in general, studies one instance (one *case*) in great detail as a means of explicating the phenomenon. Descriptive case studies are frequently conducted as an adjunct to a more broadly based inductive descriptive study from which typical cases are selected to serve as examples of the various ways in which the broader phenomenon is manifest.

A case study typically involves some direct content with the entity that is the case. If the case is a library, the investigator might visit the library, interview administrators and key constituents, examine the physical facilities of the library, analyze routinely collected data such as circulation figures, determine trends revealed by annual reports, review publicity and news information about the library, or engage in other useful activities designed to build an effectively complete picture of the case.

Study:	Selinda Adelle Berg, Kristin Hoffmann, and Diane Dawson, "Not on the Same Page: Undergraduates' Information Retrieval in Electronic and Print Books," *Journal of Academic Librarianship* 36, no. 6 (2010): 518–25.
Question/Purpose:	The study explored how students' use of electronic books is similar to and/or different from their use of print books.
Population:	University students.
Sample:	A convenience sample of 20 undergraduate students enrolled at a research university in Canada.
Personnel:	Three researchers, all university librarians.
Data Sources:	Prompted think-aloud sessions conducted with undergraduate science students selected through a convenience sampling method based on estimated saturation.
Data Gathering:	Each participant was asked to think aloud while carrying out eight information retrieval tasks, using eight books, four of which were provided as print books and four e-books. Participants were instructed to verbalize all thoughts while performing the assigned tasks. Video recordings were limited to capturing the audio of the think-aloud and filming the computer screen or book pages of the print books in order to accurately document information retrieval strategies and participant behavior. These data were supplemented by the notes taken during the session by a second researcher. The third researcher facilitated the session and prompted the participant to think aloud while performing the assigned tasks.

Figure 9.3   From the professional literature—qualitative method.   (*Continued*)

Summary:	Results indicated that, although students were generally computer literate, they were not intuitively able to effectively use electronic books. Four qualitative themes were identified: (1) students tended to use structured linear strategies when completing tasks using print books but shifted to nonlinear tactics when working with electronic books; (2) the physical nature of the print book was an aid to successful completion of tasks, but could not successfully mimic the structure of the print book when working with an electronic book; (3) familiarity with print books resulted in few unmet expectations, but students tended to set unrealistic expectations for electronic books; (4) behaviors weren't transferred between the print and electronic formats even when tools such as indexes were available in both formats.
Conclusions:	The researchers concluded that familiarity with print books and success in their use to accomplish specific tasks is not directly transferrable to the use of electronic books. Librarians should not assume that students or other patrons can automatically achieve success in using electronic books.

Figure 9.3   (*Cont.*)

Advantages of Descriptive Case Study

1. Level of detail. The purpose of a descriptive case study is to provide detail. Rather than expressing the ways in which individual cases are different (variability) or similar (centrality), a case study describes a specific case as a means of understanding one meaningful way in which the phenomenon of interest occurs. An investigator might conduct a survey by distributing questionnaires asking library administrators to describe and assess the organizational structures of the libraries for which they are responsible. After tabulating the survey data, the investigator might select a small number of libraries that represent different classes of organizational structures derived from the survey results and conduct case studies to provide expanded descriptions of those classes.

2. Potential for serendipity. An advantage of any form of case study research is the potential for learning the unexpected. Direct observation, interviews, and questionnaire-based research tend to be very focused on preidentified variables. Case study research leaves open the possibility that variables will be identified during the process of gathering data rather than in advance. Taking advantage of serendipity requires that the investigator remains open to the potential for observing the unexpected.

Disadvantages of Descriptive Case Study

1. Expense. Because case study research is typically conducted on-site, it can be expensive. If the investigator must travel to conduct the case study, the expenses of transportation, housing, meals, and other support activities can accumulate rapidly. Some case studies will require travel to more than one site.

2. Time. Most case study research is time consuming. If the goal really is to build a complete picture of the case, it may be necessary to spend substantial time conducting interviews, visiting facilities, and examining documents with no way of predicting how useful the results of the data gathering activities will be. As the complexity of the case study increases, the time required to gather data also increases.

3. Softness of data. Case study data, because it is gathered on-site in an exploratory manner, is sometimes viewed as being inherently less precise and softer than data gathered through other descriptive means. This may be especially true if the investigator has not properly accounted for the potential for bias in data gathering.

4. Potential for bias. There are two prominent sources of potential bias in case study research. The first derives from bias on the part of the case. If the case is an individual, that person may have a preference for being viewed in a particular manner that introduces a source of bias in the information he or she presents to the investigator. The investigator therefore has an obligation to search for and attempt to minimize the influence of such bias. It may be possible to reduce bias somewhat by collecting data from multiple respondents, but there is the potential for all individuals associated with a particular endeavor sharing the same biases. The second source of bias is the investigator. An investigator interested in a particular phenomenon may have a conscious or unconscious desired outcome of the case study. This requires substantial self-examination and reflection to remove investigator bias in data gathering and analysis.

5. Low potential for reliability. Case study research tends to be very personal and very individual. There is little potential for meaningful replication of case study research.

6. Uncertain potential for validity. Because the potential for reliability is low, the potential for validity in case study research is almost always an unknown. The best approach to ensuring validity in case study research is triangulation.

QUALITATIVE APPROACHES TO DIRECT OBSERVATION

Direct observation plays a major role in research and evaluation in the qualitative paradigm. Case study research can be either quantitative or qualitative in nature. Observation in the qualitative paradigm tends to emphasize immersive processes in which the level of contact between the investigator and the observed phenomenon is very high. Three techniques of particular interest in qualitative observation are unstructured observation, structured observation, and ethnographic observation.

1. Unstructured observation is a technique in which the phenomenon is identified in general terms prior to gathering data but the characteristics to be observed and the approaches taken to observing those characteristics emerge and evolve as the study is carried out.

2. Structured observation is a technique in which the characteristics of the phenomenon that will be observed and the methods for observing them are precisely defined prior to data gathering. Structured observation typically deliberately deselects certain characteristics to allow for more careful and detailed observation of the characteristics of interest to the investigator.

3. Ethnographic observation most frequently involves an investigator becoming immersed in a social, cultural, or group environment as a means of studying that environment and the individuals who are members of the society, culture, or group.

Study:	Kendall Hobbs and Diane Klare, "User Driven Design: Using Ethnographic Techniques to Plan Student Study Space," *Technical Services Quarterly* 27, no. 4 (2010): 347–63.
Question/Purpose:	The goal of this evaluation project was to explore the "real needs, desires, and behaviors" of students and "to apply that knowledge to plan for all the spaces and services" provided by the library.
Population:	University students.
Sample:	Students enrolled at a small residential university.
Personnel:	Anthropologist; team of library personnel.
Data Sources:	Photo elicitations; campus maps; architectural/design drawings.
Data Gathering:	Students took photographs from predefined lists of subjects, using disposable cameras; students used campus maps to record activities and locations and times of the activities; students drew and explained personal designs for the reuse of library space. The photograph and campus map exercises were followed by explanatory interviews.
Summary:	Students were found to mostly exploit relatively simple personal technologies during their daily lives, but expected the university to provide a variety of more sophisticated technologies for their use while on campus. Students "separate work and home spaces, social spaces and study spaces, and even differentiate study spaces based on tasks such as reading, writing, or group work." Common desires for a redesigned library included bringing nature into the building, coziness, and accommodation of group spaces of varying sizes.
Conclusions:	Although existing structural considerations limited the extent to which the ethnographically derived data were incorporated into the redesign of the library, the exercise was successful in exploring ways in which student-centered design can be used in modeling an academic library.

Figure 9.4   From the professional literature—ethnographic method.

LIST CHECKING

List checking is an established, frequently used collection evaluation process used to evaluate the quality of a collection in comparison to some external source. As opposed to direct observation of user behavior, list checking constitutes direct observation of the collection. Halliday identified six essential steps in list checking:

1. identification of the area of interest to be studied, including its relationship to organizational goals;

2. identification, examination, comparison, and selection of appropriate lists to be checked;

3. definition of terms for local application of the list checking process;

4. comparison of lists to holdings;

5. analysis to determine trends; and

6. definition of decision areas.[2]

Lists may be standard works such as the *Fiction Catalog* or the American Library Association's *Guide to Reference*. Such standard works can be used in their entirety or a section of the work can be used to examine the quality of a particular collection section or subsection. Alternatively, specialized lists can be formulated by the investigator based on definitive sources. Halliday used list checking to examine a major urban public library's holdings related to rock and roll music, using lists based on the *Rolling Stone* 200, *A Basic Music Library: Essential Scores and Sound Recordings*, *Library Journal's* Rock and Roll Hall of Fame, and the *Billboard* 200 charts.[3] Mulcahy examined the science fiction holdings of Association of Research Libraries member libraries using a list of 200 core works compiled from the listings of the winners of six major science fiction awards.[4]

Van Fleet effectively summarized the benefits and disadvantages of list checking:

> The advantage of *list checking* is that there is a great deal of apparent validity in relying on external expertise. The disadvantage is that external experts are not as familiar with the library's local constituencies and priorities for service, nor is there any attention to demand and use. Some list makers may well take need and demand into account, and some lists may create demand, but the focus is on the intrinsic quality of the item.[5]

TRANSACTION LOG ANALYSIS

A transaction log is a list of interactions between some system of interest and the users of that system. Libraries have collected transaction data for various activities since the earliest days of attempts to evaluate library collections, processes, and services. One of the simplest forms of a transaction log is the reference question check sheet in use in many libraries in which library staff members tally the numbers of reference questions answered (or at least for which an answer has been attempted)—sometimes categorized using a scheme that differentiates among subject areas, distinguishes among directional, informational, and research questions—or using some other approach to making sense of the data. Circulation counts and in-house use counts are also a traditional and widely used source of transaction data.

Study:	Karen Antell and Jie Huang, "Subject Searching Success: Transaction Logs, Patron Perceptions, and Implications for Library Instruction," *Reference & User Services Quarterly* 48, no. 1 (2008): 68–76.
Question/Purpose:	What factors affect the success of subject searchers of an online public access catalog (OPAC)?
Population:	OPAC catalog searches; university students
Sample:	Transaction logs for sixteen samples; twenty undergraduate and graduate students selected randomly
Personnel:	Two researchers, both library faculty members.
Data Sources:	Transaction logs generated by the library OPAC; observational interviews in which students were asked to perform specific tasks.
Data Gathering:	650 subject search transactions; 218 observational interview transactions
Summary:	Transaction log analysis found that keyword searching was used fourteen times more frequently than subject searching and that subject searches frequently used inappropriate search terms that yielded zero results. Observational interviews revealed that students generally found subject terms accidentally or incidentally rather than systematically. Many students simply gave up when the initial search was unsuccessful. The percentage of student searches that yielded zero results was comparable to the percentage of noted for transaction log analysis.
Conclusions:	"This study's results corroborate the findings of previous research showing that OPAC users experience great difficult with subject searching. Both the transaction log data and the observation interviews show low rates of success in subject searching." The researchers suggest that advanced subject search features and expanded "point of need" information literacy education are needed to improve subject search success.

Figure 9.5 From the professional literature—transaction log analysis and observational interviews.

The introduction during the 1950s of computerized means of controlling, managing, and monitoring library and information system operations made possible automation of the collection of an increasingly broad and flexible range of data related to system use and, by extension, user behavior. Most online public access catalog (OPAC) systems allow for some level of automatic data capture that can be interpreted at various levels, including the level of the individual transaction. Systems also exist for tracking the use of the World Wide Web.

The major advantage of automated transaction log analysis is that it is possible to use vendor-supplied or readily customized routines for gathering an enormous wealth of data. Automated transaction log analysis is, however, at best a partial approximation of direct observation of user behavior. The recordable aspects of a transaction between a library patron and an online system may include incredibly rich data at the level of individual key strokes, words, phrases, fields, and logical operations, but cannot capture the real-world human factors, such as facial expressions, body language, and environmental distractions that characterize a meaningful component in the interaction between the patron and the system. Automated transaction logs can capture apparent errors in the form of use of the delete or backspace key or aborted searches, but cannot determine whether the patron succeeded or failed in finding the information that was sought.

CONTENT ANALYSIS

Content analysis is the search for patterns in recorded information sources. White and Smith provide a good overview of the processes of both quantitative and qualitative content analyses.[6] Krippendorff defined content analysis as "a research technique for making replicable and valid inferences from texts (or other meaningful matter) to the contexts of their use."[7] The data sources may be print, audio, images, video, architecture, or any other expression of knowledge. Content analysis may be wholly qualitative or wholly quantitative; most content analyses combine elements of qualitative and quantitative data analysis. White and Smith provided an overview of library and information science content analyses published between 1991 and 2005.[8] They found substantial variability in the nature of the texts used in content analyses, which included both naturally occurring bodies of text and texts constructed for purposes of research.

THE POWER OF OBSERVATION

"Nothing has such power to broaden the mind as the ability to investigate systematically and truly all that comes under thy observation in life."[9] Observation is a fundamental human activity, if one that is present to a variable degree in different people. Observation is closely related to direct personal experience as a way of learning. One of the dangers of observation as an approach to research and evaluation, however, is that the observation process may become too much a matter of personal experience and too little a matter of gathering data for an investigation. There are clearly questions to be answered and problems to be solved that can only be effectively addressed through observation of the phenomenon of interest. When an observational study is designed with care and with an eye to appropriate avoidance of intrusion, observation has great power to yield a richness of data rarely possible with any other family of methods.

THINK ABOUT IT!

1. What library and information science phenomenon can be studied only through observation or studied best through observation?
2. What are the fundamental differences of data gathered through observation and data gathered through interview or questionnaire methods?
3. Identify a specific library department or service. What aspects of that department or service can be studied through direct observation? What aspects are not amenable to direct observation?

DO IT!

1. Find an appropriate library setting and observe a tightly defined phenomenon for a short period of time. How does the phenomenon manifest itself? What are the challenges to observing the phenomenon? How can observations be recorded in an unobtrusive manner?
2. Design an instrument for recording observations of a real library and information science phenomenon.
3. Design a protocol for teaching observers how to observe and record observations for a real library and information science phenomenon.

NOTES

1. Frank Merrett, "Reflections on the Hawthorne Effect," *Educational Psychology* 26, no. 1 (2006): 143.

2. Blane Halliday, "Identifying Library Policy Issues with List Checking," in *Library Evaluation: A Casebook and Can-Do Guide*, ed. Danny P. Wallace and Connie Van Fleet, 140 (Englewood, CO: Libraries Unlimited, 2001).

3. Ibid., 142–43.

4. Kevin R. Mulcahy, "Science Fiction Collections in ARL Academic Libraries," *College & Research Libraries* 67, no. 1 (2006): 15–34.

5. Connie Van Fleet, "Evaluating Collections," in *Library Evaluation: A Casebook and Can-Do Guide*, ed. Danny P. Wallace and Connie Van Fleet, 122 (Englewood, CO: Libraries Unlimited, 2001).

6. Marilyn Domas White and Emily E. Smith, "Content Analysis: A Flexible Methodology," *Library Trends* 55, no. 1 (2006): 22–45.

7. Klaus Krippendorff, *Content Analysis: An Introduction to Its Methodology* (Thousand Oaks, CA: Sage, 2004), 18.

8. White and Smith, "Content Analysis."

9. Marcus Aurelius, *Meditations*, 2nd century AD.

SUGGESTED READINGS

Michael V. Angrosino, ed., *Doing Cultural Anthropology: Projects for Ethnographic Data Collection* (Long Grove, IL: Waveland, 2007).

Lynda M. Baker, "Observation: A Complex Research Method," *Library Trends* 55, no. 1 (Summer 2006): 171–89.

Victor C. de Munck and Elisa J. Sobo, eds., *Using Methods in the Field: A Practical Introduction and Casebook* (Walnut Creek, CA: AltaMira, 1998).

Heidi Julien, Jen Pecoskie, and Kathleen Reed, "Trends in Information Behavior Research, 1999–2008: A Content Analysis," *Library and Information Science Research* 33, no. 1 (January 2011): 19–24.

Klaus Krippendorff and Mary Angela Bock, eds., *The Content Analysis Reader* (Thousand Oaks, CA: Sage, 2009).

Margaret Diane LeCompte and Jean J. Schensul, *Designing and Conducting Ethnographic Research: An Introduction*, 2nd ed. (Lanham, MD: Altamira, 2010).

Anne F. Lunden, "List Checking in Collection Development: An Imprecise Art," *Collection Management* 11, no. 3–4 (1989): 103–12.

Lisl Zach, "Using a Multiple-Case Studies Design to Investigate the Information-Seeking Behavior of Arts Administrators," *Library Trends* 55, no. 1 (Summer 2006): 4–21.

Ying Zhang, Bernard J. Jansen, and Amanda Spink, "Time Series Analysis of a Web Search Engine Transaction Log," *Information Processing and Management* 45, no. 2 (March 2009): 230–45.

10

EXPERIMENTAL METHODS

The absence of proof is not the proof of absence.

—Attributed to William Cowper

In This Chapter

Definition of experimentation

Factors affecting validity in experiments

Experimentation and causation

True experimental designs

Pre-experimental designs

Quasi-experimental designs

DEFINITION OF EXPERIMENTATION

In an experiment, the researcher deliberately applies a treatment (manipulation of an independent variable) to determine its relationship to a particular characteristic or behavior (a dependent variable). As defined in Chapter 1, "Knowing, Research, and Evaluation," a variable is an observable entity of interest, the value or nature of which is not known at the outset of the research project. The essence of experimentation is (1) measurement of the effect of (2) a deliberately induced change in (3) a predictable environment. Experimentation involves manipulating variables in an artificial environment to answer the question "what might happen?" If any of these three elements is absent, the design is not a true experiment.

1. Measurement. Experimentation is more closely tied to quantification than any other family of research methods. Although it is possible to integrate experimentation and qualitative approaches to gathering and analyzing data, a distinct majority of experimentation projects rely on gathering quantitative data and employing statistical tools for analysis.

2. Deliberate change. Change is a constant characteristic of the natural environment Studying change in the real world is complicated by a variety of factors: it is difficult to isolate individual variables in the real world. The involvement of multiple changes in multiple variables makes it hard to determine the impact of any particular change; changes happen in an unpredictable manner that creates difficulty in observing and gathering data. As a means of reducing the confounding impact of these complications, an experiment establishes an artificial environment in which one or more changes in a selected variable or variables can be deliberately induced while other changes are prevented.

3. Predictable environment. Measuring the impact of the induced change requires that the setting in which the change takes place is predictable. There are two fundamental tools for ensuring a predictable environment:

   a. Controls are artificially created constants, variables that are not allowed to vary or that are allowed to vary only in carefully controlled manner. There are some disciplines in the physical sciences, chemistry being a prime example, in which most experimentation involves true controls: temperature, pressure, and other environmental factors that are normally variable are carefully controlled while the relationships among other variables are observed. The use of true controls is possible in many areas of the physical sciences and in some areas of the biological and health sciences. True controls are much more difficult to apply in the social and behavioral sciences, since the variables that would need to be controlled in those fields are typically behaviors or other human characteristics. The risk of inducing harm through either the imposition of controls or the inducement of change is an especially sensitive element in any research project involving human subjects. It is unlikely to be practical, for instance, to design an experiment for which it is necessary to create laboratory emulations of a public library in which to incorporate true controls for purposes of studying user behavior.

   b. Comparable groups are a substitute for controls in experimental designs for which true controls aren't feasible. Many experimental designs involving comparable groups have their origin in agricultural research. Although it is possible to create a truly controlled environment in which to study variables such as plant growth, it is frequently undesirable to do so, since practical agriculture cannot be practiced in an artificial setting. The use of experimental designs in which the growth of different seed varieties is studied in a single environment or the same seed variety is studied in varying environments is a fundamental part of agricultural research. The use of comparable groups as a means of simulating a controlled environment is essential to experimentation in the social and behavior sciences. Although it is not practical to create a laboratory environment for studying library user behavior, it is quite practical to identify two demographically equivalent public libraries and implement an experimental design that uses one library as an experimental setting and the other as the comparable group equivalent to a control.

AN ESSENTIAL RESOURCE FOR EXPERIMENTATION DESIGN

There are some topics for which a definitive source of information exists. Experimentation in the social sciences is one of those areas. The definitive source of information regarding experimentation designs is Campbell and Stanley's *Experimental and Quasi-Experimental Designs for Research.*[1] Campbell and Stanley identified all the major categories and variations

Study:	Karen Anderson, and Frances A. May, "Does the Method of Instruction Matter? An Experimental Examination of Information Literacy Instruction in the Online, Blended, and Face-to-Face Classrooms," *Journal of Academic Librarianship* 36, no. 6 (2010): 495–500.
Question/Purpose:	Research question 1: What library research skills do incoming college students possess?
	Research question 2: Does student retention of library research skills vary based on the method of instruction (FTF vs. online vs. blended)?
	Research question 3: Does students' ability to apply library research skills to specific course assignments vary based on the method of instruction (FTF vs. online vs. blended)?
Population:	University students.
Sample:	Students enrolled in a required Introduction to Communication course in a public university.
Personnel:	Two researchers—one librarian, one faculty member.
Data Sources:	Pretest/posttest administration of a 15-question test of students' knowledge and ability to apply information from a variety of sources, knowledge of the library catalog, and ability to identify elements of a standard journal article.
Data Gathering:	Pretest administered during information literacy training session and posttest administered 5 weeks after the training session.
Summary:	Students enrolled in the course were divided into three groups. One group completed the training session in an entirely face-to-face mode; one group completed the training session in a partially face-to-face and partially online mode; one group completed the training session in an entirely online mode. Training content was the same for all three groups.
Conclusions:	Students were found to have higher-than-expected initial information literacy abilities. The mode of instruction was not significantly related to either retention of information literacy skills or students' ability to apply information literacy skills to specific course assignments. Support was given for any combination of learning modalities for information literacy training. Collaboration among librarians and faculty was viewed as essential for successful student learning.

Figure 10.1   From the professional literature—experimental method 1.

on experimentation design models and discussed in detail the challenges to validity encountered in conducting experimentation. Their work has not been surpassed by any subsequent work, nor has there been any need for an update or revision.

FACTORS AFFECTING INTERNAL VALIDITY IN EXPERIMENTS

Internal validity has to do with the extent to which relationships among variables are accurately described. Campbell and Stanley identified eight "threats" to internal validity in experimentation designs.

1. The history effect refers to unanticipated events that occur during the course of the experiment. The most critical issue in history in experiments involving comparable groups is any occurrence that damages the comparability of the groups. Imagine a research project focusing on the comparative value of two approaches to virtual reference: e-mail reference and live chat room reference. Three libraries, deliberately selected because they are substantially similar in terms of a carefully identified set of demographic and volume-of-activity variables, are identified as comparable group environments. Overall patron satisfaction with reference services is assessed in each library using a standardized questionnaire (a pretest). Following that assessment, e-mail reference service is implemented in Library One while live chat reference service is implemented in Library Two. Library Three, the control group, continues to offer only those services offered during the pretest period. The design calls for conducting a second assessment (a posttest) in each of the three libraries after the e-mail and chat services have been in effect for 12 weeks (the experimental period) and comparing pre- and posttest results to determine the impact of e-mail and chat on patron satisfaction. Unfortunately, the community served by Library Three is faced with a budget crisis that emerges in the second week of the experimental period. Library Three is forced to cut staff and reduce service hours. The result is that Library Three is no longer a comparable environment and the results of the posttest for Library Three cannot be assumed to be comparable. Any differences observed in Library One or Library Two are now lacking the context of a control group. Interpretation of the results is compromised because it is not impossible to assess what would have happened to patron satisfaction in the absence of either e-mail or live chat reference services. This is a history effect.

2. Maturation has to do with unanticipated changes directly resulting from the passage of time. The classic example of maturation arises in educational research, in which children can be expected to exhibit behavioral changes that are primarily related to advancing intellectual maturity rather than the effects of designed learning experiences. Many key indicators of student learning, such as those related to reading proficiency, are based on the assumption that, all other things being equal, a student of a given age or in a given grade will demonstrate proficiency at a predictable level. An experimental application of a technique for teaching reading that does not take normal maturation into account has great potential for yielding results suggestive of benefits that do not actually exist. In library and information science, information literacy instruction research and evaluation carries substantial risks of maturation effects. Although freshman university students can be expected to experience increased information literacy as a result of a deliberate library-sponsored instructional program, they may also experience increases simply due to the need to fulfill the information literacy requirements of university-level courses.

3. Testing, or reaction to testing, also known as pretest sensitization, is the effect of one manipulation or observation on other manipulations or observations. In particular, reaction to testing describes the impact pretesting can have on posttest performance. A freshman university student whose self-perception is that he or she performed poorly on a pretest of information literacy skills may independently elect to try to learn more prior to the posttest, even if the student has been assigned to the control group. At a minimum, the student may spend the time between the pretest and the posttest thinking about ways to do better on the posttest.

4. Instrumentation involves changes in the way in which the dependent variable is measured. Instrumentation issues frequently arise when data are gathered via direct observation of the phenomenon that is represented by the dependent variable. There is a natural tendency for human observers to become more discriminating as the number of observations increases. A researcher studying the friendliness of reference librarians by observing transactions at a reference desk may over the course of time unconsciously revise his or her definition of the set of behaviors that constitutes friendliness; this will not likely be accounted for by a control group. Instrumentation is also a critical issue in any pretest/posttest design in which the pretest and posttest do not use exactly the same instrument.

5. Regression, or regression toward the mean, is the tendency for individuals in groups to become similar, and for different groups to become similar. This is an almost inevitable problem if groups are selected on the basis of preexisting differences rather than on the basis of similarities. Imagine a test of the relationship between Miller Analogies Test (MAT) scores and a learning experience designed to encourage analog thinking. Subjects are given the MAT and their scores recorded. Subjects are then divided into a high-MAT group and a low-MAT group. Both groups participate in an analog-thinking workshop that combines lecture, discussion, and completion of a workshop. At the end of the workshop, both groups again take the MAT. Statistical probability makes it highly likely that the difference in average performance for the two groups will decrease from the pretest to the posttest, even if average performance of the two groups combined increases.

6. Selection bias describes any failure to select comparable groups. The essential assumption of any comparable group design is that comparable groups will react in a comparable manner to a controlled change in an independent variable. The obverse assumption is that noncomparable groups will not react in a comparable manner. This does not imply that groups must be absolutely identical or that they must be comparable in every conceivable way. Groups must, however, be demonstrably comparable in terms of every variable that can reasonably have an impact on the impact of the change.

7. Mortality is the unanticipated removal of subjects from the experiment. Some experimental mortality can be expected in nearly any experimental design. Imagine an experiment in which two comparable libraries are selected for a study of the impact on circulation of adult nonfiction programming. Two identical sets of new nonfiction books are added simultaneously to the collections of the two libraries and circulation of those items is recorded. In Library One, the new books are discussed at a series of adult programs; no such programs are offered in Library Two. A probable outcome is the loss or destruction of some of the books. This is a mortality problem. If the level of loss or destruction is excessive in one or both libraries, the potential for comparable circulation will be undermined and the impact of the programming will be impossible to assess.

8. The final threat to internal validity is interaction among any of the above factors. In the example described under history, the actual complication is made more complex by the resulting noncomparability of groups and by a mortality factor in which Library Three cannot be expected to produce a volume of results comparable to Library One and Library Two. In practice, failure to account for any one of the threats to internal validity is likely to result in an increased likelihood of the occurrence of other threats.

FACTORS AFFECTING EXTERNAL VALIDITY IN EXPERIMENTS

External validity is the extent to which conclusions can be generalized and applied to other environments. Campbell and Stanley describe four fundamental threats to external validity in experimental designs. The fundamental risk associated with these threats to external validity is the conclusion that the change was beneficial when it in fact was not, with the result of applying the results in another environment that are an unnecessary investment in a new way of doing things.

1. Reaction to testing is a threat to external validity as well as to internal validity. In the context of eternal validity, it is difficult to assess whether the same reaction to testing issues would be present if the experiment were carried out in another environment.

2. Selection/bias interaction occurs when the researcher, intentionally, unconsciously, or unknowingly, selects groups in a manner that biases a group in favor of a positive (or negative) reaction to the experimental treatment. If, for instance, an experiment is being conducted in which one library will implement a virtual reference service and a control library will not, and the experimental library is selected on the basis of having a superior technology environment, the experiment has been biased from the outset by the selection decision.

3. If the artificial environment is excessively different from the natural environment it is intended to mimic, the results of the experiment will be difficult or impossible to reproduce in the real world. One of the disadvantages of creating a true laboratory environment, even when it is possible to do so, is that the accidental and serendipitous factors that define natural environments may be missing.

4. Multiple treatment interference may occur when more than one experimental treatment is included in a single experiment. Unless the experiment is managed very carefully, it may be difficult to accurately assess the impact of any single experimental treatment or combination of experimental treatments. A particularly problematic situation is produced when the impact of multiple experimental treatments occurs only if the experimental treatments are induced in a specific order.

EXPERIMENTATION AND CAUSATION

Experimentation is not necessarily carried out to explore causal relationships, but experimentation is much more closely associated with exploration of causation than either historical or descriptive research. In most disciplines and domains, experimentation is the only viable approach to demonstrating causal relationships.

Definitive evidence of causation can be produced only through demonstration that a change in the independent variable is both necessary and sufficient to produce a change in the dependent variable. A change in the independent variable is necessary to a corresponding change in the dependent variable only if no change in the dependent variable can take place without the change in the independent variable. A change in the independent variable is sufficient for a corresponding change in the dependent variable if no factor other than the change in the independent variable is needed for the change in the dependent variable to occur.

Demonstration of necessity and sufficiency is difficult in all disciplines and domains outside the physical sciences and is especially problematic in the social and behavioral sciences. The most commonly employed substitute for demonstration of necessity and sufficiency is systematic rejection of alternative explanations. This requires substantial knowledge, analysis, and creativity in envisioning alternatives and establishment of compelling arguments against those alternatives.

TRUE EXPERIMENTAL DESIGNS

Campbell and Stanley identified three basic designs that represent true experimentation. There are many variations on and extensions from these basic design models, but all have their roots in these three.

Pretest/Posttest Control Group

observation	→	experimental treatment	→	observation
observation	→	no experimental treatment	→	observation

The pretest/posttest control group design is the simplest true experimental design. There are two groups: an experimental group and a control group. The nature of the dependent variable is observed in both groups, the experimental treatment affecting the independent variable is induced in the experimental group, and the dependent variable is again observed. Assuming that the groups are truly comparable (preferably through random assignment to groups), this design accounts for all the internal validity problems, but not for the external validity problems.

As an example, a study is designed to address the question "does provision of virtual reference services enhance patron satisfaction with the library?" Two comparable public libraries not currently offering virtual reference services are selected. A coin flip is used to determine which library will introduce virtual reference services and which will serve as the control. An appropriate sample of patrons from each library is selected and a questionnaire assessing patron satisfaction is administered. After the virtual reference service has been offered in the experimental library for a suitable length of time, patrons again complete a patron satisfaction questionnaire and the differences in scores between the pretest and posttest are analyzed to determine if there is a relationship between introduction of virtual reference services and satisfaction scores.

Solomon Four Group

observation	→	experimental treatment	→	observation
observation	→	no experimental treatment	→	observation
no observation	→	experimental treatment	→	observation
no observation	→	no experimental treatment	→	observation

In the Solomon Four Group design, there are two experimental groups and two control groups. A further element of control is added by eliminating the pretest (the observation)

Study:	S. L. Baker, "The Display Phenomenon: An Exploration into Factors Causing the Increased Circulation of Displayed Books," *Library Quarterly* 56, no. 3 (July 1986): 237–57.
Question/Purpose:	The study addressed two explicit hypotheses: (1) fiction books placed in a prime display location will circulate significantly more than their counterparts on the regular shelves or in a nonprime display location simply because they are more physically accessible and visible to browsers and (2) fiction books marked as "recommended" will circulate more than their counterparts in the prime display area, in the nonprime display area, or on the regular shelves because such a recommendation serves to narrow the browser's choice of materials, thus providing a type of selection guidance that overcomes the effects of information overload.
Population:	Fiction books in public libraries.
Sample:	Selected books from the fiction collections of two small public libraries.
Personnel:	One researcher.
Data Sources:	Circulation records for selected fiction books from the sample libraries.
Data Gathering:	Normal library circulation records.
Summary:	The study used a pretest/posttest control group design. During the 3-month pretest, all books studied were left in their usual locations and circulation figures were tabulated. For the first hypothesis, books in the experimental libraries were randomly divided into three groups—prime display books, nonprime display books, and nondisplay books left in their usual locations—and circulation of the books was tracked for 3 months. For the second experiment, 38 books from each display group were marked with red dots to indicate that they were "recommended." Differences in circulation for the various groups were examined using analysis of variance (ANOVA).
Conclusions:	Results of the statistical analysis revealed that circulation of books in the prime display location was significantly greater than circulation of the same books during the pretest. There was no significant difference in the circulation of "recommended" books and circulation of the same books during the pretest period. The study concluded that locating books in a prime display location was causally linked to an increase in circulation of those books.

Figure 10.2   From the professional literature—experimental method 2.

for one experimental group and one control group, thereby removing the potential for reaction to testing. This design balances the negative influence of pretests by comparing a pair of pretested groups to a pair of groups that have not been subject to the potential bias of a pretest. This is a particularly good design when naturally occurring groups must be used.

A study of the efficacy of an information literacy program in a required freshman English composition course, for instance, might be difficult to carry out without using existing sections of the course. It is, however, possible to assign roles to the sections randomly. This yields two pairs of sections, each with an experimental group and a control group. The experimental and control groups in the first pair receive a pretest, the experimental group completes an information literacy program, and a posttest is administered to both groups. In the second pair, there is no pretest, the experimental group completes an information literacy program, and both groups receive the posttest. The expectation, all other factors being equal, is that the performance of the two control groups will be comparable, as will the performance of the two experimental groups.

Posttest-Only Control Group (Random Assignment to Groups)

| no observation | → | experimental treatment | → | observation |
| no observation | → | no experimental treatment | → | observation |

The complexity and expense of the Solomon Four Group design can be eliminated by careful use of the posttest-only control group design. This design uses an experimental group and a control group but no pretest. This differs from the static group comparison pre-experimental design in that assignment to groups is random. Since pretests have a strong tendency to bias subjects, this design has a great deal of validity, if external indicators of equivalence are available. If assignment to groups is truly random, this design will account for all internal and external validity problems.

For example, two comparable libraries that have consistently conducted similar annual patron satisfaction surveys are selected. Since preexisting satisfaction data are available, there is no fundamental need for a pretest. One library is randomly selected as the experimental group and a virtual reference service is implemented. After an appropriate passage of time, both groups are administered satisfaction questionnaires to assess the impact of the virtual reference service.

PRE-EXPERIMENTAL DESIGNS

Campbell and Stanley described three major pre-experimental designs. These designs are called pre-experimental designs because, although they aren't quite experiments, they may nonetheless have some minimal validity.

One Group Posttest (One Shot Case Study)

| no observation | → | experimental treatment | → | observation |

There is an experimental group but no control group. Only one observation is made, and no controls are introduced. No explicit basis for comparison is established, and there is no way of evaluating what would have happened if the experimental treatment had not taken place.

This pre-experiment takes place in libraries on a frequent basis. There is generally some perception of a need for a change, perhaps because of a possible failure, a reported decline in use of some service, or an external pressure such as the observation that a nearby library has initiated a new service. Sometimes the message from administration is the bandwagon plaint "everyone but us is doing this." There is no systematic observation of current performance, but the implementation of the new way of doing things is felt to be more justified if performance is assessed after the change is implemented.

One Group Pretest/Posttest

observation   →   experimental treatment   →   observation

There is an experimental group but no control group. There is a basis for comparison, but there is still no way of knowing what would have happened if the experimental treatment had not taken place, and no way to determine whether any of the factors that negatively influence internal validity were present. If the independent variable is known to be both necessary and sufficient, this will work, but is probably unnecessary. This is only a slight improvement over the one group posttest.

In a library context, this design may be implemented when some performance indicator suggests a need for improvement. It may be observed, for instance, and documented with hard data, that e-books are not circulating. A response may be to launch a publicity campaign to encourage use of e-books, including a tangible reward to the patron who checks out the most e-books during a three-month period. The problem with this design is that, although there is likely to be an immediate increase in circulation as a result of the publicity campaign, the publicity campaign has not directly assessed the question of why e-books were not circulating and may have no more than a short-term impact on circulation.

Static Group Comparison (Naturally Occurring Groups)

no observation   →   experimental treatment   →   observation
no observation   →   no experimental treatment   →   observation

This is the same as the posttest-only control group true experimental design except in the assignment of members to the experimental and control groups. The two groups are naturally occurring groups. The equivalence of the two groups prior to the experimental treatment is unknown, and therefore the result of the experimental treatment is unknown.

An obvious and easy way to examine the impact of an information literacy program on university freshmen is to select two sections of a required English composition course, identify one as the experimental group and the other one as the control group, implement the information literacy program in the experimental group, and then administer a test of information literacy skills to both groups. The limitation of this design is that the comparability of the two groups is unknown and untested. There is a distinct possibility that students in the experimental group possessed higher levels of information literacy skills prior to being part of the information literacy program.

QUASI-EXPERIMENTAL DESIGNS

There are a great many almost-but-not-quite experimental designs, but very few of them are of much use for library and information science research. The key feature of a quasi-experimental design is the lack of random assignment of subjects to groups. Two such designs identified by Campbell and Stanley that have more potential for validity than the pre-experimental designs are the nonequivalent control group and the ex post facto study.

Nonequivalent Control Group (Known, Measurable Differences)

| observation | → | experimental treatment | → | observation |
| observation | → | no experimental treatment | → | observation |

This design employs an experimental group and a control group. The main characteristic of this design is that the differences in the experimental group and the control group are known and measurable. Typically, the assignment to groups is natural rather than random. The differences in the groups can be controlled through statistical manipulation of the data to compensate for the known differences. The greatest problem is that there may be unknown differences as well.

If, for instance, Library One and Library Two are demographically comparable, except that Library One has half the service population of Library Two, a design can be implemented in which the two libraries can be compared, even though the sampling base for Library Two is twice that of Library One, if the difference in bases is accounted for in the data analysis.

Ex Post Facto Study

The ex post facto study may be more properly classified as a form of historical research. The basic characteristic of this design is that it employs preexisting data, usually gathered for some purpose other than examination of the relationship between the independent and dependent variables that are the focus of the ex post facto study. An example of a possible ex post facto study in a library context is a study of the impact of the transition from a command-line interface to an online catalog to a Web interface to the same catalog. If transaction logs exist that provide consistent data for use of both versions of the catalog it may be possible to assess the impact of the transition to the Web interface on the volume and nature of catalog searches.

EXPERIMENTATION AND EXPERIENCED REALITY

Experimental research has a relationship to reality that is unique among families of research methods. Historical studies, content analysis, bibliometrics, and citation analysis explore the documented record of research. Interview and questionnaire methods examine reported knowledge, behaviors, and opinions. Observation methods place the investigator in close contact with reality and allow for flexible examination of the nature of reality. The reality of the experiment is the reality created by the investigator and experienced by participants in the experiment.

This emphasis on a designed, experienced reality that may be subtly different from object reality is both the major advantage of and the major challenge faced by experimental methods. To the extent that the artificially designed reality is reflective of objective reality, experimental methods allow for greater control of the research environment than any other methodological family. Experimentation aligns library and information science research and evaluation with the "hard," empirical sciences, which may lend enhanced credibility to experimental studies in library and information science. Experimentation is frequently viewed as the only approach to research that allows for demonstration of causation.

At the same time, experimental studies entail some of the greatest risks of all research and evaluation methods. Most other families of methodologies involve no more than a limited probability that the project will be a failure in its entirety. It is always possible, however for an experiment to simply not find a relationship between a selected dependent variable and one or more independent variables that are posited to be related to the dependent variable. Such an outcome, while not necessarily disastrous, is likely to be disappointing.

It is the nexus of control and risk, however, that lends power and precision to experimental methods that are not available from other methods. The experimenter who fails to find a hypothesized relationship has a great opportunity to step back, examine the results and the experimental design and ask "if that relationship doesn't exist, what are the driving relationships affecting the dependent variable?" Alternatively, the investigator may conclude that some aspect of the experiment itself was flawed and that there is a need for correction to a control or a measure. Experimentation at its best exploits the cyclical nature of research and evaluation to its fullest, building toward heightened understanding of what is and is not characteristic of the phenomenon of interest.

THINK ABOUT IT!

1. How can experimentation be effectively used in evaluation as well as in research?
2. Identify a real library and information science problem amenable to experimental study. How can the factors that threaten internal and external validity be minimized for an experimental study of the problem?
3. What human factors must be considered when employing experimental methods in library and information science?

DO IT!

1. Identify a real library and information science problem. Identify dependent and independent variables and select an experimental design that is appropriate for exploring the relationships among variables.
2. Identify a real library and information science problem for which a pretest/posttest control group design is appropriate. How can subjects best be assigned to the experimental and control groups for the study?
3. Identify or design an instrument for collecting data for a pretest/posttest experimental design for a topic or problem of your choice.

NOTE

1. Donald T. Campbell and Julian C. Stanley, *Experimental and Quasi-Experimental Designs for Research* (Chicago, IL: Rand McNally, 1963).

SUGGESTED READINGS

Donald T. Campbell, *Social Experimentation* (Thousand Oaks, CA: Sage, 1999).

William R. Shadish, Thomas D. Cook, and Donald T. Campbell, *Experimental and Quasi-Experimental Designs for Generalized Causal Inference* (Boston, MA: Houghton Mifflin, 2002).

C. F. Jeff Wu and Michael S. Hamada, *Experiments: Planning, Analysis, and Optimization*, 2nd ed. (Hoboken, NJ: Wiley, 2009).

11

BIBLIOMETRICS AND CITATION ANALYSIS

And for the citation of so many authors, 'tis the easiest thing in nature. Find out one of these books with an alphabetical index, and without any farther ceremony, remove it verbatim into your own . . . there are fools enough to be thus drawn into an opinion of the work; at least, such a flourishing train of attendants will give your book a fashionable air, and recommend it for sale.

—*Miguel de Cervantes*, Don Quixote, *1605*

In This Chapter

Definitions of bibliometrics and citation analysis

Origins of bibliometrics and citation analysis

Context for bibliometrics and citation analysis

Productivity

Obsolescence

Citation analysis

Uses of bibliometric studies

Uses of citation studies

Theoretical bases for bibliometrics and citation analysis

DEFINITION OF BIBLIOMETRICS AND CITATION ANALYSIS

Bibliometrics is the application of mathematical and/or statistical methods to the study of information products. Pritchard's 1969 proposal in support of the term bibliometrics stated that "The definition and purpose of bibliometrics is to shed light on the process of written communications and of the nature and course of a discipline (in so far as this is displayed through written communication) by means of counting and analysing the various facets of written communication."[1] Bibliometrics focuses on the patterns of information-related phenomena. Typical bibliometric variables include country of publication, language of publication, document type, methodological type, age, and a broad family of variables collectively known as productivity.

Citation analysis is examination of the patterns defined by the references provided in scholarly publication. The basic principle of citation analysis is that there is at least a provisionally intrinsic link between a scholarly publication and its references. Citation analysis can focus on a single work, a group of works, an author, a group of authors, an institution such as a university, a group of institutions, or a number of other factors.

ORIGINS OF BIBLIOMETRICS AND CITATION ANALYSIS

Studies that can be thought of as related to bibliometrics and citation analysis have been carried out for nearly two centuries. Although the 1873 initiation of the periodical *Shepard's Citations*, a legal citator, is frequently credited as the origin of citation indexing, Shapiro traced the origin of legal citation indexing to the 1743 publication *Raymond's Reports*.[2] Weinberg traced the use of a form of citation indexing to the Babylonian Talmud, the first printed edition of which was published between 1522 and 1524.[3]

Cole and Eales's "The History of Comparative Anatomy. Part I: A Statistical Analysis of the Literature" is generally regarded as the first research publication to present a bibliometric analysis.[4] Cole and Eales were basically conducting a historical study of a specific scientific discipline. As part of that study, they compiled a comprehensive bibliography and presented a systematic statistical analysis of the literature, including graphic presentations. Hulme, in his 1923 *Statistical Bibliography in Relation to the Growth of Modern Civilization*, coined the term "statistical bibliography," which was used for nearly 50 years to express the basic concepts of what is now known as bibliometrics. After Prichard introduced the term bibliometrics in his 1969 article "Statistical Bibliography or Bibliometrics?" bibliometrics quickly replaced the earlier term statistical bibliography. Although Otlet had introduced the similar term bibliometrie as early as 1934, it was Pritchard's work that signaled the swing to the adoption of bibliometrics to describe the application of statistical techniques to the study of recorded knowledge.[5]

A major development in citation indexing came with the 1963 introduction of the *Science Citation Index* by the Institute for Scientific Information (ISI). The index was a direct outcome of Eugene Garfield's 1955 "Citation Indexes for Science," in which he presented a model for extending the principles of *Shepard's Citations* to the sciences.[6] *Science Citation Index* was followed by *Social Sciences Citation Index* in 1973 and *Arts & Humanities Citation Index* in 1978. *Journal Citation Reports*, which began publication in 1976, based on data from the *Science Citation Index* and *Social Sciences Citation Index*, provides detailed information regarding the patterns of citation links and other evaluation data for the journals indexed in the two sources.

CONTEXT FOR BIBLIOMETRICS AND CITATION ANALYSIS

Bibliometrics can be thought of as a subfield within the larger field of informetrics. Tague-Sutcliffe defined informetrics as "the study of the quantitative aspects of information in any form, not just records or bibliographies, and in any social group, not just scientists.

Thus, it looks at the quantitative aspects of informal or spoken communication, as well as recorded, and of information needs and uses of the disadvantaged, not just of the intellectual elite."[7] Bibliometrics is related to and overlaps with scientometrics, which the *Oxford English Dictionary* defines as "the branch of information science concerned with the application of bibliometrics to the study of the spread of scientific ideas; the bibliometric analysis of science." The *OED* traces the term to Price's 1963 *Little Science, Big Science.*[8]

The emergence of the Internet and the introduction of the World Wide Web provided new and to some extent unexpected avenues for the extension of bibliometrics and citation analysis to new sources of information. Webometrics is part of "the study of the quantitative aspects of the construction and use of information resources, structures and technologies on the Web drawing on bibliometric and informetric approaches."[9] Webometrics is a subfield within the broader field of cybermetrics, "the study of the quantitative aspects of the construction and use of information resources, structures and technologies on the *whole* Internet drawing on bibliometric and informetric approaches."[10]

STUDIES OF PRODUCTIVITY

Newton is quoted as having written "if I have seen further it is only by standing on the shoulders of giants."[11] A fundamental principle of bibliometrics is that no author or publication stands completely on its own—understanding of the contribution of a given act of scholarship or creativity is interpretable only within the broader context of all such acts. Productivity refers to the contribution made by a specific entity or category of entity to a body of literature or text. Patterns of productivity are a major emphasis of bibliometric research.

Author Productivity (Lotka's Law)

Lotka was a chemist who later became an insurance actuary. Lotka's Law, originally presented in the 1926 article "The Frequency Distribution of Scientific Productivity," states that the number of authors making n contributions to a body of literature is about $1/n^2$ of the number of authors making one contribution.[12] Furthermore, the number of authors making only one contribution will be account for about 60 percent of the body of literature. Figure 11.1 presents a hypothetical example of Lotka's Law.

In practice, the number of highly productive authors tends to exceed the pattern predicted by Lotka's Law. What makes Lotka's Law interesting is the regularity of the pattern combined with the consistency with which Lotka's Law has been observed to be accurate. The regularity of the pattern can be presented graphically and is shown in Figure 11.2.

Although Lotka did not include such a graphic presentation in his article, later work in the area of author productivity revealed that this pattern prevails to the exclusion of other patterns.

Word Frequency (Zipf's Law)

Zipf was a philologist and a professor at Harvard University. While a graduate student he began studying patterns within bodies of text and presented a mathematical representation of the use of words in text. Zipf was primarily interested in other areas of language and did little to expand on his original model for the general pattern of word use. Zipf's Law was a fairly minor component in his 1949 *Human Behavior and the Principle of Least Effort.*[13]

Number of publications (in a reasonably comprehensive bibliography)		= 1,000
Number of publications by authors represented only once (60% of 1,000)	.60 * 1,000	= 600
Number of publications by authors represented n times	= $1/n^2$ * 600	
Number of publications by authors represented 2 times	= $1/2^2$ * 600	= 150
Number of publications by authors represented 3 times	= $1/3^2$ * 600	= 67
Number of publications by authors represented 4 times	= $1/4^2$ * 600	= 38
Number of publications by authors represented 5 times	= $1/5^2$ * 600	= 24
Number of publications by authors represented 6 times	= $1/6^2$ * 600	= 17
Number of publications by authors represented 7 times	= $1/7^2$ * 600	= 12
Number of publications by authors represented 8 times	= $1/8^2$ * 600	= 9
Number of publications by authors represented 9 times	= $1/9^2$ * 600	= 7
Number of publications by authors represented 10 times	= $1/10^2$ * 600	= 6
Number of publications by authors represented 25 times	= $1/25^2$ * 600	= 1

Figure 11.1 Lotka's Law example.

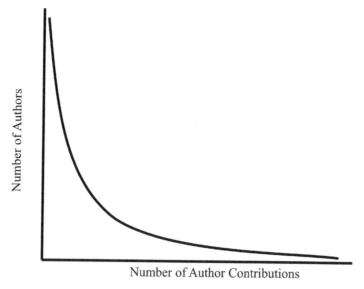

Figure 11.2 Lotka's Law graph.

Zipf's Law is based on two concepts:

1. *Word-types* are distinct words in a body of text. If the word "library" appears in the text, it counts as one word-type no matter how many times it occurs.
2. *Word-tokens* are distinct occurrences of word-types in a body of text. If the word "library" appears in the text 30 times, each constitutes a word-token for a total of 30 word-tokens.

Two measures are derived related to these concepts:

r = rank order of word-types for a given body of text

f = the frequency of word-tokens for word-types in a given body of text

Zipf's Law is stated in terms of the formula $r \times f = c$, where c is a constant that is presumed to be unique to the body of text. c is typically equal to about 1/10 the total number of word-tokens in the body of text.

A graphic representation of the Zipf distribution is presented in Figure 11.3.

Zipf presented a similar graphic representation of his law, but made little attempt to explain the distribution directly, although he did suggest that it conforms to his broader theory of the Principle of Least Effort. Note the similarity between the graphs of the Lotka and Zipf distributions.

Journal Productivity (Bradford's Law)

Bradford was a librarian at the British Museum Library (now the British Library). Unlike Lotka and Zipf, who were primarily theoreticians, Bradford was interested in solving a practical problem. He speculated that two-thirds of scholarly articles were missed by indexing

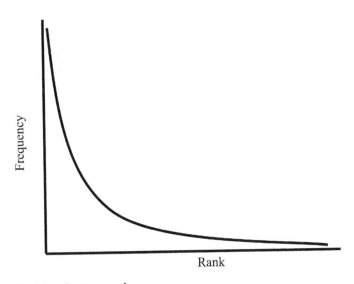

Figure 11.3   Zipf distribution graph.

and abstracting services. His hypothesis was that the ways in which articles on a given subject are distributed among the journals that publish those articles results in some articles being hidden from the attention of indexers and abstracters.

If the journals that have contributed articles to a field are ranked in order of decreasing productivity, they can be divided into zones in which the number of articles is constant and the number of journals conforms to the pattern

$$1 : n : n^2$$

where n is a constant known as the Bradford multiplier.[14]

The distribution of Bradford's example from the journal literature of applied geophysics is presented in Figure 11.4.

Although the numbers of journals in the three zones don't quite follow the predicted pattern and the number of articles varies fairly substantially across the three zones, Bradford felt that the predicted pattern was approximated well enough to support his hypothesis. Figure 11.5 presents an idealized version of the distribution into zones.

Zone	Number of Journals	Number of Articles
1	8	429
2	59	499
3	258	404

Figure 11.4   Bradford distribution table: Applied geophysics.

	Number of Source Journals	Number of Articles Per Source Journal	Total Number of Articles	Cumulative Total Number of Articles	
3	1	100	100	100	
	2	50	100	200	200
9	1	40	50	250	
	2	25	50	300	
	2	20	60	360	200
	4	10	40	400	
27	8	9	72	472	
	7	8	56	528	
	6	7	42	570	200
	10	3	30	600	

Figure 11.5   Idealized Bradford distribution table.

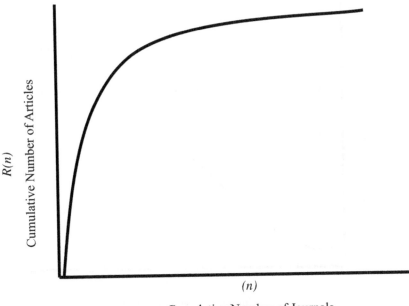

Figure 11.6   Bradford distribution graph.

Although Bradford implied that the number of zones would always be three, later researchers found that the number of zones is a function of the subject represented by the bibliography. The implications of Bradford's work have been extensively discussed in terms of collection management and sometimes directly applied. It is hardly surprising that a very small number of journals may account for a large proportion of the articles published about a given topic. What is surprising is the regularity of the pattern. Figure 11.6 is a graphic representation of the Bradford distribution.

Comparing this graph to the graphs of the Lotka and Zipf distributions reveals that they are remarkably similar except that the Bradford graph curves upwards (positively) rather than downwards (negatively). Bradford, recognizing that the curve appeared to be approximately exponential, elected to redesign the graph so that n, the cumulative number of journals, was on a logarithmic scale rather while leaving $R(n)$, the cumulative number of articles, on an arithmetic scale. A graph with one logarithmic scale and one arithmetic scale is known as a semilog plot. If the distribution were truly exponential, the impact of converting the graph to a semilog plot would be that the distribution would fall along a straight line. What Bradford found was that the semilog plot was almost a straight line. Figure 11.7 is a generalized version of a typical Bradford distribution semilog plot.

Bradford interpreted the deviation from linearity at the lower left as being indicative of those journals that are central to the discipline and that therefore contribute the most articles. Bradford did not observe the deviation from linearity at the upper right, which occurs in most Bradford plots. Groos suggested that this deviation is caused by an incomplete bibliography: there are some articles on any topic that cannot be identified and included in a Bradford analysis because they are in truly obscure journals. The deviation at the upper right has since been known as the "Groos droop."[15]

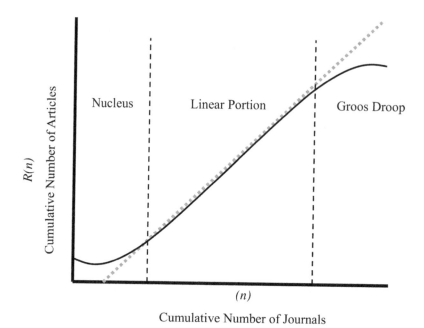

Figure 11.7 Bradford distribution semilog plot.

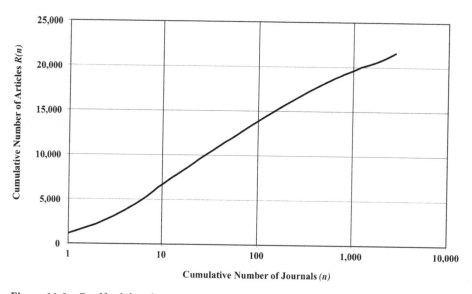

Figure 11.8 Bradford distribution semilog plot for knowledge management journals.

Figure 11.8 is a plot of the results of a comprehensive search on articles related to knowledge management. Note that the pattern is very much that of the idealized model presented above, including the Groos droop, although there is a slightly anomalous upturn at the end of the distribution. This pattern is typical of highly interdisciplinary bodies of literature.

Dimensions of the Exponential Distribution

The curiosity of the exponential curve that characterizes bibliometric distributions lies in the consistency with which it has been observed and with the range of phenomena it describes. The same basic curve has been found to apply to

1. the distribution of articles among journals in nearly every field or discipline
2. the circulation of items held in library collections (Trueswell's 80/20 rule)
3. the journals from which faculty members request photocopies from a document delivery service (Neway)
4. patron choice of databases (Evans)
5. distribution of income (Pareto)

Bradford also commented on the role of interdisciplinarity in the management of journal articles: " the articles of interest to a specialist must occur not only in the periodicals specializing in his subject, but also, from time to time, in other periodicals, which grow in number as the relation of their fields to that of his subject lessens and the number of articles on his subject in each periodical diminishes."[16] Work by Garfield and others at ISI found "that a list of 1000 journals will contain all the leading journals on any specialty list, as well as account for a large percentage of all articles published in that field."[17] Garfield's Law of Concentration suggests that there is a set of Bradford zones that describes all of scientific journal publishing. Garfield's Law of Concentration postulates that, out of all the scientific journals published worldwide, it should be possible to identify a Bradford core of 500 to 1,000 journals that are the essential core of scholarship.

OBSOLESCENCE

Obsolescence has to do with the decline in use of information products as they age. It should come as no surprise to anyone that older items in any collection tend not to be used as much as newer items. Most items receive their greatest use shortly after being added to the collection, with a rapid drop-off in use as items age. " 'Obsolescence' implies a relation between use and time, but the effects of time are revealed in different ways, which are easily confused. According to Line and Sandison, there are three fundamental dimensions of obsolescence. First, there is the influence of time past, as expressed in the current ages of the items of literature when they are studied. Secondly, the passage of time present increases the age of each item. And thirdly, of great practical interest, there is the effect of time future, which we try to foretell by extrapolations from the effects of time past and time present."[18]

Line and Sandison produced a detailed discussion of the obsolescence phenomenon in which they presented four major reasons for the decline in use over time:

1. The information contained in a work is valid, but has been incorporated into other works.
2. The information contained in a work is valid, but has been superseded by other works.
3. The information contained in a work is valid, but interest in the field to which the work belongs is declining.
4. The information contained in a work is no longer considered valid.[19]

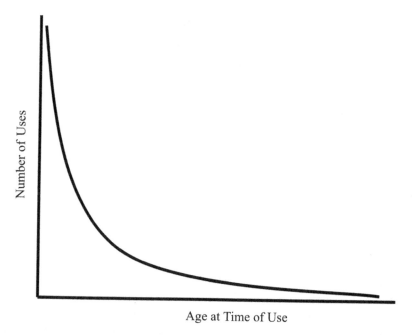

Figure 11.9 Typical obsolescence graph.

Line and Sandison also discussed the circumstances under which use of some materials may actually increase over time:

1. The information contained in a work is initially considered invalid, but becomes recognized as valid.

2. The information contained in a work is valid, but theory and/or technology doesn't allow for its exploitation at the time of its introduction.

3. The information contained in a work is valid, and interest in the field to which the work belongs is increasing.[20]

A graph of the typical relationship between ages of items at the time they are used and the number of uses of those items is presented in Figure 11.9.

In some cases, use of items starts relatively high, increases, and then declines. This is known as the *immediacy effect,* which is illustrated in Figure 11.10.

MEASURES OF OBSOLESCENCE

Line and Sandison defined three typical approaches to studying obsolescence:

1. In a diachronous study, a sample of items published at a given time is selected and use of the items in the sample is measured over time. At the end of the observation period, the midpoint of the number of uses is determined. This is the half-life of the sample. Diachronous studies can and have been done by tracing the circulation records of library materials, although current practice with regard to patron privacy and security may make such studies more difficult than they once were.

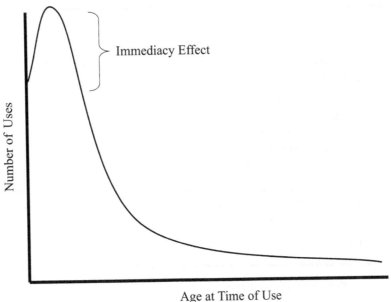

Figure 11.10   Obsolescence graph with immediacy effect.

2. In a synchronous study, a sample of items published at a given time is selected and the ages of the items listed in the references of the sample items are recorded. The midpoint of the ages of the references is the median citation age of the sample. Synchronous studies can be conducted by examining lists of references from journals, books, reports, Web pages, or other sources.

3. In a disynchronous study, multiple synchronous studies are conducted at carefully selected intervals to examine changes over time.

Line and Sandison contended that there was no inherent reason to assume that a diachronous study and a synchronous study would produce the same results. Their view was that a diachronous study was inherently superior and more accurate. Stinson, however, found that the results of a synchronous study were statistically no different from the results of a diachronous study.[21] Since a synchronous study is substantially easier to conduct, most subsequent studies of obsolescence have been synchronous.

CITATION ANALYSIS

Definition of Citation Analysis

Citation analysis is examination of the patterns defined by the references provided in scholarly publication. There is technically a definitional difference between references and citations:

1. A reference is a credit a publication gives to another source.

2. A citation is a credit a publication receives from another source.

Five Laws

S. R. Ranganathan wrote his "The Five Laws of Library Science" in 1931. The Five Laws are:

1. Books are for use.
2. Every reader his book.
3. Every book its reader.
4. Save the time of the reader.
5. The library is a growing organism.

In 1931 books and periodicals were about all that most libraries collected, and certainly school libraries—where they existed—had little beyond print. But Ranganathan's idea was on the right track. Too bad we somehow left it behind.[1]

1. Carol Simpson, "Five Laws," *Library Media Connection* 26, no. 7 (2008): 6.

Figure 11.11   Reference versus citation.

Consider the passage from a journal article presented in Figure 11.11.

Using the technical definitions, the article from which this passage was taken has provided a reference to Ranganathan's 1931 publication. Ranganathan's publication has received a citation from the article. In practice, the distinction is subtle and citation is frequently used to describe both concepts. The distinction becomes more meaningful in defining categories of research projects:

1. A citation study examines the patterns of citations to some body of work. This requires gathering data external to the body of work, usually from a citation index. A diachronous study of obsolescence is an example of a citation study.
2. A reference study examines the patterns of the references included in a body of work. This requires gathering data from the reference lists, footnotes, or endnotes included in the works themselves. A synchronous study of obsolescence is an example of a reference study.

Sources of Citation Data

Conducting a reference study is relatively easy: an appropriate body of literature is gathered, references listed in the literature are recorded, and the resulting body of data is then examined to determine patterns or test a hypothesis. Conducting a citation study is more difficult because the basic question has to do with what happens to works after they are published. The major source of data for citation studies is found in the citation indexes published by ISI. The policies and practices of ISI have a direct influence on the nature of the data available for use in citation studies:

1. ISI subscribes to about 8,000 journals, which are the source materials for the indexing process.
2. Indexing is done by trained employees who are *not* professional indexers in that they have completed no formal educational process, are not required to have even a

bachelor's degree, and are usually not knowledgeable of any indexing processes beyond their own jobs.

3. For each article in each issue of each journal, an indexer enters into a database the complete bibliographic information using a style unique to ISI and data for each reference included in the article. Only the first reference to a given work is entered: if a work is referenced multiple times in the article, only one citation link is recorded. For the *Arts & Humanities Citation Index,* implicit references are also recorded.

4. ISI indexers work only with the article itself, recording data as they appear in the article. There are no authority control or error-correction processes. If there is an error in the article, that error will appear in the citation index. If the data in the article are incomplete, the entry in the citation index will be incomplete.

5. All author names are recorded as part of the bibliographic data for the article being indexed, but only the first author of each publication included in a reference is recorded.

    Although it is possible to conduct limited subject searches and title keyword searches in the citation indexes, their real purpose is to facilitate *citation searches.* A citation search typically answers questions such as

    a. How many times has a specific article been cited by later works?

    b. How many times have the works of a specific author been cited?

    c. How many times have the works of a group of authors been cited?

    d. Who (usually by category rather than by individual) has cited a specific work, author, or group of authors?

    e. What works are related to a specific article?

Additionally, ISI publishes an adjunct publication, *Journal Citation Reports,* which provides summary data for the journals indexed in the citation indexes.

Assumptions of Citation Studies

Smith, in what is perhaps the definitive discussion of citation analysis, has identified five critical assumptions of citation studies:

1. Citation implies use.

2. Citation reflects merit.

3. Citations are made to the best possible works.

4. Citing and cited documents are inherently linked.

5. All citations are equal.[22]

As Smith pointed out, none of these assumptions can be accepted without question. Examples of citation practices that violate any or all of the assumptions are easy to identify. Nonetheless, it is apparent that there is *some* relationship between citing and cited documents and that citation reflects *some* form of recognition of the cited document by the citing document. As tenuous as these five assumptions may be, they are not sufficient to completely undermine the meaning and usefulness of citation studies.

Garfield identified 15 prominent motives for citation:

1. Paying homage to pioneers. This motive provides recognition for the origin of an idea, theory, method, technique, or other critical contribution, even though the work in which the contribution had its origin may not have been directly used in the citing work.

2. Giving credit for related work (homage to peers). Many scholars feel that they have an obligation to provide readers with contextual information that positions their work with in the discipline or subject area in which the work takes place.

3. Identifying methodology, equipment, and so on. In the sciences, it may be important to identify the specific laboratory equipment used in a study. In the social and behavioral sciences, authors frequently credit the sources of standardized assessment instruments.

4. Providing background reading. This is a convenience for the reader in which the author provides a means of "getting up to speed" so that the reader can understand the work at hand.

5. Correcting one's own work. As a researcher's knowledge of a subject increases through research a series of publications may emerge, each of which adds to and corrects previous works by the same author.

6. Correcting the works of others. The research literature is frequently viewed as a scholarly discussion in which researchers question, refute, and correct each other in print.

7. Criticizing previous work. This extends from the sixth motive. The term criticism doesn't necessarily imply a negative assessment. Most fields place some emphasis on review articles (such as those published in Library Trends) that attempt to provide an overview and critical analysis of the literature related to a field.

8. Substantiating claims. This is the process of providing evidence to support conclusions or assertions presented elsewhere.

9. Alerting to forthcoming work. This is especially important as a means of alerting readers to additional sources of information, either by the author of the work being read or by others, that will be added to the literature on the subject. A problem sometimes arises when works identified as forthcoming are not subsequently published or are published with a different title or in a different source.

10. Providing leads to poorly disseminated, poorly indexed, or uncited work. When an author is aware of potentially important works and believes them to be unknown or unavailable to the field, identifying and providing links to such works is a beneficial service.

11. Authenticating data and classes of fact. This is the process of defining terms and establishing that external data sources are valid.

12. Identifying original publications in which an idea or concept was discussed. Many authors feel that the original mention of a concept necessitates a reference even if that source was not only not used in preparing the author's own work but perhaps not even examined.

13. Identifying sources of eponymic concepts or terms. Mentioning the original article in which Bradford's Law was presented may be viewed by an author as an essential component in a publication reporting on a Bradford analysis, even though Bradford's 1934 article was a very limited contribution to the study of journal productivity.

14. Disclaiming work or ideas of others (negative claims). This is basically the process of contending that another scholar's work is flawed and should be rejected.

15. Disclaiming priority claims of others (negative homage). This is the process of contending that someone who claimed to be first wasn't.[23]

Brooks, extending from Garfield's delineation, studied actual citer motives, finding that they were multifaceted, complex, and essentially impossible to deduce from publications in which references are included.[24]

Smith identified nine problems related to citation studies, many of which derive from the limitations of the citation indexes published by ISI:

1. Multiple authorship. This is a problem in two ways: (a) The ISI citation indexes provide citation entries only for first authors. Identifying all citations to the works of a given individual requires reference to a complete bibliography of that person's works as a means of tracking citations to works for which he or she was not the first author. This is conceptually simple but may be pragmatically difficult. (b) Some researchers have expressed concern that acting as sole author of a work should carry more credit than acting as a coauthor. Some very complex methods have been developed for allocating credit for citations to multiple-author works. In many of these allocation schemes, it is assumed that the first author listed should receive the greatest credit and that the last author listed should receive the least credit. Some authors have responded by deliberately listing their names in alphabetical order and stating in a note that they have done so.

2. Self-citation. Self-citation, in which an author cites his or her own work, can be a function of vanity but can also be an act of citing the best available source. Some researchers (and many college and university administrators) treat all self-citations as automatically invalid and eliminate them in citation counts. This is easily done when the self-citing author is the first author of the cited work, but otherwise involves the problems encountered in gathering all citation data for an individual who is not always first author.

3. Homographs. The ISI citation indexes employ an abbreviated version of authors' names in which the last name is recorded in full, but only the first letter of the first and (sometimes) middle name are recorded. Furthermore, last names recorded during the earlier years during which the indexes were published were truncated at eight letters. This means that there can be many authors represented by a single last name, first initial combination. The *Social Sciences Citation Index*, as of July 2011, included 6,358 citation entries for authors whose names can be represented as SMITH J. It is possible to reduce some of the confusion by adding an author's discipline or institution to the search, assuming that they are known. Even that is uncertain: there are two authors whose names can be represented as CARPENTER M, both of whom published works in the INFORMATION SCIENCE & LIBRARY SCIENCE category while at the University of California-Berkeley. There is no way to eliminate this specific homograph problem other than by searching for citations to specific works.

4. Synonyms. ISI employs no authority control for author names. Indexers are officially charged with recording the name as it appears in the publication being indexed, but there are inconsistencies. Furthermore, there are variations in the ways in which authors' names appear in the source publications. Some authors use their middle initials always while others sometimes use a middle initial and sometimes don't. Author's names sometimes change: in July 2011 there were 82 citation references to MCCOOK K, at least some of which are to Dr. Kathleen McCook, a faculty member at the University of South Florida, but there were 266 references to HEIM K, at least some of which are to Dr. McCook's previous name, Kathleen Heim. Furthermore, under her previous name, Dr. McCook sometimes but not always used the middle initial M.

5. Types of sources. A variety of studies have indicated that, regardless of discipline, authors of journal articles tend to cite journal articles rather than other types of publications. Since the ISI citation indexes rely entirely on references listed in journal articles, authors of nonjournal publications are unlikely to be as well represented in the citation indexes as authors of journal articles.

6. Implicit citations. In indexing the *Science Citation Index* and *Social Sciences Citation Index,* ISI indexers examine only lists of references, bibliographies, endnotes, and footnotes. They do not examine the text of an article and will not record any reference that is incorporated into the text but not reflected in the source material from which index data are drawn. Implicit citations are included in the *Arts & Humanities Citation Index,* but the rate at which they are successfully observed and recorded is an unknown.

7. Fluctuations with time. Citation rates for individual publications or authors tend to vary from year to year. Total citation counts are probably more useful than other measures such as citations per year.

8. Field variations. Citation rates vary across fields or disciplines in two ways: (a) Citation and other publishing practices differ among fields. Some fields emphasize comprehensive documentation of sources while others prefer very brief reference lists. (b) Coverage in the ISI indexes varies substantially across fields and subfields. In library and information science, subfields related to information science, information technology, and management are relatively well represented, but subfields related to school library media centers and youth services are very poorly represented.

9. Errors. ISI makes mistakes: Dr. Connie Van Fleet is represented correctly as VANFLEET C but is also represented as FLEET CV. Finding all synonyms for an author whose name has varied is difficult; accounting for all indexing errors in a citation search is nearly impossible.[25]

USES OF BIBLIOMETRIC DATA

A number of pragmatic uses of bibliometric data have been proposed, most of which have never been implemented on any meaningful scale:

1. Identification of core literatures. This is an extension from Bradford's original motive for the division of a bibliography into zones. If the Bradford nucleus truly does constitute the central core of important literature in a field, conducting a Bradford analysis should enable a library, indexing or abstracting service, or other information agency to precisely identify the most important journals or other publications that need to be included in a collection. This application has been employed in a variety of environments but has not become a central approach to collection management.

2. Estimating completeness of a database. If, as Groos suggested, the deviation in the Bradford graph is an indicator of an incomplete bibliography, then conducting a Bradford analysis should provide an indicator of database completeness. This has been done experimentally but does not appear to have been used in any practical manner.

3. Ranking publications. Since the Bradford graph represents a continuum of productivity, it is possible to use a Bradford analysis to explicitly assign ranks of importance to individual journals.

4. Ranking authors. The Lotka distribution has frequently been assumed to reflect author importance in that the most frequently published authors in a field may be the most important authors. If publications can be ranked and the ranking is an indicator of importance, then it should also be possible to rank authors according to the journals in which they have been published.

5. Ranking institutions. Just as authors can be ranked based on the journals in which they have been published, institutions such as universities can be ranked by creating

composite rankings based on the journals in which authors affiliated with the institutions have been published.

6. Guiding retention policies. It should be possible to use obsolescence data to make determinations regarding retention of items in a collection. Standard retention and weeding policies and practices tend to use age in a very arbitrary manner. Conducting a true obsolescence study should be very easy in an automated catalog environment and could be used to provide more precise data for retention decisions.

7. Predicting use. If a Bradford ranking is truly an indicator of quality, it should be possible to predict item use based on rankings. Similarly, it should be possible to use an obsolescence study to predict when an item will no longer be likely to attract a meaningful level of use.

8. Sociometric and scientometric studies. Regardless of the potential for incorporation of bibliometric techniques into library and information system operations, bibliometrics provides a very useful set of tools for understanding the ways in which information products are used. Bibliometrics is especially useful in comparing different groups of scholars or consumers of information products.

USES OF CITATION STUDIES

Citation data can be used in a number of different ways:

1. Sociological studies

   Citation links are clearly reflective of the processes of communication among scholars. Sociological studies based on citation analysis address such issues as

   a. mapping the communication process to identify structural patterns within scholarly communication or trace the history of ideas

   b. comparing literatures by subject area or by publication type

   c. comparing author groups by subject area or by category of employment

   d. comparing geographic areas

   e. defining disciplines through identification of citation clusters

2. Evaluation studies

   The use of citation data in evaluation is among the most frequent applications and among the most controversial.

   a. Evaluating the performance of individuals. Citation counts are frequently included as indicators of quality or success in the evaluation of college and university faculty members. Citation counts can also be used to compare individuals or to identify the most productive contributors to a specific field or discipline.

   b. Evaluating the performance of groups. Aggregate data can be used in a comparative manner to evaluate the performance of academic departments or entire institutions.

   c. Evaluating the importance of publications. There is a frequently assumed correlation between the quality of a publication and the number of times it is cited. This can be applied at the level of individual articles or as a tool in comparing the importance of journals.

   d. Predicting other types of use. If there is a valid correlation between citation and importance and it can be expected that the most important publications will also

Study:	Danny P. Wallace, Connie Van Fleet, and Lacey J. Downs, "The Research Core of the Knowledge Management Literature," *International Journal of Information Management* 31, no. 1 (2011): 14–20.
Question/Purpose:	Research question 1: What are the basic bibliometric characteristics of the research literature of knowledge management, as revealed by a Bradford analysis?
	Research Question 2: What methodologies are used in the research literature of knowledge management?
Population:	The research literature of knowledge management.
Sample:	630 refereed articles judged to be about knowledge management.
Personnel:	Three researchers: two library and information science faculty members and one library and information science student.
Data Sources:	Search results from *Social Sciences Citation Index*; references drawn from articles related to knowledge management.
Data Gathering:	20 journals were selected based on citation in *Social Sciences Citation Index* and/or inclusion of the expression "knowledge management" in the journal's title. References were gathered from all refereed articles published in the journals during a 3-year period. Content analysis was done to identify references that were truly related to knowledge management. Three Bradford analyses were conducted. Content analysis was done to categorize research methods used in the knowledge management literature.
Summary:	Three Bradford analyses found that the 21,596 references drawn from articles from 20 journals, 3,037 candidate articles, and 630 articles determined to be truly related to knowledge management all conformed to the Bradford distribution. A quarter of the articles identified as related to knowledge management employed no recognizable research method. The five most frequently used research methods were case study, survey/questionnaire, literature review, framework, and interview.
Conclusions:	The study concluded that the bibliometric characteristics of the literature of knowledge are consistent with those of other fields that have been studied using Bradford analysis. Empirical research using standard social sciences research methods does not appear to be the dominant mode for the scholarly literature of bibliometrics.

Figure 11.12 From the professional literature—bibliometric analysis.

be the publications most frequently used, it should be possible to predict use from citation data. This could be very helpful in managing library collections.

3. Information retrieval

The original motivation for citation indexing was efficiency in information retrieval. *Shepard's* was designed to ease the fundamental processes of searching for precedent in legal research. The ISI citation indexes were designed to facilitate searching for related publications. Although the nature of the relationship among a citing article and a cited publication is variable, there is clearly *some* relationship. It can be assumed that a scholar interested in a specific article may be interested both in the items included in that article's list of references and in those later publications that cite the article of interest. In addition to simple citation searching, two additional citation-based retrieval measures have been proposed:

a. Co-citation refers to the extent to which two or more publications are cited together. A high rate of co-citation can be assumed to be an indication of a strong link among the co-cited publications. Simple co-citation searches can be conducted using the ISI citation indexes, but there is no current facility for calculating co-citation coefficients.

b. Bibliographic coupling refers to the extent to which two or more publications share the same list of references. Again, the assumption is that a high rate of bibliographic coupling is an indication of a strong link among coupled publications. The ISI citation indexes do not support any approach to searching for bibliographically coupled publications.

THEORETICAL BASES FOR BIBLIOMETRICS AND CITATION ANALYSIS

The regularity of patterns observed in bibliometric and citation studies has prompted substantial interest in exploration of the shared causes of the distributions of bibliometric and citation data. Two general principles that appear to be related are the Principle of Least Effort and the Cumulative Advantage Principle.

The Principle of Least Effort

Zipf believed the pattern he observed related to the use of words in text was a function of a larger process he termed the Principle of Least Effort. The Principle of Least Effort can be summarized in terms of two basic principles:

1. All human activities are interrelationships among *tasks* to be performed and the *tools* developed to perform those tasks.

2. Any human being charged with using a tool to perform a task will attempt to do so in the manner that requires the *least effort.*

In the context of Zipf's studies of language, he concluded that the Principle of Least Effort dictated that, rather than using a large vocabulary, authors choose to use a more limited vocabulary in a repetitive manner. The Principle of Least Effort may also govern citation practices and lead scholars to cite those items to which they have the most convenient access rather than those items that are best.

The Cumulative Advantage Principle

The Cumulative Advantage Principle was extensively discussed by Price.[26] A simple explanation of the cumulative advantage principle is that the single greatest predictor of and influence on future use for any item in an information system is prior use. The cumulative advantage principle has been extensively studied in the form of urn games. An urn game is a computer simulation of an experiment in which the basic model is a container full of numbered ping-pong balls, each of which represents an item in an information system. In each round of the game a randomly selected ball is removed. In the simplest form of the game, any ball that is drawn is replaced by two balls: the ball that was drawn and a second ball with the same number. As multiple rounds are played, any number that has been drawn has an increasingly greater chance of being drawn again. Over a sufficiently large number of rounds, the pattern of the distribution of the numbers in the container that emerges is the exponential distribution observed in studying bibliometric phenomena.

Price related the cumulative advantage principle to Merton's notion of the Matthew effect, which draws on a passage from the Christian Bible.[27]

> For whosoever hath, to him shall be given, and he shall have more abundance: but whosoever hath not, from him shall be taken away even that he hath.

—Matthew 13:12

MAKING INFORMATION COUNT

Bibliometrics and citation analysis have substantial applicability to both research and evaluation. The inherently quantitative nature of bibliometrics and citation analysis allows for the application of sophisticated statistical analyses and effective data visualization. Bibliometrics and citation analysis are inherently unobtrusive and nonreactive; an attraction of this family of methods for some investigators is avoidance of the need for Institutional Review Board human subjects review.

The range of possibilities for bibliometric and citation studies is virtually unlimited. Even when specific areas have been explored, the evolving nature of scholarly productivity makes new studies of old topics valuable. The entire field of webometrics is new and is itself emerging and rapidly evolving. Bibliometrics and citation analysis have both broad-ranging research applications and sharply focused evaluation possibilities. Many of the uses of bibliometrics and citation analysis that have been proposed by researchers have been applied no more than incompletely in the world of library and information science practice. Studies of obsolescence, for instance, have great potential for determining library collection retention policies and for guiding the need to digitize older collections.

Bibliometric and citation studies can be tedious and time consuming to conduct, but they can also be designed to yield large databases that can be mined to explore a variety of questions over time. Bibliometric databases can fairly easily be updated over time to add depth and a dimension of time to analysis. Although not by any means new, bibliometrics and citation analysis are a potentially important part of the research and evaluation toolkit for library and information science that is currently underutilized.

THINK ABOUT IT!

1. What are the similarities and differences of Lotka, Zipf, and Bradford's Laws?
2. How might a Bradford analysis for a well-established discipline differ from an analysis for a newly emerging multidisciplinary field?
3. How can citation analysis be applied to nonscholarly literatures?

DO IT!

1. Conduct a literature search for a topic of interest to you; a good target is about 100 articles. Conduct a Bradford analysis to determine the distribution of articles among the journals that produced them.
2. Gather the bibliographic references from the articles used for the Bradford analysis. Build a spreadsheet with the dates of the articles and the dates of the references and determine the median age of the references.
3. Use **Web of Science** or one of the ISI citation indexes to track a scholar whose work is known to you. Are there any surprises in the pattern of the articles that have cited that author?

NOTES

1. Alan Pritchard, "Statistical Bibliography or Bibliometrics?" *Journal of Documentation* 20, no. 4 (1969): 348.

2. Fred R. Shapiro, "Origins of Bibliometrics, Citation Indexing, and Citation Analysis: The Neglected Legal Literature," *Journal of the American Society for Information Science* 43, no. 5 (1992): 337–39.

3. Bella Haas Weinberg, "The Earliest Hebrew Citation Indexes," *Journal of the American Society for Information Science* 48, no. 4 (1997): 318–30.

4. F. J. Cole and N. B. Eales, "The History of Comparative Anatomy. Part I: A Statistical Analysis of the Literature," *Science Progress* 11 (1917): 578–96.

5. Paul Otlet, *Traite De Documentation. Le Livre Sur Le Livre. Theorie Et Pratique* (Brussels: Van Keerberghen, 1934).

6. Eugene Garfield, "Citation Indexes for Science," *Science* 122, no. 3159 (1955): 108–11.

7. Jean Tague-Sutcliffe, "An Introduction to Informetrics," *Information Processing & Management* 28, no. 1 (1992): 1.

8. Derek J. de Solla Price, *Little Science, Big Science* (New York: Columbia University Press, 1963).

9. Lennart Björneborn and Peter Ingwersen, "Toward a Basic Framework for Webometrics," *Journal of the American Society for Information Science & Technology* 55, no. 14 (2004): 1217.

10. Ibid.

11. Isaac Newton, letter to Robert Hooke, February 15, 1676.

12. A. J. Lotka, "The Frequency Distribution of Scientific Productivity," *Journal of the Washington Academy of Science* 16 (1926): 317–23.

13. G. K. Zipf, *Human Behavior and the Principle of Least Effort* (New York: Hafner, 1949).

14. S. C. Bradford, "Sources of Information on Specific Subjects," *Engineering* 137 (1934): 85–86.

15. Ole V. Groos, "Bradford's Law and the Keenan-Atherton Data," *American Documentation* 18, no. 1 (1967): 46.

16. S. C. Bradford, *Documentation* (Washington: Public Affairs Press, 1950), 110.

17. Eugene Garfield, "The Mystery of the Transposed Journal Lists: Wherein Bradford's Law of Scattering Is Generalized According to Garfield's Law of Concentration," in *Essays of an Information Scientist* (Philadelphia: ISI Press, 1977), 223.

18. Maurice B. Line and A. Sandison, "'Obsolescence' and Changes in the Use of Literature with Time," *Journal of Documentation* 30, no. 3 (1974): 286.

19. Ibid., 283.

20. Ibid., 284.

21. Eddie Ray Stinson, "Diachronous vs. Synchonous Study of Obsolescence." Ph.D. Dissertation, University of Illinois at Urbana-Champaign, 1981.

22. Linda C. Smith, "Citation Analysis," *Library Trends* 30 (1981): 87–89.

23. Eugene Garfield, "Can Citation Indexing Be Automated?" in *Statistical Association Methods for Mechanized Documentation*, ed. Mary E. Stevens, 189 (Washington: National Bureau of Standards, 1965).

24. Terry A. Brooks, "Evidence of Complex Citer Motivations," *Journal of the American Society for Information Science* 37 (1986): 34–36.

25. Ibid., 86–93.

26. Derek J. de Solla Price, "A General Theory of Bibliometric and Other Cumulative Advantage Processes," *Journal of the American Society for Information Science* 27 (1976): 292–306.

27. R. K. Merton, "The Matthew Effect in Science," *Science* 159 (1968): 56–63.

SUGGESTED READINGS

Lutz Bornmann and Loet Leydesdorff, "Which Cites Produce More Excellent Papers than can be Expected? A New Mapping Approach, Using Google Maps, Based on Significance Testing," *Journal of the American Society for Information Science and Technology* 62, no. 10 (October 2011): 1954–62.

Nicola De Bellis, *Bibliometrics and Citation Analysis: From the* Science Citation Index *to Cybermetrics* (Lanham, MD: Scarecrow, 2009).

Virgil Diodato, *Dictionary of Bibliometrics* (New York: Haworth, 1994).

Michael J. Kurtz and Johan Bollen, "Usage Bibliometrics," *Annual Review of Information Science and Technology* 44 (2010): 3–64.

Hank F. Moed, *Citation Analysis in Research Evaluation* (Dordrecht: Springer, 2005).

Christoph Neuhaus and Hans-Dieter Daniel, "Data Sources for Performing Citation Analysis: An Overview," *Journal of Documentation* 64, no. 2 (2008): 193–210.

Taemin Kim Park, "The Visibility of *Wikipedia* in Scholarly Publications," *First Monday* 16, no. 8 (August 1, 2011), http://firstmonday.org/htbin/cgiwrap/bin/ojs/index.php/fm/article/view/3492/3031.

Mike Thelwall, "Bibliometrics to Webometrics," *Journal of Information Science* 34, no. 4 (August 2008): 605–21.

Michael Thelwall, *Introduction to Webometrics: Quantitative Web Research for the Social Sciences* (San Rafael, CA: Morgan and Claypool, 2009).

Howard D. White, Sebastian K. Boell, Hairong Yu, Mari Davis, Concepcion C. Wilson, and Fletcher T. H. Cole, "Libcitations: A Measure for Comparative Assessment of Book Publications in the Humanities and Social Sciences," *Journal of the American Society for Information Science and Technology* 60, no. 6 (June 2009): 1083–96.

Dietmar Wolfram, *Applied Informetrics for Information Retrieval Research* (Westport, CT: Libraries Unlimited, 2003).

12

DATA ANALYSIS
AND PRESENTATION

It is a capital mistake to theorize before one has data. Insensibly one begins to twist facts to suit theories, instead of theories to suit facts.

—*Sir Arthur Conan Doyle,* "A Scandal in Bohemia," *1892*

Human thought is the process by which human ends are ultimately answered.

—*Daniel Webster,* "Address on Laying the Corner-Stone
of the Bunker Hill Monument," *1825*

In This Chapter
Purposes of data analysis
Data analysis concerns
Data matrix model
Implementation of the data matrix model
Analytical tools
Tables
Graphs and charts

PURPOSES OF DATA ANALYSIS

Data analysis serves two purposes, both of which are fundamental to the research or evaluation process:

1. The first purpose of data analysis is to prepare data for use. Data do not generally come ready to use and rarely automatically fall into interpretable patterns. There is almost always some necessary process of making the data usable. Unfortunately, there are also no all-purpose data. The processes employed in making data usable are largely a function of decisions made in the design of the research or evaluation

process regarding the ways in which the data will be analyzed. In a very real sense, data analysis begins not after the data have been gathered as a matter of application of analytical tools, but before the project has been undertaken as a matter of design decision making.

2. The second purpose of data analysis is making sense of data. It is a very rare occurrence for data and the patterns data describe to have an obvious meaning. Generally speaking, data have meaning only in the context of the steps taken to interpret the data. The investigator must use appropriate analytical tools and processes to extract sense and meaning from the data. It is of paramount importance to explain not only the meaning of the data but also explain the processes whereby meaning was assigned. Data, regardless of their origin in quantitative or qualitative methods, are of little or no use if they do not lead to some logical conclusion. In most instances inference plays a key role in that the data are representative of the phenomenon being studied rather than comprehensive. A carefully stated conclusion and discussion of the implications of the research or evaluation are important even if it is ultimately possible to say no more than that nothing can be inferred from the data at hand. Negative results are not necessarily a negative outcome—the investigator must be willing to say, "the data appear to mean nothing." It is, of course, much more gratifying to be able to say precisely what the data do mean. An unfortunate social artifact of the research or evaluation process is that researchers and evaluators are frequently reluctant to report negative results—no one wants to be led to the point of saying, "I tried this and it didn't work." Such negative results are, however, very valuable in that they inform future researchers or evaluators of avenues not to explore.

DATA ANALYSIS CONCERNS

There are a number of considerations and concerns to be addressed in the processes of data analysis. Among the foremost concerns are missing data, faulty data, data organization, and the process of questioning the data.

Missing Data

No matter how carefully the project is designed and executed, there will typically be some data that are, for reasons beyond the investigator's control, missing. It is extremely important to identify missing data and deal with them in a manner that is appropriate to the study and that preserves the validity and reliability of the data. Missing data fall into two major categories:

1. Missing cases. A case is a complete set of data for one entity of interest—a person, place, thing, or event. The sampling process assists the investigator in identifying those cases for which data will be sought. Ideally, data are gathered from all those cases selected, but in the real world things are rarely that perfect. A targeted respondent can decline to participate, a questionnaire can be lost or irretrievably damaged, an electronic recording device can fail. There are three dominant courses of action the investigator can take when data for one or more cases are missing in their entirety.

   a. In some cases it is possible to obtain the data desired for a case by returning to the data-gathering process. A person who failed to respond to a questionnaire can be nagged to complete it, for instance. The risk in doing so is that those individuals who respond willingly may in some meaningful way differ from those who respond only when further prompted to do so.

b. It may be possible to replace the case with another case by resampling. This yields the desired number of cases but risks undermining the integrity of the sample, particularly if any sort of randomization is desired.

c. If the case cannot be obtained or replaced, or if the risks to data integrity of obtaining or replacing the data are viewed as being unacceptably high, the investigator may choose to ignore the absence of the case. This is in many cases the most appropriate thing to do. The risk in ignoring data is that the sample is no longer of the desired size. It is sometimes possible to anticipate this problem by oversampling—deliberately selecting a sample that is larger than is needed to account for case mortality. Doing so doesn't really reduce the risk much, however, in that there is still the possibility that any missing cases are systematically different from cases for which data are available.

2. Missing variables or incomplete cases. Even if data are available for a given case, there may be one or more variables for which data are not available. An individual may neglect or decline to answer a question, an observation may be missing, there may be a glitch in an electronic recording. There are three major options for handling an incomplete case.

a. If the missing variable is viewed as absolutely critical to data analysis, it may be necessary to exclude the case from the analysis in its entirety.

b. If the analysis can proceed in a meaningful manner with only those variables for which data are available, it may be possible to exclude the variable for the specific case while retaining data for all other variables.

c. If the variable in question is missing from a substantial number of cases in a manner that appears to be systematic, it may be necessary to exclude the variable from the study.

Faulty Data

Just as it is essential to identify and handle missing data, it is also important to identify faulty data. Faulty data fall into two major categories: out-of-range values and incorrect or suspect in-range values.

1. Out-of-range values are recorded data that do not make sense given the nature of the variable. If the variable on a questionnaire for a descriptive study is "year of birth," for instance, 9157 is probably not a valid value. In most cases the only truly appropriate thing to do with an out-of-range value is to treat it is a missing value and employ one of the options for handling incomplete cases. It may be tempting to assume that 9157 is a transposition of 1957, but the validity of that assumption cannot be assured. It may in some instances be possible to return to the original source of the data to correct out-of-range values or to consult some other source for the correct value, but even that must be approached very carefully.

2. Incorrect in-range values are the most difficult to identify. If 1967 is recorded when the correct date of birth is 1957, the investigator may have little or no opportunity to identify the value as being flawed. One of the motives for selecting an adequate sample size is to minimize the effect of incorrect in-range values.

Data Organization

Organizing the data for effective analysis and interpretation is a process that must begin before any data are collected. "Don't pick something up until you know where you are going to put it down" is a common parent–child admonition. In research or evaluation terms, that translates into, "don't gather data until you know what you are going to do with it." Qualitative data are frequently recorded and organized in the form of structured field notes and thematic maps. Quantitative data, particularly if they are to be analyzed using statistical processes, must be carefully organized in a manner that will facilitate numeric processing. The data matrix model described later in this chapter is a typical approach to organizing quantitative data.

Questioning the Data

Questioning, querying, or interrogating the data is the process of engaging in a dialectical process designed to make sense of the data. The questioning process in qualitative research or evaluation tends to be interactive and flows from the ongoing research or evaluation process, although some set of guiding questions is an essential part of the planning process for qualitative research or evaluation. In quantitative research or evaluation, the questions to be asked of the data are normally formulated as part of the design process and directly influence the nature of the data to be gathered and the processes used to gather them. Questioning the data can take a number of forms.

1. The search for patterns is a fundamental component in both qualitative and quantitative research or evaluation.

2. Calculations are numeric expressions derived from quantitative data. Calculations and statistics are explored in Chapter 13, "Descriptive and Inferential Statistics".

3. Tables are tools used to summarize data. Tables are most frequently used for quantitative data, but may be used effectively for some forms of qualitative data.

4. Graphs are visual tools used to summarize data. Graphs are used almost exclusively for quantitative data, although the thematic maps sometimes used in qualitative research or evaluation are also a form of graph.

THE DATA MATRIX MODEL

The data matrix model is a conceptual tool for organizing quantitative data. The data matrix model is also referred to as a datasheet and bears a strong resemblance to a spreadsheet. The data matrix model can easily be implemented in a spreadsheet such as Excel or Quatro Pro, but the model itself precedes spreadsheet productivity software by many decades. The general model is presented in Figure 12.1.

Each row in the matrix represents a case for which data are available; a row records all the data available for that case. Each column represents a variable for which data are available; a column represents all the data available for that variable. The intersection of a row and a column defines a specific value of the specified variable for the specified case.

The example presented in Figure 12.2 provides a matrix for an incredibly simplistic study in which 10 librarians were each asked a set of three reference questions and the time required for each librarian to answer each question was recorded. Ten cases obviously aren't very many and are unlikely to be sufficient for any real purpose, but it's a convenient number to use as an example.

Case	Variable 1	Variable 2	Variable n
Case 1	Value (C1, V1)	Value (C1, V2)	Value (C1, Vn)
Case 2	Value (C2, V1)	Value (C2, V2)	Value (C2, Vn)
Case 3	Value (C3, V1)	Value (C3, V2)	Value (C3, Vn)
Case 4	Value (C4, V1)	Value (C4, V2)	Value (C4, Vn)
Case 5	Value (C5, V1)	Value (C5, V2)	Value (C5, Vn)
Case 6	Value (C6, V1)	Value (C6, V2)	Value (C6, Vn)
Case 7	Value (C7, V1)	Value (C7, V2)	Value (C7, Vn)
Case 8	Value (C8, V1)	Value (C8, V2)	Value (C8, Vn)
Case 9	Value (C9, V1)	Value (C9, V2)	Value (C9, Vn)
Case 10	Value (C10, V1)	Value (C10, V2)	Value (C10, Vn)
Case n	Value (Cn, V1)	Value (Cn, V2)	Value (Cn, Vn)

Figure 12.1   The data matrix model.

Case	Question 1	Question 2	Question 3
Librarian 1	6	2	10
Librarian 2	6	8	8
Librarian 3	5	3	9
Librarian 4	4	2	8
Librarian 5	5	3	9
Librarian 6	5	2	8
Librarian 7	4	3	9
Librarian 8	5	5	10
Librarian 9	4	2	12
Librarian 10	5	4	4

Figure 12.2   Data matrix example: time to answer each of three reference questions.

ANALYTICAL TOOLS

Data analysis doesn't require the use of a computer, but computer-based analytical tools are dominant in all forms of research or evaluation and have been since the first electronic spreadsheet was developed in the early 1960s. The introduction of VisiCalc, the first spreadsheet program for personal computers, in 1978 truly revolutionized the way in which simple statistical analysis of quantitative data could be performed. There are many computer-based tools that can be used in data analysis.

General Purpose Spreadsheets

Simple quantitative analysis is easily accomplished using any standard spreadsheet, such as Excel, Quattro Pro, or Numbers. More advanced statistical analysis is possible but is tedious with a spreadsheet and requires substantial understanding of statistics. Spreadsheets can also be used for organizing qualitative data. A general beginner's tutorial for using spreadsheets can be found at http://spreadsheets.about.com/. Help and tutorials for Excel can be found at http://office.microsoft.com/en-us/excel-help/. Apple provides video tutorials for Numbers at http://www.apple.com/iwork/tutorials/numbers.

Statistical Software

Complex statistical analysis is best accomplished with specialized statistical analysis software. Statistical products such as *The Statistical Package for the Social Sciences,* more frequently known as *SPSS, Statpac,* and *Statistica* allow the investigator to concentrate on the data and its meaning rather than knowledge of statistical calculations. There is still, however, an imperative that the investigator understand the meaning and outcome of any statistical process used.

Qualitative Software

Software for qualitative analysis constitutes a rapidly growing and changing market that has been subject to substantial instability. Widely used qualitative analysis products include *NVivo (Non-numerical Unstructured Data Indexing Searching & Theorising), Ethnograph,* and *ATLAS.ti.*

The Data Matrix Model Implemented in a Spreadsheet

The starting point for using a spreadsheet to analyze qualitative data is entering the data into the spreadsheet. The data from the study of reference question times are presented in spreadsheet form in Figure 12.3. Just as in the generic data matrix model, the rows are cases and the columns are variables. Rows are identified by numbers; columns are identified by letters. The intersection of a row and a column is a cell that is identified by a combination of a letter and a number. The value for Librarian 1's time for Question 1 is in cell B2.

Simple calculations are defined functions within the spreadsheet. Typical statistical functions include average (mean), median, mode, standard deviation, and other tasks that will be addressed later in this chapter. Inclusion of the mean is illustrated in Figures 12.4 and 12.5. Figure 12.4 shows the formula for calculating the mean: = average (beginningvalue:endingvalue); in this case = average(b2:b11). Pressing the Enter key results in the calculation being performed and the result displayed. As shown in Figure 12.5, the mean for all librarians for Question 1 is 4.9 min.

The Data Matrix Model Implemented in a Statistical Analysis Program

The Statistical Package for the Social Sciences (SPSS) is one of the oldest and most powerful statistical analysis programs. The simplest of several approaches to data entry

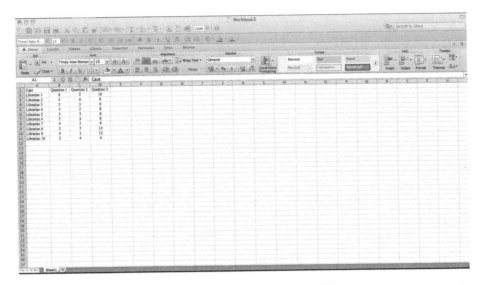

Figure 12.3 The data matrix model implemented in a spreadsheet.

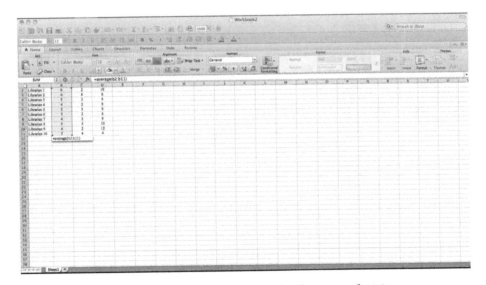

Figure 12.4 Using a spreadsheet to calculate a mean—the average function.

looks much like a spreadsheet. IBM SPSS Statistics is an SPSS product designed to provide basic to moderately complex statistical analysis capabilities. IBM SPSS Statistics can import data from most spreadsheet and database programs. The IBM SPSS Statistics Data Editor, with values for the data from the study of reference question times, is shown in Figure 12.6.

Figure 12.6 is the data view; Figure 12.7 is shows the variable view, which is used to name and define variables for analysis. Four variables are defined: Librarian, Question1, Question2, and Question3. Librarian is a string or alphanumeric variable. Question1, Question2,

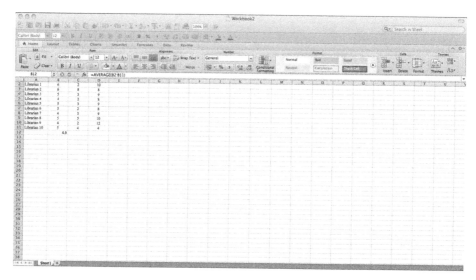

Figure 12.5   Using a spreadsheet to calculate a mean—calculated mean.

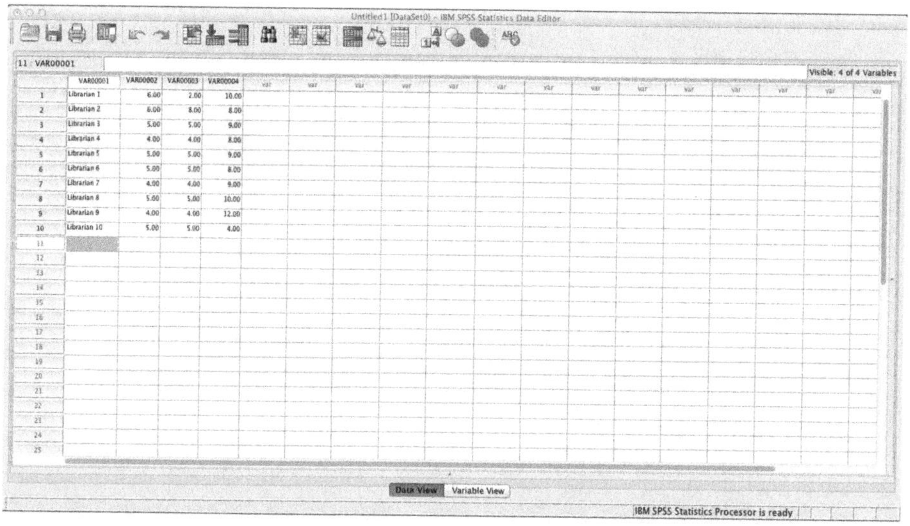

Figure 12.6   The data matrix model implemented in a statistical analysis package.

and Question3 are numeric variables. The IBM SPSS Statistics default values for numeric variables reserve space for eight-digit numbers with two decimal places. Since the reference study data are all one- or two-digit integers, the default values have been changed to match the nature of the data.

Rather than embedding calculations in the work sheet, SPSS uses dropdown menus to define calculations. Simple calculations such as mean, median, mode, and standard deviation are found under the "Descriptive Statistics" menu, shown in Figure 12.7. A further advantage of SPSS and similar programs is that there are multiple ways to display results.

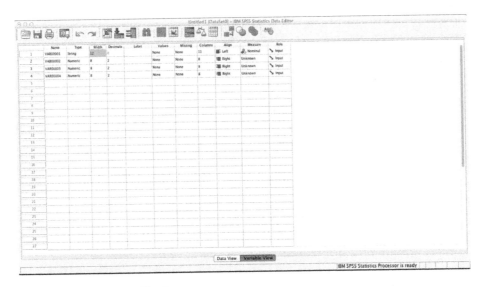

Figure 12.7 SPSS variable view.

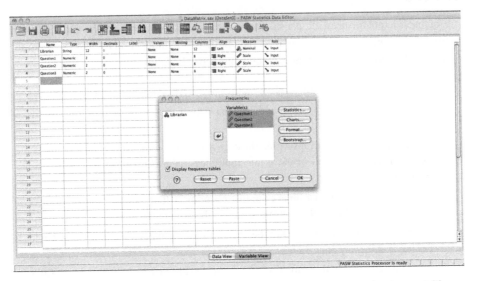

Figure 12.8 Using a statistical analysis package to calculate a mean—selecting variables.

The dialog box under "Frequencies" allows the user to individually select those variables for which results are desired (Figure 12.8).

The default report from Frequencies in Figure 12.9 shows basic descriptive statistics for the specified variables as well as a frequency distribution for each specified variable. SPSS allows the user to save both the command file that identifies calculations to be made and the output file. There is also a Report function for generating more attractive output.

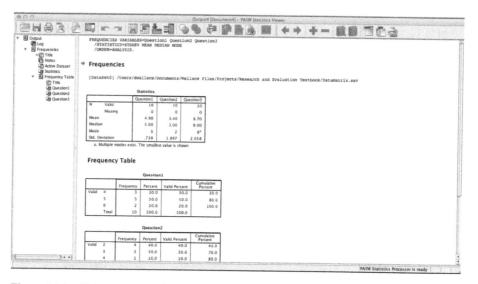

Figure 12.9   Using a statistical analysis package to calculate a mean—results.

TABLES

A table is a tool for presenting a summary of data, usually but not always quantitative in nature. The purpose of a table is to make data more easily understood by creating a simplified view of a complex phenomenon. Good tables have the following basic elements:

1. A title that is indicative of the purpose and content of the table and simple enough to be easily understood. The reader should never have to struggle to grasp the purpose of the table.

2. An emphasis on relationships within the data. A table typically either presents multiple aspects of a single variable or shows how multiple variables (usually no more than two) are related to each other.

3. A table usually has at least three columns. A summary that requires fewer than three columns can usually be effectively presented in the form of text.

4. Clear, expressive headings. As with the title, the headings for columns and rows should be simple and easily understood.

5. No blank cells. Even if there are no cases represented by a cell, the cell should have some content to make it clear that it has not accidentally been left blank. This might be a zero to indicate that were no cases for that value of the variable or a dash to indicate that there is no valid value for the cell.

6. Limited decimal places. It's fairly rare for the number of digits to the right of the decimal place to exceed two. More tends to imply a false level of precision.

7. Decimal alignment rather than left, center, or right justification. This makes it easier to scan columns of data.

8. Careful use of footnotes, if any. People tend not to read footnotes associated with tables. It's better to use meaningful titles and headings.

9. An indication of the number of cases represented by the table. Showing the number of cases helps the reader understand the total to which cell values are related.

Table Number Table Title
(n = number of cases)

Category Heading	Column Heading	Column Heading
Row Heading	Value	Value
Row Heading	Value	Value
Row Heading	Value	Value
Row Heading	Value	Value

Figure 12.10   Table layout basics.

Table 1 Success in Answering Questions

Subject Area	Number of Correct Answers	Percent of Total Correct Answers
Arts and Humanities	114	31
Social Sciences	156	43
Science and Technology	97	26
Total	367	100

Figure 12.11   Table layout example.

Table 2 Success in Answering Questions
(n = 600)

Subject Area	Number of Correct Answers	Number of Incorrect Answers	Percent Answered Correctly
Arts and Humanities	114	86	57
Social Sciences	156	44	78
Science and Technology	97	103	49
Total	367	233	63

Figure 12.12   Improved table example.

The general layout for a typical table is presented in Figure 12.10. Style varies considerably among style manuals, institutions, and publishers. The examples presented here are based on the *Chicago Manual of Style*.

Figure 12.11 shows the results of a study in which 200 librarians were each asked three reference questions—one arts and humanities question, one social sciences question, and one science and technology question—and the numbers of correct answers were tabulated. Note that this is an example of how to do a table, not of a good design.

Table 1 basically gets the job done, but there are some things missing. It's not directly possible from the table to tell how many questions were asked, how many were answered incorrectly, or can those figures be calculated from the data provided. It's also not clear that the percentage of total correct answers accounted for by each subject area is the most meaningful data. Table 2, presented in Figure 12.12, improves on Table 1 by providing more explicit information, providing the number of cases, and indicating not the percentage of total correct answers but the percent in each subject category answered correctly.

1. Exclude values for effect. Ideally, a table should present all the pertinent data. Totals should represent all the data in the distribution.

2. Exclude categories for effect. A table usually presents all categories of data for a variable. When only selected categories are included, an explanation should be provide and care should be taken to ensure that any totals are not deceptive.

3. Use extensive decimals to imply precision. Extensive decimal places make tables more difficult to read while at the same time implying greater meaning. The reader may be left with the impression that the table is difficult to interpret because he or she lacks the ability to comprehend the data.

4. Include misleading statistics. An easy way to mislead with statistics in a table is to report percentages with meaningless bases. Another way is to use the term "average" without explaining what it means. Statistics are explored in detail in Chapter 13, "Descriptive and Inferential Statistics."

5. Include misleading headings that don't really indicate the nature of the row or column. Row and column headings are meant to be informative, not catchy. Abbreviations should be used sparingly and, when used, should conform to standard approaches to abbreviation.

Figure 12.13   How to lie with tables.

GRAPHS AND CHARTS

Graphs and charts are tools for presenting data, usually quantitative in nature, visually. Graphs and charts serve many of the same purposes as tables, but present the data such that relationships are emphasized through visual cues. Creating an effective graph requires attention to a number of basic concerns:

1. selecting a type of graph appropriate to the data being presented
2. setting an appropriate scale for the graph
3. using titles and legends effectively to convey the nature of the content
4. employing an appropriate level of numeric precision
5. ensuring that the graph is complete within the context of the purpose it is intended to serve
6. striving to make the graph as visually expressive as possible

All of the examples of graphs used here were created using Microsoft Excel. Statistical analysis programs can also be used to create graphs.

Column Graphs

Column graphs are useful for displaying relationships among variables. Typically one variable is nominal level and the other is ordinal, interval, or ratio level. Figure 12.14 is an example that shows the distribution of public libraries in the United States by type of service outlet for Fiscal Year 2008.[1]

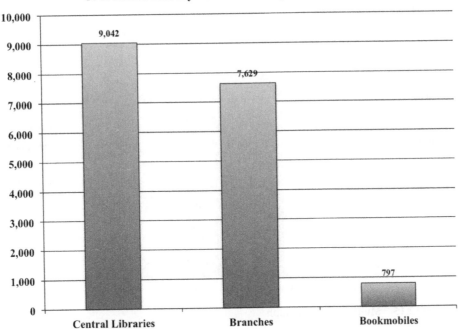

Figure 12.14   Column graph.

Multiple Column Graph

It is sometimes useful to display multiple columns in a single graph. This can be effective in showing more than one factor across time periods, as is in Figure 12.15, which shows expenditures by Association of Research Libraries members in four categories at 4-year intervals.[2]

Stacked Column Graph

A stacked column graph shows the same data as a multiple line graph but emphasizes the contribution of each category to the total; Figure 12.16 provides an example of a stacked column graph for the Association of Research Libraries data previously presented in Figure 12.15.

100 Percent Column Graph

A 100 percent column graph shifts the focus from numbers to percentages and is good for showing the relative contribution of each category to the total. A 100 percent column graph is shown in Figure 12.17 based on the Association of Research Libraries data from Figure 12.15. A 100 percent graph tends to be more difficult to interpret than other graph types. A 100 percent graph invites the reader to assume that the total values are all the same, when the reality is that the total percentages are and have to be the same.

Figure 12.17 is a three-dimensional graph, a feature that adds visual effect but may also add an element of deception in that the third dimension seems to add depth to the data as well as the visualization. Generally speaking, the simplest possible graph design is the best design.

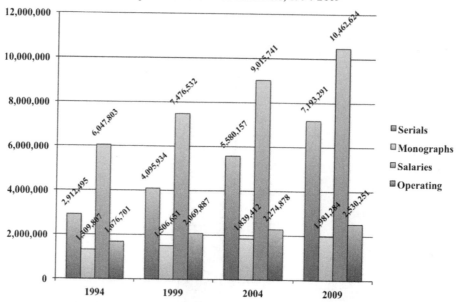

Figure 12.15 Multiple column graph.

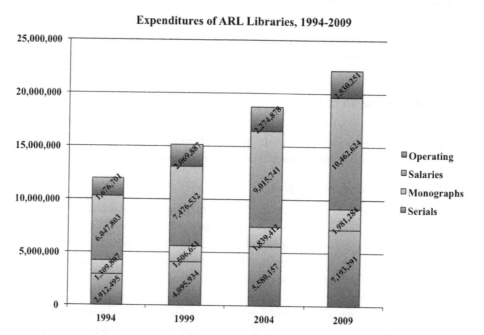

Figure 12.16 Stacked column graph.

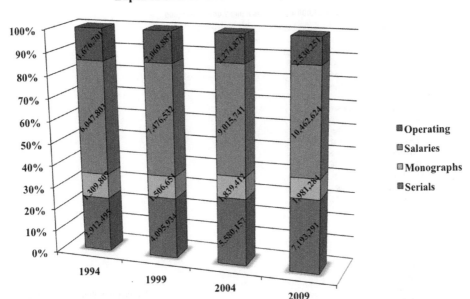

Figure 12.17   100 percent column graph.

Bar Graphs

A bar graph shifts the emphasis from vertical to horizontal alignment. Stacked and 100 percent versions of bar graphs are also possibilities. The stacked bar graph in Figure 12.18 shows the numbers of schools with and without school library media centers for all 50 U.S. states and the District of Columbia for Fiscal Year 1999–2000, in descending order based on the total number of schools in each state.[3]

Column Graphs versus Bar Graphs

Column graphs and bar graphs are both used to illustrate the relationship between two variables, in this case mean circulation per hour and circulation location. So, if a column graph and a bar graph can both be used to display the same information, how does one decide which to use? There are two basic guiding principles:

1. Because texts in Western languages are generally read left to right, the variable on the horizontal scale of any column or bar graph tends to be emphasized.
2. The labels for the horizontal scale of any column or bar graph necessarily need to be very terse to fit on the page or display. Although it is possible to rotate the labels to allow for more text, people mostly don't like to read rotated labels. It makes sense then, to place the variable with the longest labels along the vertical scale.

In practice, it is frequently a matter of looking at the graph both ways, which is easily done, and making a judgment call about the layout that seems to most effectively get the message across.

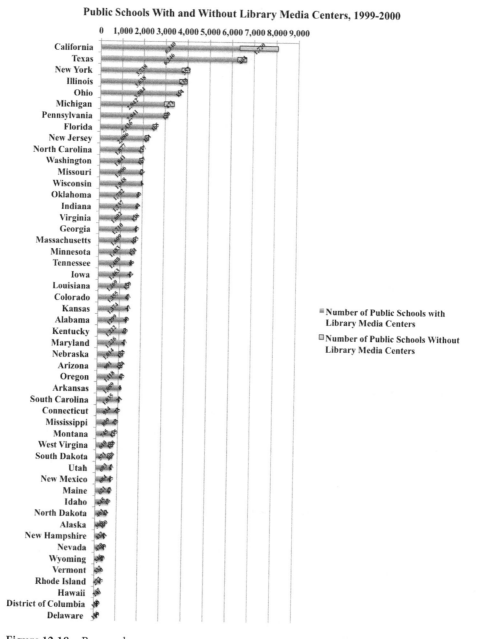

Figure 12.18   Bar graph.

Pie Charts

A pie chart emphasizes proportions of values within a single nominal-level variable. Pie charts are simple to construct and interpret but are limited in their expressiveness. Pie charts always represent 100 percent of the values in the distribution. A pie chart with more than a few values is very difficult to read. Although it is possible to present a pie chart as a three-dimensional object, doing so exaggerates the impact of large values; two-dimensional pie charts are always preferred. Figure 12.19 provides a breakdown of

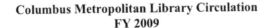

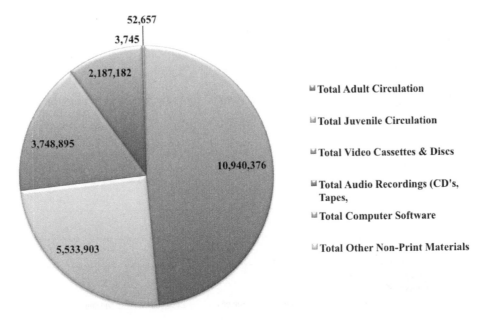

Figure 12.19 Pie chart.

circulation for the Columbus, Ohio, Metropolitan Library for Figure 2009 in the form of a pie chart. The chart makes it easy to assess the relative impact of different components of the collection at a glance, but some categories are so small in relative terms that they are hard to see.[4]

Scatter (*XY*) Plots

A scatter plot provides detailed information on the relationship between two variables, each of which is ordinal, interval, or ratio level. Figure 12.20 is a scatter plot showing the relationship between circulation and reference transactions for Ohio public libraries serving populations of less than 100,000 for fiscal year 2009.[5]

Scatter Plot with Trend Line

This variation on the scatter plot removes the frequencies and imposes a trend line based on linear regression. Figure 12.21 adds a trend line to the data for Ohio circulation and reference transactions.

Line Graphs

A line graph shows a relationship between two or more variables, one of which is typically nominal level while the others are ordinal, interval, or ratio level. Unlike a column or bar graph, a line graph shows the ordinal-, interval-, or ratio-level variable as a continuum. Line graphs are particularly useful for illustrating trends over time; trend line graphs almost always place time on the horizontal axis and another variable or variables on the vertical axis.

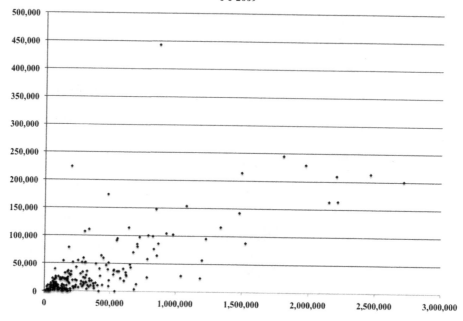

Figure 12.20   Scatter plot.

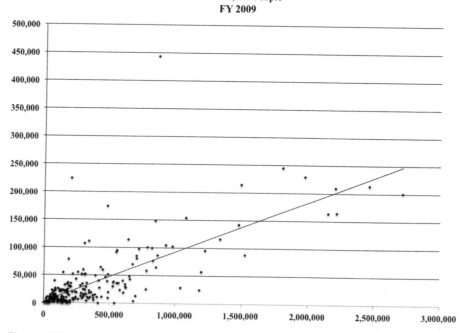

Figure 12.21   Scatter plot with trend line.

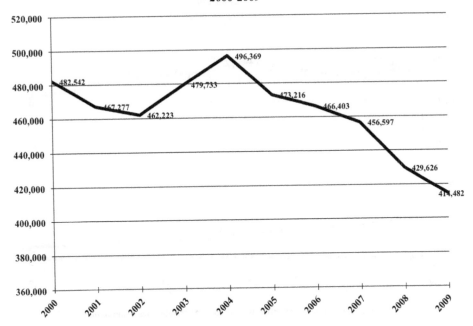

Total Circulation in ARL Libraries, 2000-2009

Figure 12.22   Line graph.

Figure 12.22 graphs total circulation in Association of Research Libraries member libraries across a 10-year period.

Multiple Line Graphs

Multiple lines can easily be incorporated into a line graph with appropriate care. Too many lines or lines that track at too many different levels can be difficult to interpret. Figure 12.23 adds interlibrary loan borrowing and reference transactions to the Association of Research Libraries data presented in Figure 12.22.

Scaling

The impression made by a graph can easily be influenced by altering the scale on which the data are presented. Contrast the line graph presented in Figure 12.22 with the line graph in Figure 12.24. They provide exactly the same data, but the image conveyed is very different. Where the differences across circulation points in the former seem dramatic, the differences appear to be trivial in the latter.

Perspective

Graphs are also subject to the influence of the perspective or aspect ratio applied. Figure 12.25 is a third version of the same line graph presented in Figures 12.22 and 12.24. Notice how the change in perspective makes the differences among the circulation points appear even more dramatic.

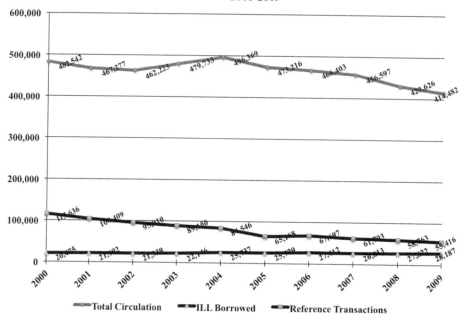

Figure 12.23   Multiple line graph.

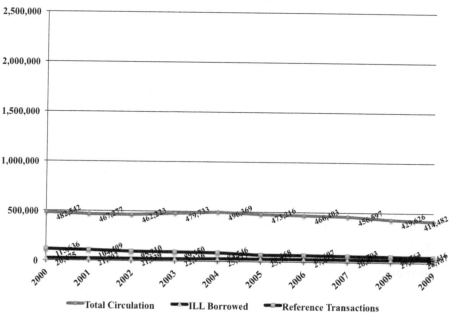

Figure 12.24   Impact of scale on a line graph.

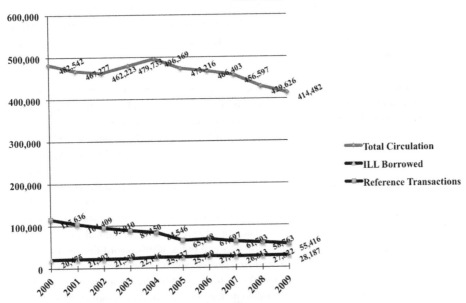

Figure 12.25 Impact of perspective on a line graph.

1. Exclude values for effect. A time series based on relatively long intervals may produce a graph that is easier to read, but if a time series based on 10-year intervals excludes noticeable peaks or troughs, the result is deceptive.

2. Exclude categories for effect. This is especially useful in pie charts, which are correct and meaningful only if they include all categories of the variable of interest.

3. Alter the scale for effect. Figure 12.24 depicts the effect of an exaggerated scale on a line graph.

4. Alter the perspective for effect. Figure 12.25 shows the impact of compressed perspective on a line graph.

5. Use misleading symbols. Selecting a marker for a line graph that shows "happy faces" for one variable and "sad faces" for another adds an element of emotion that may misguide the reader.

6. Use misleading labels. Labels should be expressive of the nature of the data. Catchiness is not a desirable characteristic of labels for graphs.

7. Use an inappropriate graph type. Line graphs imply time series, but can be used for other types of data. Bar charts and histograms, on the other hand, imply discrete categories. Selection of the correct type of graph is essential to honesty in presenting data graphically.

Figure 12.26 How to lie with graphs.

ANALYSIS OF QUALITATIVE DATA

Making sense of qualitative data is a very different process from that used in analyzing quantitative data. The processes of analysis may be the most significant way in which qualitative and quantitative research differ. Some aspects of analysis that are characteristic of qualitative research are:

1. Emphasis on field notes. Much, perhaps most, qualitative research is based on direct observation, with the researcher typically serving as the sole observer. Field notes in qualitative research are much like the field notes recorded by naturalists. In both cases, extensive recording of data while actually in the field tends to be intrusive. There is therefore an emphasis on minimal note-taking while in the field coupled with extensive post-observation expansion of the notes. Most qualitative researchers spend a substantial amount of time refining their field notes as soon as possible after the observation. The process of recording data in the field may be augmented by audio or video recording, but even when electronic recording devices are used they are normally a backup and adjunct to manual field notes. In addition to recording observational data in field notes, a qualitative researcher may use personal notes, which record the researcher's reactions to and thoughts on the research process much in the manner of a diary, or methodological notes, which record the methods used in observation with particular emphasis on any changes in methodology that occur as the observational phase progresses.

2. Thematic analysis. A major process in qualitative data analysis is the search for themes in field notes. Thematic analysis can take two major forms. In the first, thematic categories are predefined based on some preexisting structure or derived from the researcher's perception of the theoretical basis for the study. The researcher then matches field note data to the categories and assesses the extent to which the categories are representative of the data and the data are representative of the categories. In the second approach, thematic categories are derived directly from the field notes with no predetermined or predefined classification or categorization scheme.

3. Dialectical processing. Qualitative data analysis can be viewed as a dialog between the researcher and the data in which the researcher asks questions of the data, derives answers, and uses those answers to formulate additional questions. This is a creative process with the goal of exhaustively mining the data for meaning. The dialog ends when the researcher either can formulate no more questions or finds that the data cannot answer any additional questions.

4. Visualization. Reports of quantitative research frequently present results visually in the form of graphs and tables. Visualization in qualitative research tends to be more conceptual in nature. Idea maps or thematic maps are one form of visualization used in qualitative research. A generic thematic map is presented in Figure 12.27. The differing sizes of the balloons are intended to suggest the relative contribution of each subtheme. A thematic map can be much more complex than this, although excessive complexity makes the map difficult to interpret. Another difference in the use of visualization in qualitative research is that visual tools are frequently used directly by the researcher as part of the process of understanding and analyzing data, not just to present results at the report stage.

In most quantitative research, data analysis begins only after all the data have been collected and determined to be valid and useful. A fundamental way in which qualitative

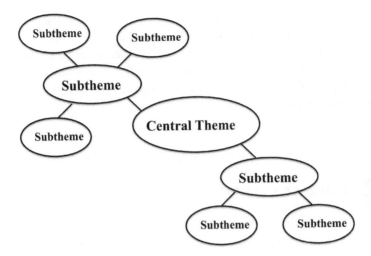

Figure 12.27   Thematic map.

analysis differs from most quantitative analysis is that the process of analysis takes place continuously as the data are gathered. As the researcher refines and expands field notes following observations, preliminary analysis is conducted as an approach to making sense of the data. That analysis changes as the field notes are compiled and analyzed.

ANALYSIS AS REFLECTION

Data analysis is the most reflective component in research and evaluation. Although the emphasis on the processes of cleaning data, preparing data for use, selecting tools for analysis, and applying the tools to the data may seem quite mechanical, the real focus of that emphasis is ensuring that the investigator takes a thoughtful and insightful approach to making sense of the data. Donald Schön, who was introduced in Chapter 2, "Research and Evaluation Processes," emphasized the role of the practitioner in both "reflection-in-action" and "reflection-on-action."[7] Reflection-in-action is the process of thinking while doing or thinking on one's feet. To the reflective practitioner there are no routine or rote activities. Research and evaluation are tools used by reflective practitioners to ensure that they are engaging in reflection-in-action. Research and evaluation are also tools for use in reflection-on-action. A central purpose of research and evaluation in library and information science is revisiting what the profession knows and does and reflecting on the possibility that the knowledge base needs restructuring or that the policies, practices, and tools of an institution need revision or improvement.

Although reflection may seem a passive, cerebral, or unemotional activity, Schön assigned a more active, engaged, and affective role to reflection:

> The practitioner allows himself to experience surprise, puzzlement, or confusion in a situation which he finds uncertain or unique. He reflects on the phenomenon before him, and on the prior understandings which have been implicit in his behavior. He carries out an experiment which serves to generate both a new understanding of the phenomenon and a change in the situation.[8]

Although Schön's view of the roles of reflection applies broadly to research and evaluation, it is of particular importance in considering and understanding the purposes of data analysis. The core goal of data analysis is not to render data ready for the application of analysis tools, but to question the data and search reflectively and creatively for answers. Only through application of the principles of active reflection can data analysis lead to enhanced understanding and improved practice.

 ## THINK ABOUT IT!

1. How does data analysis differ for qualitative data and quantitative data? Should the difference play a role in the selection of a qualitative versus a quantitative approach to research or evaluation?
2. How does data analysis differ for a research project and for an evaluation project? How does that difference influence the impact of analysis?
3. What are some ways in which a library and information science professional can enhance his or her understanding of and facility with analytical tools?

 ## DO IT!

1. Identify the data needed for a study of a real library and information science research or evaluation project. What are the potentials for missing data? What are the potentials for faulty data?
2. Identify the data needed for a study of a library and information science research or evaluation project. What questions can be asked of the data? How do the data need to be organized to yield useful answers?
3. Download the "Public Library State Totals and Selected Tables (2009–2010 Fiscal Year)" Excel spreadsheet file from http://www.library.ca.gov/lds/docs/CA_Tables.xls. Select a table and generate a bar graph for one variable.

NOTES

1. E. Henderson, K. Miller, T. Craig, S. Dorinski, M. Freeman, N. Isaac, J. Keng, P. O'Shea, and P. Schilling, *Public Libraries Survey Fiscal Year 2008* (Washington: Institute of Museum and Library Studies, 2010).

2. Martha Kyrillidou and Shaneka Morris, *ARL Statistics 2008–2009* (Washington: Association of Research Libraries, 2011).

3. Barbara Holton, Yupin Bae, Susan Baldridge, Michelle Brown, and Dan Heffron, *The Status of Public and Private School Library Media Centers in the United States: 1999–2000* (Washington: National Center for Education Statistics, U.S. Department of Education, 2004).

4. "2009 Ohio Public Library Statistics," State Library of Ohio, http://www.library.ohio.gov/sites/default/files/LPD_09_Ohio_Library_Statistic_Full_File.xls (accessed June 1, 2011).

5. Ibid.

6. Kyrillidou and Morris, *ARL Statistics 2008–2009.*

7. Donald A. Schön, *The Reflective Practitioner: How Professionals Think in Action* (New York: Basic Books, 1983).

8. Ibid., 68.

SUGGESTED READINGS

Craig K. Enders, *Applied Missing Data Analysis* (New York: Guilford, 2010).

David C. Hoaglin, Frederick Mosteller, and John W. Tukey, *Exploring Data Tables, Trends, and Shapes* (Hoboken, NJ: Wiley-Interscience, 2006).

George A. Miliken, *Analysis of Messy Data* (Boca Raton, FL: CRC Press, 2009).

Andrew K. Shenton, "The Analysis of Qualitative Data in LIS Research Projects: A Possible Approach," *Education for Information* 22, no. 3/4 (December 2004): 143–62.

DESCRIPTIVE AND INFERENTIAL STATISTICS

There are three kinds of lies: lies, damned lies, and statistics.

—Attributed to Benjamin Disraeli in The Times *(London), 1895*

He uses statistics as a drunken man uses lamp posts—for support rather than illumination.

—Attributed to Andrew Lang in Alan L. Mackay, Harvest of a Quiet Eye, *1977*

In This Chapter

The nature of statistics
Functions of statistics
Descriptive statistics
he normal curve
Statistical testing
Inferential statistics

THE NATURE OF STATISTICS

Definition of Statistic

The term *statistic* has a number of possible meanings, depending on the context in which the term is used. It is important to realize that statistics, like any other technical or professional area (library and information science is no exception), has its own technical jargon that uses ordinary words in a very specific and carefully controlled manner. Understanding statistics requires a willingness to accept the notion that terms may mean something different in a statistical context than in other contexts.

1. In everyday language, the term statistic frequently means an item of information expressed in a numeric format. Libraries often refer to their use statistics, citing counts for circulation, reference questions, attendance at meetings, and other static factors that

are most easily understood if expressed in a numeric format. This usage of the term has no validity in the field of statistics, in which an item of information expressed in a numeric format is variously referred to as a data point or a value.

2. In a technical sense, a statistic is a characteristic of a sample used as an indicator of a corresponding population parameter. This definition, which was first discussed in the context of sampling, is a highly precise use of the term valid only within a very specific context and will be largely ignored in this discussion of statistics.

3. The sense of the term statistic that is most applicable to the current discussion is that a statistic is the result of a statistical procedure or calculation. If a group of numbers is aggregated and an average of some kind is calculated (more on averages later), that average is a statistic. In this sense of the term, average daily circulation for a library is a statistic. Note that, generally speaking, a statistic is a summarization of the characteristics of a group of data points or values used to represent the group. The statistic has no meaning independent of the aggregated values. Average daily circulation for a library is meaningful only to the extent that it is related to other factors such as minimum and maximum daily circulation and variations over time.

FUNCTIONS OF STATISTICS

Two functions define the fundamental categories of statistical procedures: description and inference.

1. Descriptive statistics, sometimes referred to as summarizing statistics, norming statistics, or normative statistics, are procedures used primarily for description and summarization of a group of values. In a technical sense, descriptive statistics reveal the nature of the specific values included in the procedure and have no direct implications outside the context of those values studied. Generally speaking, the concept of statistical significance does not apply to descriptive statistics.

2. Inferential statistics are procedures used primarily to draw conclusions about a population based on the values of a carefully selected sample. Inferential statistics allow for estimation of statistical significance as a means of establishing confidence that statistics based on a sample truly represent the characteristics of a population.

In practice, the distinction between description and inference isn't quite so clear-cut and rigid. Descriptive statistics are often employed to imply the characteristics of a population: weather forecasts, for example, often mention a normal high or low temperature that is an average drawn from available data that is clearly intended to represent the specific day of the year across all years. Inferential processes are sometimes used to assess the accuracy or reliability of sample data with no specific inference to the broader context. It is nonetheless important to understand the domain in which a particular procedure is designed to function and to recognize the limitations of applying that procedure in any other domain.

DESCRIPTIVE STATISTICS

The general purpose of descriptive statistics is to determine the basic characteristics of variables. There are three major categories of descriptive statistics:

1. Measures of proportion serve to describe the extent to which a single category within a variable characterizes the variable as a whole. Measures of proportion include ratio, proportion, and percentage.

2. Measures of centrality or central tendency describe the extent to which the values of a variable are alike. The generic term for a measure of central tendency is average and technically all measures of central tendency are averages. Because the term average has a somewhat different meaning in general usage, it is generally best in the research or evaluation context to refer to directly to the specific measure and assiduously avoid use of the term average. Measures of central tendency include mean, median, and mode.

3. Measures of dispersion or variability describe the extent to which the values of a variable are different. Frequently used measures of variability include range, variance, and standard deviation.

Measures of Proportion

Ratio. A ratio is one number divided by another. The notation for ratios can take a number of forms:

- x/y
- $x{:}y$
- x to y
- x per y

As an example, if the reference staff at Any Library answered 4,352 directional and 3,256 informational questions during 2011 it is possible to calculate the following ratios:

- 1.34 directional questions per informational question (4,352 divided by 3,256)
- .75 informational questions per directional question (3,256 divided by 4,352)
- a ratio of directional questions to informational questions of 1.34:1 (4,352 divided by 3,256)
- an informational/directional question ratio of .75 (3,256 divided by 4,352)

Ratios are used primarily for determining rates and trends and establishing bases for comparison. The value of any ratio is independent of the overall size of the dataset from which it is derived, which makes ratios very useful for comparing different datasets through time series or across major categories within a variable.

Proportion. A proportion is a ratio in which a number representing a part is divided by a number representing the whole. The notation for a proportion is typically

- part/whole or
- part out of whole

As an example, if the reference staff at Any Library answered a total of 7,608 questions during 2011, of which 3,256 were informational questions, it is possible to calculate the following proportions:

- the proportion of questions that were informational questions was .43 (3,256 divided by 7,608)
- out of 7,608 questions, 3,256 were informational questions

Proportions are used to express the portion of a whole accounted for by a specified part. A limitation of proportions is that the decimal fraction format of the calculation can be difficult to read.

Percentage. A percentage is a proportion with a base of 100; a percentage is calculated by multiplying a proportion by 100. The typical notation for a percentage is

- *n*% or
- *n* percent

Extending from the example used in describing proportions,

- Forty-three percent of the questions answered at Any Library during 2011 were informational questions.
- Of 7,608 questions answered at Any Library during 2011, 43% were informational questions.

Percentages are used primarily to make proportions more easily understandable by expressing them in whole numbers rather than as decimal fractions.

Statistical Tests for Ratios, Proportions, and Percentages

There are no tests for determining the significance of ratios, proportions, or percentages. If 30 percent of Library A's circulation is accounted for by children's materials and 60 percent of Library B's circulation is accounted for by children's materials, there is clearly a substantial difference, but there is no way of assigning a numeric significance value to that difference. There are inferential procedures for comparing proportions, which will be described in the discussion of inferential statistics.

How to Lie with Ratios, Proportions, and Percentages[1]

- The easiest way to deceive with any statistical procedure is to deliberately fail to provide context. If the reader has no understanding of the nature of the dataset or the way in which it was assembled, it is very difficult for the reader to determine what statistics really mean and easy to influence how the reader is likely to interpret the statistics.
- Round up or down to achieve effect. Percentages of 43.49 and 43.50 are only one one-hundredth of a percentage point apart. If they are converted to whole numbers, however, 43.49 typically rounds down to 43 and 43.50 rounds up to 44. Now the two figures are an entire percentage point apart.
- Report extensive decimal places to imply precision. There isn't really any difference between percentages of 43.493568 and 43.493570, but a reader can easily be led to believe that those last two digits really make a difference.
- Select ratios for effect. A ratio of directional questions to research questions of 10:1 implies that research questions play a very limited role in comparison to directional questions. Without the raw numbers, though, the ratio is difficult to completely interpret. If the total number of research and directional questions is 11, the ratio means very little. If the total number is 11,000, it implies that 1,000 research questions were answered, which may in context be a very meaningful number.
- Report nonexhaustive statistics. How might that interpretation of the ratio of directional to research differ if the overall distribution includes 3,350 directional questions, 335 research, and 17,358 informational questions? The ratio of directional questions to research is 10:1, but the fact that the overwhelming preponderance of questions were informational is ignored.
- Report percentages for small bases. Percentages really only apply when the overall base is large enough for percentage differences to be interesting. Knowing that 10 percent of

questions answered were research is of very little interest if the dataset consists of a total of 10 questions answered. The base simply isn't large enough for the statistic to be meaningful.

- Compare noncomparable data. The ratio of the number of reference questions answered during 2011 in the Anytown Public Library to the number of children registered for the summer reading program is easily calculated, but what does it actually mean? Does the ratio in any way imply the relative importance of reference services and summer reading programs?

- Fail to account for missing data. In businesses, libraries, and other environments that keep gate counts for both entering and exiting customers or patrons, it is frequently the case that the daily entrance count and the daily exit count don't match. What is actually implied if, over a substantial period of time, the number of counted entrances is 2 percent greater than the number of counted exits? What could account for such a difference? The answer is almost undoubtedly that the difference implies nothing because it is the result of missing data. Any comparison of entering and exiting counts must take into account the possibility of differences caused by missing data.

- Use inappropriate statistical tests. The fact that there are no statistical tests that can appropriately be used to determine the significance of ratios, proportions, and percentages doesn't imply that there are no tests that can be manipulated to produce inappropriate statistics. One of the dangers of statistical analysis software systems such as the Statistical Package for the Social Sciences is that it is amazingly easy to produce meaningless statistical output.

Centrality and Dispersion

Centrality, the extent to which values of a variable are similar, and dispersion, the extent to which values of a variable are dissimilar, work together to help characterize the distribution of values across the variable. Centrality and dispersion can best be understood from the hypothetical distribution shown in Figure 13.1.

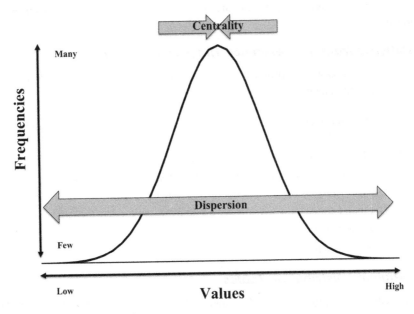

Figure 13.1 Centrality and dispersion.

	Question 1	Question 2	Question 3
Librarian 1	6	2	10
Librarian 2	6	8	8
Librarian 3	5	3	9
Librarian 4	4	2	8
Librarian 5	5	3	9
Librarian 6	5	2	8
Librarian 7	4	3	9
Librarian 8	5	5	10
Librarian 9	4	2	12
Librarian 10	5	4	4

Figure 13.2 Data matrix example: Time to answer each of three reference questions.

The horizontal axis of the graph shows the range of observed values of the variable, usually displayed with the lowest value to the left and the highest value to the right. The vertical axis shows the number of times each value occurs, which is the frequency of that value. The graph presented here conforms to the pattern of the normal curve, which will be discussed in greater detail later.

The height of the curve provides an indication of the extent to which the values are similar: the greater the extent to which a single central value dominates the distribution, the more similar the values are across the variable. The width of the curve provides an indication of the extent to which the values are dissimilar: the greater the extent to which the values are distributed across the range from lowest to highest, the more dissimilar the values are across the variable.

This data matrix of the time required for 10 reference librarians to answer each of three questions, first presented as Figure 12.2 and reproduced as Figure 13.2, will be used in a number of examples. Note that 10 cases are absolutely not adequate except for purposes of demonstration.

Statistics from the Reference Times Data Matrix

The following measures of proportion are examples of statistics that can be derived from the reference times data matrix:

- Ratio of answers requiring five or more minutes to answers requiring fewer than 5 minutes = 18/12 = 1.5
- Proportion of answers requiring 5 or more minutes = 18/30 = .6
- Percentages of answers requiring 5 or more minutes = 18/30 × 100 = 60%
- Percentage of answers requiring 5 or more minutes, by answer
  - Question 1: 7/10 = 70%
  - Question 2: 2/10 = 20%
  - Question 3: 9/10 = 90%

Frequency Distribution Tables

It is frequently helpful as part of data analysis to develop a frequency distribution table for each variable in a study. Information included in a frequency distribution table typically includes

Number of Minutes (Value)	Number of Cases (Frequency)	Percent of Total	Cumulative Percent
4	3	30	30
5	5	50	80
6	2	20	100
Total	10	100	

Figure 13.3 Frequency distribution table: Time to answer each of three reference questions.

- each value recorded for the variable
- the frequency with which each value was recorded
- the frequency of each value as a percentage of the total number of values
- the cumulative percentage accounted for by ascending values

The frequency distribution table for Question 1 from the data matrix is presented in Figure 13.3.

The first column of Figure 13.3 lists the observed values for the time needed to answer Question 1: 4 minutes, 5 minutes, and 6 minutes. The second column shows the number of librarians who required each of the observed values: three librarians required 4 minutes, five librarians required 5 minutes, and two librarians required 6 minutes. The third column is the number of librarians requiring each of the observed values divided by 10, the total number of cases. The fourth column provides a cumulative percent; this column can be read as 30 percent of librarians required 4 minutes to answer Question 1, 80 percent required 4 or 5 minutes to answer, and 100 percent required 4, 5, or 6 minutes to answer.

It's actually possible to make some preliminary assessments of centrality and dispersion by simple examination of the frequency distribution table. There are only three recorded values for the time required to answer Question 1 and they span a range of only 2 minutes, which seems to suggest that variability is limited. Half the librarians required 5 minutes to answer the question, which suggests that the distribution centers around 5 minutes as the typical time needed to answer the question.

Measures of Centrality

Mode. The mode is the most frequently occurring value in the distribution of values for a variable. The mode for Question 1 is 5 minutes, which was recorded for five cases. The mode for Question 2 is 2 minutes, which was recorded for four cases. For Question 3, however, both 8 minutes and 9 minutes were recorded for three cases. This is a bimodal distribution; multimodal distributions are also possible. The mode is expressive of the distribution of the variable only to the extent that values really cluster around one prevalent value but can be used with any level of measurement (nominal, ordinal, interval, or ratio). There are no statistical tests that can appropriately or effectively be used to compare modes across variables.

Median. The median is the midpoint of a distribution. It is helpful in determining the median to arrange the values for a variable in descending order.

It is clear that the median for the distribution of values for Question 1 is five. There are two rules for determining the median:

Question 1
6
6
5
5
5
5
4
4
4
4

Figure 13.4   Calculating the median: Time to answer reference Question 1.

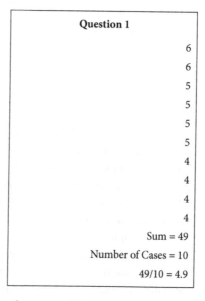

Figure 13.5   Calculating the mean 1: Time to answer reference Question 1.

1. For an odd number of cases, the median is the value of the true midpoint.
2. For an even number of cases, the median is either
   a. the value below which half the values lie or
   b. the value above the midpoint plus the value below the midpoint, divided by 2.

Most statistical analysis software employs the second approach to calculating the median for an even number of cases.

The median is insensitive to extreme values (outliers) but is expressive of the distribution as a whole only to the extent that values really cluster at the center of the distribution. The median can be used with ordinal-, interval-, and ratio-level data. Statistical tests for comparing medians across variables are of limited expressiveness.

Mean. The mean, more accurately called the arithmetic mean, is the sum of all values for a distribution divided by the number of values.

The mean for Question 1 is 4.9 minutes.

Notation for the Mean

The mean is the first statistic examined here for which there is explicit mathematical notation. The formula for calculating the mean is:

$$\bar{x} = \frac{\sum x}{n}$$

where

- $\bar{x}$, the symbol for the mean, is an x with a bar across the top; a lower case x with a bar denotes a sample mean while an upper case X with a bar denotes a population mean.
- Σ, sigma, is the summation symbol and means add together the following elements.
- x is the value of each case.
- Σx is the sum of values for all cases.
- n is the number of cases.

The formula then means sum the values of all cases and divide by the number of cases.

The mean incorporates all values but is highly sensitive to extreme values. Consider the example shown in Figure 13.6, which differs by only one value from the values for Question 1.

The highest recorded value is clearly not typical of the distribution as a whole but has a great influence on calculation of the mean.

The mean can be used with interval- and ratio-level data and can be used with care with ordinal-level data. There are many highly sophisticated statistical tests for comparing means across variables.

Question x
10
6
5
5
5
5
4
4
4
4
Sum = 57
Number of Cases = 10
49/10 = 5.7

Figure 13.6 Calculating the mean 2: Time to answer reference Question x.

1. Report a single mode for a bimodal or multimodal distribution or for a distribution with no clear prevalent value.

2. Report the median for values that do not cluster at the center of a distribution.

3. Report the mean for a distribution that is influenced by extremely high or extremely low values.

4. Use the word *average* without further definition.

Figure 13.7   How to lie with measures of centrality.

Measures of Dispersion

Range. Range has two prominent meanings:

1. An expression of the lowest and highest values for a distribution. Using this meaning, the range for Question 1 is 4–6 minutes.

2. The difference between the lowest and highest values for a distribution. This is the meaning reported by statistical analysis programs. Using this meaning, the range for Question 1 is 6–4 = 2 minutes.

The range can be used with ratio-level data and can be used with interval-level data with care. The range for a distribution provides a very rudimentary indicator of the dispersion of the overall distribution. Because the range uses only two values, the maximum and the minimum, it is quite possible for radically different overall distributions to have exactly the same range. The range is expressive only to the extent that the range of possible values is known. There are no useful statistical tests for comparing ranges across variables.

Standard Deviation. The standard deviation is a measure of the mean distance of individual scores from the overall mean for the distribution. Like the mean, the standard deviation uses all values of the distribution.

Notation for the Standard Deviation

By convention, there are two different symbols for the standard deviation:

σ = lower case sigma, the population standard deviation

s = the sample standard deviation used as an indicator of the population standard deviation or used when no inference about the population is being made

The formula for the standard deviation is:

$$s = \sqrt{\frac{\sum (x - \bar{x})^2}{n-1}}$$

where

s = the symbol for the sample standard deviation

$\bar{x}$ = the distribution mean

x = each value of the variable

n = the number of cases

$n-1$ = the number of cases minus 1 (This is also known as the *degrees of freedom* for n or the *unbiased* equivalent to n. Subtracting 1 from n produces a slightly higher, or more conservative calculation of the standard deviation.)

The basic process involves

1. subtracting the population mean from each value of the variable
2. squaring the difference to eliminate negative numbers
3. summing the squared differences
4. dividing the sum by the number of cases
5. calculating the square root of the sum to eliminate the effect of having squared the differences

Calculation of the standard deviation for Question 1 is shown in Figure 13.8.

So, the mean for Question 1 is 4.9 minutes and the standard deviation is 0.74 minutes, which lends support to the earlier surmise that there isn't much dispersion in the answer times for Question 1.

The standard deviation can be used only with ratio-level data and assumes a normal distribution or a close approximation thereof. The further the distribution deviates from normal the less expressive is the standard deviation. There are no useful tests for comparing standard deviations across variables.

x	$x-\bar{x}$	$(x-\bar{x})^2$
6	1.1	1.21
6	1.1	1.21
5	0.1	0.01
5	0.1	0.01
5	0.1	0.01
5	0.1	0.01
5	0.1	0.01
4	−0.9	.81
4	−0.9	.81
4	−0.9	.81

$$\sum (x-x)^2 = 4.9$$

$$\sum (x-\bar{x})^2 / n-1 = 4.9/9 = 0.54$$

$$\sqrt{\sum (x-\bar{x})^2 / n-1} = 4.9/9 = 0.54 = 0.74$$

Figure 13.8   Calculating the standard deviation: Time to answer reference Question 1.

1. Report the range as the difference between minimum and maximum values without reporting the minimum and maximum values.
2. Report the standard deviation without reporting the mean.
3. Report dispersion for data other than ratio-level data.

Figure 13.9   How to lie with measures of dispersion.

Variance. The variance is the square of the standard deviation or the standard deviation minus the final step of canceling out the squaring of the differences between values and the mean. The notation for variance is

σ^2 = the population variance

s^2 = the sample variance

For Question 1, $s^2 = .54$.

Variance can be used only with ratio-level data and is used primarily in calculating other statistics and has little use on its own. There are no useful statistical tests for comparing variance across variables or distributions.

THE NORMAL CURVE

Most statistical tests assume that the values under consideration are distributed according to the pattern known as the normal curve. Figure 13.10 is a graphic representation of a normal curve.

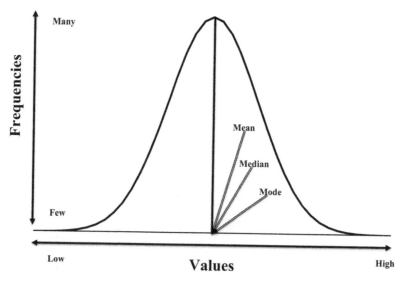

Figure 13.10   The normal curve.

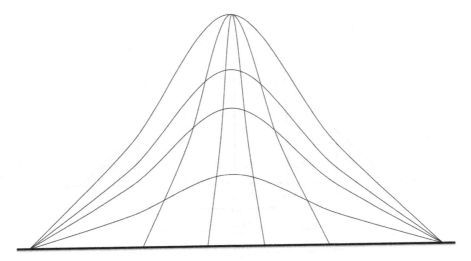

Figure 13.11 Normal curves.

A normal curve has two fundamental characteristics:

1. The mean, median, and mode all have the same value.
2. Values are distributed in exactly the same manner above and below the central point defined simultaneously by the mean, median, and mode.

If enough values are examined, the variables defined by the characteristics of most naturally occurring phenomena fall into the pattern of the normal curve. There are major exceptions to this pattern, some of which are systematic and important. Furthermore, the assumption of the normal curve can frequently be violated fairly liberally.

The relationship between centrality and dispersion defines the specific shape of any normal curve. The distributions shown in Figure 13.11 are all normal curves with identical means, medians, and modes but influenced by varying dispersions.

Areas under the Normal Curve

One of the interesting characteristics of the normal curve is that the proportions of values that fall at specified distances from the mean, measured in standard deviations, are always the same regardless of the specific shape of the curve. The areas under the normal curve are shown in Figure 13.12. Working from this chart of the areas under the normal distribution, it can be seen that 68 percent of all values are within one standard deviation on either side of the mean. So, if the mean, standard deviation, minimum, and maximum are known, it is possible to determine the percentage of values associated with the distance from the mean defined by each standard deviation.

Regardless of the specific distribution, 68 percent of all values will fall within one standard deviation above and below the mean, 95 percent will fall within two standard deviations, and 99 percent will fall within three standard deviations.

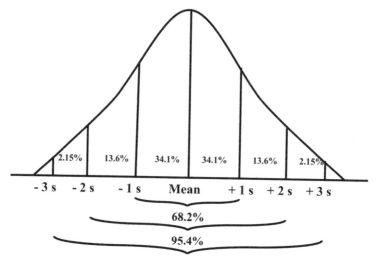

Figure 13.12   Areas under the normal curve.

Why Is the Normal Curve Important?

Although the importance of the normal curve can easily be overstated, there are three fundamental ways in which the normal curve is important:

1. Many naturally occurring phenomena, including many social sciences phenomena, naturally conform to the normal curve.

2. Random and pseudorandom phenomena tend to conform to the normal curve to the extent that one approach to assessing randomness is conformity to the normal curve.

3. Most inferential statistical procedures assume that the data being examined conform to the normal curve. Although this assumption can frequently be violated, understanding that is being consciously violated is essential. In some cases conformity to the normal curve determines the form of statistical test that can be used with a particular dataset.

Non-normal Curves

There aren't any formally recognized abnormal curves. The normal curve gets its name because of its *normative* nature in which the mean, median, and mode are all congruent. There are, however, major identified categories of non-normal curves.

Negatively Skewed Curve

A negatively skewed curve is characterized by a large frequency of lower values, resulting in the mean being lower than the median and mode; the median and mode in a negatively skewed curve are frequently but not necessarily the same.

Positively Skewed Curve

A positively skewed curve is characterized by a large frequency of higher values, resulting in the mean being higher than the median and mode. Positively skewed curves are very common in social sciences, educational, and information research or evaluation.

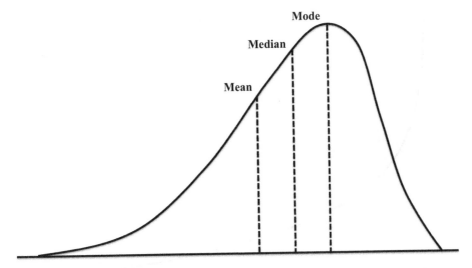

Figure 13.13   Negatively skewed curve.

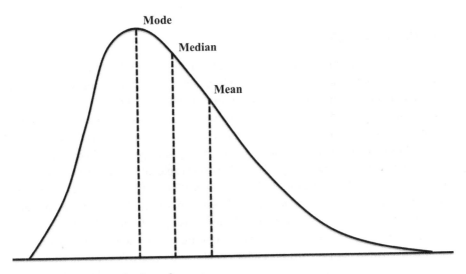

Figure 13.14   Positively skewed curve.

Exponential Curve

A particular type of positively skewed curve that is extremely common in studying in-formation phenomena is the exponential or logarithmic curve, which almost always applies when time is one of the variables, such as when plotting the circulation of items in a collec-tion in relationship to the ages of the items at the time of use. Note the extremely steep initial rise followed by the regular curve of the long tail.

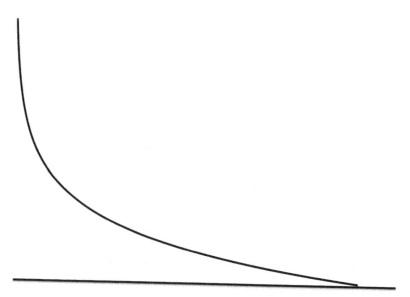

Figure 13.15   Logarithmic (J-shaped) curve.

STATISTICAL TESTING

Statistical testing and inferential statistics are primarily about establishing relationships, sometimes among the values of a single variable, but more frequently across variables. The basic question is either "how are the values for this variable related to each other?" or "how are these variables related to each other?" There are, of course many possible relationships, depending on the nature of the variables being examined. If the question is "how is circulation distributed among nonfiction, adult fiction, young adult books, and children's books in the Anytown Public Library?" the relationship being explored is among values of a single variable, circulation. If the question is "how is circulation distributed among nonfiction, adult fiction, young adults books, and children's books in all member libraries of the Large Metropolitan Public Library Consortium?" the relationship adds the additional variable of the different libraries that are members of the consortium. The question "how has circulation of nonfiction, adult fiction, young adults books, and children's books in all member libraries of the Large Metropolitan Public Library Consortium varied during the last ten years?" the variable of time has been added. The search for relationships in statistical testing is a very systematic and demanding process in which the nature of the relationship, the significance of the relationship, and the potential for error are all very thoroughly explored.

An Example of a Relationship: Driver Behavior and Traffic Fatalities

Driver behavior and traffic fatalities are of ongoing public concern. In addition to the historical problems of driver fatigue and drunk driving, recent attention has been focused on the potential hazards of driving while distracted. Figure 13.16 provides data from the U.S. Department of Transportation for traffic fatalities during 2009 related to three categories of driver behavior.

Number of Fatalities			Number of Fatalities
Group 1	Group 2	Group 3	
20,961	1,905	10,839	33,705

Figure 13.16 Traffic fatalities, 2009.

A very clear pattern emerges in the data in Figure 13.14. Drivers in Group 1 accounted for 62 percent of all reported traffic fatalities in the United States in 2009. Drivers in Group 3 were responsible for slightly more than half as many deaths as drivers in Group 1 at 32 percent of all reported fatalities. Drivers in Group 2 appear to have been the safest drivers, having been responsible for only six percent of the 33,705 fatalities during the year. A logical conclusion based on the data is that the behavior exhibited by drivers in Group 1 should be actively discouraged, while the behavior characteristic of Group 2 should be fostered as highly beneficial to traffic safety.

A different picture emerges, however, when the nature of the three patterns of behavior is revealed. The missing behaviors are shown in Figure 13.17.

Number of Fatalities			
Driver blood alcohol concentration = 0.00	Driver blood alcohol concentration = 0.01–0.07	Driver blood alcohol concentration = 0.08 or above	Number of Fatalities
20,961	1,905	10,839	33,705

Source: "Traffic Safety Facts 2009." U.S. Department of Transportation. Washington: National Highway Traffic Safety Administration, 2010.

Figure 13.17 Traffic fatalities and blood alcohol concentration, 2009.

The added information that the three behavior groups have to do with alcohol consumption prior to or during driving reshapes the interpretation of the data substantially. There is clearly some relationship between blood alcohol concentration and traffic fatalities, but what is the nature of the relationship? Is the relationship in any way significant? Based on the table, it appears to be the case that the safest drivers, those who are involved in the fewest fatal accidents, are those who have very small blood alcohol concentrations, while the most dangerous are clearly those who haven't consumed any alcohol at all. How can that be?

The answer is that there simply aren't enough data within this table to infer anything interesting at all. The relationship between alcohol consumption and traffic fatalities is more complex. Among other things, there is no way to know what to expect, although most people probably expect that the incidence of fatalities involving alcohol consumption is in some way significantly worse than the incidence of fatalities involving no alcohol consumption.

Statistical Testing and Error

Statistical testing, more properly referred to as hypothesis testing but more frequently called simply statistical testing, is the process of determining the statistical or probabilistic likelihood that a hypothesis of interest can be supported. Statistical or hypothesis testing takes place in the context of a null hypothesis. A null hypothesis is framed in terms of

	Accept Null Hypothesis	Reject Null Hypothesis
Null Hypothesis is True	Null hypothesis is correctly accepted	Type I error: null hypothesis is incorrectly rejected
Null Hypothesis is False	Type II error: null hypothesis is incorrectly accepted	Null hypothesis is correctly rejected

Figure 13.18   Null hypothesis truth table.

anticipation of the existence of no relationship between stated variables. Any null hypothesis should be accompanied by one or more alternative hypotheses that offer potential explanations for the situation in which the null hypothesis is rejected. Statistical hypothesis involves determining the probability that the null hypothesis is true—that there is in fact no relationship between the variables of interest.

There are two possible states of the null hypothesis: it is either (1) true or (2) false. Although probability plays a strong and essential role in statistical testing, the binary nature of the truth of the null hypothesis is fundamental and essential. There are no states of partial truth associated with the null hypothesis.

There are also two possible outcomes of statistical testing: (1) the test supports the null hypothesis, in which case the null hypothesis is accepted and the alternative hypothesis is rejected without further consideration or (2) the test rejects the null hypothesis, in which case the investigator proceeds to attempt to demonstrate the viability of the alternative hypothesis.

The null hypothesis and error table presented in Figure 13.18 defines the four possible relationships between the true nature of the null hypothesis and the outcome of hypothesis testing.

1. The null hypothesis is true and the results of hypothesis testing indicate that the null hypothesis should be accepted. This is a correct assessment of the state of the null hypothesis.

2. The null hypothesis is true and the results of hypothesis testing indicate that the null hypothesis should be rejected. The null hypothesis has been incorrectly rejected; this is a Type I error.

3. The null hypothesis is false and the results of hypothesis testing indicate that the null hypothesis should be rejected. This is a correct assessment of the state of the null hypothesis.

4. The null hypothesis is false and the results of hypothesis testing indicate that the null hypothesis should be accepted. The null hypothesis has been incorrectly accepted; this is a Type II error.

The Impact of Error

The primary impact of Type I error is exploration of alternative hypotheses that are in fact of little or no value. Having rejected the null hypothesis, the investigator assumes substantial confidence in the alternative hypothesis.

The primary impact of the Type II error is suppression of exploration of the alternative hypothesis. Having accepted the null hypothesis, the investigator abandons the alternative hypothesis as being unjustified.

In most medical, biological, and social sciences research or evaluation—in fact, in most research or evaluation environments in which action is an anticipated outcome of the research or evaluation—reduction of Type I error is emphasized. The general assumption is that the temporary suppression of further exploration of the alternative hypothesis is less harmful than implementation of an ineffective solution. That assumption may vary based on the social significance of the problem at hand. Implementing a solution based on Type I error may be expensive and harmful, but the expense and harm may be worth the risk in the case of something such as a cure for AIDS or a means of preventing suicide bombings.

Significance and Power

Statistical significance is an estimate of the probability of Type I error, in which the null hypothesis is true and there is no relationship between the variables being studied but the null hypothesis is incorrectly rejected, lending false support to the alternative hypothesis. Significance is also known as alpha (α).

Power is an estimate of the probability of Type II error, in which the null hypothesis is false and there is a relationship between the variables being studied but the null hypothesis is incorrectly rejected, resulting in abandonment of the alternative hypothesis. Power is also known as beta (β).

Unfortunately, significance and power are linked in a negative reciprocal relationship—any action that reduces Type I error increases Type II error; any action that reduces Type II error increases Type I error.

Components of Statistical Testing

There are four fundamental components to statistical testing:

1. data to be analyzed
2. a test to be applied to the data
3. a probability threshold to be used in applying and interpreting the test
4. the number of degrees of freedom that characterize the test

Typical Probability Thresholds

The probability threshold defines statistical significance, the probability of Type I error. A probability threshold is usually expressed as the number of chance of Type I error.

- A probability threshold of .001 (one chance in 1,000 of Type I error) is employed for most biomedical research. This is a very conservative threshold designed to absolutely minimize the likelihood of adopting a counterproductive alternative hypothesis.
- A probability threshold of .01 (one chance in 100 of Type I error) is generally considered to be suitable for social sciences research with large samples.
- A probability threshold of .05 (five chances in 100 of Type I error) is the norm for most social sciences research, except those studies involving large samples.

Probability Notation

- p (always italicized) is the symbol for a Type I error probability threshold; p is an indicator of the significance of the results of the test.

- $p < .05$ means the exact probability of Type I error is less than five chances in 100.
- $p = .042$ means the exact probability of Type I error is exactly 4.2 chances in 100.

Degrees of Freedom

Degrees of freedom is one of the most difficult concepts in statistical testing and to some extent may need to simply be taken on faith. Given an overall distribution of values, degrees of freedom is

- an indication of how the value of any given case is influenced by the values of other cases
- an indication of how many values must be known to derive all values
- a mathematically derived indicator of how to interpret a statistic

Notation for Degrees of Freedom

df_n denotes that the degrees of freedom for a particular test design $= n$.

Degrees of Freedom: One Cell

The concept of degrees of freedom can effectively be presented graphically as a table that defines the relationships within values for a variable in a distribution or the relationships among multiple variables. Think of a very uninteresting study in which all of the cases have the same value. There is no variability at all and the mean, median, and mode are all the same. The overall distribution of values for a one-cell distribution is shown graphically in Figure 13.19.

The row total and the overall total are known. How much additional information is needed to determine the unknown value of the cell? For instance, if the row total and the overall total are both 15, what is the unknown value?

As shown in Figure 13.20, if the row total is 15 and the column total is 15, the overall total also has to be 15. The unknown value also has to be 15. No additional information is needed. The degrees of freedom for this design = 0.

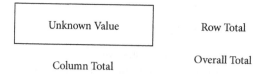

Figure 13.19   Degrees of freedom: One cell.

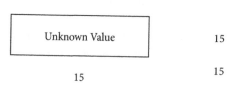

Figure 13.20   Degrees of freedom: One-cell solution.

Degrees of Freedom: Two Cells

Let's expand to a single variable with two values. The overall distribution of values is shown in Figure 13.21.

If the row total and the overall total are known, how much additional information is needed to determine the unknown values of the cells? For instance, if the row total and the overall total are both 30, as shown in Figure 13.22, how much information is needed to determine all values?

If the value of the first cell is 20, as indicated in Figure 13.23, what is the value of the second cell?

The answer has to be 10. If the value of one cell is known, no additional information is needed. The degrees of freedom for this design = 1

Degrees of Freedom: Univariate Tests

A pattern starts to emerge here. For any test that involves only one variable the number of degrees of freedom is the number of values (the number of cells) minus 1.

- $df_1 = 1-1 = 0$
- $df_2 = 2-1 = 1$
- $df_9 = 9-1 = 8$

Unknown Value	Unknown Value	Row Total
Column Total	Column Total	Overall Total

Figure 13.21   Degrees of freedom: Two cells.

Unknown Value	Unknown Value	30
Column Total	Column Total	30

Figure 13.22   Degrees of freedom: Two cells, known row totals.

20	Unknown Value	30
20	Column Total	30

Figure 13.23   Degrees of freedom: Two-cell solution.

Degrees of Freedom: Bivariate Test: Four Cells

Now let's move on to two related variables, each of which has two possible values, as shown in Figure 13.24.

If both row totals and the overall total are known, how much additional information is needed to determine all unknown values? If, for instance, it is known that both row totals are 20 and the overall total is 40?

If the value of the first cell is 10, what are the values of the other cells?

The values of all the other cells have to be 10 as well. If the value of one cell is known, no additional information is needed. The degrees of freedom for this test design = 1.

Degrees of Freedom: Bivariate Tests

A definite pattern emerges for bivariate tests as well: for any bivariate test, the degrees of freedom is equal to the number of values of the first variable minus 1 multiplied by the number of values of the other values of the other variable minus 1.

Unknown Value	Unknown Value	Row Total
Unknown Value	Unknown Value	Row Total
Column Total	Column Total	Overall Total

Figure 13.24   Degrees of freedom: Four cells.

Unknown Value	Unknown Value	20
Unknown Value	Unknown Value	20
Column Total	Column Total	40

Figure 13.25   Degrees of freedom: Four cells, known row totals.

10	Unknown Value	20
Unknown Value	Unknown Value	20
Column Total	Column Total	40

Figure 13.26   Degrees of freedom: Four-cell solution.

- $df_{\text{rows,columns}} = (\text{rows-1}) \times (\text{columns-1})$
- $df_{2,2} = (2\text{-}1) \times (2\text{-}1) = 1 \times 1 = 1$
- $df_{3,3} = (3\text{-}1) \times (3\text{-}1) = 2 \times 2 = 4$
- $df_{5,4} = (5\text{-}1) \times (4\text{-}1) = 4 \times 3 = 12$

INFERENTIAL STATISTICS

Standard Assumptions of Inferential Statistics

There are certain assumptions that apply to most inferential statistical procedures. The standard assumptions are

1. Data are from a normally distributed population; that is, the values conform to a normal curve. Note that it is the distribution of the population that is important, not the distribution of the sample.
2. Data are from a sample. Inferential statistics are not designed for use with census-level data and are frequently undermined by application to overly large datasets.
3. The sample is random. Random sampling in inferential statistics has the dual benefits of ensuring that the data are representative and ensuring that the sample, like the population, is normally distributed.
4. Assignment to groups is random. There is no systematic process in use to influence the likelihood of a case being assigned to any particular group such as an experimental group or a control group.
5. Groups being compared have equal variances. Many inferential statistical processes essentially test the question "are these groups part of the same population?" That becomes more difficult—although not necessarily impossible—to test when sample variances are not equal.

Major Families of Inferential Statistics

Inferential statistics fall into two major levels of statistics:

1. Parametric statistics are used with interval- or ratio-level variables and are closely associated with the assumption of a normally distributed population.
2. Nonparametric statistics are more frequently used with nominal- or ordinal-level variables and are associated with no assumption of a normally distributed population.

Selected Inferential Statistical Tests: Goodness of Fit and Proportion

Chi-Square Test of Goodness of Fit

Variables: one nominal-level variable

Question: Is the distribution of cases across categories the result of chance?

Example: Fifty librarians each answered one question and the success of each answer was tabulated. The distribution of results is presented in Figure 13.27.

The number of degrees of freedom for any univariate test is the number of categories minus 1; since there are three categories in this test—correct, partially correct, and incorrect—the number of degrees of freedom is two.

Correct	Partially Correct	Incorrect
15	25	10

Figure 13.27   Success in answering reference questions, 50 librarians.

Notation for the Chi-Square Test of Goodness of Fit

$$\chi^2 = \sum \frac{(O-E)^2}{E}$$

χ^2 = chi-square, the name of the test

O = observed value for each cell

E = expected value for each cell

The calculation involves the following steps:

1. record the observed and expected value for each cell as described below
2. subtract the expected value from the observed value
3. square the difference to eliminate negative numbers
4. divide the squared difference by the expected value
5. sum the dividends

There are two approaches to determining observed values:

1. Logically determine observed values based on prior knowledge of the phenomenon being studied.
2. Statistically derive observed values based on what chance predicts with all other factors being equal.

For the example, the statistical approach has been used. Chance would predict that each category would be equally represented. The needed data are presented in Figure 13.28.

So, the calculated value of χ^2 is 6.988. How, then, do we know if that is meaningful? The traditional way is to consult a table of Critical Values of chi-square. A sample of a portion of such a table is reproduced in Figure 13.29.[2] This is just a fragment of the table; the table from which this was drawn actually extends to 100 degrees of freedom.

Question	O	E	$(O-E)^2$	$(O-E)^2/E$
Correct	15	16.7	2.89	.173
Partially Correct	25	16.7	68.89	4.125
Incorrect	10	16.7	44.89	2.69
Sum of $(O-E)^2/E$				6.988

Figure 13.28   Data needed for chi-square analysis, success in answering reference questions, 50 librarians.

Degrees of Freedom (*df*)	Probability of Exceeding the Critical Value			
	.10	.05	.01	.001
1	2.706	3.841	6.635	10.827
2	4.605	5.991	9.210	13.815
3	6.251	7.815	11.345	16.266
4	7.779	9.488	13.277	18.467
5	9.236	11.070	15.086	20.515
6	10.645	12.592	16.812	22.458
7	12.017	14.067	18.475	24.322
8	13.362	15.507	20.090	26.125
9	14.684	16.919	21.666	27.877
10	15.987	18.307	23.209	29.588

Figure 13.29   Critical values of chi-square.

Each cell in the table shows the critical value of chi-square for a particular level of significance (.10, .05, .01, .001) for a particular number of degrees of freedom. For the example, the number of degrees of freedom is equal to the number of values minus 1 = 3-1 = 2. If the .05 level of significance is chosen, the critical value of chi-square is 5.991. The notation for that is

$$_{.05}\chi^2_2$$

which simply means the critical value of chi-square at the .05 level of significance with two degrees of freedom. If the observed value exceeds the critical value, then the results of the test are statistically significant.

In the case of the example, the calculated value is 6.986 and the critical value is 5.991, so the null hypothesis is rejected and the alternative hypothesis, which is that there is a systematic pattern that defines how successfully questions are answered, is supported.

Assumptions of Chi-Square Tests

Any form of chi-square test is expected to conform to certain assumptions. The fundamental ones are:

1. The data are drawn from a random sample. This assumption can be violated fairly freely.
2. Cells are independent. This means that no value can be represented in more than one cell.
3. There are no expected frequencies less than one. This is an absolute and cannot be violated.
4. No more than 20 percent of expected frequencies are less than five. This is an absolute and cannot be violated.
5. Chi-square is not valid for very large samples where very large typically means no more than 100 values per cell and no more than a few hundred values total. Although the critical value of chi-square doesn't vary with the size of the sample, the calculated value increases as the size of the sample increases.

Chi-Square Test of Proportion

Chi-square defines not a single statistical test, but a family of tests all based on the distribution of the value of chi-square. A single statistic may serve different roles in different tests.

The chi-square test of proportion is slightly more complicated and therefore more expressive than the chi-square test of goodness-of-fit.

Variables: Two or more nominal-level variables. Although it is somewhat difficult to visualize a relationship that includes three or more variables, there is no theoretical limit to the number of variables that can be examined using the chi-square test of proportion.

Question: Is the distribution of cases among cells the result of chance?

Example: One hundred librarians each answered two questions on the same topic, one requiring a strictly factual answer and the other requiring some analysis and interpretation. The research question is "Is there a relationship between success in answering a factual question and success in answering an interpretive question?" The results are presented in Figure 13.30.

For any bivariate test, the degrees of freedom is equal to the number of values of the first variable minus 1 multiplied by the number of values of the other values of the other variable minus 1. The degrees of freedom for this distribution, then, is $(3-1) \times (3-1) = 2 \times 2 = 4$. Expected values for the distribution are shown in Figure 13.31.

Although the calculation for the chi-square test isn't presented here, the calculated value of chi-square is 2.387. The critical value of chi-square with four degrees of freedom at the .05 probability level from Figure 13.29 is 9.488. Since the observed value does not exceed the critical value, the null hypothesis that there is no relationship between success in answering the two related kinds of questions must be accepted.

		Question 2		
		Correct	Partially Correct	Incorrect
	Correct	6	8	18
Question 1	Partially Correct	14	10	20
	Incorrect	8	10	10

Figure 13.30   Success in answering two related reference questions, 100 librarians.

		Question 2		
		Correct	Partially Correct	Incorrect
	Correct	6.0	8.0	18.0
	Expected	7.8	7.8	12.3
Question 1	Partially Correct	14.0	10.0	20.0
	Expected	12.3	12.3	19.4
	Incorrect	8.0	10.0	10.0
	Expected	7.8	7.8	12.3

Figure 13.31   Expected values, success in answering two related reference questions, 100 librarians.

Selected Inferential Statistical Tests: Correlation

Correlation refers to a family of statistical procedures that measure the extent to which two or more variables vary together. A positive correlation is observed when a low value on one variable corresponds to a low value on the other variable(s) and a high value corresponds with a high value(s), as shown in Figure 13.32.

A negative correlation is observed when a low value on one variable corresponds to a high value on the other variable(s) and a high value corresponds to a low value(s). A negative correlation is illustrated in Figure 13.33.

The results of a test of correlation are useful for examining both positive and negative relationships but may be deceptive when there is no real relationship. The distribution shown in Figure 13.34 would yield a negative correlation, but the relationship between the two variables is far from smooth.

Tests of correlation are also potentially deceptive when there is a systematic nonlinear relationship such as that shown in Figure 13.35.

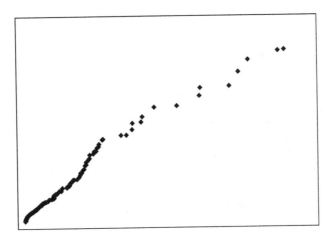

Figure 13.32   Positive correlation.

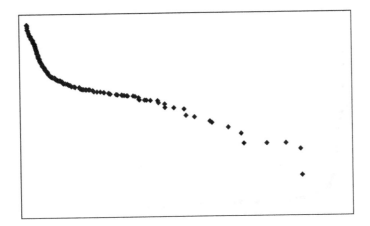

Figure 13.33   Negative correlation.

Frequency Correlation

This is the most commonly used form of test of correlation. The basic goal of a frequency correlation is to examine the consistency with which two variables vary together. All tests of correlation yield a correlation coefficient, which is always a decimal fraction in the range of -1.00 to +1.00, where -1.00 denotes a perfect negative correlation and +1.00 denotes a perfect positive correlation. A perfect correlation graphs as a 45° straight line.

Variables: Two or more interval- or ratio-level variables. Frequency correlation is most valid when the variables are ratio-level, but can be used with interval-level variables with care. Frequency correlation cannot be used with nominal- or ordinal-level variables.

Question: Is there a systematic relationship between (or among) the distributions of the variables?

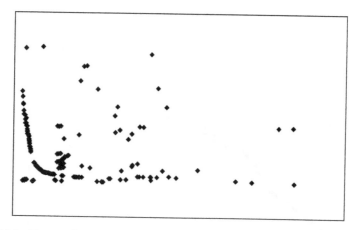

Figure 13.34   No correlation.

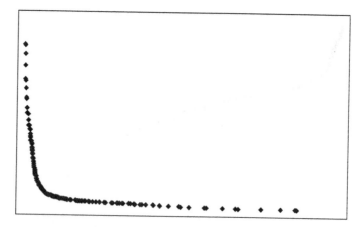

Figure 13.35   Nonlinear relationship.

Librarian	Factual Questions Answered Correctly	Interpretive Questions Answered Successfully
1	6	2
2	6	8
3	5	3
4	4	2
5	5	3
6	5	2
7	5	3
8	4	5
9	5	4
10	4	2

Figure 13.36 Results of success in answering paired factual/interpretive question, 10 librarians.

Example: Ten reference librarians were each asked 10 factual questions and 10 interpretive questions, each pair related to the same topic. Answers were recorded as correct or incorrect. The research question is "Is there a systematic relationship between the number of factual questions answered correctly and the number of interpretive questions answered correctly?" Results are presented in Figure 13.36.

The most commonly used frequency correlation is the Pearson product-moment correlation. The formula for the Pearson correlation is

$$r = \frac{\sum XY - n\overline{X}\,\overline{Y}}{(\sum X^2 - n\overline{X}^2)(\sum Y^2 - n\overline{Y}^2)}$$

Although the formula may appear to be very complex, it can easily be broken down into its component parts.

n = number of cases

X = value of variable X, in this case the number of factual questions answered correctly, for each case

Y = value of variable Y, in this case the number of interpretive questions answered correctly, for each case

XY = value of X multiplied by the value of Y, for each case

$\sum XY$ = sum of all values of XY

$\overline{X}$ = mean for all values of X

$\overline{Y}$ = mean for all values of Y

X^2 = value of X multiplied by itself, for each case

Y^2 = value of Y multiplied by itself, for each case

$\sum X^2$ = sum of squares for X—the sum of all values of X^2

$\sum Y^2$ = sum of squares for Y—the sum of all values of Y^2

Case	X	Y	X^2	Y^2	XY
1	6	2	36	4	12
2	6	8	36	64	48
3	5	3	24	9	15
4	4	2	16	4	8
5	5	3	25	9	15
6	5	2	25	4	10
7	5	3	25	9	15
8	4	5	16	25	20
9	5	4	25	16	20
10	4	2	16	4	8
Sums	Not needed	Not needed	$\Sigma X^2 = 244$	$\Sigma Y^2 = 148$	$\Sigma XY = 171$
Means	$\overline{X} = 4.9$	$\overline{Y} = 3.4$	$\overline{X^2} = 24.4$	$\overline{Y} = 14.8$	Not needed

Figure 13.37 Tables of values for calculating Pearson correlation.

$\overline{X^2}$ = mean of squares of X—the mean of all values of X^2

$\overline{Y^2}$ = mean of squares of Y

The raw numbers, sums, and means for the sample question are shown in Figure 13.37. From the table, the following values are needed to calculate the Pearson correlation:

$n = 10$

$\Sigma XY = 171$

$\overline{X} = 4.9$

$\overline{Y} = 3.4$

$\Sigma X^2 = 244$

$\Sigma Y^2 = 148$

$\overline{X}^2 = 25.01$

$\overline{Y}^2 = 11.56$

$$r = \frac{\sum XY - n\overline{X}\overline{Y}}{(\sum X^2 - n\overline{X}^2)(\sum Y^2 - n\overline{Y}^2)}$$

$$= \frac{171 - (10 \times 4.9 \times 3.4)}{(244 - (10 \times 24.01)) \times (148 - (10 \times 11.56))}$$

$$= \left[\frac{4.4}{12.6}\right]$$

$$= .349$$

The Pearson correlation coefficient, then is .349, a positive correlation, but not a very interesting one. A typical interpretation of the meaningfulness of the Pearson correlation coefficient is

- −1.0 to −0.7 is a strong negative association.
- −0.7 to −0.3 is a weak negative association.
- −0.3 to +0.3 connotes little or no association.
- +0.3 to +0.7 is a weak positive association.
- +0.7 to +1.0 is a strong positive association.

This is a rule of thumb, not an official interpretation. According to this interpretation, there is a weak positive correlation between the number of factual questions answered correctly and the number of interpretive questions answered successfully.

Other Tests of Correlation

There are many tests for correlation, each designed for a specific purpose and for a specified combination of variables. Rank correlations are used with ordinal-level data and don't require as precise a linear relationship as a Pearson correlation. Commonly used rank correlation tests are Kendall's tau (τ) and Spearman's rho (ρ). Rank-frequency correlations are common in library and information science research. A simple rank-frequency correlation looks at the relationship between one ordinal-level variable (a rank) and one interval- or, usually, ratio-level variable (a count). Rank-frequency correlation analysis is frequently used with bibliometric data (see Chapter 11, "Bibliometrics and Citation Analysis").

Correlation and Causation

Causation is a special case of correlation. Loosely defined, causation refers to the situation in which a change in one variable not only is related to a change in another variable, but actually effects the change. If the variables are not correlated, then there can be no causal link, but the presence of a correlation does not in and of itself imply causation. Causation usually implies that a change in the independent variable is both necessary and sufficient for a change in the dependent variable.

Necessary means that the dependent variable will not change unless influenced by the independent variable. So, if it is posited that taking longer to answer reference questions will cause an increase in accuracy, there should be no other factors at work that can result in an increase in accuracy.

Sufficient means that no influence other than that of the independent variable is required for the change in the dependent variable. If it is posited that taking longer to answer reference questions will cause an increase in accuracy, spending more time should by and of itself result in an increase in accuracy.

The most common flaw in research is the assumption that correlation implies causation; this is closely related to the post hoc fallacy. Post hoc, ergo propter hoc loosely translates as "after this, therefore as a result of this."

An anonymous e-mail that circulated widely in the 1990s addressed the relationship between bread and global warming. A version of that warning is presented in Figure 13.38.[3]

The implication of the relationships between bread consumption and other factors is clearly that bread consumption results in criminal behavior, poor test scores, catastrophic illnesses, and other calamitous events. Although there may truly be such a correlation, however, causation is a very different phenomenon.

The Dangers of Bread

A recent *Cincinnati Enquirer* headline read, "Smell of baked bread may be health hazard." The article went on to describe the dangers of the smell of baking bread. The main danger, apparently, is that the organic components of this aroma may break down ozone (I'm not making this stuff up).

I was horrified. When are we going to do something about bread-induced global warming? Sure, we attack tobacco companies, but when is the government going to go after Big Bread?

Well, I've done a little research, and what I've discovered should make anyone think twice . . .

1. More than 98 percent of convicted felons are bread eaters.

2. Fully HALF of all children who grow up in bread-consuming households score below average on standardized tests.

3. In the 18th century, when virtually all bread was baked in the home, the average life expectancy was less than 50 years; infant mortality rates were unacceptably high; many women died in childbirth; and diseases such as typhoid, yellow fever, and influenza ravaged whole nations.

4. More than 90 percent of violent crimes are committed within 24 hours of eating bread.

5. Bread is made from a substance called "dough." It has been proven that as little as one pound of dough can be used to suffocate a mouse. The average American eats more bread than that in one month!

6. Primitive tribal societies that have no bread exhibit a low occurrence of cancer, Alzheimer's, Parkinson's disease, and osteoporosis.

7. Bread has been proven to be addictive. Subjects deprived of bread and given only water to eat begged for bread after only two days.

8. Bread is often a "gateway" food item, leading the user to "harder" items such as butter, jelly, peanut butter, and even cold cuts.

9. Bread has been proven to absorb water. Since the human body is more than 90 percent water, it follows that eating bread could lead to your body being taken over by this absorptive food product, turning you into a soggy, gooey bread-pudding person.

10. Newborn babies can choke on bread.

11. Bread is baked at temperatures as high as 400 degrees Fahrenheit! That kind of heat can kill an adult in less than one minute.

12. Most American bread eaters are utterly unable to distinguish between significant scientific fact and meaningless statistical babbling.

In light of these frightening statistics, we propose the following bread restrictions:

1. No sale of bread to minors.

2. No advertising of bread within 1,000 feet of a school.

3. A 300 percent federal tax on all bread to pay for all the societal ills we might associate with bread.

4. No animal or human images, nor any primary colors (which may appeal to children) should be used to promote bread usage.

5. A $4.2 zillion fine on the three biggest bread manufacturers. Please send this e-mail on to everyone you know who cares about this crucial issue.

Figure 13.38   Is bread causing global warming?

Continuing with the example of the relationship between the times required to answer reference questions and the accuracy of the answers, suppose that the following scenario is put into place:

1. First, the time spent in answering reference questions and the accuracy of the answers are assessed for a statistically valid number of reference transactions in a large public library at which the reference desk is staffed by three employees at all times.

2. Next, an additional employee is added at all times to make it possible for reference staff to spend more time answering questions and the head of the reference department meets several times with all the reference staff to encourage them to spend more time on questions.

3. There is then a second round of assessment of the time spent answering questions and the accuracy of the answers is conducted and it is found that both time and accuracy have increased.

What can be concluded as a result?

It is very tempting to assume that the increase in time has caused the increase in accuracy, but there are at least three confounding factors:

1. The increase in accuracy may be a result of the addition of reference staff, which both provides more time and relieves existing staff members of a source of stress and burnout.

2. Both the increase in time and the increase in accuracy may be the result of increased positive attention from the head of reference—the reference staff feel that someone actually cares whether they do a good job and, individually and not completely consciously, make a collective effort to do a better job.

3. The increases in both time and accuracy are effected primarily by the new staff members, who are not affected by the stress and burnout experienced by longer-term staff members and who additionally fear that they will receive poor performance evaluations and face dismissal if they don't do well in their new jobs.

By simply reflecting on these confounding factors it becomes clear that devoting increased time to answering questions is not a necessary condition for an improvement in accuracy and may not be a sufficient factor for improvement. This experimental process, although it yielded pragmatically beneficial and interesting results, does not demonstrate that increasing the time spent in answering reference questions produces greater accuracy in answering reference questions.

Correlation can be tested and verified through a variety of quantitative and qualitative means; causation is extremely difficult to examine and can never be proven, not even in the physical and biological sciences. Even approaching proof of causation is extremely difficult in the social and behavioral sciences.

Selected Inferential Statistical Tests: Comparison of Means

Comparing means for variables of interest adds a level of sophistication to the simpler calculation of a correlation coefficient. Comparison of means is especially useful for examining the relationships between the performance of defined groups or assessing changes in performance between measurements. Means may be compared in a variety of ways. The simplest involve comparing means for two groups.

The t-Test (Student's t)

The *t*-test is a procedure for exploring the relationship between means for two groups. The *t*-test was developed and researched by William Sealy Gosset, a statistician who worked for the Guinness brewery in the early part of the 20th century. To avoid any risk of publication of proprietary information, the brewery's management allowed Gosset to publish the results of his work on the *t*-test only on the condition that he publish under a pseudonym. The pen name Gosset chose was student. There are two prominent forms of the *t*-test: the *t*-test for paired samples and the *t*-test for independent samples.

t-Test for Paired Samples

Variables: One binary nominal-level independent variable and one ratio-level dependent variable.

Question: Is the difference in means for two observations of one set of cases the result of chance?

Example: Ten librarians were each asked 10 questions and the numbers of correct answers were recorded. The 10 librarians then completed an intensive continuing education seminar focusing on approaches to ensuring success in answering questions. The librarians were then each asked 10 different questions and the numbers of correct answers were recorded. The research question is "Is there any relationship between completion of an intensive continuing education experience focusing on approaches to ensuring success in answering questions and the mean number of correct answers?"

This is the dominant form of test for comparison of means in single group pretest/posttest experimental and quasi-experimental designs. The basic question is "was there a change between the pretest and the posttest?"

The mean number of correct answers for the posttest is clearly greater than that for the pretest, but there is no self-evident means of determining whether that difference is

Librarian	Number of Correct Pretest Answers	Number of Correct Posttest Answers
1	10	10
2	5	9
3	4	7
4	9	8
5	5	8
6	9	10
7	4	5
8	4	7
9	8	9
10	6	10
Mean	6.4	8.3

Figure 13.39   Results of success in answering pretest/posttest questions, 10 librarians.

significant. That is the role of the paired-samples *t*-test. The probability of a Type I error (incorrect rejection of the null hypothesis) for the test results is .026, substantially less than the typical probability threshold of .05. The null hypothesis can therefore be rejected and the alternative hypothesis that there is a relationship between the continuing education experience and success in answering questions is supported.

t-Test for Independent Samples

The *t*-test for independent samples is used to compare performance for two groups. The levels of the variables to be included in the test and the fundamental question are the same as for the paired-sample test, but the binary variable defines two groups rather than two tests of a single group.

Example: Twenty librarians were randomly assigned to two different groups. Group A participated in an intensive continuing education experience focusing on approaches to ensuring success in answering questions. Group B did not participate in the continuing education experience. Both groups were then asked 10 reference questions and the numbers of correct answers were recorded. The research question is "will librarians who have completed an intensive continuing education experience focusing on approaches to ensuring success in answering questions and perform differently on a test of ability to answer questions correctly than librarians not participating in the continuing education experience?"

Other Tests of Differences in Means

The *t*-test is limited to comparison of two groups. There is a broad family of additional tests of differences in means based on the principles of analysis of variance, also known as ANOVA. One-way analysis of variance extends the principles of the *t*-test for independent samples to tests involving a single dependent variable and an independent variable with three or more groups. The continuing education test, for instance, might be extended to include three groups, with Group A participating in one form of continuing education experience, Group B participating in a different continuing education experience, and Group C (the control group) participating in no continuing education experience.

There are many variations on ANOVA. *n*-Way analysis of variance allows for the inclusion of two or more nominal-level independent variables and a single ratio-level dependent variable. Multiple analysis of variance (MANOVA) allows for two or more ratio-level dependent variables. Analysis of covariance (ANCOVA) looks at the relationships between the variables from the more stringent standard of covariance, which is a measure of the extent to which the deviation from the mean is correlated for two or more distributions.

Selected Inferential Statistical Tests: Regression

Regression refers to a substantial family of statistical procedures that use the values of a predictor (independent) variable or variables to predict or explain the values of a criterion (dependent) variable or variables. Regression is closely tied to correlation and involves graphing a regression line that summarizes the correlation of two or more variables. A regression line is shown in Figure 13.40.

Regression results in the expression of the regression line in terms of a formula based on the slope of the regression line, as shown in Figure 13.41.

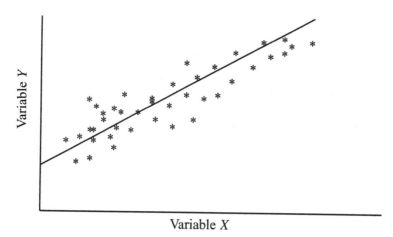

Figure 13.40 Regression line.

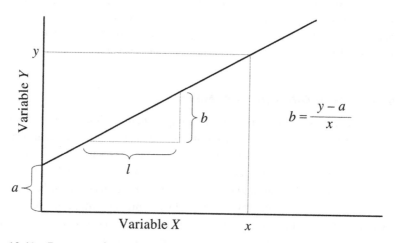

Figure 13.41 Regression line calculation.

There are many forms of regression analysis. Simple regression involves one dependent variable, usually ratio-level, and one independent variable, usually ratio-level to address the question "how can values of the predictor (independent) variable be used to predict values of the criterion (dependent) variable?" Multiple regression includes one dependent variable, usually ratio-level, and two or more independent variables, usually ratio-level to address the question "how can values of the predictor (independent) variables be used to predict values of the criterion (dependent) variable?"

Outliers

Outliers are isolated values that do not fit the pattern of other values. Although outliers are problematic in all statistical testing, they are perhaps most noticeable in linear regression. Figure 13.42 shows a distribution with an outlier.

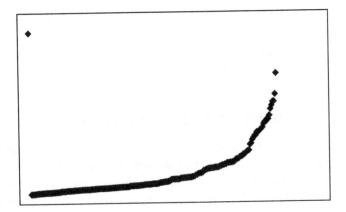

Figure 13.42   Outlier example.

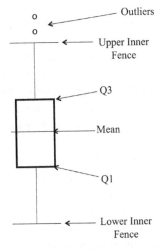

Figure 13.43   Box plot.

There are two prominent sources of outliers: errors and rare events. A common motive for viewing data graphically is to examine patterns for potential errors. The cause for the outlier in Figure 13.42 could simply be that the data were encoded improperly. Errors can usually be easily corrected. Rare events are potentially more difficult. If the outlier represents a correct encoding of data, the question then becomes one of whether the data were collected incorrectly or the data are indeed real. It is often difficult to reconstruct the data collection process at the point of analysis. As a result, there may be lingering uncertainty regarding the legitimacy of an outlier. When many outliers occur in a single distribution, the problem is intensified.

Identification of Outliers

Visualization, as in the distribution graph presented in Figure 13.42, is one approach to identifying outliers. A different, more precise visualization is that of box plot. A box plot is a tool for summarizing the core characteristics of a distribution. Box plots, also known as box and whisker plots, were introduced by Tukey in 1977.[4] An example of a box plot is presented in Figure 13.43. The box plot identifies the mean of the distribution, expresses centrality through the box centered on the first and third quartiles of the distribution (the boundaries that exclude the lowest fourth and highest fourth of the recorded values), and establishes upper and lower fences that demark the normal or expected range of values. Any values outside the fences are viewed as outliers.

UNRAVELING THE MYSTERY OF STATISTICS

Statistics, particularly statistical analysis and inferential statistics, are to many people an intimidating and confounding concept. It is important to recognize that statistics and statistical procedures are tools. As is the case with all tools, knowing how and when to use the tool is essential to the effective use of statistics. Knowing how and when to use a tool, however, does not require knowing the details of the inner workings of the tool. Effective use of a library's Integrated Online System (IOLS) to support cataloging or circulation functions does not require knowing how to program such a system or knowing how the specific system is programmed. It does require knowing the functions and options necessary for getting the job done and the library's policies, protocols, and rules for using the system. Similarly, using the chi-square test of goodness-of-fit does not require knowing the theoretical distribution of the chi-square statistic nor how that distribution was created. It does require knowing that the chi-square test of goodness-of-fit is the appropriate tool for the task, how to generate the analysis, and how to interpret the results. These are not purely mechanical processes, but they do not require advanced understanding of mathematics or the theoretical underpinnings of statistics.

Similarly, using a word processing package on a personal computer does not require any particular understanding of the inner workings of computers, how operating systems work, how the word processing package was programmed, or functional linguistics. Effective use of a word processing package does require understanding how documents are structured, how to effectively and efficiently apply a structure to a document, how language can be effectively used in written communication, and how to influence the appearance of document elements. Similarly, using a statistical analysis package does not require understanding of the formulas that underlie statistical analysis routines, how the statistical analysis package was programmed, or advanced statistical reasoning. Effective use of a statistical analysis package does require understanding the logic of statistical analysis, being able to select a statistical test or procedure, and knowing how to implement that test or procedure.

Ultimately, a great deal of the statistical analysis essential to evaluation and some of the statistical analysis necessary for research involve relatively simple statistical calculations that are used repetitively and sometimes routinely. A great deal can be expressed about a body of quantitative data using a fairly limited set of descriptive statistics. Generally speaking, inferential statistics are used only for research projects that involve explicit testing of hypotheses. A gentle grounding in the basics of descriptive statistics and the ability to use a statistical analysis package or a spreadsheet to generate basic summary statistics constitutes the core of what most library and information science practitioners need to know about statistics.

THINK ABOUT IT!

1. Library X has gathered data by asking members of the community how frequently they use the library, which library services they use most frequently, and which library services they think are overall most beneficial to the community. In what sense are the aggregated answers to those questions statistics?
2. Libraries frequently gather counts of core activities such as circulation of materials, reference questions answered, and attendance at library-sponsored programs. How can basic measures of centrality be used to summarize those data?
3. What are some ways in which a library's administration can effectively compare the library to other libraries that serve demographically similar communities?

DO IT!

1. Record the number of pages (paper or digital) you read in a week. Calculate the mean, median, and mode for the number of pages per day.
2. Identify the data needed for a study of a real library and information science problem. What measures of central tendency and dispersion can best be used to summarize those data?
3. Download the "Public Library State Totals and Selected Tables (2009–2010 Fiscal Year)" Excel spreadsheet file from http://www.library.ca.gov/lds/docs/CA_Tables.xls. Select a table and calculate the statewide mean, median, and mode for all variables included in the table. Search the World Wide Web to see what public library data are available for the state in which you live.

NOTES

1. The sections of this book on "How to Lie …" were inspired by Darrell Huff, *How to Lie with Statistics* (New York: Norton, 1954).

2. Adapted from "Critical Values of the Chi-Square Distribution," *Engineering Statistics Handbook*, National Institute of Standards and Technology, http://www.itl.nist.gov/div898/handbook/eda/section3/eda3674.htm (accessed April 4, 2011).

3. "The Dangers of Bread," http://www.geoffmetcalf.com/bread.html (accessed July 18, 2011).

4. John W. Tukey, *Exploratory Data Analysis* (Reading, MA: Addison-Wesley, 1977).

SUGGESTED READINGS

Leo L. Egghe and Ronald Rousseau, *Elementary Statistics for Effective Library and Information Service Management* (London: Aslib-AMI, 2001).

David R. Gerhan, "Statistical Significance: How it Signifies in Statistics Reference," *Reference & User Services Quarterly* 40, no. 4 (Summer 2001): 361–74.

Stan Gilibisco, *Statistics Demystified* (New York: McGraw-Hill, 2004).

Arthur W. Hafner, *Descriptive Statistical Techniques for Librarians*, 2nd ed. (Chicago, IL: American Library Association, 1998).

Peter Hernon, *Statistics: A Component of the Research Process* (Norwood, NJ: Ablex, 1994).

David M. Levine and David F. Stephan, *Even You Can Learn Statistics: A Guide for Everyone Who Has Ever been Afraid of Statistics* (Upper Saddle River, NJ: FT Press, 2010).

John Mulberg, *Figuring Figures: An Introduction to Data Analysis* (New York: Prentice Hall, 2002).

Neil J. Salkind, *Statistics for People Who (Think They) Hate Statistics*, 4th ed. (Thousand Oaks, CA: 2011).

Peter Stephen and Susan Hornby, *Simple Statistics for Library and Information Professionals* (London: Library Association, 1995).

14

FUNDING FOR RESEARCH AND EVALUATION

A billion here, a billion there, and pretty soon you're talking about real money.

—*Attributed to Everett M. Dirksen by John Kriegsman,* New York Times, *1975*

In This Chapter

Funding for research and evaluation

What makes a project fundable?

Funding agencies

Governmental and quasi-governmental agencies

Foundations

Associations

Corporations and businesses

FUNDING FOR RESEARCH AND EVALUATION

Research and evaluation aren't free. Research and evaluation require time, effort, materials, and equipment. There are three prominent possible sources of funding for research and evaluation:

1. Personal. There was historically a time when scientific research and evaluation was conducted by individuals rather than institutions and funded either by the investigator or by an individual acting in the role of patron to the investigator. This is perhaps epitomized in the fictional works of H. G. Wells, such as *The Invisible Man* and *The Time Machine,* or Robert Louis Stevenson's *Dr. Jekyll and Mr. Hyde,* in which it is never quite clear how the radical research and evaluation projects of the main characters are funded. This is the kind of research and evaluation that Derek J. de Solla Price characterized as "little science."[1] There are some situations in which personal funding naturally plays a meaningful role in research and evaluation. Student researchers, for instance, frequently

contribute at least some of the costs of the research efforts that lead to master's theses and doctoral dissertations. Employees, though, should not normally be expected to directly fund research and evaluation projects carried out on behalf of the institutions for which they work, nor should they be expected to contribute indirectly by devoting personal time to such activities.

2. Institutional. The institutional commitment to evaluation tends to be very different from the institutional commitment to research. Evaluation projects are almost always funded internally by the institution that is expected to benefit from the outcomes of the evaluation. Evaluation activities should be included—and often are—in normal administrative budgets. Some of the costs of research may be included in an institution's operating budget—it is generally assumed, for instance, that university faculty members will receive some departmental or institutional support for their research and evaluation efforts—but in many environments, including most libraries, research is not part of the normal budget. Even in those circumstances in which there is institutional support for research efforts, individual research projects are likely to carry costs that exceed the institution's dedicated budget. These additional costs, known as the *incremental costs* of research, must be covered from some source other than the normal institutional budget. In some cases it may be possible to allocate special funds to support research efforts or to seek additional allocations from the institution's primary funding body.

3. External. In many cases institutional support for research and evaluation is either unavailable or insufficient to fund the incremental costs of meaningful research and evaluation. In those circumstances the investigator has little choice other than to abandon the project or to seek funding from some source external to the institution. Most external funding sources have some expectation that the institution will contribute to the research and evaluation effort at least in the form of "in kind" contributions—contributions such as the investigator's time that entail no direct cash cost to the institution other than the investigator's normal salary and benefits. Most of this chapter centers on external funding as a source of support for research and evaluation, with particular emphasis on funding for research. Most funding agencies are not interested in answering local questions or solving local problems—the local environment is of interest primarily or solely as a microcosm of some larger phenomenon. External funding for research and evaluation is generally restricted to demonstration projects that have the potential for applicability beyond the local institution. External funding may be available for evaluation projects but does not generally play a major role in locally based evaluation activities that are part of management and administrative decision making.

WHAT MAKES A PROJECT FUNDABLE?

A proposal for funding is necessarily a persuasive document that builds a case for the project for which funding is being sought. Gwinn described six major characteristics that make a proposed project appeal to a funding agency, from which the following notes are adapted.[2]

1. A good idea. It seems rather obvious that a fundable idea must be a good idea, but the definition of good is variable. In this context, a good idea has three basic elements of appeal:

   a. Need. There is an identified, readily apparent, and compelling need for the proposed project. This can be stated in the form of a question for which there is no answer or a problem in need of a solution. The old saying, "Think Globally, Act Locally" applies very directly to making the case for the need to carry out a particular project. Demonstrating that addressing the question will serve broader societal purposes is an important part of demonstrating that the idea is a good one that needs to be addressed.

b. Originality. A good idea has some element of originality. That doesn't mean that the question has never before been asked or that no one has attempted to find a solution to the problem. It may simply mean that the question hasn't been asked in the particular way in which it will be addressed in the proposed project or that the solution hasn't been attempted in the specific type of environment in which it will be tested in the proposed project. It could even mean that the project will directly emulate a previous project in the interest of updating research that is perceived to be out of date. The investigator does have an obligation to directly explain to the funding agency what makes the proposed project original and different.

c. Honesty. The proposed idea must be presented with absolute honesty. Exaggerated claims or overstated benefits can easily undermine the appeal of the proposal. The investigator's obligation is to identify exactly what the project will and will not accomplish. The principle of honesty applies to every aspect of the proposal.

2. Relationship to the funder's interests. Most funding agencies have identified specific areas within which awards can be made. These may be topical, geographic, tied to the type of institution to which awards can be made, or any combination of those and other factors. One of the major challenges of seeking external funding is identifying the right funding agency. The primary sources of information about funding agency interests are:

a. Published directories. There are several important directories and other sources of information. In addition to contact information, directories may directly indicate areas of interest and may also provide examples of recently funded projects.

b. Agency publications. Most, but not all, funding agencies provide paper or electronic sources of information about funding opportunities. Some are greatly detailed, while others are extremely vague. Examining agency publications is essential but may not be sufficient.

c. Preliminary inquiries. Most funding agencies welcome preliminary inquiries as a means of helping an investigator determine whether to submit a proposal. Some agencies require preliminary inquiries. Some agencies explicitly will not respond to preliminary inquiries. If the agency is open to preliminary inquiries, the investigator is generally best served by making a phone call or sending an e-mail to determine whether the agency would consider the proposed project to be within its scope of interest. Verifying that the project is within scope does not, of course, guarantee that the project will be funded.

3. Preproposal research. This is the process of demonstrating that the investigator has done his or her homework. A competent literature review is a key element of the preproposal research and evaluation process. Preproposal research has two major goals:

a. To demonstrate understanding. The proposal must demonstrate that the investigator truly understands the domain in which the proposed project lies.

b. To document the need for the proposed project. The proposal must build a convincing case for the importance of further investigation. This relates directly to the concept of originality and further grounds the proposed project in the need for an answer or a solution.

4. A plan of action. Every funding agency expects that the investigator will have carefully explored the course of action that will lead to an answer to the question or a solution to the problem. Many funding agencies provide explicit, detailed guidelines for the plan of action, but some provide little or no guidance. The Institute of Museum and Library Services requires a plan of action that includes a Gantt chart such as that in Figure 14.1 and a narrative explanation. No matter what the funding agency formally requests in a proposal, the agency expects a precise and understandable plan of action that is:

   a. Pragmatic. It must be clear that the proposed work can actually be done and that there are no technical, institutional, or societal barriers to carrying out the project.

   b. Realistic. The goals of the project must be attainable and the proposed work must devolve directly and logically from the goals.

   c. Timely. The scope of the proposed work must be attainable within the stated timeframe of the project and it must be possible to complete all aspects of the project within that timeframe.

5. A reasonable budget. Reasonable doesn't necessarily mean *cheap*. A reasonable budget is

   a. Sufficient to carry out the proposed project. There is no point in requesting funding that is inadequate to effectively answer the question or explore the solution;

   b. Free from padding. The project budget should request the funding actually needed to carry out the work and no more;

   c. Negotiable. The funding agency may challenge items within the budget without rejecting the proposal outright, may ask for a reduction in the scope of the project with an accompanying reduction in the budget, or may in rare cases request an expansion of the scope of the project with an accompanying increase in the budget.

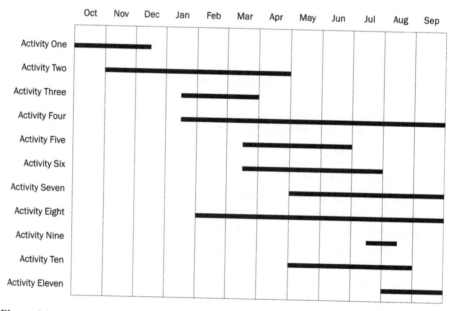

Figure 14.1   IMLS schedule of completion.

The investigator should anticipate the need to address any of these revisions of the budget.

6. A qualified investigator. Naturally enough, every funding agency wants to be assured that the investigator is capable of carrying out the project. There are three basic elements that contribute to instilling confidence in the qualifications of the investigator:

   a. Institutional affiliation. With few exceptions, agencies provide funding to institutions, not to individuals. The investigator therefore needs to demonstrate to the funding agency that the institution that will serve as home to the proposed project has the capacity to support the project and is an appropriate environment to serve as the project's base. There does not have to be a direct match between the nature of the project and the nature of the investigator's institutional affiliation—it is quite possible for a public librarian to carry out a study of the information seeking practices of high school students, but that does increase the burden for demonstrating capacity and appropriateness.

   b. Background. The investigator must demonstrate that his or her background experiences are sufficient and appropriate to the proposed project. This may be a combination of documenting work history, demonstrating knowledge of the research and evaluation process (acquired, perhaps, via a research and evaluation methods book), and demonstrating knowledge of the specific topical area via an effective literature review and discussion. This is obviously more of a challenge for a beginning investigator than for an experienced investigator, but everyone is a beginning investigator at some time.

   c. Connections. Even when most of the work will be carried out by a single investigator, that investigator doesn't have to do everything alone. Identifying formal consultants or informal advisors who will be involved in the research and evaluation process can contribute tangibly to the success of a proposal.

FUNDING AGENCIES IN THE UNITED STATES

This discussion provides an introduction to and overview of prominent sources of funding for research and evaluation and other projects. It is strongly recommended that students explore each of the listed websites as a means of expanding understanding of the information available from each source.

GOVERNMENTAL AND QUASI-GOVERNMENTAL AGENCIES

Governmental and quasi-governmental agencies are among the most conspicuous sources of funding. Quasi-governmental agencies are entities that are responsible for reporting to a government oversight body but are not officially government agencies. The Smithsonian Institution, for instance, is a quasi-governmental agency that operates independently but is responsible for reporting to the Executive Branch of the U.S. government. Such agencies exist at the federal, state, county, and local levels. The policies and processes of governmental and quasi-governmental agencies tend to be very formal and in some cases quite complex, especially at the federal level. Most federal agencies are characterized by multiple funding programs that are generally available only to carefully specified categories of institutions.

Sources of Information about Governmental and Quasi-Governmental Agencies

The central resource for U.S. government grants is Grants.gov, which was established in 2002 to act as a central information resource and clearinghouse for federal grants.[3] Grants.gov includes a search feature, although it is relatively primitive. Note that many of the grant opportunities listed in the Grants.gov database are not explicitly research or evaluation grants. Ultimately, all applications for federal grants have to be submitted online via the Grants.gov system.

The *U.S. Government Manual* "provides comprehensive information on the agencies of the legislative, judicial, and executive branches. It also includes information on quasi-official agencies, international organizations in which the United States participates, and boards, commissions, and committees."[4] The *Manual* provides overview information of agencies, including brief information about grant and other funding programs.

The *Federal Register* is "the official daily publication for rules, proposed rules, and notices of Federal agencies and organizations, as well as executive orders and other presidential documents."[5] As such, it is the source in which announcements of federal funding opportunities must be published to become part of the formal record of federal government activities. The *Federal Register* provides very basic information on grant program actions but is of limited use beyond that. Search features within the *Federal Register* are somewhat primitive.

The *Catalog of Federal Domestic Assistance* "provides a full listing of all Federal programs available to State and local governments (including the District of Columbia); federally-recognized Indian tribal governments; Territories (and possessions) of the United States; domestic public, quasi-public, and private profit and nonprofit organizations and institutions; specialized groups; and individuals."[6] *CFDA* has reasonably good search features and is a good tool to use when a project might be fundable from more than one agency. Try doing a simple keyword search in *CFDA* for libraries to see the range of agencies that potentially fund projects related to libraries.

Specific Governmental and Quasi-Governmental Agencies

Most governmental and quasi-governmental agencies produce various kinds of publications and maintain comprehensive Web presences. A few selected examples are presented here.

1. The Institute of Museum and Library Services "is the primary source of federal support for the nation's 123,000 libraries and 17,500 museums. The Institute's mission is to create strong libraries and museums that connect people to information and ideas. The Institute works at the national level and in coordination with state and local organizations to sustain heritage, culture, and knowledge; enhance learning and innovation; and support professional development."[7] The National Leadership Grants for Libraries program includes a Research and evaluation and Demonstration subprogram explicitly intended to support research and evaluation.[8] Figure 14.2 lists the major library-related programs sponsored by the Institute of Museum and Library Services.

2. The U.S. Department of Education supports research through the Institute of Education Sciences, whose "overarching priority is research that contributes to improved academic achievement for all students, and particularly for those whose education

Connecting to Collections: Statewide Implementation Grants

Laura Bush 21st Century Librarian Program

Learning Labs in Libraries and Museums

National Arts and Humanities Youth Program Awards

National Leadership Grants

Sparks! Ignition

Figure 14.2   Library funding programs of the Institute of Museum and Library Services.

prospects are hindered by inadequate education services and conditions associated with poverty, race/ethnicity, limited English proficiency, disability, and family circumstance," and other subagencies.[9]

3. The *National Science Foundation* "is an independent federal agency created by Congress in 1950 'to promote the progress of science; to advance the national health, prosperity, and welfare; to secure the national defense.'"[10] "With an annual budget of about $5.5 billion, we are the funding source for approximately 20 percent of all federally supported basic research and evaluation conducted by America's colleges and universities. In many fields such as mathematics, computer science and the social sciences, NSF is the major source of federal backing." Although NSF is perhaps best known for its funding of projects in the biological and physical sciences, the Directorate for Social, Behavioral & Economic Sciences provides funding in such areas as "humans spanning areas of inquiry including brain and behavior, language and culture, origins and evolution, and geography and the environment."[11]

Other federal agencies with potential for funding projects in library and information science are numerous and include the National Endowment for the Arts, the National Endowment for the Humanities, nearly every other federal agency, and perhaps surprisingly, all branches of the armed forces. In many cases, parallel agencies exist at the state level, including state library agencies and state arts, humanities, and history agencies.

FOUNDATIONS

Foundations are nonprofit institutions that exist primarily as sources of philanthropy and community support. Foundations are typically supported by some combination of endowed funds and donations. The policies and procedures of foundations vary widely from highly formal to uninformatively informal.

Sources of Information about Foundations

The most comprehensive source of information about foundations is the *Foundation Center*, which is "is the leading source of information about philanthropy worldwide."[12] The Foundation Center serves as a clearinghouse for information about foundations of all kinds and philanthropy in general.

The Foundation Center supports Cooperating Collections of foundation information in each of the U.S. states, the District of Columbia, and Puerto Rico. "Cooperating Collections are free funding information centers in libraries, community foundations, and other nonprofit resource centers that provide a core collection of Foundation Center publications and a variety of supplementary materials and services in areas useful to grantseekers."[13] A list of all Cooperating Collections is provided at the Foundation Center website.

The Foundation Center generates a number of publications. The central publication is the *Foundation Directory*, a comprehensive guide to foundations in the United States. The *Foundation Grants Index* provides information on foundation grants that have actually been awarded. The *Foundation Directory* identifies stated funding interests; the *Foundation Grants Index* describes actual funding actions.

The Foundation Center is not the only source of information about foundations and their programs. The *Annual Register of Grant Support* is an Information Today publication that is similar in intent to the *Foundation Grants Index*.[14] The *Library and Book Trade Annual* provides some information on grant information in library and information science.[15]

Specific Foundations

The Council on Library and Information Resources (CLIR) "is an independent, nonprofit organization. Through publications, projects, and programs, CLIR works to maintain and improve access to information for generations to come. In partnership with other institutions, CLIR helps create services that expand the concept of 'library' and supports the providers and preservers of information."[16] CLIR is largely a pass-through organization that redistributes funding obtained from other foundation sources.

The W.K. Kellogg Foundation "supports children, families, and communities as they strengthen and create conditions that propel vulnerable children to achieve success as individuals and as contributors to the larger community and society."[17] This very broad mission has frequently included funding for library-related projects; research and evaluation projects are generally, although not exclusively, funded as part of larger projects.

The Gannett Newspaper Foundation "supports non-profit activities in the communities in which Gannett does business."[18] Although the Gannett Foundation tends to support programs and projects rather than research and evaluation, research and evaluation can be incorporated as a component within a proposal to the foundation.

ASSOCIATIONS

Professional associations have something of a vested interest in supporting research and evaluation related to their specific areas of professional concern. Many professional associations have very fully developed research and evaluation grant programs. Associations tend to have moderately formal policies and processes for awarding grants.

Sources of Information about Associations

The most important single source of information about associations is the *Encyclopedia of Associations*, published by Gale Research. The *Encyclopedia of Associations* is the "only comprehensive source for detailed information on nonprofit American membership organizations of national scope."[19] Very brief notes on the grant and award programs of listed associations are provided. The *Library and Book Trade Annual* also provides some brief information on grant and award programs of associations.

Specific Associations

The American Library Association supports a number of research and evaluation grant programs both centrally and through the association's divisions.[20] Examples include the following:

- The *Carroll Preston Baber Research Grant* which "is given annually to one or more librarians or library educators who will conduct innovative research and evaluation that could lead to an improvement in services to any specified group(s) of people."

- The *Loleta D. Fyan Grant* "for the development and improvement of public libraries and the services they provide."

- The *Ingenta Research Award*, which "is given annually by the Library Research Round Table of the American Library Association to support research and evaluation projects about acquisition, use, and preservation of digital information."

- The *SIRSI Leadership in Library Technology Grant*, which is "given to encourage and enable continued advancements in quality library services for a project that makes creative or groundbreaking use of technology to deliver exceptional services to its community."

- The *AASL/Highsmith Research Grant*, which is "awarded to conduct innovative research aimed at measuring and evaluating the impact of school library media programs on learning and education."

Other professional associations also sponsor research and evaluation grants. The following are selected examples:

- The American Society for Information Science & Technology sponsors the *Thomson ISI Citation Analysis Research Grant*, which has the very specific purpose of supporting "research based on citation analysis by encouraging and assisting individuals in this area of study with their research and evaluation."[21]

- The Association for Library and Information Science Education supports a number of research opportunities through its Research Competitions program.[22]

Many state and regional professional associations also sponsor grants for research or evaluation.

CORPORATIONS AND BUSINESSES

Corporations and businesses are rarely interested in providing primary funding for research and evaluation projects, but may be called up to support very specific aspects of a research and evaluation project. A business supply, for instance, might be persuaded to provide paper on which to print questionnaires. Although there are published guides to corporate giving, the greatest success in obtaining support from corporations and businesses comes from direct contact and good public relations. Becoming involved in civic organizations and making presentations to the business community can be effective approaches to building the community network necessary for obtaining this kind of support.

THE BOTTOM LINE ISN'T NECESSARILY THE BOTTOM LINE

One of the frequently cited reasons that libraries and other institutions do not engage in systematic evaluation comes down to the question "who will pay for it?" In some instances, this concern may be well justified. Evaluation can easily be viewed as a drag on institutional resources, especially when the impetus for evaluation comes from outside the institution. The unfunded student performance assessment demands of the federal No Child Left Behind Act of 2001 at a time when school districts nationwide were experiencing extreme financial hardships were intimidating. Even when the impetus for evaluation is local and immediate, administrators have to balance the resources necessary for evaluation with the resources available for other operations.

The emphasis on external funding that defined the era of big science and the philanthropic generosity of entrepreneurs such as Andrew Carnegie, Henry Ford, and John D. Rockefeller have in some institutions instilled a sense that a project is not worth doing if it is not accompanied by a major infusion of funding. At some universities, faculty members are—in some cases tacitly, in others explicitly—expected to buy back their salaries through grant activities. At the extreme of this phenomenon, all funding for the direct costs of research is expected to come from grants and the task of the faculty member is to bring in sufficient external funding to pay for his or her salary and benefits through indirect costs.

The real question to be asked, for both research and evaluation, is "what will be the benefit of this project?" If there is no perceivable benefit, no amount of funding from any source will make the project worthwhile. The news media frequently call attention to federally funded projects that seem to have such limited impact or are so seemingly far-fetched that it is difficult for the casual reader to understand how the funding was justified. In some cases, this is matter of the spin given to the news coverage and the project is indeed warranted. On the other hand, proposals for external funding are sometimes initiated by the perception that "the funding is there to be had, and our institution should go after it, whether we have a beneficial project in mind or not."

The purpose of funding for research and evaluation for library and information science projects, whether from internal or external sources, is to achieve goals and objectives and to yield human-centered improvements. The merit of a research or evaluation project lies in the benefits to be derived from the project. Although some projects can be expected to yield economic benefits, many library and information science projects do not. The process should begin with the project, not with the money. A good starting question is "is this project worth doing if some source of funding can be found for it?" For some projects, the question is "will we attempt to do this project even if no additional funding can be found?" To return to Gwynn's notion that a fundable research project begins with a good idea, it is easy to extrapolate that every worthwhile project begins with a good idea. It is bringing that idea to fruition that is the appropriate goal of research and evaluation, not the fiscal bottom line.

THINK ABOUT IT!

1. How does the availability of funding affect the scalability of research or evaluation projects?
2. How would a library and information science professional go about contacting a local foundation or corporate source for support for a library project?
3. How does the political climate affect governmental support for library and information science projects?

 DO IT!

1. Visit the Foundation Center at http://www.foundationcenter.org/. What resources from the Foundation Center are particularly important in identifying sources of external funding for library and information science projects?
2. Use the Foundation Finder at http://www.foundationcenter.org/findfunders/foundfinder/ to search for foundations in your state. Try to locate foundations in your state that have an explicit interest in providing funding for libraries.
3. Search Grants.gov (http://www.grants.gov) for federal grant opportunities related to libraries. What kinds of opportunities are listed? Can you find information related to a specific library project or program of interest to you?

NOTES

1. Derek J. de Solla Price, *Little Science, Big Science* (New York: Columbia University Press, 1965).

2. Nancy E. Gwinn, "Funding Library Research and Evaluation," *College and Research and evaluation Libraries* (May 1980): 207–09.

3. Grants.gov, www.grants.gov/ (accessed April 4, 2011).

4. U.S. Government Manual, http://www.gpoaccess.gov/gmanual/index.html (accessed April 4, 2011).

5. Federal Register, http://www.gpoaccess.gov/fr/index.html (accessed April 11, 2011).

6. Catalog of Federal Domestic Assistance, https://www.cfda.gov/ (accessed April 11, 2011).

7. Institute of Museum and Library Services, http://www.imls.gov/ (accessed April 11, 2011).

8. National Leadership Grants, http://www.imls.gov/applicants/grants/nationalLeadership.shtm (accessed April 11, 2011).

9. Institute of Education Sciences, http://www2.ed.gov/about/offices/list/ies/index.html (accessed April 4, 2011).

10. National Science Foundation, http://www.nsf.gov/about/ (accessed April 11, 2011).

11. National Science Foundation, Directorate for Social, Behavioral & Economic Sciences, http://www.nsf.gov/div/index.jsp?div=BCS (accessed April 11, 2011).

12. About the Foundation Center, http://www.foundationcenter.org/about/;jsessionid=2VR4 P1ZMQBNJLLAQBQ4CGW15AAAACI2F (accessed April 11, 2011).

13. Cooperating Collections, http://foundationcenter.org/collections/ (accessed April 4, 2011).

14. *Annual Register of Grant Support*, Information Today, Inc., annual.

15. *Library and Book Trade Annual*, Information Today, Inc., annual.

16. Council on Library and Information Resources, http://www.clir.org/about/about.html (accessed April 4, 2011).

17. W. K. Kellogg Foundation, http://www.wkkf.org/ (accessed April 4, 2011).

18. Gannett Newspaper Foundation, http://www.gannettfoundation.org/ (accessed April 4, 2011).

19. Encyclopedia of Associations: national organizations of the U.S., Gale, annual.

20. Grants, http://www.ala.org/ala/aboutala/offices/wo/woissues/washfunding/grants/grants. cfm (accessed April 4, 2011).

21. ASIS&T Awards, http://www.asist.org/awards.html (accessed April 4, 2011).

22. ALISE Research Competitions, http://www.alise.org/mc/page.do?sitePageId=55547 (accessed April 11, 2011).

SUGGESTED READINGS

Jane C. Geever, *The Foundation Center's Guide to Proposal Writing*, 5th ed. (New York: Foundation Center, 2007).

Ellen Karsh, *The Only Grant-Writing Book You'll Ever Need* (New York: Basic Books, 2009).

Deborah Koch, *How to Say It: Grantwriting: Write Proposals that Grantmakers Want to Fund* (New York: Prentice Hall, 2009).

Herbert B. Landau, *Winning Library Grants: A Game Plan* (Chicago, IL: American Library Association, 2011).

Pamela H. MacKellar and Stephanie K. Gerding, *Winning Grants: A How-to-Do-It Manual for Librarians with Multimedia Tutorials and Grant Development Tools* (New York: Neal-Schuman, 2010).

Gail M. Staines, *Go Get That Grant! A Practical Guide for Libraries and Nonprofit Organizations* (Lanham, MD: Scarecrow, 2010).

Mary W. Walters, *Write and Effective Funding Application: A Guide for Researchers and Scholars* (Baltimore, MD: Johns Hopkins University Press, 2009).

15

RESEARCH, EVALUATION, AND CHANGE

Results are what you expect, and consequences are what you get.

—*Ladies' Home Journal, 1942*

The end of man is an action and not a thought, though it were the noblest.

—*Aristotle, quoted in Thomas Carlyle,* Sartor Resartus, *1837*

The future cannot be predicted, but futures can be invented.

—*Dennis Gabor,* Inventing the Future, *1963*

In This Chapter

The purpose of research and evaluation

Research, evaluation, and the informed consumer

Characteristics of useful research and evaluation

Creating a culture of research and evaluation

Research, evaluation, and managing change

Research, evaluation, and the reflective practitioner

THE PURPOSE OF RESEARCH AND EVALUATION

This book began with a discussion of the many ways of knowing and argued that research and evaluation activities are designed for the purpose of deepening understanding, enhancing knowledge, and improving decision making. It emphasized the characteristics of formal research and evaluation, particularly the cyclical nature of these activities and the ultimate goal of informing evidence-based professional practice. In short, research and evaluation activities are an integral part of the reflective practitioner's professional life, not a sporadic series of isolated, one-time events.

RESEARCH, EVALUATION, AND THE INFORMED CONSUMER

Many library and information science professionals will never conduct a formal research project, although most will engage in some sort of evaluation activities on a regular basis. The utility of evaluation will be evident to most—at least in principle. Evaluation outcomes influence how something is done in a local environment. Evaluation results, however, should be contextualized to be of greatest use in decision making. More generalizable, broad-scale research is used to develop theories, policies, standards, and best practices. It enhances understanding in a way that influences direct practice. It may also stimulate the individual's curiosity and creativity. It keeps the librarian in contact with the larger professional community of practice.

This habit of lifelong learning is a key strategy for intellectual and emotional effectiveness in coping with change. "Learning to learn is one of the great inventions of living things."[1] Although *Knowledge Into Action: Research and Evaluation in Library and Information Science* naturally focuses on library and information studies research, the benefits of understanding the fundamentals of research and evaluation extend to all aspects of an individual's life. Knowing how to approach research literature with a critical eye, understanding how methodology can influence outcomes, and being aware of the ways in which data analysis and presentation can distort results, leads to active engagement with information that influences decision making in all arenas of life whether that information is presented in professional literature, newspapers of newscasts, or websites. Individuals who understand the professional literature become more informed self-advocates in all of the roles they inhabit—librarian, student, patient, investor, consumer, parent, or citizen.

CHARACTERISTICS OF USEFUL RESEARCH AND EVALUATION

Given the overwhelming benefits of understanding and using professional research and evaluation, why is there often resistance to even reading and using these reports, much less active engagement in conducting investigations? For the outcome of research and evaluation to be used, it must meet three criteria: it must be accessible, both intellectually and physically; it must be relevant to a perceived need; and it must be valued. These characteristics are summarized in Figure 15.1.

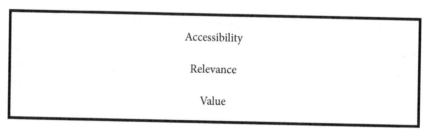

Figure 15.1   Factors in putting results to work.

Accessibility

Accessibility comprises two facets: the literature must be understandable (intellectually accessible) and available (physically accessible). Research and evaluation reports must be intellectually accessible for people to make use of them. Making results understandable carries with it two subrequirements: (a) researchers and evaluators must present results in a manner that can be understood by practitioners and (b) practitioners must strive to be able to understand research and evaluation results. That is, authors of reports must make some attempt to reach a middle ground between technical sophistication and simplistic reporting. Not every incarnation of a report can or should meet this middle ground; sometimes a single project can produce multiple reports geared to different audiences. Einstein is quoted as having said, "Most of the fundamental ideas of science are essentially simple, and may, as a rule, be expressed in a language comprehensible to everyone." Practitioners, however, cannot accept reports at face value. They must approach the literature as informed consumers; to this end they should learn the basics of research and evaluation processes. To expect either group of participants in the research and evaluation process to operate entirely within the language constraints or preferences of the other group is unreasonable and impractical. Investigators and practitioners must engage in a collaborative effort to build a knowledge base that enhances professional understanding and service to constituents.

Research and evaluation reports must be physically and temporally accessible for people to make use of them. It is no more than common sense to observe that an individual who can benefit from the results of research or evaluation will not do so if those results are not available to him or her. Availability has two essential components: Information must be available where and when it is needed.

Results cannot be put to work if they are not physically available to those individuals, groups, and institutions responsible for practice. In the past, many employers maintained professional collections, most frequently consisting of subscription runs of professional journals, for use by employees. Actual use of such collections was, of course, variable across individuals, across employers, and across professional groups. Smaller organizations rarely allocate scarce resources to provide extensive access to the professional literature unless providing such access is viewed as essential to the continued performance of the organization. In larger organizations, budgetary factors frequently allow for the development and maintenance of such collections, sometimes in the form of formally organized libraries, but making materials directly available to the people who can most benefit from them becomes increasingly difficult and complex as organizations grow. The availability of digital access to the research and evaluation literature has ameliorated some of these problems, but much of the literature is still costly. Less formal modes of access, however, have emerged in the digital era that can to some extent take the place of access to published literature.

Many research projects and some evaluation projects are accompanied by websites that provide access to project details, working documents, interim reports, and final reports. Some project websites provide access to study instruments and data files. Although there are many benefits, there are several caveats regarding the use of project websites. The information may not have been synthesized and condensed in a manner conducive to quick reading; reams of detail have not been distilled into a neatly and succinctly presented article or report. Unlike work appearing in scholarly journals, the reports posted on a project website have not been vetted through a peer-review process. And, finally, maintenance and organization of the project website may suffer as a project progresses and the priority of the project team shifts to completion of the investigation. Posting of results of internal evaluation projects, even on institutional intranets, may not be viewed as an appropriate activity by some administrators, who view the results as only one element in decision making and may be concerned about the impact of decontextualized data.

Networking, whether in person, by telephone, by e-mail, or via Internet social networking tools, also adds to the extent to which information about research and evaluation projects can be shared. Durrance and Van Fleet note the importance public library administrators place on these networking activities.[2] Price, Crane, and others described the "invisible college" phenomenon that emerged in the 1950s.[3] The basic premise of the invisible college model is that, "although the formal communication methods of publication and professional associations continue to be valuable, they are insufficient to provide the knowledge-sharing networks required by scholars."[4] The invisible college phenomenon among scientists can be thought of as a precursor to the social networking websites of the 21st century. In the research and evaluation community, it is increasingly convenient for individuals to share ideas, reports, questions, answers, and data as a means of ensuring the physical availability of results.

A second aspect of availability relates to timeliness. Results must be available at the time when they are needed. A confounding factor is that it is not always possible to adequately predict just when any kind or source of information may be needed. Nearly everyone has personally experienced the phenomenon of having read something in the past that suddenly becomes very pertinent in the context of a newly arisen problem or need. Nearly everyone has also experienced the phenomenon of working out a complex and time-consuming solution to a problem and then reading something that presents a fully formulated and perhaps superior solution that was developed elsewhere. Larger organizations have frequently attempted to solve this problem through selective dissemination of information (SDI) programs in which individual employees, preferably in consultation with an information professional, create profiles that describe their specific ongoing information needs so that, through either automated or manual processes, information potentially of interest is pushed to them.

In recent years, there has been a great deal of emphasis in the library, information, and knowledge professions on the distinction between just-in-case approaches and just-in-time approaches. Although the just-in-time principle is immensely appealing, there is some extent to which professionals must maintain contact with the literature on a just-in-case basis. Van Fleet and Durrance observe that public library administrators tend to combine the two approaches by skimming current literature and networking with other administrators on a regular basis and by undertaking focused topical information searches when the need presented.[5] They suggest that this pattern be accommodated with increased opportunities for regular interaction between researchers and practitioners and the publication of an increased number of comprehensive literature reviews. The resources and tools of the Internet greatly enhance a skilled individual's ability to gain access to important information and make it possible for investigators to disseminate results in a timely manner.

Relevance

A recurring problem in professional areas is that there is at least the perception, and sometimes the reality, that researchers and practitioners have very different priorities and perspectives. Practitioners accuse scholars of being overly theoretical and not adequately focused on the day-to-day problems of practice. Scholars accuse practitioners of being too occupied with local problem solving to appreciate the broader context and of being too entrenched in traditional practice to embrace change. Hildreth and Aytac's study of the research literature of library and information science, however, found that there are actually few differences between research projects carried out by practitioners and projects conducted by academics and that research projects involving a combination of practitioners and academics are not uncommon.[6] Within the context of an individual institution, employees on the front lines may look on evaluation projects as being at best a distraction and at worst busy work, while managers and administrators with responsibility for evaluation may view those on the front lines as impeding progress and improvement.

Perceptions of relevance rarely happen spontaneously, accidentally, or automatically. An investigator, in addition to communicating in advance the answer to the general "so what?" question should make clear the value of the project to the practitioner. As noted in Chapter 4, "Published Reports and the Professional as Consumer," every stakeholder has the right to know "what does this mean to me?" This imperative applies throughout the life cycle of the project. Staff members responsible for contributing data to an evaluation project need to know before they begin collecting data what the goals and projected outcomes of the project are and how they as employees will be affected both by the evaluation process and by any decisions that may result from the evaluation. A researcher must address the required elements of informed consent, but he or she also has an ethical and pragmatic responsibility of letting respondents or other human participants know why they are being included in the study and how the society of which they are members may benefit from the outcomes of the study.

Effective reporting of results is essential to establishing the relevance of a project. No library employee is likely to react positively to participating in an evaluation project but never learning the outcomes or being informed of the impact of the results on decision making. If participants do not see the results of their activities, they are likely to have a negative view not only of the specific project, but of evaluation activities in general, resulting in an unwillingness to engage in future projects, careless data gathering, or even deliberate sabotage. Researchers who do not actively disseminate results in the literature, at a conference, on a website, or through some other active approach suggest that they do not think the project is good enough to make it available to peer scrutiny or valuable enough to share with the professional community.

Ultimately, making results relevant requires an active effort by the investigator or appropriate administrators to disseminate and explain the nature of the project and the implications of the results. Relevance is a matter of perception and an outgrowth of openness and transparency.

Value

It sometimes appears that practitioners are actively resistant to the results of research and evaluation. Lynam, Slater, and Walker observe that "in some way, being a formally qualified library worker acts as a deterrent to appreciation of research."[7] Responding to practitioners who devalue research results, Van Fleet and Wallace stated that "This is analogous to the person who, as a result of being tone deaf, concludes that music is of no value."[8] They conclude with a call for action: "librarians must strive to make research and practice two sides of the same coin."[9]

Individuals in managerial, decision-making, and leadership roles in organizations must overtly recognize the value of research and evaluation, encourage employees to use research and evaluation, and create environments in which the use of research and evaluation is openly and conspicuously viewed as valuable. In essence, administrators must foster the concept of evidence-based practice. Employees in an environment that does not actively foster the use of research and evaluation are unlikely to value participation in such activities or appreciate the outcomes. Even worse, they may view their own interests in the use of research and evaluation as being covert, unsanctioned, and antithetical to the core values of the organization. Unfortunately, it is difficult and in many cases impossible for employees who value research and evaluation to engage in any kind of ground-up, grassroots encouragement of practice in the face of a sincere lack of administrative respect for the use of research and evaluation in practice. It is incumbent on administrators and managers to create an organizational climate in which research and evaluation activities are integral and provide a basis for reflective practice and a means for managing change.

CREATING A CULTURE OF RESEARCH AND EVALUATION

If library and information science is to remain a viable profession that grows and prospers in the future, it is essential to encourage a culture of research and evaluation. In no other way can members of the community, whether researchers or practitioners, deepen understanding of information needs and behaviors and make appropriate decisions to address those needs. Van Fleet and Durrance commented on the ways in which the research and evaluation literature of library and information science can be made more accessible to public librarians and several subsequent articles have reiterated their methodology in other areas of library and information science. They make five explicit recommendations based on principles that support integration of research and practice: interaction, collaboration, and mutual respect among those who investigate library and information phenomena and those who apply the results to practice.

1. Make research and evaluation literature easily available to librarians by recognizing and accommodating the manner in which they use the literature.
2. Enhance opportunities for interaction in library settings, with investigators and librarians each contributing from their areas of strength.
3. Develop a formalized framework at the association level for interaction between librarians, researchers, and evaluators.
4. Emphasize state library and other cooperative research and evaluation ventures.
5. Develop a research and evaluation perspective at the master of library and information science level.[10]

It is unclear to what extent the first four recommendations have been transformed into action, but O'Connor and Park's exploration of the role of research and evaluation in graduate programs in library and information science suggests that the fifth is still an unmet goal, given that 62 percent of the programs they examined did not require a research methods course.[11] Nevertheless, the principles upon which the recommendations are based are common strategies for creating an organizational culture of reflective practice and change. These principles are echoed in the five targets for change Schlosser identified in The Ohio State University Libraries' initiative to build a renewable and self-regenerating culture:

1. nurturing a culture of assessment
2. empowering collaboration
3. encouraging innovation
4. participating in and leading scholarly communication
5. making the materials and services of the libraries "available, accessible, and apparent to our patrons at the point that they need them"[12]

These are lofty goals, goals that clearly represent a substantial investment in organizational change, but not unattainable goals for an institution that appears to be philosophically aligned with the integration of evaluation and research that is a core value of *Knowledge Into Action: Research and Evaluation in Library and Information Science*.

Although such a culture may be more easily instituted in an academic setting in which ties to scholarship are self-evident and there is an obvious need to fit into the academic milieu, the fundamental principles can be adapted to any environment.

RESEARCH, EVALUATION, AND MANAGING CHANGE

The infusion of research and evaluation into practice is problematic in many fields and has been a frequent topic for discussion in such varied disciplines as medicine, law, education, and psychology as well as in library and information science. One of the inherently intimidating characteristics of research and evaluation is their association with change. The library and information professions are no more resistant to change than any other professional domain; all professionals are subject to the fears and demands that accompany change.

It is ironic that some practitioners will be reluctant to embrace a culture of research and evaluation because they fear the changes that such a culture might entail. Lifelong learning—the essential purpose of research and evaluation—is perhaps the most effective means of coping with personal, organizational, and societal change. Knowledge gained from continuous learning is the mechanism not just for passively understanding change and anticipating the future, but for actively managing change and shaping the future.

Hirshon outlined the eight steps of change management:

1. a trigger situation that suggests that change may be necessary or desirable
2. planning to set goals and objectives for change
3. communication to share the plans for change with appropriate constituents
4. restructuring of the organization to facilitate and support the planned change
5. process and policy analyses determine any changes necessary at the policy, procedure, or process level
6. training of staff and other constituents to address new tasks and responsibilities
7. monitoring and assessing the success of the implemented change
8. cultural change to achieve a state in which the new way of doing things is ingrained and seems organic and natural[13]

These steps, interestingly, parallel the fundamental characteristics of the research and evaluation culture and process. Both change management and the research and evaluation process begin with an impetus, require planning and goal setting, benefit from communication with stakeholders, result in decision making and action, and maintain the cycle by monitoring and assessing the impact of those actions. In addition, change management and research and evaluation activities are carried out most effectively and benefit the organization most greatly when based in an organizational culture that values those activities and recognizes them as essential, organic, and natural.

RESEARCH, EVALUATION, AND THE REFLECTIVE PRACTITIONER

In *Library Evaluation: A Casebook and Can-Do Guide,* Wallace and Van Fleet describe an ideal situation in which "evaluation becomes a basic social and societal system of the library and a *culture of evaluation* permeates the library and all its functions and activities."[14] Wallace and Van Fleet describe an evaluation action plan that guides evaluation decision making. The evaluation action plan is summarized in Figure 15.2. *Knowledge Into Action* extends that ideal to include research activities as well. Research and evaluation are intimately related, with shared purposes, characteristics, and processes that vary only in focus, scope, and application. Ultimately, ensuring that the cycle of research and evaluation becomes self-perpetuating has to be a matter of individual recognition, determination, and commitment within the context of an institutional setting that encourages and recognizes individual, team, and institution-wide contributions to advancing understanding and practice. Although much of this text deals with explanations of methods and processes, our primary purpose has been to create an appreciation for evidence-based practice and to foster a critical and reflective approach to the profession.

A culture of research and evaluation is one that embraces curiosity, reflection, and creativity. It is one that recognizes that change is inevitable and that lifelong learning is a key strategy not only in managing change and providing enhanced service, but also in shaping the future for both the profession and those we serve.

> What's the problem?
>
> Why am I doing this?
>
> What exactly do I want to know?
>
> Does the answer already exist?
>
> How do I find out?
>
> Who's involved?
>
> What's this going to cost?
>
> What will I do with the data?
>
> Where do I go from here?

Figure 15.2   The evaluation action plan.

THINK ABOUT IT!

1. How can local institutions encourage a cyclical culture of research and evaluation?
2. What is the role of local, regional, national, and international professional associations in fostering research and evaluation?
3. What can you as an individual do to enhance your ability to contribute to research and evaluation in library and information science?

DO IT!

1. Find the policy manual or similar document for a library or other information agency? What does the manual convey about the importance of research and/or evaluation for the institution?
2. Visit the website for a professional association of your choice. What does the association convey regarding its role in supporting research and evaluation?
3. Develop a 5-year plan for your professional development in the areas of research and evaluation.

NOTES

1. Ralph W. Girard, "The New Computerized Shape of Education," in *Inventing Education for the Future*, ed. W. Z. Hirsch (San Francisco: Chandler, 1967).

2. Joan C. Durrance and Connie Van Fleet, "Public Library Leaders and Research: Mechanisms, Perceptions, and Strategies," *Journal of Education for Library and Information Science* 34 (Spring 1993): 137–52.

3. Derek J. de Solla Price, *Little Science, Big Science* (New York: Columbia University Press, 1963); Diana Crane, *Invisible Colleges: Diffusion of Knowledge in Scientific Communities* (Chicago: University of Chicago Press, 1972).

4. Danny P. Wallace, *Knowledge Management: Historical and Cross-Disciplinary Themes* (Westport, CT: Libraries Unlimited, 2007), 111.

5. Connie Van Fleet and Joan C. Durrance, "Public Library Research and evaluation: Use and Utility," Chapter 1, in *Research and Evaluation Issues in Public Librarianship: Trends for the Future*, ed. Joy M. Greiner, 1–16 (Westport, CT: Greenwood Press, 1994).

6. Charles R. Hildreth and Selenay Aytac, "Recent Library Practitioner Research: A Methodological Analysis and Critique," *Journal of Education for Library and Information Science* 48, no. 3 (2007): 236–58.

7. Peter Lynam, Margaret Slater, and Rennie Walker, *Research and the Practitioner: Dissemination of Research Results Within the Library-Information Profession*, ASLIB Occasional Publication No. 27 (London: ASLIB, 1982), 6.

8. Ibid., 301.

9. Connie Van Fleet and Danny P. Wallace, "Beals Revisited: Sad Tidings, Lamentations, and Anti-Research," *RQ* 31, no. 3 (1992): 305.

10. Van Fleet and Durrance, "Public Library Research and evaluation: Use and Utility."

11. Dan O'Connor and Soyeon Park, "Research and Methods as Essential Knowledge," *American Libraries* 33 (January 2002): 50.

12. Melanie Schlosser, "OSUL2013: Fostering Organizational Change through a Grassroots Planning Process," *College & Research Libraries* 72, no. 2 (2011): 158.

13. Arnold Hirshon, "Libraries, Consortia, and Change Management," *Journal of Academic Librarianship* 25, no. 2 (1999): 124–25.

14. Danny P. Wallace and Connie Van Fleet, *Library Evaluation: A Casebook and Can-Do Guide* (Englewood, CO: Libraries Unlimited, 2001), 1.

GLOSSARY

Abstract: a brief summary of a proposal or publication that serves as a representation of the proposal or publication. *See also* Executive summary.

Accidental sample: *See* Convenience sample.

Action research: *See* Applied research

Alternative hypothesis: a hypothesis used to explain rejection of a null hypothesis.

Analysis of variance (ANOVA):   a statistical procedure for assessing the significance of the relationship between three or more distributions based on ratio-level variables. *See also* Statistical testing; Inferential statistics; Significance.

Anonymity: any research or evaluation process in which the identities of subjects are unknown to the investigator. *See also* Confidentiality.

ANOVA: *See* Analysis of variance.

Applied ethics: *See* Practical ethics.

Applied research: research carried out primarily to improve some body of practice; also known as action research or decision-making research.

Aristotelian logic: a system of deductive reasoning based on categorical syllogisms.

Artistic research: the contributions artistic or other creative activities make to the advancement of knowledge; the application of principles adopted from the arts and humanities to the kinds of questions more usually explored through quantitative research; research that examines artistic practices and products. *See also* Qualitative methods.

Assent: a child's agreement to participate in a study. *See also* Informed consent.

Assumption: a conclusion or assertion that is "taken on faith" and is not subjected to the gathering or analysis of evidence.

Axiom: a maxim or statement generally accepted as being true.

Basic research: research carried out primarily to increase understanding of some phenomenon; also known as pure research or theoretical research. *See also* Applied research.

Belmont Report: a statement of fundamental ethical principles related to research involving human subjects adopted by the National Commission for the Protection of Human Subjects of Biomedical and Behavioral Research in 1979.

Benchmarking: the process of evaluating an activity or service in comparison to a standard, guideline, or external criterion.

Beneficence: the ethical principle that researchers have an obligation to protect and preserve the well-being of human subjects. *See also* Belmont Report; Justice; Respect for Persons.

Best practices: accepted approaches to action that are based on the shared understanding and collective evaluation outcomes of a professional body.

Bibliometrics: the application of mathematical and/or statistical methods to the study of information products.

Bimodal distribution: a distribution that has two modes. *See also* Mode.

Binomial variable: *See* Dichotomous variable.

Bivariate: involving two variables. *See also* Multivariate; Variable.

Calibration: the process of determining or influencing the accuracy and precision of a measurement tool or technique. *See also* Measure; Measurement.

Case study: a research process in which an investigator studies one instance in great detail as a means of explicating a phenomenon. *See also* Descriptive methods.

Causation: the situation in which a change in one variable not only is related to a change in another variable, but actually effects the change.

Census: a descriptive study of an entire population.

Central tendency: *See* Measures of centrality.

Centrality: *See* Measures of centrality.

Chi-square: a probability distribution used in a wide variety of inferential statistics. *See also* Inferential statistics; Statistics.

Chi-square test of goodness-of-fit: a test of whether the distribution of cases across categories of a nominal-level variable is the result of chance. *See also* Chi-square; Inferential statistics; Statistics.

Chi-square test of proportion: a test of whether the distribution of cases among cells for the relationship among two or more nominal-level variables is the result of chance. *See also* Chi-square; Inferential statistics; Statistics.

Citation analysis: examination of the patterns defined by the references provided in scholarly publication.

Classification: the process of assigning different manifestations of a phenomenon to discrete categories as a means of understanding fundamental differences or variations within that phenomenon.

Closed-ended question: a question that requires a respondent to select from a list of predetermined answer categories. *See also* Descriptive methods; Open-ended question.

Collaboration conflicts: conflicts that arise when research or evaluation is a shared responsibility of a team rather the responsibility of an individual. *See also* Conflict of interest; Dishonesty; Misconduct.

Collective biography: quantitative historical method that focuses on analysis of the demographic characteristics of carefully defined groups. *See also* Historical methods; Quantitative history.

Concept map: *See* Thematic map.

Conceptual definition: a definition that characterizes a phenomenon in general terms but is not precise enough to directly advance a research question or hypothesis.

Confidentiality: an agreement between the investigator and human subjects that, although the identities of subjects will be known, those identities will not be revealed. *See also* Anonymity.

Conflict of interest: any situation in research or evaluation in which the interests of the investigator are in conflict with the interests of honesty, integrity, and ethical behavior.

Constant: an observable entity, the value or nature of which is known at the outset of the research project and does not vary throughout the research process.

Construct validity: the extent to which variables are accurately identified and described.

Content analysis: examination of patterns in recorded information sources.

Context data: data that provide a framework in which to understand primary data. *See also* Primary data.

Contextualization: the process of identifying relationships within primary and context data and tying results to what is already known about the phenomenon being studied.

Contingency table: a table showing the distribution of values of one variable as rows and the distribution of values for a second variable as columns.

Continuous measure: a measure that, at least theoretically, can be measured with an infinite level of precision. *See also* Discrete measure; Measure; Measurement.

Control: an artificially constructed constant, the value or nature of which is deliberately designed to influence interaction among variables.

Convenience sample: a sample for which members of the population are selected because they are readily or easily available. *See also* Sample.

Correlation: a systematic, consistent, predictable relationship between variables.

Cost-effectiveness: comparison of achievement of objectives to expense.

Covariance: a measure of the correlation between the deviance from the mean for two or more distributions based on ratio-level variables. *See also* Correlation; Analysis of variance.

Criterion variable: in regression analysis, a variable that may be influenced by other variables; a dependent variable. *See also* Dependent variable; Predictor variable; Regression.

Data: unanalyzed observations of a phenomenon.

Data consolidation: the process of coordinating and aggregating data drawn from multiple sources.

Data matrix model: a two-dimensional representation of the relationship between two variables.

Data reduction: the process of reducing a complex concept to a simpler, more manageable representation.

Debriefing: in studies involving deception, the investigator's obligation, once participation has ended, to inform the subject of the existence and nature of the deception, to describe and explain in detail the true nature and methodology of the study, to allow the subject to comment on his or her reaction to the deception, and possibly to disallow use of data gathered through deception of the subject. *See also* Deception; Human subjects; Informed consent.

Deception: any research or evaluation process in which subjects are deliberately misled regarding any aspect of the process. *See also* Debriefing; Human subjects; Informed consent.

Decision-making research: *See* Action research.

Declaration of Helsinki: a set of internationally accepted ethical principles related to experimentation with human subjects published by the World Medical Association in 1964.

Deduction: the systematic application of general principles to specific cases.

Degrees of freedom: an indication of how the value of any given case is influenced by the values of other cases; an indication of how many values must be know to derive all values; a mathematically derived indicator of how to interpret a statistic. *See also* Inferential statistics.

Dependent variable: a variable that may be influenced by other variables; the value of a dependent variable may be the effect of the influence of other variables.

Description: the process of generating a general understanding of a phenomenon of interest by encapsulating the fundamental characteristics of the phenomenon, usually in the form of a narrative. *See also* Descriptive methods.

Descriptive methods: Research or evaluation methods that are based on observation of the present.

Descriptive statistics: statistical procedures used primarily for description and summarization of a group of values.

Design research: a subcategory of artistic research that focuses on the application of systematic principles to the processes of design. *See also* Artistic research; Qualitative methods.

Dialectical processing: a technique in which the investigator asks questions about a phenomenon, derives answers, and uses the answers to build further questions for which answers are also sought.

Dichotomous variable: a nominal-level variable that can assume one of two values. *See also* Multinomial variable; Nominal-level variable.

Discrete measure: an integer measure that can be used to count objects, but cannot be used to draw precise comparisons at a fine level. *See also* Continuous measure; Measure; Measurement.

Dishonesty: any deliberate act or effort to misrepresent research or evaluation. *See also* Collaboration conflicts; Conflict of interest; Fabrication; Falsification; Misconduct; Plagiarism.

Dispersion: *See* Measures of dispersion.

Effectiveness: measurement of achievement of goals and objectives.

Efficiency: assessment of the appropriateness of resource allocation.

Emergent theory: a theory that arises from understanding the phenomenon of interest. *See also* Forced theory; Theory.

Empirical methods: processes for deriving data from observation or experience.

Epistemology: the study of the nature of knowledge.

Eponym: a term based on the personal name of the origin of an idea, concept, theory, or other entity.

Estimation: the process of establishing an approximation of a value rather than obtaining a precise value through measurement. *See also* Measurement.

Ethics: a moral code or set of rules for conduct.

Ethnographic methods: a research process in which an investigator becomes immersed in a social, cultural, or group environment as a means of studying that environment and the individuals who are members of the society, culture, or group.

Evaluation: the process of assigning value to things, institutions, processes, or individuals.

Evidence: verifiable observations.

Executive summary: a brief summary of an evaluation plan or report that serves as an overview of the plan or report. *See also* Abstract.

Experiment: measurement of the effect of a deliberately induced change in a predictable environment. *See also* Experimental methods.

Experimental methods: research or evaluation methods that are based on manipulation of the present. *See also* Experiment.

Experimental mortality: *See* Mortality.

External validity: the extent to which conclusions can be generalized and applied to other environments.

Fabrication: creation of data or results without a legitimate research process. *See also* Dishonesty; Falsification; Misconduct; Plagiarism.

Fact: an item of evidence that has been verified and replicated, and can therefore be generalized.

Falsification: alteration of data to achieve a desired effect. *See also* Dishonesty; Fabrication; Misconduct; Plagiarism.

Feminist research: research that is carried out from a feminist perspective and/or addresses issues or concerns related to feminism.

Field notes: observations recorded by an investigator, usually as part of a qualitative study, in the course of field-based research.

Focus group: a type of group interview in which a discussion is used to assess shared perceptions of some phenomenon of interest.

Forced theory: a theory that is derived from acceptance of a preformulated hypothesis. *See also* Emergent theory; Theory.

Formative evaluation: use of evaluation results for improvement through assessing the adequacy or appropriateness of existing performance targets, determining the necessity of desirability of establishing new targets, and identifying methods or mechanisms for meeting new targets. *See also* Evaluation; Summative evaluation.

Generalizability: the extent to which results produced in one environment or by one study can be considered broadly applicable. *See also* External validity.

Grounded theory: a social sciences research method, used primarily with qualitative methods, in which theory is derived from data. *See also* Qualitative methods; Theory.

Health Research Extension Act: a 1985 act of the U.S. Congress requiring administrative oversight to minimize fraud in scientific research. *See also* Dishonesty; Fabrication; Falsification; Misrepresentation; Misconduct; Plagiarism.

Historical methods: research or evaluation methods that are based on observation of the past.

History effect: unanticipated events that occur during the course of an experiment. *See also* Experimental methods.

Historicism: assignment of values to historical events. *See also* Ethics; Historical methods.

Homogeneity: the extent to which members of a population or sample are similar.

Homogeneous sample: a sample whose members are, for purposes of a specific study, substantially similar. *See also* Sample.

Human subjects: people who are the subject of research or evaluation. *See also* Informed consent; Institutional review board; Vulnerable populations.

Humanistic research: a subcategory of artistic research that raises "questions about the meanings of consciousness, conduct, and culture in a context of diversity and change."[1] *See also* Artistic research; Qualitative methods.

Hypothesis: a statement of a problem area that builds on existing understanding, states an expectation regarding the unknown, and can be tested in a manner conducive to replication.

Hypothesis testing: *See* Statistical testing.

Idea map: *See* Thematic map.

Ideological analysis: tracing an idea through literature. *See also* Historical methods.

Image analysis: examination of imagery and its impact on society, politics, or other factors. *See also* Historical methods.

Impressionistic research: research conducted to produce an overview or general sense of the phenomenon of interest.

Independent variable: a variable that may have some influence on other variables; an independent variable may be the cause of some change in another variable.

Indirect costs: overhead items that are necessary to support the institution in which a project is to take place.

Induction: the formulation of general principles based on information about specific cases.

Inference: the use of data gathered from a sample to draw conclusions about a population. *See also* Inferential statistics.

Inferential statistics: statistical procedures used primarily to draw conclusions about a population based on the values of a carefully selected sample. *See also* Inference.

Informed consent: the principle that human participants in research projects should know and understand that they are research subjects and should be aware of the nature, extent, and likelihood of any risks to them as a result of their participation. *See also* Assent; Human subjects.

Insider/outsider phenomenon: the situation in which different investigators may have differing access to subjects based on the characteristics of the investigators.

Institutional Review Board (IRB): an administrative and oversight body of a specific institution that has comprehensive responsibility for ensuring the protection and ethical treatment of human research subjects.

Instrumentation: in experimentation, changes in the way in which the dependent variable is measured. *See also* Experimental methods.

Intercoder reliability: the extent to which two or more observers agree on what has been observed and how to describe what has been observed.

Internal validity: the extent to which relationships among variables are accurately described.

Interpretation: the process of applying meaning to observations of a phenomenon.

Interval-level variable: a variable that allows for the division of the phenomenon of interest into nameable categories, assigns order among the categories, and establishes fixed intervals between categories. *See also* Nominal-level variable; Ordinal-level variable; Ratio-level variable.

Interview: direct interaction between an investigator and a subject, in-person, via telephone, or by other means. *See also* Descriptive methods; Questionnaire.

Interview schedule: a list of topics used by an investigator in conducting an interview. *See also* Interview.

Jargon: the specialized language of a professional field.

Justice: the ethical principle that human subjects should be treated equitably. *See also* Belmont Report; Beneficence; Respect for Persons.

Law: a hypothesis that has been supported to the extent that it can be assumed to be true.

Likert scale: a scale used in questionnaire and interview methods that typically asks the respondent to rate degree of agreement or disagreement with a statement. *See also* Descriptive methods; Questionnaire.

Linkage: the process of making associations and identifying relationships.

List checking: a collection evaluation process used to evaluate the quality of a collection in comparison to some external source.

Literary analysis: examination of literature as a source of social history. *See also* Historical methods.

Literature review: an analytical synthesis of published literature included in a proposal or report that addresses confirmation of need, establishment of focus, identification of the specific subject and context, identification of the theoretical base, and identification of the methodological base for a research or evaluation project.

Logical positivism: an early-20th-century movement to apply the precision and predictability of mathematics to all areas of understanding and particularly to philosophy.

Maturation: in experimentation, unanticipated changes directly resulting from the passage of time. *See also* Experimental methods.

Mean: the sum of all values for a distribution divided by the number of values.

Measure: an approach to describing, summarizing, and representing the entities that have been defined as the focus of a research or evaluation activity.

Measurement: "deliberate observations of the real world for the purpose of describing objects and events in terms of the attributes composing a variable."[2] *See also* Estimation.

Measures of centrality: measures that describe the extent to which the values of a variable are alike. *See also* Mean; Median; Mode.

Measures of central tendency: *See* Measures of centrality.

Measures of dispersion: measures that describe the extent to which the values of a variable are different. *See also* Standard deviation; Variance.

Measures of proportion: measures that describe the extent to which a single category within a variable characterizes the variable as a whole. *See also* Percentage; Proportion; Ratio.

Measures of variability: *See* Measures of dispersion.

Median: the value that defines the midpoint of a distribution.

Method: a general approach to research.

Methodology: a specific plan for conducting a research or evaluation project.

Milgram obedience studies: a series of laboratory studies conducted by Stanley Milgram during the 1960s and 1970s designed to explore the concept of obedience in the context of the willingness of subjects to harm others in the interest of following instructions from a perceived authority figure.

Misconduct: dishonesty, collaboration conflicts, or conflicts of interest in research or evaluation.

Multimodal distribution: a distribution that has three or more modes. *See also* Mode.

Multinomial variable: a nominal-level variable that can assume one of three or more values. *See also* Dichotomous variable; Nominal-level variable.

Multivariate: involving more than one variable. *See also* Bivariate; Variable.

Mode: the most frequently occurring value in the distribution of values for a variable.

Mortality: in experimentation, unanticipated removal of subjects from an experiment. *See also* Experimental methods.

Multiple response list: a question structure in which the respondent is allowed to identify more than one answer to the question and has no obligation to identify any answer as being more important or more prominent than any other. *See also* Questionnaire.

National Research Act: a 1974 act of Congress authorizing the National Commission for the Protection of Biomedical and Behavioral Research.

Naturalistic methods: *See* Qualitative methods.

Nominal-level variable: a variable that allows for the division of the phenomenon of interest into nameable categories. *See also* Internal-level variable; Ordinal-level variable; Ratio-level variable.

Nonnumeric research: research that explicitly does not employ quantitative methods. *See also* Qualitative methods.

Nonparametric statistics: statistical procedures frequently used with nominal- or ordinal-level variables and not associated with an assumption of a normally distributed population. *See also* Parametric statistics.

Nonprobability sample: a sample selected using a process in which the probability of any given member of the population being included in the sample is irrelevant. *See also* Probability sample; Sample.

Nonquantitative research: *See* Nonnumeric research.

Normal curve: *See* Normal distribution.

Normal distribution: a symmetrical distribution in which the values of the mean, median, and mode are identical.

Null hypothesis: a hypothesis is framed in terms of anticipation of the existence of no relationship between stated variables.

Nuremberg Code: the first generally accepted core statement on humane principles in research, adopted by the American Medical Association in 1947.

Ontology: the study of being or existence.

Open-ended question: a question for which the respondent is charged with formulating an answer. *See also* Descriptive methods; Closed-ended question.

Operational definition: a specific way of defining a concept for purposes of advancing a research question or hypothesis.

Ordinal-level variable: a variable that allows for the division of the phenomenon of interest into nameable categories. *See also* Internal-level variable; Nominal-level variable; Ratio-level variable.

Outlier: values in a distribution that do not fit the pattern of other values.

Paradigm: a model or pattern used in understanding a particular domain of interest.

Parameter: a naturally occurring constant, the value or nature of which may influence interaction among variables.

Parametric statistics: statistical procedures used with interval- or ratio-level data and based on the assumption of a normally distributed population. *See also* Nonparametric statistics; Normal distribution.

Pearson product–moment correlation: a commonly used statistical procedure for examining correlation between two or more ratio-level variables.

Peer-reviewed journal: a journal for which the contributions of scholars are reviewed by other scholars prior to acceptance for publication and dissemination.

Percentage: a proportion with a base of 100; a proportion multiplied by 100.

Perceived reality: in qualitative research, the premise that there is no objective reality and reality is defined by the relationship between the observer and the environment.

Phenomenological research: in qualitative methods, methods and techniques used to describe the "lived experience" of a phenomenon. *See also* Qualitative methods.

Plagiarism: nonexistent, inadequate, or inappropriate attribution of sources, word, or ideas. *See also* Dishonesty; Fabrication; Falsification; Misconduct.

Population: all those entities that are the focus of interest of the research study.

Power: an estimate of the probability of Type II error in hypothesis testing. *See also* Type II error.

Post hoc fallacy: the tendency to infer that correlation implies causation; post hoc, ergo propter hoc loosely translates as after this, therefore as a result of this.

Practical ethics: application of the principles of ethics to problem solving or decision making.

Predictor variable: in regression analysis, a variable that may influence other variables; an independent variable. *See also* Independent variable; Criterion variable; Regression.

Primary data: those data that are truly of interest to an investigator. *See also* Context data.

Primary source: in historical investigation, an account of an event by a witness to the event. *See also* Historical methods; Secondary source.

Principles of warrant: the five fundamental principles of human subjects research.

Probability sample: a sample selected by a process in which the probability of any given member of the population being included in the sample is a factor. *See also* Nonprobability sample; Random sample; Sample.

Probability threshold: an indicator of the degree of Type I error that will be used to define significance in hypothesis testing. *See also* Hypothesis testing; Significance; Type I error.

Problem statement: a brief summary of a research or evaluation goal that defines the boundaries that encompass the problem, identifies subproblems, delineates questions and hypotheses, and states implications for action.

Profession: an occupation characterized by self-regulation, advancement of knowledge, social goals and advancing the public good, and avoidance of harm.

Project plan: *See* Proposal.

Project timeline: *See* Work plan.

Proof: an assertion that has been proven and has the status of being definitively, immutably, and irrefutably true. *See also* Fact.

Proportion: a number representing a part divided by a number representing the whole.

Proportional sample: an approach to sampling in which subcategories within the population are identified and subsamples are drawn randomly from within the subcategories to reflect the proportional representation of subcategories within the population. *See also* Random Sample; Sample; Stratified sample.

Proposal: a detailed plan for the conduct of a research or evaluation project.

Psychohistory: the use of psychological methods to examine historical events. *See also* Historical methods.

Purposive sample: a sampling technique in which members are selected from the population to serve some specific, presumably logical purpose. *See also* Sample.

Pure research: *See* Basic research.

Qualitative methods: research or evaluation methods that focus on in-depth examination of the nature of the entities being studied.

Quantitative history: examination of numeric evidence related to historical events. *See also* Collective biography; Historical methods.

Quantitative methods: research or evaluation methods that focus on measuring and summarizing the characteristics of the entities being studied.

Questionnaire: a set of questions designed to be answered by participants in a research or evaluation study. *See also* Descriptive methods; Interview.

Quota sample: a sampling technique in which subcategories within the population are identified, subsample sizes determined and data are gathered until each subsample size has been reached. *See also* Sample.

Random sample: a sampling technique in which each member of the population has a known probability of being included in the sample. *See also* Sample; Simple random sample.

Ranked list: a question structure that requires the respondent to apply an ordinal value to pre-identified categories. *See also* Questionnaire.

Rating scale: *See* Likert scale.

Ratio: any number divided by another number.

Ratio-level variable: a variable that allows for the division of the phenomenon of interest into nameable categories, assigns order among the categories, establishes fixed intervals between categories, and is based on a true zero that defines the absence of the characteristic of interest. *See also* Interval-level variable; Nominal-level variable; Ordinal-level variable.

Refereed journal: *See* Peer-reviewed journal.

Reaction to testing: *See* Testing.

Reflective practice: the process of reflexively assessing professional action while engaged in it in the interest of improving professional performance.

Regression: a family of statistical procedures that use the values of a predictor (independent) variable or variables to predict or explain the values of a criterion (dependent) variable or variables. *See also* Criterion variable; Predictor variable; Inferential statistics.

Regression toward the mean: in experimentation, the tendency for individuals in groups to become similar, and for different groups to become similar over time. *See also* Experimental methods.

Reliability: a measure of how consistently a variable represents what the phenomenon it is intended to represent.

Replicability: a measure of the extent to which another researcher could carry out the same research process and produce the same results.

Research: systematic investigation intended to increase knowledge of some phenomenon.

Research question: a general query that guides research but does not necessarily establish a formal structure for an anticipated outcome.

Respect for persons: the ethical principle that human subjects should be allowed to act as autonomous agents and that persons with diminished autonomy are entitled to special protections. *See also* Belmont Report; Beneficence; Justice.

Sample: a subset of a population selected to represent that population for purposes of a particular research or evaluation project. *See also* Population; Sample. Frame.

Sampling frame: a source of information about a population used to make it possible to select a sample. *See also* Population; Sample.

Saturation sample: a sampling technique in which subcategories within the population are identified and data are gathered until each subsample is determined to have been saturated. *See also* Sample.

Schedule of completion: *See* Work plan.

Scientific methods: *See* Quantitative methods.

Secondary source: in historical investigation, any source of historical data that is not an account of an event by a witness to an event is a secondary source. *See also* Historical methods; Primary source.

Selection bias: in experimentation, failure to select comparable groups.

Self-plagiarism: republishing one's own work, in whole or in part, without proper attribution. *See also* Plagiarism; Misconduct.

Significance: an estimate of the probability of Type I error in hypothesis testing. *See also* Power; Type I error.

Simple random sample: a sampling technique in which each member of the population has a known, equal probability of being included in the sample.

Single response forced choice: a question structure that requires the respondent to select one and only one answer from a list. *See also* Questionnaire.

Social informatics: the study of the social aspects of computers and information technology.

Spreadsheet: a computer program that allows for the definition of data in the form of a data matrix.

Standard deviation: a measure of the mean distance of individual scores from the overall mean for the distribution.

Standard error of the mean: an indication of the variability of sample data used in sampling and statistical analysis.

Stanford Prison Experiment: a 1971 experiment carried out at Stanford University to study "interpersonal dynamics in a prison-like setting" using a "functional simulation of a prison."[3]

Statistic: an item of information expressed in a numeric format; a characteristic of a sample used as an indicator of a corresponding population parameter; the result of a statistical procedure or calculation.

Statistical significance: *See* significance

Statistical testing: the process of determining the statistical or probabilistic likelihood that a hypothesis of interest can be supported.

Statistics: the process of analyzing numeric data for purposes of description or inference. *See also* Hypothesis testing; Statistic.

Stratified sample: an approach to sampling in which subcategories within the population are identified and subsamples are drawn randomly from within the subcategories. *See also* Proportional sample; Random sample; Sample.

Structured observation: a technique in which the characteristics of the phenomenon that will be observed and the methods for observing them are precisely defined prior to data gathering.

Student's *t*: *See* *t*-test.

Summative evaluation: assessment of the extent to which existing targets for performance are being met. *See also* Evaluation; Formative evaluation.

Summarization: the process of rendering analyzed data understandable for purposes of reporting.

Surprisal: the process of producing unexpected results.

Survey: a descriptive study of a sample conducted as an approach to understanding the qualities of a population. *See also* Census.

Symbolic interactionism: the study of the role of symbols in social interaction.

Syllogism: in deduction, an argument with two premises and a conclusion.

Synergy: increased effectiveness resulting from the contributions of multiple factors.

Systematic sample: an approach to sampling in which members of the population are selected for the sample on the basis of a numeric interval. *See also* Random sample; Sample.

Systems thinking: the process of identifying and analyzing the systems and structures that define a phenomenon or activity of interest.

***t*-test:** a statistical procedure for assessing the significance of the relationship between two distributions based on ratio-level variables. *See also* Hypothesis testing; Inferential statistics; Significance.

Testing: in experimentation, the effect of one manipulation or observation on other manipulations or observations. *See also* Experimental methods.

Thematic analysis: in qualitative methods, the search for themes in field notes.

Thematic map: a visualization tool used to summarize nonquantitative relationships in a body of data, usually used in qualitative research. *See also* Visualization.

Theoretical research: *See* Basic research.

Theoretical sample: an approach to data gathering in which the nature of the sample emerges as data are gathered rather than being predetermined prior to data gathering.

Theory: a body of interrelated assumptions, facts, laws, and hypotheses that can, as a whole, be interpreted as a summary of a particular area of interest.

Time series: a series of observations of a variable conducted at different times.

Transaction log analysis: examination of the patterns of interactions between some system of interest and the users of that system.

True/false: a question structure that requires the respondent to supply a dichotomous answer. *See also* Questionnaire.

Truth: the state of being true.

Tuskegee Syphilis Study: a study of the effects of untreated syphilis sponsored by the U.S. Public Health Service from 1932 to 1972.

Type I error: incorrect rejection of a null hypothesis as a result of hypothesis testing.

Type II error: incorrect acceptance of a null hypothesis as a result of hypothesis testing.

Typology: a classification of some phenomenon according to type.

Unobtrusive study: the use of measures that do not require direct contact between the investigator and the subject, or in which the subject is unaware of the investigator's presence.

Unstructured observation: a technique in which the phenomenon is identified in general terms prior to gathering data but the characteristics to be observed and the approaches taken to observing those characteristics emerge and evolve as the study is carried out.

Validity: a measure of the extent to which a variable represents what the phenomenon is intended to represent.

Variability: *See* Measures of dispersion.

Variable: an observable entity, the value or nature of which is not known at the outset of the research project. The essential nature of a variable is that its value or nature can vary.

Variance: the square of the standard deviation, used in statistical testing.

Verification: in qualitative methods, the processes of testing beliefs, assumptions, theories, or previous interpretations. *See also* Qualitative methods.

VisiCalc: the first computer spreadsheet program, introduced by Personal Software in 1979.

Visualization: presentation of results in a visual form such as a graph or illustration.

Vulnerable populations: defined groups of individuals who merit special consideration in research or evaluation involving human subjects.

Work plan: a detailed description of the sequence and flow of the tasks necessary to carry out the project and the timing of the project.

NOTES

1. Scott D. Churchill, "Humanistic Research in the Wake of Postmodernism," *The Humanistic Psychologist* 33, no. 4 (2005): 331.

2. Earl Babbie, *The Practice of Social Research*, 12th ed. (Belmont, CA: Cengage, 2010), 125.

3. Philip G. Zimbardo, "On the Ethics of Intervention in Human Psychological Research: With Special Reference to the Stanford Prison Experiment," *Cognition* 2, no. 2 (1974): 244.

BIBLIOGRAPHY

Aaron, Shirley L. "Apply Drott's Criteria for Reading Research." *School Library Media Quarterly* 13 (Winter 1985): 64–68.

"About ORI—History." Office of Research Integrity, U.S. Department of Health and Human Services, http://ori.dhhs.gov/about/history.shtml.

Adler, Emily Stier, and Roger Clark. *An Invitation to Social Research: How It's Done*. Belmont, CA: Cengage, 2011.

Alkadry, Mohmad G., and Matthew T. Witt. "Abu Ghraib and the Normalization of Torture and Hate." *Public Integrity* 11, no. 2 (2009): 135–53.

Altman, Ellen, and Peter Hernon, eds. *Research Misconduct: Issues, Implications, and Strategies*. Greenwich, CT: Ablex, 1997.

Anderson, Karen, and Frances A. May. "Does the Method of Instruction Matter? An Experimental Examination of Information Literacy Instruction in the Online, Blended, and Face-to-Face Classrooms." *Journal of Academic Librarianship* 36, no. 6 (2010): 495–500.

Angrosino, Michael V., ed. *Doing Cultural Anthropology: Projects for Ethnographic Data Collection*. Long Grove, IL: Waveland, 2007.

Antell, Karen. "Why Do College Students Use Public Libraries? A Phenomenological Study." *Reference & User Services Quarterly* 43, no. 3 (2004): 227–36.

Antell, Karen, and Jie Huang. "Subject Searching Success: Transaction Logs, Patron Perceptions, and Implications for Library Instruction." *Reference & User Services Quarterly* 48, no. 1 (2008): 68–76.

"ASIS&T Professional Guidelines." Washington: American Society for Information Science & Technology, 1992.

Asselin, Marilyn E. "Insider Research: Issues to Consider When Doing Qualitative Research in Your Own Setting." *Journal for Nurses in Staff Development* 19, no. 2 (2003): 99–103.

Babbie, Earl. *The Practice of Social Research*. 12th ed. Belmont, CA: Cengage, 2010.

Baker, Lynda M. "Observation: A Complex Research Method." *Library Trends* 55, no. 1 (Summer 2006): 171–89.

Baker, Sharon L. "The Display Phenomenon: An Exploration into Factors Causing the Increased Circulation of Displayed Books." *Library Quarterly* 56 (1986): 237–57.

Baker, Sharon L., and F. Wilfrid Lancaster. *The Measurement and Evaluation of Library Services.* 2nd ed. Arlington, TX: Information Resources Press, 1991.

Beals, Ralph A. "Implications of Communications Research for the Public Library." In *Print, Radio, and Film in a Democracy*, edited by Douglas Waples, 165–67. Chicago, IL: University of Chicago Press, 1942.

Bellesiles, Michael A. "The Origins of Gun Culture in the United States, 1760–1865." *Journal of American History* 83, no. 2 (1996): 425–55.

Bellesiles, Michael A. *Arming America: The Origins of a National Gun Culture.* New York: Alfred A Knopf, 2000.

"The Belmont Report: Ethical Principles and Guidelines for the Protection of Human Subjects of Research." National Commission for the Protection of Human Subjects of Biomedical and Behavioral Research. Washington: Government Printing Office, 1979.

Berg, Selinda Adelle, Kristin Hoffmann, and Diane Dawson. "Not on the Same Page: Undergraduates' Information Retrieval in Electronic and Print Books." *Journal of Academic Librarianship* 36, no. 6 (2010): 518–25.

Berger, Peter L., and Thomas Luckmann. *The Social Construction of Reality: A Treatise in the Sociology of Knowledge.* New York: Doubleday, 1967.

Bertot, John Carlo, and Paul T. Jaeger. "Survey Research and Libraries: Not Necessarily Like in the Textbooks." *Library Quarterly* 78, no. 1 (January 2008): 99–105.

Biemer, Paul P., and Lars E. Lyberg. *Introduction to Survey Quality.* Hoboken, NJ: Wiley, 2003.

Bierce, Ambrose. *The Devil's Dictionary.* Cleveland, OH: World Publishing Company, 1948.

Blass, Thomas, ed. *Obedience to Authority: Current Perspectives on the Milgram Paradigm.* Mahwah, NJ: Lawrence Erlbaum Associates, 2000.

Blumberg, Stephen J., and Julian V. Luke. "Wireless Substitution: Early Release of Estimates from the National Health Interview Survey, January–June 2010." National Center for Health Statistics Division of Health Interview Statistics. Washington: Centers for Disease Control and Prevention, 2010.

Blumer, Herbert. "What Is Wrong with Social Theory?" In *Symbolic Interactionism: Perspective and Method*, edited by Herbert Blumer, 140–52. Englewood Cliffs, NJ: Prentice Hall, 1954.

Bornmann, Lutz, and Loet Leydesdorff. "Which Cites Produce More Excellent Papers than can be Expected? A New Mapping Approach, Using Google Maps, Based on Significance Testing." *Journal of the American Society for Information Science and Technology* 62, no. 10 (October 2011): 1954–62.

Boyce, Bert R., Charles T. Meadow, and Donald H. Kraft. *Measurement in Information Science.* San Diego, CA: Academic Press, 1994.

Bradford, S. C. "Sources of Information on Specific Subjects." *Engineering* 137 (1934): 85–86.

Bradford, S. C. *Documentation.* Washington: Public Affairs Press, 1950.

Braquet, Donna M. "Library Experiences of Hurricane Katrina and New Orleans Flood Survivors." *LIBRES Library and Information Science Research Electronic Journal*, no. 1 (2010), http://libres.curtin.edu.au/.

Brooks, Terry A. "Evidence of Complex Citer Motivations." *Journal of the American Society for Information Science* 37 (1986): 34–36.

Bui, Yvonne L. *How to Write a Master's Thesis.* Thousand Oaks, CA: Sage, 2009.

Burchard, Waldo W. "Lawyers, Political Scientists, Sociologists—and Concealed Microphones." *American Sociological Review* 23, no. 6 (1958): 686–91.

Buschman, John E., and Gloria J. Leckie, eds. *The Library as Place: History, Community, and Culture.* Westport, CT: Libraries Unlimited, 2007.

Calabrese, Raymond L. *The Dissertation Desk Reference: The Doctoral Student's Manual to Writing the Dissertation.* Lanham, MD: Rowman & Littlefield Education, 2009.

Callison, Daniel. "Action Research." *School Library Media Activities Monthly* 23, no. 10 (2007): 40–43.

Campbell, Donald T. *Social Experimentation*. Thousand Oaks, CA: Sage, 1999.

Carlyle, Thomas. *Sartor Resartus*. Boston, MA: J. Monroe and Company, 1837.

Celsus, Aulus Cornelius. *De Medicina*. Florence: Nicolaus Laurentii, 1478.

Chatman, Elfreda A. "Life in a Small World: Applicability of Gratification Theory to Information-Seeking Behavior." *Journal of the American Society for Information Science* 42, no. 6 (1991): 438–49.

Churchill, Scott D. "Humanistic Research in the Wake of Postmodernism." *The Humanistic Psychologist* 33, no. 4 (2005): 321–34.

"Code of Ethics of the American Library Association." Chicago, IL: American Library Association, 2008.

Cole, F. J., and N. B. Eales. "The History of Comparative Anatomy. Part I: A Statistical Analysis of the Literature." *Science Progress* 11 (1917): 578–96.

Conan Doyle, Arthur. *Adventures of Sherlock Holmes*. New York: Harper and Brothers, 1892.

Connaway, Lynn Silipigni, and Ronald R. Powell. *Basic Research Methods for Librarians*. 5th ed. Santa Barbara, CA: Libraries Unlimited, 2010.

Connell, Tschera Harkness. "Writing the Research Paper: A Review." *College & Research Libraries* 71, no. 1 (2010): 6–7.

Cook, Douglas, and Lesley Farmer, eds. *Using Qualitative Methods in Action Research: How Librarians Can Get to the Why of Data*. Chicago, IL: Association of College and Research Libraries, 2011.

Coontz, Stephanie. "Let Scholars Bring Realism to the Debates on Family Values." *Chronicle of Higher Education* 39, no. 9 (1992): B1–B2.

Crane, Diana. *Invisible Colleges: Diffusion of Knowledge in Scientific Communities*. Chicago, IL: University of Chicago Press, 1972.

Cuseo, Allan A. *Homosexual Characters in YA Novels: A Literary Analysis, 1969–1982*. Metuchen, NJ: Scarecrow, 1992.

Dain, Phyllis. "Ambivalence and Paradox: The Social Bonds of the Public Library." *Library Journal* 100, no. 3 (1975): 261–66.

Dain, Phyllis. "The Historical Sensibility." *Libraries & Culture* 35, no. 1 (Winter 2000): 240–43.

Dattalo, Patrick. *Strategies to Approximate Random Sampling and Assignment*. New York: Oxford University Press, 2010.

David, Daniel. "Letter to the Editor: Duplication Spreads the Word to a Wider Audience." *Nature* 452, no. 7183 (2008): 29.

Day, Ronald E. *The Modern Invention of Information: Discourse, History, and Power*. Carbondale: Southern Illinois University Press, 2001.

De Bellis, Nicola, *Bibliometrics and Citation Analysis: From the* Science Citation Index *to Cybermetrics*. Lanham, MD: Scarecrow, 2009.

de Munck Victor C., and Elisa J. Sobo, eds. *Using Methods in the Field: A Practical Introduction and Casebook*. Walnut Creek, CA: AltaMira, 1998.

Dillman, Don A., Jolene D. Smyth, and Leah Melani Christian. *Internet, Mail, and Mixed-Mode Surveys: The Tailored Design Method*. 3rd ed. Hoboken, NJ: Wiley, 2009.

Diodato, Virgil. *Dictionary of Bibliometrics*. New York: Haworth, 1994.

Ditzion, Sidney. *Arsenals of a Democratic Culture: A Social History of the American Public Library Movement in New England and the Middle States from 1850 to 1900*. Chicago, IL: American Library Association, 1947.

Divelko, Juris Divelko. "An Ideological Analysis of Digital Reference Service Models," *Library Trends* 50, no. 2 (Fall 2001): 218–44.

Dougherty, William C. "The Google Books Project: Will It Make Libraries Obsolete?" *Journal of Academic Librarianship* 36, no. 1 (January 2010): 86–89.

Durrance, Joan C., and Connie Van Fleet. "Public Library Leaders and Research: Mechanisms, Perceptions, and Strategies." *Journal of Education for Library and Information Science* 34 (1992): 137–52.

Dwyer, Sonya Corbin, and Jennifer L. Buckle. "The Space Between: On Being an Insider–Outsider in Qualitative Research." *International Journal of Qualitative Methods* 8, no. 1 (2009): 54–63.

Edwardy Jeffrey M., and Jeffrey S. Pontius. "Monitoring Book Reshelving in Libraries Using Statistical Sampling and Control Charts. *Library Resources & Technical Services* 45, no. 2 (April 2001): 90–94.

Egghe, Leo L., and Ronald Rousseau. *Elementary Statistics for Effective Library and Information Service Management.* London: Aslib-AMI, 2001.

Enders, Craig K. *Applied Missing Data Analysis.* New York: Guilford, 2010.

Endersby, James W. "Collaborative Research in the Social Sciences: Multiple Authors and Publication Credit." *Social Science Quarterly* 77, no. 2 (1996): 375–92.

Eves, Howard W. *Mathematical Circles Adieu: A Fourth Collection of Mathematical Stories and Anecdotes.* Boston, MA: Prindle, Weber, and Schmidt, 1977.

Garfield, Eugene. "Citation Indexes for Science." *Science* 122, no. 3159 (1955): 108–11.

Garfield, Eugene. "Can Citation Indexing Be Automated?" In *Statistical Association Methods for Mechanized Documentation*, edited by Mary E. Stevens. Washington: National Bureau of Standards, 1965.

Garfield, Eugene. "The Mystery of the Transposed Journal Lists: Wherein Bradford's Law of Scattering Is Generalized According to Garfield's Law of Concentration." In *Essays of an Information Scientist*, vol. 1, *1962–1973*, 222–23. Philadelphia, PA: ISI Press.

Geever, Jane C. *The Foundation Center's Guide to Proposal Writing.* 5th ed. New York: Foundation Center, 2007.

Gerhan, David R. "Statistical Significance: How it Signifies in Statistics Reference." *Reference & User Services Quarterly* 40, no. 4 (Summer 2001): 361–74.

Gilibisco, Stan. *Statistics Demystified.* New York: McGraw-Hill, 2004.

Gillham, Bill. *Developing a Questionnaire.* New York: Continuum, 2007.

Girard, Ralph W. "The New Computerized Shape of Education." In *Inventing Education for the Future*, edited by W. Z. Hirsch. San Francisco, CA: Chandler, 1967.

Given, Lisa, ed., *The Sage Encyclopedia of Qualitative Research Methods.* Thousand Oaks, CA: Sage, 2008.

Glaser, Barney G., and Anselm L. Strauss. *The Discovery of Grounded Theory: Strategies for Qualitative Research.* Chicago, IL: Aldine, 1967.

Goldhor, Herbert. *An Introduction to Scientific Research in Librarianship* Washington: U.S. Department of Education Bureau of Research, 1969.

Goldhor, Herbert. "The Effect of Prime Display Location on Public Library Circulation of Selected Titles." *Library Quarterly* 42, no. 4 (1972): 371–89.

Gregory, Ian. *Ethics in Research.* New York: Continuum, 2003.

Greifeneder, Elke, and Michael S. Seadle. "Research for Practice: Avoiding Useless Results." *Library Hi Tech* 28, no. 1 (2010): 5–7.

Greenwood, Judy T., Alex P. Watson, and Melissa Dennis. "Ten Years of LibQUAL: A Study of Quantitative and Qualitative Survey Results at the University of Mississippi 2001–2010." *Journal of Academic Librarianship* 37, no. 4 (July 2011): 312–18.

Groos, Ole V. "Bradford's Law and the Keenan-Atherton Data." *American Documentation* 18, no. 1 (1967): 46.

Grose, M. W., and M. B. Line. "On the Construction and Care of White Elephants." *Library Association Record* 70 (January 1968): 2–5.

Gupta, A. K. *Theory of Survey Sampling.* New York: World Scientific, 2011.

Gwartney, Patricia A. *The Telephone Interviewer's Handbook: How to Conduct Standardized Conversations.* San Francisco, CA: Jossey-Bass, 2007.

Hafner, Arthur W. *Descriptive Statistical Techniques for Librarians.* 2nd ed. Chicago, IL: American Library Association, 1998.

Halliday, Blane. "Identifying Library Policy Issues with List Checking." In *Library Evaluation: A Casebook and Can-Do Guide*, edited by Danny P. Wallace and Connie Van Fleet, 140–52. Englewood, CO: Libraries Unlimited, 2001.

Hamaker, Charles A. "Time Series Circulation Data for Collection Development; Or, You Can't Intuit That." *Library Acquisitions* 19 (Summer 1995): 191–95.

Harris, Michael H. "Purpose of the American Public Library: A Revisionist Interpretation of History." *Library Journal* 98, no. 16 (1973): 2509–14.

Hauptman, Richard. *Ethics and Librarianship.* Jefferson, NC: McFarland, 2003.

Hawley, Mary B. "Reference Statistics." *RQ* 10 (1970): 143–47.

Hernon, Peter. *Statistics: A Component of the Research Process.* Norwood, NJ: Ablex, 1994.

Hernon, Peter, and Candy Schwartz. "Research by Default." *Library and Information Science Research* 31, no. 3 (2009): 137.

Hernon, Peter, and Candy Schwartz. "What Is a Problem Statement?" *Library and Information Science Research* 29, no. 3 (2007): 307–09.

Hernon, Peter, and Charles R. McClure. "Unobtrusive Reference Testing: The 55 Percent Rule." *Library Journal* 111 (1986): 37–41.

Hernon, Peter, and Charles R. McClure. *Evaluation and Library Decision Making.* Norwood, NJ: Ablex, 1990.

Hildreth, Charles R., and Selenay Aytac. "Recent Library Practitioner Research: A Methodological Analysis and Critique." *Journal of Education for Library and Information Science* 48, no. 3 (2007): 236–58.

Hirshon, Arnold. "Libraries, Consortia, and Change Management." *Journal of Academic Librarianship* 25, no. 2 (1999): 124–26.

Hoaglin, David C., Frederick Mosteller, and John W. Tukey. *Exploring Data Tables, Trends, and Shapes.* Hoboken, NJ: Wiley-Interscience, 2006.

Hobbs, Kendall, and Diane Klare. "User Driven Design: Using Ethnographic Techniques to Plan Student Study Space." *Technical Services Quarterly* 27, no. 4 (2010): 347–63.

Holstein James A., and Jaber F. Gubrium, eds. *Inside Interviewing: New Lenses, New Concerns.* Thousand Oaks, CA: Sage, 2003.

Huff, Darrell. *How to Lie with Statistics.* New York: W. W. Norton, 1954.

Information Power: Guidelines for School Library Media Programs. Chicago, IL: American Library Association, 1988.

"Integrity and Misconduct in Research: Report of the Commission on Research Integrity." Washington: U.S. Government Printing Office 1995.

Israel, Mark and Iain Hay. *Research Ethics for Social Scientists: Between Ethical Conduct and Regulatory Compliance.* Thousand Oaks, CA: Sage, 2006.

Julien, Heidi, Jen Pecoskie, and Kathleen Reed. "Trends in Information Behavior Research, 1999–2008: A Content Analysis." *Library and Information Science Research* 33, no. 1 (January 2011): 19–24.

K'Meyer, Tracy E., and A. Glenn Crothers. "'If I See Some of This in Writing, I'm Going to Shoot You:' Reluctant Narrators, Taboo Topics, and the Ethical Dilemmas of the Oral Historian." *Oral History Review* 34, no. 1 (2007): 71–93.

Karsh, Ellen. *The Only Grant-Writing Book You'll Ever Need*. New York: Basic Books, 2009.

Kaser, David. *A Book for a Sixpence: The Circulating Library in America*. Pittsburgh, PA: Beta Phi Mu, 1980.

Kayongo, Jessica, and Clarence Helm. "Graduate Students and the Library: A Survey of Research Practices and Library Use at the University of Notre Dame." *Reference & User Services Quarterly* 49, no. 4 (2010): 341–49.

Kipling, Rudyard. *Just So Stories for Little Children*. Leipzig: Tauchnitz, 1902.

Kirkpatrick, David D. "2 Say Stephen Ambrose, Popular Historian, Copied Passages." *New York Times*, January 5, 2002, 8.

Koch, Deborah. *How to Say It: Grantwriting: Write Proposals that Grantmakers Want to Fund*. New York: Prentice Hall, 2009.

Korn, James H. *Illusion of Reality: A History of Deception in Social Psychology*. Albany, NY: State University of New York Press, 1997.

Krathwohl, David R. *How to Prepare a Dissertation Proposal: Suggestions for Students in Education and the Social and Behavioral Sciences*. Syracuse, NY: Syracuse University Press, 2005.

Krathwohl, David R. *Methods of Educational and Social Science Research: An Integrated Approach*. 2nd ed. New York: Harlow, 1998.

Krippendorff, Klaus. *Content Analysis: An Introduction to Its Methodology*. Thousand Oaks, CA: Sage, 2004.

Krippendorff, Klaus, and Mary Angela Bock, eds. *The Content Analysis Reader*. Thousand Oaks, CA: Sage, 2009.

Kuhlthau, Carol C. "Inside the Search Process: Information Seeking from the User's Perspective." *Journal of the American Society for Information Science* 42, no. 5 (1991): 361–71.

Kuhn, Thomas. *The Structure of Scientific Revolutions*. Chicago, IL: University of Chicago Press, 1962.

Kurtz, Michael J., and Johan Bollen. "Usage Bibliometrics." *Annual Review of Information Science and Technology* 44 (2010): 3–64.

Kyrillidou, Martha, and Les Bland. "ARL Statistics 2007–2008." Washington: Association of Research Libraries, 2009.

Kyrillidou, Martha, and Shaneka Morris. "ARL Statistics 2008–2009." Washington: Association of Research Libraries, 2011.

Lance, Keith Curry. "The Impact of School Library Media Centers on Academic Achievement." *School Library Media Quarterly* 22 (Spring 1994): 167–70.

Lance, Keith Curry. "Still Making an Impact: School Library Staffing and Student Performance." *Colorado Libraries* 25, no. 3 (Fall 1999): 6–9.

Lance, Keith Curry. "Impact of School Library Media Programs on Academic Achievement." *Teacher Librarian* 29, no. 3 (February 2002): 29–34.

Lance, Keith Curry, and Becky Russell. "Scientifically Based Research on School Libraries and Academic Achievement: What is It? How Much of It Do We Have? How Can We Do It Better?" *Knowledge Quest* 32, no. 5 (May/June 3004): 13–17.

Lance, Keith Curry, Marcia J. Rodney, and Bill Schwarz. "The Impact of School Libraries on Academic Achievement: A Research Study Based on Responses from Administrators in Idaho." *School Library Monthly* 36, no. 9 (May 2010): 14–17.

Lancaster, F. W. *If You Want to Evaluate Your Library* .... 2nd ed. Champaign: University of Illinois Graduate School of Library and Information Science, 1993.

Landau, Herbert B. *Winning Library Grants: A Game Plan*. Chicago, IL: American Library Association, 2011.

Lee, Robert E. *Continuing Education for Adults through the American Public Library, 1833–1964*. Chicago, IL: American Library Association, 1966.

LeCompte Margaret Diane, and Jean J. Schensul. *Designing and Conducting Ethnographic Research: An Introduction.* 2nd ed. Lanham, MD: Altamira, 2010.

Lee, Deborah. "Survey Research: Reliability and Validity." *Library Administration & Management* 18, no. 4 (Fall 2004): 211–12.

Leedy, Paul D., and Jeanne Ormrod. *Practical Research: Planning and Design.* Upper Saddle River, NJ: Pearson, 2005.

Levine David M., and David F. Stephan. *Even You Can Learn Statistics: A Guide for Everyone Who Has Ever been Afraid of Statistics.* Upper Saddle River, NJ: FT Press, 2010.

Library History Round Table, American Library Association, "American Library History: A Comprehensive Guide to the Literature," http://www.ala.org/ala/mgrps/rts/lhrt/popular resources/amerlibhis.cfm.

Lindgren, James. "Fall from Grace: Arming America and the Bellesiles Scandal." *Yale Law Journal* 111, no. 8 (2002): 2195–249.

Line, Maurice B., and A. Sandison. "'Obsolescence' and Changes in the Use of Literature with Time." *Journal of Documentation* 30, no. 3 (1974): 283–350.

Locke, Lawrence F., Waneen Wyrick Spirduso, and Stephen J. Silverman. *Proposals that Work: A Guide for Planning Dissertations and Grant Proposals.* 5th ed. Thousand Oaks, CA: Sage, 2007.

Lotka, A.J. "The Frequency Distribution of Scientific Productivity." *Journal of the Washington Academy of Science* 16 (1926): 317–23.

Lunden, Anne F. "List Checking in Collection Development: An Imprecise Art." *Collection Management* 11, no. 3–4 (1989): 103–112.

Lyons, E. Stina. "Researching Race Relations: Myrdal's American Dilemma from a Methodological Perspective." *Acta Sociologica* 47, no. 3 (2004): 203–17.

Lyons, Ray. "Statistical Correctness." *Library and Information Science Research* 33, no. 1 (2011): 92–95.

Mackay, Alan L. *The Harvest of a Quiet Eye: A Selection of Scientific Quotations.* Bristol: Institute of Physics, 1977.

MacKellar, Pamela H., and Stephanie K. Gerding. *Winning Grants: A How-to-Do-It Manual for Librarians with Multimedia Tutorials and Grant Development Tools.* New York: Neal-Schuman, 2010.

Marcovitch, Harvey. "Coping with Publication Misconduct." *Serials Librarian* 57, no. 4 (2009): 334–41.

Mastroianni, Anna, and Jeffery Kahn. "Remedies for Human Subjects of Cold War Research: Recommendations of the Advisory Committee." *Journal of Law, Medicine, and Ethics* 24 (1996): 118–26.

McKechnie, Lynne. "Observations of Babies and Toddlers in Library Settings." *Library Trends* 55, no. 1 (2006): 190–201.

Merrett, Frank. "Reflections on the Hawthorne Effect." *Educational Psychology* 26, no. 1 (2006): 143–46.

Mertens, Donna M., and Pauline E. Ginsberg, eds. *The Handbook of Social Research Ethics.* Thousand Oaks, CA: Sage, 2009.

Merton, Robert K. *On the Shoulders of Giants: A Shandean Postscript.* New York: Free Press, 1965.

Merton, R.K. "The Matthew Effect in Science." *Science* 159 (1968): 56–63.

Merton, Robert K. "Insiders and Outsiders: A Chapter in the Sociology of Knowledge." *American Journal of Sociology* 78, no. 1 (1972): 9–47.

Milgram, Stanley. "Behavioral Study of Obedience." *Journal of Abnormal and Social Psychology* 67, no. 4 (1963): 371–78.

Milgram, Stanley. "Some Conditions of Obedience and Disobedience to Authority." *Human Relations* 18 (1965): 57–76.

Milgram, Stanley. *Obedience to Authority: An Experimental View*. New York: Harper and Row, 1974.

Miliken, George A. *Analysis of Messy Data*. Boca Raton, FL: CRC Press, 2009.

Moed, Hank F. *Citation Analysis in Research Evaluation*. Dordrecht: Springer, 2005.

Mulberg, John. *Figuring Figures: An Introduction to Data Analysis*. New York: Prentice Hall, 2002.

Mulcahy, Kevin R. "Science Fiction Collections in ARL Academic Libraries." *College & Research Libraries* 67, no. 1 (2006): 15–34.

Myrdal, Gunnar. *An American Dilemma: The Negro Problem and Modern Democracy*. New York: Harper, 1944.

Nardi, Peter M. *Doing Survey Research: A Guide to Quantitative Methods*. Boston, MA: Allyn and Bacon, 2003.

"National Leadership Grants—FY 2011 Guidelines." Washington: Institute of Museum and Library Services, 2010.

Neuhaus, Christoph, and Hans-Dieter Daniel. "Data Sources for Performing Citation Analysis: An Overview." *Journal of Documentation* 64, no. 2 (2008): 193–210.

Nietzsche, Friedrich Wilhelm. *Thus Spake Zarathustra: A Book for All and None*. Edinburgh: T. N. Foulis, 1909.

Nilsen, Kirsti, and Catherine Ross. "Evaluating Virtual Reference from the Users' Perspective." *The Reference Librarian* no. 95/96 (2006): 53–79.

Nixon, Richard M. *Six Crises*. Garden City, NY: Doubleday, 1962.

O'Connor, Dan, and Soyeon Park. "On My Mind: Research Methods as Essential Knowledge." *American Libraries* 33, no. 1 (2002): 50.

O'Neill, Edward T., Patrick D. McClain, and Brian F. Lavoie. "A Methodology for Sampling the World Wide Web." *Journal of Library Administration* 34, no. 3/4 (2001): 279–71.

O'Neill, Onora. "Applied Ethics: Naturalism, Normativity and Public Policy." *Journal of Applied Philosophy* 26, no. 3 (2009): 219–30.

"On Preventing Conflicts of Interest in Government Sponsored Research at Universities." Washington: American Association of University Professors, 1997.

Orcher, Lawrence T. *Conducting Research*. Glendale, CA: Pyrczak, 2005.

Otlet, Paul. *Traite De Documentation. Le Livre Sur Le Livre. Theorie Et Pratique*. Brussels: Van Keerberghen, 1934.

Park, Taemin Kim. "The Visibility of *Wikipedia* in Scholarly Publications." *First Monday* 16, no. 8 (August 1, 2011), http://firstmonday.org/htbin/cgiwrap/bin/ojs/index.php/fm/article/view/3492/3031.

Pasteur, Louis. In *Compte Rendus des Travaux du Congres Viticole et Sericole de Lyon*. Lyon, 1872.

Pawley, Christine "History in the Library and Information Science Curriculum: Outline of a Debate." *Libraries & Culture* 40, no. 3 (Summer 2005): 223–38.

Pearson, Edmund Lester. In *The Librarian: Selections from the Column of That Name*, edited by Jane B. Durnell and Norman B. Stevens. Metuchen, NJ: Scarecrow, 1976.

Peshkin, Alan. "The Goodness of Qualitative Research." *Educational Researcher* 22, no. 2 (1993): 23–29.

Porter, Stephen R., *Overcoming Survey Research Problems*. San Francisco, CA: Jossey-Bass, 2004.

Price, Derek J. de Solla. *Little Science, Big Science*. New York: Columbia University Press, 1963.

Price, Derek J. de Solla. "A General Theory of Bibliometric and Other Cumulative Advantage Processes." *Journal of the American Society for Information Science* 27 (1976): 292–306.

Pritchard, Alan. "Statistical Bibliography or Bibliometrics?" *Journal of Documentation* 20, no. 4 (1969): 348–49.

Rea Louis M., and Richard A. Parker. *Designing and Conducting Survey Research: A Comprehensive Guide*. San Francisco, CA: Jossey-Bass, 2005.

"Protection of Human Subjects." Washington: Department of Health and Human Services, Government Printing Office, 2005.

Pyrczak, Fred. *Evaluating Research in Academic Journals*. 4th ed. Glendale, CA: Pyrczak, 2008.

"Qualitative Research," ed. Gillian M. McCombs and Theresa M. Maylone, special issue, *Library Trends* 46, no. 4 (Spring 1998).

Reference & User Services Association. "Reference & User Services Association, Guidelines for Behavioral Performance of Reference and Information Service Providers." http://www.ala.org/ala/mgrps/divs/rusa/resources/guidelines/guidelinesbehavioral.cfm.

Reich, Eugenie Samuel. "Self-Plagiarism Case Prompts Calls for Agencies to Tighten Rules." *Nature* 468, no. 7325 (2010): 745.

Rentschler, Eric. "The Fascination of a Fake: The Hitler Diaries." *New German Critique*, no. 90 (2003): 177–92.

"Research in Librarianship," ed. Mary Jo Lynch, special issue, *Library Trends* 32, no. 4 (Spring 1984).

Robert S. Taylor. "Question-Negotiation and Information Seeking in Libraries." *College & Research Libraries* 29 (1968): 178–94.

"Responsibilities of Awardee and Applicant Institutions for Dealing with and Reporting Possible Misconduct in Science." Washington: Department of Health and Human Services, Government Printing Office, 1989.

"Responsible Science: Ensuring the Integrity of the Research Process." Washington: Committee on Science Engineering and Public Policy, Panel on Scientific Responsibility and the Conduct of Research, National Academies of Science, 1992.

Reverby, Susan M. *Examining Tuskegee: The Infamous Syphilis Study and Its Legacy*. Chapel Hill: University of North Carolina Press, 2009.

Ritchey, Donald A. ed. *The Oxford Handbook of Oral History*. New York: Oxford University Press, 2011.

Roig, Miguel. "The Debate on Self-Plagiarism: Inquisitional Science or High Standards of Scholarship?" *Journal of Cognitive and Behavioral Psychotherapies* 8, no. 2 (2008): 245–58.

Sales Bruce D., and Susan Folkman, eds. *Ethics in Research with Human Participants*. Washington: American Psychological Association, 2000.

Salkind, Neil J. *Statistics for People Who (Think They) Hate Statistics*. 4th ed. Thousand Oaks, CA: Sage, 2011.

Salkind, Neil J. *Tests and Measurement for People Who (Think They) Hate Tests and Measurement*. Thousand Oaks, CA: Sage, 2006.

Samuelson, Pamela. "Self-Plagiarism or Fair Use?" *Communications of the ACM* 37, no. 8 (1994): 21–25.

Schlosser, Melanie. "OSUL2013: Fostering Organizational Change through a Grassroots Planning Process." *College & Research Libraries* 72, no. 2 (2011): 152–65.

Schön, Donald A. *The Reflective Practitioner: How Professionals Think in Action*. New York: Basic Books, 1983.

Schweitzer, Albert. *Civilization and Ethics*. London: A & C Black, 1923.

Seaman, Scott. "Salary Compression: A Time Series Analysis of ARL Position Classifications." *portal: Libraries and the Academy* 7, no. 1 (January 2007): 7–24.

Seidman, Irving. *Interviewing as Qualitative Research: A Guide for Researchers in Education and the Social Sciences*. 3rd ed. New York: Teachers College Press, 2006.

Shadish, William R., Thomas D. Cook, and Donald T. Campbell. *Experimental and Quasi-Experimental Designs for Generalized Causal Inference*. Boston, MA: Houghton Mifflin, 2002.

Shamoo, Adil E. *Responsible Conduct of Research*. New York: Oxford University Press, 2002.

Shapiro, Fred R. "Origins of Bibliometrics, Citation Indexing, and Citation Analysis: The Neglected Legal Literature." *Journal of the American Society for Information Science* 43, no. 5 (1992): 337–39.

Sheikh, Simon. "Objects of Study or Commodification of Knowledge? Remarks on Artistic Research." *Art and Research* 2, no. 2 (2009).

Shenton, Andrew K. "The Analysis of Qualitative Data in LIS Research Projects: A Possible Approach." *Education for Information* 22, no. 3/4 (December 2004): 143–62.

Shiflett, Lee. "Clio's Claim: The Role of Historical Research in Library and Information Science." *Library Trends* 32 (Spring 1984): 385–406.

Shiflett, Lee. "Louis Shores and Library History." *Libraries & Culture* 35, no. 1 (Winter 2000): 35–40.

Sidgwick, Henry. *Practical Ethics: a Collection of Addresses and Essays*. New York: Macmillan, 1898.

Sieber, Joan E. "Deception in Social Research I: Kinds of Deception and the Wrongs They May Involve." *IRB: Ethics and Human Research* 4, no. 9 (1982): 1–5.

Simon, Julian L., and Paul Burstein. *Basic Research Methods in Social Science: The Art of Empirical Investigation*. 3rd ed. New York: McGraw-Hill, 1985.

Singleton, Royce A. Jr., and Bruce C. Straits. *Approaches to Social Research*. 5th ed. New York: Oxford University Press, 2010.

Slater, Mel, Angus Antley, Adam Davison, David Swapp, Christopher Guger, Chris Barker, Nancy Pistrang, and Maria V. Sanchez-Vives. "A Virtual Reprise of the Stanley Milgram Obedience Experiments." *PLoS ONE*, no. 1 (2006).

Smith, Linda C. "Citation Analysis." *Library Trends* 30 (1981): 83–106.

Sommer, Robert. *A Practical Guide to Behavioral Research: Tools and Techniques*. 5th ed. New York: Oxford University Press, 2002.

Staines, Gail M. *Go Get That Grant! A Practical Guide for Libraries and Nonprofit Organizations*. Lanham, MD: Scarecrow, 2010.

Stanford, Phil. "Roots and Grafts on the Haley Story." *Washington Star*, April 8 1979, F4.

Stanley, Donald T., and Julian C. Campbell. *Experimental and Quasi-Experimental Designs for Research*. Chicago, IL: Rand McNally, 1963.

Steneck, Nicholas H. "Fostering Integrity in Research: Definitions, Current Knowledge, and Future Directions." *Science and Engineering Ethics* 12, no. 1 (2006): 53–74.

Stephen, Peter, and Susan Hornby. *Simple Statistics for Library and Information Professionals*. London: Library Association, 1995.

Stevens, Wallace. "Description without Place." *Sewanee Review* 53, no. 4 (1945): 559–65.

Stinson, Eddie Ray. "Diachronous Vs. Synchonous Study of Obsolescence." Ph.D. Dissertation, University of Illinois at Urbana-Champaign, 1981.

Strunk, William, and E. B. White. *The Elements of Style*. Ithaca, NY: Thrift Press, 1958.

Suarez, Doug. "Evaluating Qualitative Research Studies for Evidence Based Library and Information Practice." *Evidence Based Library and Information Practice* 5, no. 2 (2010), http://ejournals.library.ualberta.ca/index.php/EBLIP/article/view/7418.

Swisher, Robert, and Charles R. McClure. *Research for Decision Making: Methods for Librarians*. Chicago, IL: American Library Association, 1984.

Tague-Sutcliffe, Jean. "An Introduction to Informetrics." *Information Processing & Management* 28, no. 1 (1992): 1–3.

Tague-Sutcliffe, Jean. *Measuring Information: An Information Services Perspective*. San Diego, CA: Academic Press, 1995.

Tasker, Elizabeth, and Frances B. Holt-Underwood. "Feminist Research Methodologies in Historic Rhetoric and Composition: An Overview of Scholarship from the 1970s to the Present." *Rhetoric Review* 27, no. 1 (2009): 54–71.

Taylor, Helen. "The Griot from Tennessee:' the Saga of Alex Haley's Roots." *Critical Quarterly* 37, no. 2 (1995): 46–62.

Taylor, Robert S. "Question-Negotiation and Information Seeking in Libraries." *College & Research Libraries* 29 (May 1968): 178–94.

Thomas, Fannette H. "The Black Mother Goose: Collective Biography of African-American Children's Librarians." In *Culture Keepers: Enlightening and Empowering Our Communities, Proceedings of the First National Conference of African American Librarians, September 4–6, 1992, Columbus, Ohio*, edited by Stanton F. Biddle and Members of the BCALA NCAAL Conference Proceedings Committee. Chicago, IL: American Library Association, 1992.

Thelwall, Michael. *Introduction to Webometrics: Quantitative Web Research for the Social Sciences*. San Rafael, CA: Morgan and Claypool, 2009.

Thelwall, Mike. "Bibliometrics to Webometrics." *Journal of Information Science* 34, no. 4 (August 2008): 605–21.

Thompson, C. Seymour. "Director's Introduction." In *A Survey of Libraries in the United States*, 9–14. Chicago, IL: American Library Association, 1926.

Thompson, C. S. "Do We Want a Library Science?" *Library Journal* 56, no. 13 (1931): 581–88.

Thurston, Zora Neale. *Dust Tracks on a Road: An Autobiography*. Philadelphia, PA: J. B. Lippincott, 1942.

"Traffic Safety Facts 2009." Washington: U.S. Department of Transportation, National Highway Traffic Safety Administration, 2010.

Tucker, John Mark. "Clio's Workshop: Resources for Historical Study in American Librarianship." *Libraries & Culture* 35, no. 1 (Winter 2000): 192–214.

Tukey, John W. *Exploratory Data Analysis*. Reading, MA: Addison-Wesley, 1977.

"2009 Ohio Public Library Statistics." State Library of Ohio, http://www.library.ohio.gov/sites/default/files/LPD_09_Ohio_Library_Statistic_Full_File.xls.

Van Fleet, Connie. "Evaluating Collections." In *Library Evaluation: A Casebook and Can-Do Guide*, edited by Danny P. Wallace and Connie Van Fleet, 117–28. Englewood, CO: Libraries Unlimited, 2001.

Van Fleet, Connie, and Joan C. Durrance. "Public Library Research: Use and Utility." In *Research Issues in Public Librarianship: Trends for the Future*, edited by Joy Greiner, 1–16. Westport, CT: Greenwood, 1994.

Van Fleet, Connie, and Danny P. Wallace. "Beals Revisited: Sad Tidings, Lamentations, and Anti-Research." *RQ* 31, no. 3 (1992): 301–05.

Veblen, Thorstein. "Evolution of the Scientific Point of View." *University of California Chronicle* 10 (1908): 32.

Wagner, Cassie, Meseret D. Gebremichael, Mary K Taylor, and Michael J Soltys. "Disappearing Act: Decay of Uniform Resource Locators in Health Care Management Journals." *Journal of the Medical Library Association* 97, no. 2 (2009): 122–30.

Walker, Shannon. "Career Motivations of the Scientist-Turned-Librarian: A Secondary Analysis of WILIS Data." *Issues in Science and Technology Librarianship* 64 (Winter 2011), http://www.istl.org/11-winter/refereed4.html.

Wallace, Danny P. *Knowledge Management: Historical and Cross-Disciplinary Themes*. Westport, CT: Libraries Unlimited, 2007.

Wallace, Danny P., and Connie Van Fleet. *Library Evaluation: A Casebook and Can-Do Guide*. Englewood, CO: Libraries Unlimited, 2001.

Wallace, Danny P., Connie Van Fleet, and Lacey J. Downs. "The Research Core of the Knowledge Management Literature." *International Journal of Information Management* 31, no. 1 (2011): 14–20.

Walters, Mary W. *Write and Effective Funding Application: A Guide for Researchers and Scholars*. Baltimore, MD: Johns Hopkins University Press, 2009.

Weber, Robert L. *More Random Walks in Science: An Anthology.* Bristol: Institute of Physics, 1982.

Weinberg, Bella Haas. "The Earliest Hebrew Citation Indexes." *Journal of the American Society for Information Science* 48, no. 4 (1997): 318–30.

Weller, Toni, ed. *Information History in the Modern World: Histories of the Information Age.* New York: Palgrave Macmillan, 2011.

Wertheimer Andrew B., and Donald G. Davis, Jr., eds. *Library History Research in America: Essays Commemorating the Fiftieth Anniversary of the Library History Round Table, American Library Association.* Washington: Library of Congress Center for the Book, 2000.

White, Howard D., Sebastian K. Boell, Hairong Yu, Mari Davis, Concepcion C. Wilson, and Fletcher T. H. Cole. "Libcitations: A Measure for Comparative Assessment of Book Publications in the Humanities and Social Sciences." *Journal of the American Society for Information Science and Technology* 60, no. 6 (June 2009): 1083–96.

White, Marilyn Domas, and Emily E. Smith. "Content Analysis: A Flexible Methodology." *Library Trends* 55, no. 1 (2006): 22–45.

Whittier, John Greenleaf. *The Complete Works of John Greenleaf Whittier.* Boston, MA: Houghton Mifflin, 1894.

Wiegand, Shirley A., and Wayne A. Wiegand. *Books on Trial: Red Scare in the Heartland.* Norman: University of Oklahoma Press, 2007.

Wiegand Wayne A., and Donald G. Davis, eds. *Encyclopedia of Library History.* New York: Garland, 1994.

Wilcox, Linda J. "Authorship: The Coin of the Realm, the Source of Complaints." *Journal of the American Medical Association* 280, no. 3 (1998): 216–17.

Wilson, Louis R. *The Geography of Reading: A Study of the Distribution and Status of Libraries in the United States.* Chicago, IL: American Library Association and University of Chicago Press, 1938.

Wolfram, Dietmar. *Applied Informetrics for Information Retrieval Research.* Westport, CT: Libraries Unlimited, 2003.

Wu C. F. Jeff, and Michael S. Hamada. *Experiments: Planning, Analysis, and Optimization.* 2nd ed. Hoboken, NJ: Wiley, 2009.

Young, Arthur P. *Books for Sammies: The American Library Association and World War I*, Beta Phi Chapbook. Pittsburgh, PA: Beta Phi Mu, 1981.

Zach, Lisl. "Using a Multiple-Case Studies Design to Investigate the Information-Seeking Behavior of Arts Administrators." *Library Trends* 55, no. 1 (Summer 2006): 4–21.

Zboray, Ronald J. *A Fictive People: Antebellum Economic Development and the American Reading Public.* New York: Oxford University Press, 1993.

Zhang, Ying, Bernard J. Jansen, and Amanda Spink. "Time Series Analysis of a Web Search Engine Transaction Log." *Information Processing and Management* 45, no. 2 (March 2009): 230–45.

Zimbardo, Philip G. *The Lucifer Effect: Understanding How Good People Turn Evil.* New York: Random House, 2007.

Zimbardo, Philip G. "On the Ethics of Intervention in Human Psychological Research: With Special Reference to the Stanford Prison Experiment" *Cognition* 2, no. 2 (1974): 243–56.

Zimbardo, Philip G. "Revisiting the Stanford Prison Experiment: A Lesson in the Power of Situation." *The Chronicle of Higher Education* 53, no. 30 (2007): B6.

Zipf, G. K. *Human Behavior and the Principle of Least Effort.* New York: Hafner, 1949.

INDEX

AASL/Highsmith Research Grant, 339
Abu Ghraib Prison, 74
Academic Libraries Survey, 146
Accessibility, 345–46; intellectual, 345; physical, 345
Action, 22, 61, 63, 145, 350; and evaluation, 63; and research, 61
Action plan, 46, 131, 334, 350
"Address on Laying the Corner-Stone of the Bunker Hill Monument," 265
Administrative review, 63
ALISE. *See* Association for Library and Information Science Education
Alternative hypothesis, 308–9, 315, 325
Ambrose, Stephen, 85
American Association of School Librarians, 99
American Association of University Professors, 87
American Council on Education, 87
American Libraries, 98–100, 103, 110
American Library Association, 10–11, 87, 98, 162, 173, 190–91, 221, 339; Code of Ethics, 11, 87, 191; Library History Round Table, 173
"*American Library History: A Comprehensive Guide to the Literature*," 173
American Medical Association, 70
American Society for Information Science & Technology, 87, 98, 339
Analysis of covariance, 325
Analysis of variance, 325

Analytical tools, 25, 50, 53, 56, 85, 105, 121, 266, 269
ANCOVA. *See* Analysis of covariance
Animal subjects, 69, 115
Annual Register of Grant Support, 338
Annual Review of Information Science & Technology, 98
Anonymity, 80, 82, 181, 187, 206–7
ANOVA. *See* Analysis of variance
Anthropology, 23, 26, 160
Apology (Socrates), 1
Archaeology, 160
Aristotle, 343
Arithmetic mean. *See* Mean
ARL. *See* Association of Research Libraries
ARL Statistics. See Association of Research Libraries
Arming America: The Origins of a National Gun Culture, 172
Artificial environment, 227, 228, 232
Artistic research, 27
Arts & Humanities Citation Index, 242, 253, 256
Assent, 80; definition, 80
Association for Library and Information Science Education, 146, 339
Association of Research Libraries, 13, 15, 146, 163, 173, 175, 221, 277; *ARL Statistics*, 13, 15, 163
Assumption, 28, 30, 43, 49–50, 106, 121; definition, 49
ATLAS.ti, 270

Authority, parental, 9–10, 80

Authors: qualifications, 108

Authorship, 86–87, 255; characteristics, 86; honorary, 87; multiple, 86, 255

Babylonian Talmud, 242

Bancroft Prize, 172

Beals, Ralph A., 99

Belief, 8, 10–12, 28, 137, 167, 181–82; derived from authority, 10–11; derived from experience, 10; personal, 10

Bellesiles, Michael A., 172

Belmont Report, 74–77; basic ethical principles, 75

Beneficence, 75–77

Berger, Peter L., 6

Bias, 8, 20, 85, 102, 106–7, 162, 164, 181, 219, 231–32, 235; in historical research, 167–68

Bibliographic coupling, 259

Bibliometrics, 36, 123, 237, 241–60; context, 242; definition, 241; origins, 242; uses, 256

Bierce, Ambrose, 159, 175

Books in Print, 97

Boston Public Library, 168

Box plot, 327–28

Bradford, Samuel C., 245–47, 249, 254

Bradford multiplier, 246

Bradford's Law, 245–49, 254

British Library, 245

British Museum Library, 245

Budget, 90, 115, 118, 124–28, 132, 145, 334–35

Burstein, Paul, 23, 31–32

Byproducts of research and evaluation projects, 34, 123

Calculations,137, 142, 270, 272–73, 292, 328; definition, 268

Calibration, 141, 143–44, 215

Campbell, Donald T., 228, 230, 232–33, 235, 237

Carlyle, Thomas, 343

Carnegie, Andrew, 340

Carroll Preston Baber Research Grant, 339

Case study, 23, 180, 213, 216–19; advantages, 218; disadvantages, 218–19

Catalog of Federal Domestic Assistance, 336

Causation, 24, 227, 232–33, 238, 321–23; and correlation, 321, 323

Cell size, 151

Celsus, 67, 69

Census, 145–49, 313; definition, 145

Centrality, 143, 218, 293, 295, 297–300, 303, 327; definition, 295; measures, 297, 298, 299

Central tendency. *See* Centrality

Cervantes, Miguel de, 241

CFDA. See Catalog of Federal Domestic Assistance

Change, 349

Charts. *See* Graphs

Chatman, Elfreda, 33

Chicago Manual of Style, 275

Children, 6, 9, 49, 72, 75, 78, 80, 91–92, 230, 338; definition, 80

Chi-square, 313–16, 328

Chi-square test of goodness of fit, 313, 328; notation, 314

Chi-square test of proportion, 315

Chi-square tests: assumptions, 315

Citation, 85; distinguished from reference, 251; motives, 253, 254

Citation analysis, 237, 241–43, 251–60; assumptions, 253; context, 242–43; definition, 242, 251–52; origins, 242; problems, 255, 256; sources of data, 252; uses, 257, 259

Citation indexes and indexing, 242, 252–53, 255–56, 259

Citation study. *See* Citation analysis

Civilization and Ethics, 67, 92

Classification, 23–24

Clinton, Bill, 72

CLIR. *See* Council on Library and Information Resources

Co-citation, 259

Codes of ethics, 11, 68, 87, 191

Coefficient, 318, 320, 323

Collaboration, 43, 84, 86–87; conflicts, 84, 86–87

Collective biography, 166

College & Research Libraries, 58, 98

Colloquialisms, 109

Commission on Research Integrity, 84–85

Common Rule. *See* 45 CFR 46

Comparable groups, 228, 230–31: definition, 228

Comparison, 24, 31

Compliance, 43, 60, 78, 92, 128, 132

Conan Doyle, Sir Arthur, 136, 265

Conclusion: deduction, 11

Conference proposals, 61

Conferences and other meetings, 61

Confidentiality, 80, 82, 85, 162, 181, 187, 203, 206–7

Conflicts of interest, 84, 87–89

Content analysis, 166, 223
Context, 7, 20, 29, 45, 254, 294, 344
Contextualization, 56, 344, 346
Control group, 20, 32, 230–31, 233, 235–37, 313, 325
Controls: definition, 228, 235
Convenience sample, 151, 152
Coontz, Stephanie, 97
Copernican theory. *See* Copernicus, Nicolaus
Copernicus, Nicolaus, 6
Core literatures, 256
Correlation, 16, 22, 257, 317–23; calculation, 319, 320; and causation, 321; formula, 319; frequency, 318; negative, 317; Pearson product-moment, 319; positive, 317; rank, 321; rank-frequency, 321
Cost/benefit analysis, 60
Cost-effectiveness, 33–34, 102
Council on Library and Information Resources, 338
Cowper, William, 227
Criterion variable, 325
Critical value, 315
Critical values, table of, 314
Cultural assumptions, 167
Culture of evaluation, 63
Culture of research and evaluation, 348
Cumulation, 21
Cumulative Advantage Principle, 33, 43, 260
Curiosity, 8, 9, 20, 41, 344, 350
Cybermetrics, 243

Data, 50–51, 53, 82; context, 51, 53, 121, 198; personal, 82; primary, 50–51, 53, 56, 82, 121, 198; sources, 51
Data analysis, 3, 40, 50, 53–56, 58, 63, 84, 100, 104, 121, 171–72, 223, 237, 265–74, 286–88, 296, 344; concerns, 266, 267; purposes, 265
Data analysis plan, 50, 121
Data consolidation, 53
Data gathering, 3, 12, 16, 18, 39, 40, 49–52, 63, 73, 91–92, 104, 121, 146, 148, 152, 160, 171–73, 182, 214, 218–19, 223, 228, 252, 266, 347
Data gathering plan, 50, 121
Data gathering tools, 51
Data interpretation, 53, 56, 105, 107, 165–68, 172, 193, 230, 268, 307
Data matrix model, 268–69, 296–97; implemented in a spreadsheet, 270; implemented in IBM SPSS Statistics, 270–74
Data organization, 268
Data presentation, 274–85

Data reduction, 25, 28, 137
Data summarization, 56
Data validation, 53
Debriefing, 83–84
Deception, 82–84; levels, 83; motivations, 83
Decision making, 14–15, 19–22, 24, 39, 40, 49, 58–60, 63, 69, 132, 266, 332, 343–44, 346–48, 350
Declaration of Helsinki, 74
Deduction, 8, 11–15, 29
Deductive reasoning. *See* Deduction
Definition of terms, 49
Degrees of freedom, 301, 309–16; bivariate tests, 312; notation, 310; univariate tests, 311, 313
De Medicina, 67
Dependent variable, 227, 231–33, 236–38, 321–26
Description, 23, 25, 28–29, 31, 56, 100, 136, 180, 292; contrasted with measurement, 136
"Description Without Place," 179
Descriptive research and evaluation, 15, 26–31, 48, 104, 120, 145–46, 172, 179–223, 232, 267; categories, 180; definition, 31, 179, 180
Design research, 27
Developmentally disabled subjects, 80
Devil's Dictionary, The, 159
Diachronous study of obsolescence, 250
Dialectical processing, 286
Dirac, Paul, 97
Direct observation, 180, 211–15; advantages, 213; disadvantages, 21–14; implementing, 212; qualitative approaches, 219
Dirksen, Everett M., 331
Discovery, 110
Dishonesty, 8, 84–88, 106–7, 145
Dispersion, 143, 149, 150, 187, 218, 223, 293, 295, 297, 300–303; definition, 295; measures, 300, 301, 302
Display phenomenon, 32, 91
Disraeli, Benjamin, 291
Disynchronous study of obsolescence, 251
Don Quixote, 241
Dr. Jekyll and Mr. Hyde, 331
Dust Tracks on a Road, 39

80/20 Rule, 249
Eisenhower, Dwight D., 113
"Elephant's Child, The," 113
Emergent theory, 30
Encyclopedia of Associations, 338
Epistemology, 6

Error, 51, 102, 105, 148, 161, 199, 203, 223, 256, 306, 327; in research reports, 107. *See also* Statistical testing
Estimation, 23, 53, 292
Ethics, 11, 51, 67–89, 92, 172–73, 191, 214; definition, 67, 68; practical, 68; professional values, 68
Ethnograph, 270
Ethnographic observation, 219
Ethnography, 20, 23, 26, 219
Evaluation: definition, 18; historical methods, 173
Eves, Howard W., 97
Evidence-based practice, 1, 348, 350
"Evolution of the Scientific Point of View," 5
Excel (spreadsheet), 154, 268, 270, 276
Experience, 7, 9–10; personal, 8–9; vicarious, 9–10
Experienced reality, 237
Experimental and Quasi-Experimental Designs for Research, 228
Experimental designs, 228, 232–35, 324
Experimental group, 233, 235–37, 313
Experimental research, 12, 15, 20, 24, 28, 30–32, 48, 104, 120, 123, 160, 168, 172, 227–37; definition, 31, 227–28
Exponential curve, 247, 249, 260, 305
Exponential Distribution. *See* Exponential curve
Ex Post Facto Study, 237

Fabrication, 85
Fact, 7–8, 30, 188–91, 254
Fakery, 162
Falsification, 85, 172
Faulty data, 58, 101, 121, 266–67
Feasibility, 60, 123
Federal Register, 336
Feminist research, 27
Fetuses, 78, 80
Fiction Catalog, 221
Field notes, 53, 161, 268, 286–87
Focus groups, 26, 51, 173, 186
Forced theory, 30
Ford, Henry, 340
45 CFR 46, 77, 78, 80, 83
Foundation: definition, 337
Foundation Center, 337–38; cooperating collections, 338
Foundation Directory, 338
Foundation Grants Index, 338
Frequency distribution table, 296–97
Funding for research and evaluation, 77–78, 86, 88, 90, 92, 114–16, 119, 123–26, 128, 130, 132–33, 149, 331–40; agencies, 335; associations, 338–39; corporations and businesses, 339–40; criteria, 332–34; external, 332; foundations, 337, 338; governmental and quasi-governmental agencies, 335–37; institutional, 332; personal, 332; sources, 331

Gabor, Dennis, 343
Gantt chart, 121
Garfield's Law of Concentration, 249
Goldhor, Herbert, 18, 65, 197
Google Docs, 203
Gosset, William Sealy, 324
Graphs, 276; bar, 279; column, 276–77, 279; concerns, 276; definition, 276; line, 281, 283; pie charts, 280
Groos, Ole V., 247
Groos droop, 247
Grounded theory, 30
Group interviews, 186
Guidelines, professional, 11, 15, 34, 56, 100, 212
Guidelines for Behavioral Performance of Reference and Information Service Providers, 212
Guide to Reference, 221
Gwynn, Nancy, 332, 340

Haley, Alex, 85, 162
Harm, avoidance of, 33, 68–69, 72, 75–78, 80, 82, 115, 288, 309
Harvest of a Quite Eye, 291
Hawthorne effect, 215
Health Research Extension Act, 84
Hippocratic Oath, 69
Historians, 160–61, 173
Historical analysis: nontraditional, 166; traditional, 164–65
Historical distance, 160
Historical research, 16, 26, 31, 159–75, 200, 232, 237; bias, 167; context, 168; data analysis, 172; deadlines, 172; definition, 31; interpretation, 165, 166, 167, 168; project conclusion, 171, 172; research question, 168, 171
Historical sources: accuracy, 163; authenticity, 162; bias, 164; corroboration, 163; detail, 164; evaluation, 162, 163, 164; meaning, 163; style, 164; witness competence, 164; witness credibility, 163
Historicism, 6, 167
History: as discipline, 175; definition, 159, 160, 161; origin of word, 160

History effect, in experimental research, 230

"History of Comparative Anatomy. Part I: A Statistical Analysis of the Literature, The," 242

Hitler, Adolf, 85, 162

Holmes, Sherlock, 136

House Science and Technology Committee, 84

How to Lie With Statistics, 145

Huff, Darrell, 145

Human Behavior and the Principle of Least Effort, 243

Humane treatment, 69–84

Humanistic research, 27

Human radiation studies, 72

Human subjects, 69–84, 90, 128, 132, 228, 260

Hurston, Zora Neale, 39

Hypothesis, 14–16, 20, 117, 121, 145, 252; definition, 48. *See also* Alternative hypothesis; Null hypothesis

Hypothesis testing. *See* Statistical testing

Ideological analysis, 166

Ideology, 90, 167

If-then sequences, 198–200

Image analysis, 166

IMLS. *See* Institute of Museum and Library Services

Impressionistic research, 27

Incomplete cases. *See* Missing variables

Independent variable, 227, 231–33, 236, 238, 321, 324–26

Induction, 8, 12–15, 29

Induction-deduction cycle, 13–15

Information Seeking Behavior Model, 33

Information Technology & Libraries, 100

Informed consent, 69, 74, 76–80, 82–83, 347; waiver, 83

Informetrics, 242

Ingenta Research Award, 339

In-person interviews, 180–83; advantages, 180–84, 186; definition, 180; disadvantages, 181–82

Insider/outsider phenomenon, 91–92

Institute for Scientific Information, 242, 249, 252–53, 255–56, 259, 339

Institute of Museum and Library Services, 145–46, 334, 336

Institutional repository, 61

Institutional review board, 51, 78–80, 83, 132, 205, 260; exemption from review, 80

Instrumentation, in experimental research, 231

Interval measurement scale, 105, 137, 140–43, 195, 276, 281, 297–300, 313, 318, 321

Interview schedule, 182

Introduction to Scientific Research in Librarianship, An, 18

Inventing the Future, 343

Investigations and Oversight Subcommittee, House Science and Technology Committee, 84

Investigator: qualifications, 335

Invisible college, 346

Invisible Man, The, 331

IRB. *See* Institutional review board

ISI. *See* Institute for Scientific Information

Jargon, 109, 115, 120, 196, 197, 203, 291

Journal Citation Reports, 242, 253

Journal of Documentation, 110, 262

Journal of the American Society for Information Science & Technology, 97, 98, 100, 110, 262, 263

Journal publication, 61

Justice, 75–77

Just So Stories, 113

Keats, John, 6

Kellogg Foundation. *See* W. K. Kellogg Foundation

Kendall's Tau, 321

Kipling, Rudyard, 113, 120, 121

Knowledge, 6, 8–12, 21, 24–25, 27, 39, 45, 56, 58, 63–64, 68–69, 89, 91–92, 103, 106, 115, 118–19, 133, 189–91, 223, 237, 242, 287; advancement of, 21, 24, 27, 68, 133, 287, 336, 343, 345–46, 349; sociology of, 6

Knowledge-eliciting questions. *See* Questions, knowledge-eliciting

Kriegsman, John, 331

Kuhlthau, Carol, 33

Kuhn, Thomas, 25

Ladies' Home Journal, 343

Lang, Andrew, 291

Learning: approaches to, 8–15

Libraries: as a public good, 7, 33

Libraries Unlimited, 110

Library and Book Trade Annual, 338, 339

Library & Information Science Editors group, 86

Library Evaluation: A Casebook and Can-Do Guide, 350

Library History Round Table, 173

Library Hotline, 99

Library Journal, 98, 99, 103, 221
Library Quarterly, 97, 110, 209
Library Trends, 98, 100
Library Visit Study, The, 107
Library War Service, 162
Likert scale. *See* Questions, Likert scale
Lippmann, Walter, 135
List checking, 221; benefits and disadvantages, 221; steps, 221
Literary analysis, 166
Literature: categorization, 99–100
Literature review, 12, 44–46, 56, 100, 102–104, 106–7, 118–20, 165, 333, 335, 346
Literature search, 44–46, 261; purposes, 44
Little Science, Big Science, 115, 243
Logic, 11–15, 27, 103, 107–8, 200, 328
Logical positivism, 25, 28–29
Loleta D. Fyan Grant, 339
Lotka, Alfred J., 243, 245
Lotka's Law, 243, 245, 247, 256
Luckmann, Thomas, 6

Mackay, Alan L., 291
MANOVA. *See* Multiple analysis of variance
Mathematical Circles Adieu, 97
Matthew Effect, 260
Maturation, in experimental research, 230
Mean, 13, 140–41, 150, 270, 272, 279, 298–99, 302–4, 310, 323; comparison, 323–25; formula, 299; notation, 299
Measure: definition, 50
Measurement, 15–17, 23–24, 31, 104–5, 135–45, 156, 215, 227; characteristics, 136, 137; concerns, 143, 144; continuous, 143; deception, 144; definition, 135, 136; direct, 136; discrete, 143; indirect, 136; manifestations, 137; scales, 137–42, 297
Median, 56, 142–43, 251, 270, 272, 293, 297–98, 303–4, 310
Medical research, 70–72
Mentally disabled subjects, 80
Method: definition, 30
Methodology, 30, 45, 48–50, 56, 84, 98, 100, 103–6, 117–18, 120–21, 123, 254, 286, 344, 348; definition, 30; design, 48–50, 56
Milgram, Stanley, 72
Million Random Digits with 100,000 Normal Deviates, A, 153
Misinterpretation, 188
Missing cases, 266–67
Missing data, 171, 266–67, 295
Missing variables, 267
Mode, 270, 272, 297, 303–4, 310

"Models of Collaboration & Competition: The University Expectation," 211
More Random Walks in Science, 135
Mortality, in experimental research, 231
Multiple analysis of variance, 325
Multiple treatment interference, 232
Myrdal, Gunnar, 91

Narrative, 23, 29, 118, 121, 128, 159, 160, 163, 165, 173, 334
National Center for Education Statistics, 15, 146, 163, 173
National Commission for the Protection of Human Subjects of Biomedical and Behavioral Research, 74
National Endowment for the Arts, 337
National Endowment for the Humanities, 337
National Institutes of Health, 77
National Research Act, 72
National Science Foundation, 337
Natural history, 160
Naturalistic research, 27
Natural Sciences and Engineering Research Council, 85
NCES. *See* National Center for Education Statistics
Necessity in causation, 232–33, 236, 321–23
Negatively skewed curve, 304
Neonates, 78, 80
Newton, Sir Isaac, 6
New York Public Library, 168
Nietzsche, Friedrich, 5, 18
Nixon, Richard, 113
No Child Left Behind Act of 2001, 340
NOIR mnemonic, 142
Nominal measurement scale, 105, 137–39, 142–43, 276, 280–81, 297, 313, 316, 318, 324–25
Nonequivalent control group design, 237
Nonlinear relationship, 317
Nonnumeric research, 28
Nonprobability sample: definition, 151
Nonverbal cues, 184, 185
Normal curve, 296, 302–4, 313; areas under, 303; characteristics, 303; importance, 304
Normal distribution. *See* Normal curve
Normative statistics. *See* Statistics, descriptive
Null hypothesis, 307–9, 315–16, 325
Numbers, 270
Nuremberg Code, 70, 74
Nuremberg Medical Trials, 70
NVivo, 270

Obedience studies, 72
Objectivity, 8, 20, 26–27, 106, 160
Obsolescence, 249; definition, 249; measures, 250
"Ode on a Grecian Urn," 6
Office of Human Subjects Research, 77
Office of Research Integrity, 84
One group posttest design, 235, 236
One group pretest/posttest design, 236
One shot case study. *See* One group posttest design
Ontology, 6
Open-ended interviews, 186
Operationalization, 49, 137
Oral history, 160, 173
Ordinal measurement scale, 105, 137, 139–40, 142–43, 276, 281, 297–99, 313, 318, 321
Outliers, 298, 326–28; identification, 327
Out-of-range values, 267
Ownership of data, results, reports, and byproducts, 123

Paleontology, 160
Paradigm, 25–30, 137, 186, 219
Pareto distribution, 249
Pasteur, Louis, 24, 211
Peer review, 97, 98
Percentage, 107, 195, 277, 292, 294–97, 303
Person: personnel, 123; in proposal writing, 130
Perspective, 283
Peshkin, Alan, 28
Phobias, 7
Plagiarism, 85–86; self, 85–86
Policy, 14–15, 22, 61, 63, 102–3, 349
Politics, 89–92; and locales for study, 89; and what can be studied, 89; and who can be studied, 90; and who can conduct studies, 90; and who must conduct studies, 92
Population, 33, 49, 69, 75, 77–78, 90–91, 103–4, 106–7, 120, 145–56; definition, 49, 145; homogeneity, 149; size, 149
Positively skewed curve, 304–5
Post hoc fallacy, 321
Posttest-only only control group design, 235
Power, 309
Prediction, 21, 121, 175
Predictor variable, 325–26
Pre-Experimental Designs, 235
Pregnant women, 78–80
Preplanning, 40, 44, 63
Pretest/posttest control group design, 32, 233

"Preventing Conflicts of Interest in Government Sponsored Research at Universities," 87
Price, Derek J. de Solla, 33, 115, 331
Primary source, 31, 160–61, 165–66, 172; assessment, 161; confidentiality, 162; lapse of time between event and account, 161; purpose, 162
Principle of Least Effort, 243, 245, 259
Prisoners, 79
Pritchard, Alan, 241
Probability, 151–52, 231, 308–10, 316, 325; notation, 309
Probability sample, 151–52
Probability threshold, 309, 325
Problem solving, 2, 63, 114, 347
Problem statement, 44–46, 48, 56, 100, 103–4, 106, 118–19
Productivity, 242–48; author, 243; journal, 245–48; word frequency, 243–45
Professional literature, 61, 97–110, 344–45
Project plan. *See* proposal
Project timeline. *See* Work plan
Proof, 8
Proportion, 280, 292–95
Proportional sample, 154–56
Proposal, 61, 80, 85, 107, 113–33, 332–35, 338, 340; costs, 133; elements, 116, 117, 118, 119, 120, 121, 123, 124, 125, 126, 127, 128, 130; as investment, 132–33; negotiation and revision, 132; as persuasive writing, 113, 116, 128, 130–31, 332; purposes, 113, 114, 115, 116; review and approval, 132; as technical document, 130; writing, 130, 131
Psychobiography, 166
Psychohistory, 166
Public good, 7, 33, 68–69
Public Libraries, 99
Public Library Association, 99
Public Library Survey, 146
Public Opinion, 135
Purposive sample, 152

Qualitative interviews, 186
Qualitative paradigm, 26–30, 186, 219
Qualitative research, 25–30, 50, 53, 136, 152, 180, 216, 223, 266, 268, 286–87, 323; characteristics, 27; contrasted with quantitative research, 29; data analysis, 53, 56, 268, 270, 286–87; focuses, 28; foundations, 28; purposes, 28
Qualitative software, 270
Quantitative history, 166

Quantitative paradigm, 26
Quantitative research, 12, 15, 25–30, 50, 53, 56, 105, 136–37, 143, 152, 171–72, 180, 186–87, 195, 214, 219, 223, 227, 242–43, 260, 266, 268, 270, 286–87, 323, 328; contrasted with qualitative research, 29
Quantity across values, 138–42
Quantity within values, 138–42
Quasi-experimental designs, 236–37, 324
Quasi-governmental agency: definition, 335
Quattro Pro (spreadsheet), 270
Questionnaire, 25, 31, 48, 51, 53, 73, 82, 90, 121, 124, 126, 186–207; administration, 203, 205–7; advantages, 186–87; analysis, 203; answer space, 201; appearance, 201; cover letters, 205; design, 189–204; disadvantages, 187–88; distribution, 205–6; expert advice, 203; follow-up, 206–7; incentives, 205–6; instructions, definitions, and directions, 199; layout, 200; multiple-page, 201; online, 201–3; online, administration, 203; online, advantages, 202; online, disadvantages, 202; pretesting, 203; size, 200
Questions, 26–28, 31, 33–36, 41, 85, 180–84, 186–202; arrangement, 199–200; attitude, 191; behavioral, 190, 191; categorization, 189; categorization by purpose, 189; categorization by structure, 191; closedended; factual, 189, 190; independence, 198; knowledge-eliciting, 190; Likert scale, 194, 195, 196; multiple response list, 192, 193; open-ended, 192; opinion, 191; personal, 197; projection, 191; ranked list, 193; self-assessment, 191; single response forced choice, 193; true/false, 193, 194; wording, 196
Quota sample, 152

Rand Corporation, 153
Random number generator, 154
Random numbers, 153–54
Random sample, 152–54, 183, 315; simple, 152–53
Ranganathan, S. R., 252
Range, 300
Rare events, 327
Rating scale. *See* Questions, Likert scale
Ratio, 292–96
Ratio measurement scale, 105, 137, 141–43, 276, 281, 283, 297–302, 313, 318, 321, 324–26
Raymond's Reports, 242
Recording processes, 182, 184, 214, 286

Redundant check, 198
Reference: distinguished from citation, 251
Reference analysis, 252
Reference & User Services Association, 100, 212; Guidelines for Behavioral Performance of Reference and Information Service Providers, 212
Reference & User Services Quarterly, 98, 100, 110, 330
Reflective practice, 4, 41, 63, 287, 343, 348, 350
Regression, 281, 325–26
Regression toward the mean, experimental research, 231
Reliability, 3, 15–20, 50, 53, 56, 104, 161, 163, 172, 181, 184, 187, 213, 215, 219, 266, 292; intercoder, 17, 215
Reports, 26, 60, 86, 97–110, 123, 165, 286, 345–46; elements, 100–101; evaluation criteria, 101–9; literary qualities, 108
Resampling, 267
Research and evaluation: benefits, 32; benefits to society, 33; benefits to the institution, 34; benefits to the investigator, 35; benefits to the profession, 33; characteristics, 19, 344; as a cycle, 2, 29; definition, 18; levels, 23; methodologies, 30; nature, 6; origins of ideas, 41, 43; process, 13, 16, 40, 333, 335, 350; purpose, 343; relationship, 1, 35, 36, 40, 63
Research and evaluation literature, 2, 97–110, 202, 345, 348
Research conduct, 84–89
Research methods courses, 98, 348
Research question, 14–15, 20, 44, 48, 104, 117, 145, 168, 171, 316, 319, 324–25; definition, 48; research, applied, 24, 160; research, basic, 24, 337
Respect for persons, 75–77
Respondent stress, 181
Response rate, 187–88
"Responsibilities of Awardee and Applicant Institutions for Dealing With and Reporting Possible Misconduct in Science," 84
Results, 15–22, 24, 26, 31, 33–48, 40, 43, 45–46, 50, 53–58, 60, 118, 132, 148, 150, 156, 165, 167, 206–7, 230, 232, 266, 286, 328; anticipated, 118, 121–23; implications, 58; limitations, 58; negative, 266; and policy, 15; processing, 53; reporting, 56–58, 60–61, 63, 69, 72, 77, 85, 88, 100–101, 103, 105–7, 109, 114, 115, 123, 126
Reverence for life, 92

Rockefeller, John D., 340
Roots: The Saga of an American Family, 85

Sabotage, 188–89, 347
Sample, 3, 12, 14, 15, 16, 49, 73, 104, 105, 107, 120, 135, 145, 146, 147, 148, 149, 150, 151, 152, 153, 154, 157, 158, 184, 188, 189, 199, 204, 234, 251, 252, 268, 293, 300, 301, 303, 314, 315, 316, 321; definition, 49, 146; nonprobability, 151; quality, 148
Sample size, 148; calculators, 150; determination, 150–51; factors, 148–50; tables, 150
Sampling, 20, 104, 107, 146–56, 183–85, 266, 292, 313; avoidance of waste, 147; data handling, 148; ease of analysis, 148; economics, 147; purpose, 147; timeliness, 148
Sampling frame, 147, 154; definition, 146, 147
Santa Claus, 7
Sartor Resartus, 343
Saturation sample, 152
Scaling, 283
"Scandal in Bohemia, A," 265
Scarecrow Press, 110
Scatter plot, 281
Schedule of completion. *See* Work plan
Schön, Donald, 41, 287, 288
Schweitzer, Albert, 67, 92
Science, 110
Science Citation Index, 242, 256, 262
Scientific American, 110
Scientometrics, 244
Secondary source, 161, 172
Selection bias, 231
Selection/bias interaction, 232
Self-addressed stamped envelope, 205
Self-regulation, 68
Serendipity, 180–81, 192, 218
Shepard's Citations, 242, 259
Sidgwick, Henry, 68
Significance, 53, 56, 121, 292, 309; practical, 53, 58, 101, 309; statistical, 53, 58, 101, 292, 294, 306, 309, 315
Simon, Julian L., 23, 31–32
Single group pretest/posttest design, 324
SIRSI Leadership in Library Technology Grant, 339
Six Crises, 113
Small World Theory, 33
Social Construction of Reality, The, 6
Social history, 160
Social Psychology Network, 154
Social Sciences Citation Index, 242, 255, 256
Socrates, 1

Solomon four group design, 233, 235
Spearman's Rho, 321
Spreadsheet, 53, 268–70, 288, 328
SPSS. *See* Statistical Package for the Social Sciences
Standard deviation, 150, 270, 272, 293, 300–301; calculation, 301; formula, 300; notation, 300
Standard error of the mean, 150
Standards, 11–12, 34, 36, 53, 56, 60, 68, 78, 87–89, 92, 100, 139, 190–91, 212, 344
Stanford Prison Experiment, 72, 73, 74
Stanley, Julian T., 228, 230, 232–33, 235, 237
"Statement of Ethics for Editors of Library and Information Science Journals, A," 86
Static group comparison design, 236
Statistica, 154, 270
Statistical Analysis System, 154
Statistical Bibliography in Relation to the Growth of Modern Civilization, 242
Statistical Package for the Social Sciences, 154, 270–74, 295
Statistical software, 270
Statistical testing, 12, 16, 21–22, 30, 105, 137, 291, 294–95, 297–300, 302, 304 306–13, 326, 328; components, 309
Statistics, 1, 4, 13, 80, 145, 196, 268, 270, 273, 289, 291–328; assumptions, 313; definition, 291; descriptive, 292–305, 328; functions, 292; inferential, 13, 15, 25, 142, 143, 150, 178, 268, 271–72, 292, 296, 313, 328, 330; nonparametric, 313; parametric, 313
StatPac, 154, 270
Stern, 85
Stevens, Wallace, 179
Stevenson, Robert Louis, 331
Stratified sample, 154
Structure of Scientific Revolutions, The, 25
Strunk, William, 109
Style, 61, 98, 107–10, 127, 129, 131, 164, 275
Subproblems, 45–48, 118
Sufficiency in causation, 232–33, 236, 321–23
Sullivan, J.W.N., 135
Summarizing statistics. *See* Statistics, descriptive
Survey, 12, 25, 31, 50, 80, 82, 90, 146–47, 173, 186, 202–3, 218, 235; definition, 146; satisfaction, 25–26, 35, 80, 90, 140, 230, 233, 235
Survey Monkey, 203
Survey research. *See* Descriptive research and evaluation
Swain, Mary Ann, 211
Syllogism, 11

Symbolic interactionism, 29
Synchronous study of obsolescence, 251
Systematic sample, 154
Systems thinking, 19–20

Tables, 56, 107, 268, 274–75; definition, 268;
   elements, 274; layout, 275
Telephone directory, 154
Telephone interviews, 180, 183–85; advan-
   tages, 183–84; disadvantages, 184
Testing, reaction to, experimental research,
   231–32, 235
Thematic analysis, 286
Thematic map, 286
Theory, 12, 18–19, 21–22, 30, 33–34, 43, 45,
   102, 250, 253; definition, 43; development,
   18–19, 22, 30, 102
Third Reich, 70
*Thomson ISI Citation Analysis Research
   Grant*, 339
Thus Spake Zarathustra, 5
Time Machine, The, 331
Time series, 21, 24, 31, 56, 173, 175, 293
"To William Lloyd Garrison," 159
Transaction log analysis, 221–23
Transferability, 21
Trend line, 281
Truth, 6–8, 11, 20, 25, 160–61; chronoligical
   influences, 6; personal influences, 7; soci-
   etal influences, 6
t-test, 324–25
Tukey, John W., 327
Tuskegee Syphilis Study, 70, 72, 74
Type I error, 308–10; impact, 308
Type II error, 308–9; impact, 308

Ulrich's International Periodicals Directory,
   97
University of Chicago: Graduate Library
   School, 30
University of Illinois: Graduate School of
   Library and Information Science, 98; Li-
   brary Research Center, 18
Urn game, 260
U.S. Code of Federal Regulations, 77

U.S. Department of Education, 336
U.S. Department of Transportation, 306
U.S. Government Manual, 336
U.S. Public Health Service, 70

Validity, 15–20, 50–51, 53, 56, 104, 148,
   161–63, 172, 182, 184, 187, 195, 214–15,
   219, 221, 230–33, 235–37, 266; construct,
   16, 187; external, 16, 232; internal, 16, 230;
   relationship to reliability, 17
Valley-Redot, R., 211
Variability. *See* Dispersion
Variable, 16, 53, 105, 135, 137–44; charac-
   teristics, 137–42, 151, 187, 193, 195, 218,
   227–28, 230–38, 242, 267–68, 270–74,
   276, 279–80, 292–328; definition, 16
Variance, 293, 302, 313; definition, 302
Veblen, Thorstein, 5
Verbal cues, 184
Vie de Pasteur, La, 211
VisiCalc (spreadsheet), 269
Visualization, 56, 260, 277, 286, 327
Vulnerable populations, 75, 77–80

War of the Worlds, 10
War Service Committee, 162
Watson, Dr. John, 136
Weasel words, 131
Weber, Robert L., 135
Webometrics, 243
Wells, H. G., 10, 331
White, E. B., 109
Whittier, John Greenleaf, 159
Wild Blue, The, 85
Wireless telephones, 185
W. K. Kellogg Foundation, 338
Word frequency. *See* Productivity
Word-token, 245
Word-type, 245
Work plan, 121
World Medical Association, 74

Zimbardo, Philip G., 73
Zipf, George K., 243, 245
Zipf's Law, 243, 245

About the Authors

DANNY P. WALLACE, BSEd (Southwest Missouri State University), MALS (University of Missouri-Columbia), PhD (University of Illinois at Urbana-Champaign) is EBSCO Chair of Library Service and professor in the School of Library and Information Science, University of Alabama. He has also held administrative and academic appointments at the University of Oklahoma, Kent Sate University, Louisiana State University, Indiana University, and the University of Iowa. His primary teaching and research interests are in the areas of library and information science research and evaluation, bibliometrics, and the impact of technological innovation on library and information organizations. He is responsible for more than 100 publications, including *Knowledge Management: Historical and Cross-Disciplinary Themes* (Libraries Unlimited, 2007). His professional service includes the American Library Association Committee on Accreditation and the boards of directors of the Association for Library and Information Science Education and Beta Phi Mu, the international library and information science honor society. Dr. Wallace was the recipient of the 2000 Association for Library and Information Science Education Award for Teaching Excellence in the Field of Library and Information Science Education and the 2008 Beta Phi Mu/Information Use Management and Policy Institute Distinguished Lecture Award. A complete vita is available at http://bama.ua.edu/~dpwallace/.

CONNIE VAN FLEET, BA (University of Oklahoma), MLIS (Louisiana State University), PhD (Indiana University) is professor, School of Library and Information Studies, University of Oklahoma. She previously served on the faculties of Kent State University and Louisiana State University. Her primary teaching and research interests are in the areas of library evaluation, equitable access to information, readers' advisory services, public library administration, and services to older adults, people with disabilities, and African American audiences. She is the author of numerous publications addressing these topics, among them *Preparing Staff to Serve People with Disabilities: A How-to-Do-It Manual* (Neal-Schuman,

1995) with Courtney Deines-Jones and *African American Literature: A Guide to Reading Interests* (Libraries Unlimited, 2004) co-edited with Alma Dawson. Van Fleet has held offices in the American Library Association and the Association for Library and Information Science Education (ALISE), in state library organizations and within the university. She is the recipient of the ALA/RUSA Margaret E. Monroe Library Adult Services Award, LSU SLIS Outstanding Alumna Award, ALISE Award for Teaching Excellence in Library and Information Science, and the ALISE Service Award. A complete vita is available at http://faculty-staff.ou.edu/V/Connie.J.Van-Fleet-1/.

Drs. Wallace and Van Fleet have been frequent collaborators since 1985. They served as co-editors of *RQ* (1991–1997) and *Reference & User Services Quarterly* (2000–2006), the official journal of the American Library Association Reference and Users Service Association. They are have been co-investigators on several federal grants as well as co-authors of numerous publications, with their work appearing in such venues as *Journal of the American Society for Information Science, Library Trends, Advances in Library Administration and Organization,* and the *International Journal of Information Management.* Their previous book collaborations include *A Service Profession, a Service Commitment: A Festschrift in Honor of Charles D. Patterson* (Scarecrow Press, 1992) and *Library Evaluation: A Casebook and Can-Do Guide* (Libraries Unlimited, 2000).

CPSIA information can be obtained at www.ICGtesting.com
Printed in the USA
BVOW09s1328130814

362734BV00005B/77/P